STUDIES IN THE HISTORY OF CHRISTIAN MISSIONS

R. E. Frykenberg
Brian Stanley
General Editors

STUDIES IN THE HISTORY
OF CHRISTIAN MISSIONS

Susan Billington Harper

*In the Shadow of the Mahatma: Bishop V. S. Azariah
and the Travails of Christianity in British India*

Kevin Ward and Brian Stanley, *Editors*

The Church Mission Society and World Christianity, 1799-1999

THE CHURCH MISSION SOCIETY
AND WORLD CHRISTIANITY,
1799–1999

Edited by

Kevin Ward and Brian Stanley

WILLIAM B. EERDMANS PUBLISHING COMPANY
GRAND RAPIDS, MICHIGAN / CAMBRIDGE, U.K.

CURZON PRESS LTD
RICHMOND, SURREY, U.K.

© 2000 Wm. B. Eerdmans Publishing Co.
All rights reserved

Published jointly 2000 by
Wm. B. Eerdmans Publishing Co.
255 Jefferson Ave. S.E., Grand Rapids, Michigan 49503 /
P.O. Box 163, Cambridge CB3 9PU U.K.
and by
Curzon Press Ltd
15 The Quadrant, Richmond, Surrey, TW9 1BP, UK

Printed in the United States of America

05 04 03 02 01 00   7 6 5 4 3 2 1

Library of Congress Cataloging-in-Publication Data

The Church Mission Society and World Christianity, 1799-1999 /
edited by Kevin Ward and Brian Stanley.
p.   cm.   (Studies in the history of Christian missions)
Includes bibliographical references.
Eerdmans ISBN 0-8028-3875-8 (cloth: alk. paper)
1. Church Missionary Society — History.
2. Mission — Theory — History of doctrines — 19th century.
3. Mission — Theory — History of doctrines — 20th century.
I. Ward, Kevin. II. Stanley, Brian, 1953-   . III. Series.
BV2500.C48   2000
266'.306 — dc21   99-41460
CIP

British Library Cataloguing in Publication Data

A catalogue record for this book is available from the British Library.
Curzon Press ISBN 0-7007-1208-9

Contents

PART 1
THE CMS: HISTORICAL AND
THEOLOGICAL THEMES

v

CONTENTS

Contents

Foreword
by the General Secretary of the
Church Mission Society

I am delighted to have been invited to write the foreword to *The Church Mission Society and World Christianity*. In this selection of essays from five continents, Kevin Ward, Brian Stanley, and their team of authors make an important contribution to the marking of the CMS Bicentenary. As Dr. Ward himself explains, the idea was not to produce a history of a mission institution but to offer historical insights about the meaning of Christian mission and about the appropriation of Christianity in some of the varied contexts in which CMS has worked over the last two hundred years. These insights from the past throw light on the practice of cross-cultural mission in our contemporary world; thus the book is of value to anyone who is concerned with mission, not only to those who may have a particular interest in CMS.

The diversity and complexity of the work of CMS over the last two hundred years is such that it has not been possible to include references to every major theme or even geographical area in a work of this size, but many crucial mission issues are addressed and the principles that emerge from the particularity of the essays are of wide general relevance. The very fact that the authors themselves come from around the world reflects a central message of the book, that mission, even at the height of the "sending" activity of the West, was always a shared enterprise. As Dr. Ward says, the planting of churches could never have been accomplished without the active initiatives of local people who freely appropriated the Christian message for themselves and shared that message within their own society and beyond.

The crucial importance of this local witness has never been as clearly demonstrated as in the case of China after the expulsion of missionaries earlier this century. Far from being weakened by this, the church grew faster during the years of isolation from the outside world than ever before. When I had the privilege of meeting with the doyen of the church in China, Bishop K. H. Ting, founding father of the Three-Self Patriotic Movement and the China Christian Council, he delighted in reminding me that it was a former general secretary of CMS who first articulated the three-self principle for churches, a principle that had been central in enabling Chinese Christians to find their Chinese identity. Although there is no essay on China, the strategic vision of Henry Venn, the keystone in the life of CMS, has been well documented by Peter Williams.

Mission is becoming truly multidirectional across the world in our day and new models of mission are being discovered, perhaps most freely by those who are unencumbered by a legacy of traditional patterns. However, critical reflection on the past undoubtedly enables past mistakes to be avoided and provides important insights into the direction of mission for the future. The celebrations of the CMS Bicentenary will include thanksgiving to God for the past and recommitment to his mission for the future. This book will undoubtedly play a significant part in enabling the society to discern the new task to which we believe God is calling us.

The editors have thanked many people for their help in their list of acknowledgments. I would like to thank the editors and all the authors for this important contribution to the life and thinking of the society.

DIANA K. WITTS
9 November 1998

Acknowledgments

This book grew out of the work of the Bicentenary Publications Committee of the Church Mission Society, set up in 1996 to explore ways of commemorating two hundred years of work. Throughout, Peter Williams has given expert guidance as chairperson, and, as the editors responsible for bringing the book to completion, we would like particularly to thank him for the wisdom with which he has guided the work and the encouragement he has shown. We would like to thank all who have participated in the planning for the book, particularly Sue Parks and Caroline Davis, who have successively served as secretaries to the committee. In addition to those contributors who served on the committee, we would also like to thank Tim Yates, Rosemary Keen, and John Martin for their advice and enthusiasm about the project. We are also grateful to Diana Witts, the general secretary, and Mark Oxbrow, the regional director, Europe and Mission consultant of the Church Mission Society, for their keen interest in the progress of the work.

We owe a special debt of gratitude to the Research Enablement Program of The Pew Charitable Trusts, administered by the Overseas Ministries Study Center in New Haven, Connecticut, for the award of a generous grant to enable us to hold a missiological consultation. We were able to gather scholars and establish a sense of common identity in the project. Particular thanks are due to Gerald Anderson, the director of the center, and to Geoffrey Little, the coordinator, for their support and encouragement.

We would particularly like to thank Sarojini Henry, Yidan Shao, and Alex Kagume, who gave stimulating presentations at Mukono, and E. C. John for his written contribution. They have helped us immensely to focus our attention on the varied aspects of mission in which the CMS has had a part.

Kevin Ward has been involved as editor of this volume from the beginning. Brian Stanley (the joint editor of the Curzon-Eerdmans series on mission history) became progressively more involved in the editorial process as time went on. As editors of this volume, we thank also Mongezi Kapia and Carrie Pemberton for the help given in preparing the manuscript for publication. It is no small task to create some uniformity out of the bewildering array of computer styles and formats. Jeremy Pemberton gave invaluable help in the compilation of the bibliography, and Jocelyn Murray performed the noble task of creating the index. We should also like to thank R. E. Frykenberg, the other joint editor of the Curzon-Eerdmans series, William B. Eerdmans, Jr., and Jennifer Hoffman of Wm. B. Eerdmans Publishing Co., and Jonathan Price of Curzon Press for their encouragement, support, and guidance.

KEVIN WARD
BRIAN STANLEY
May 1999

Contributors

JOHN CLARK is secretary for the Church of England's Partnership for World Mission (PWM). He served with the CMS in Iran from 1976 to 1979 and has also worked for the CMS in London as secretary for the Middle East and Pakistan, and as communications officer.

BISHOP KENNETH CRAGG, a scholar of Islam, has had a long association with the Middle East. He has written extensively on Islam and on relations between the Christian and Muslim faiths. He now lives in retirement in Oxford.

ALLAN K. DAVIDSON teaches church history at St. John's College, Auckland, New Zealand. His special areas of research are nineteenth-century Protestant missionary history and Christianity in New Zealand and the Pacific.

GULI FRANCIS-DEHQANI was born in Iran. She has worked in radio and has completed a doctorate on CMS women missionaries in Persia. She has been ordained recently and is a curate in Mortlake, London.

PAUL JENKINS is archivist of the Basel Mission. He has a particular interest in the rich photographic collection of missionary work.

JOHN KARANJA, a priest of the Anglican Church of Kenya, is lecturer in history at Nairobi University. He completed his doctoral research on Kenyan Christianity at Cambridge University in 1993.

GRAHAM KINGS, a former CMS mission partner in Kenya, is the Henry Martyn Lecturer in Missiology in the Cambridge Theological

Federation, affiliated lecturer in the University of Cambridge, and founding director of the Henry Martyn Centre for the Study of Mission and World Christianity. He is a vice president of the Church Mission Society.

JOCELYN MURRAY, born in New Zealand, served as a CMS missionary in Kenya (1954-67). She is the author of *Proclaim the Good News*, a history of the CMS published in 1985.

GEOFFREY A. ODDIE was senior lecturer in history in the University of Sydney, Australia, and is now an honorary research associate there. He has researched and written extensively on missionaries and Christianity in India.

LAMIN SANNEH is D. Willis James Professor of Missions and World Christianity and professor of history at Yale University. He has written numerous books on West African religion and on missiological themes.

BRIAN STANLEY is director of the Currents in World Christianity Project and a fellow of St. Edmund's College in the University of Cambridge. He has published extensively on the missionary movement, including *The History of the Baptist Missionary Society, 1792-1992*.

KEVIN WARD served with CMS from 1975 to 1991. He is ordained in the Church of Uganda and has written on East African Christianity. He is lecturer in African Religious Studies in the Department of Theology and Religious Studies at the University of Leeds.

PETER WILLIAMS is a student of nineteenth-century missionary theory and practice and has published work on Henry Venn and his successors. He is vicar of All Saints' Ecclesall, Sheffield.

List of Illustrations

LIST OF ILLUSTRATIONS

Photographs from the Church Mission Society, London, and the Church Missionary Society archives, Birmingham, are reproduced by kind permission of the Church Mission Society. Photographs from the Royal Commonwealth Society collection, University of Cambridge, are reproduced by kind permission of the Syndics of Cambridge University Library.

Abbreviations

BCMS	Bible Churchmen's Missionary Society
BFSS	British and Foreign Schools' Society
BMS	Baptist Missionary Society
CEZMS	Church of England Zenana Missionary Society
CIM	China Inland Mission
CMI	*Church Missionary Intelligencer*
CMJ	Church's Mission to the Jews (later Church's Ministry Among the Jews)
CMS	Church Missionary Society (from 1995 Church Mission Society)
CMSA	Church Missionary Society Archives
FES	Female Education Society
Hewitt	Gordon Hewitt, *The Problems of Success: A History of the Church Missionary Society, 1910-1942*. 2 vols. (London: SCM Press, 1971 and 1977)
IFNS	Indian Female Normal Schools and Instruction Society
IVF	Inter-Varsity Fellowship
LMS	London Missionary Society
NDP	Niger Delta Pastorate
PGS	*Proceedings of General Synod*
Record	*Church Missionary Record*
SCM	Student Christian Movement
SPCK	Society for Promoting Christian Knowledge
SPFEE	Society for Promoting Female Education in the East
SPG	Society for the Propagation of the Gospel in Foreign Parts

ABBREVIATIONS

Stock	Eugene Stock, *The History of the Church Missionary Society*. 4 vols. (London: CMS, 1899 and 1916)
SVMU	Student Volunteer Missionary Union
USPG	The United Society for the Propagation of the Gospel
WMC	World Missionary Conference, Edinburgh, 1910
YWCA	Young Women's Christian Association
ZBMM	Zenana Bible and Medical Mission

Introduction

KEVIN WARD

The Church Missionary Society began its life on Friday, 12 April 1799. On that day a group of sixteen evangelical clergymen (the historian of the society, Eugene Stock, emphasizes that only four of them were incumbents[1]) and nine laymen (largely from the professions) gathered in an upper room of the Castle and Falcon Inn in Aldersgate Street, and resolved that, it "being a duty highly incumbent upon every Christian to endeavour to propagate the knowledge of the Gospel among the Heathen," a society to achieve that end be constituted: the Society for Missions to Africa and the East.

John Venn, rector of Clapham, was in the chair. The society was not the first Anglican missionary society: the Society for Promoting Christian Knowledge (founded 1699) and the Society for the Propagation of the Gospel in Foreign Parts (1701) had already been in existence for a century. Nor was the CMS the only evangelical society created at this time. Rather, it was a response from within the established Church of England to the widespread rediscovery of the obligation laid on Christians to engage in mission, which had been one of the important consequences of the eighteenth-century evangelical awakening in Britain. The CMS began as a small voluntary society, professing loyalty to the established church, but regarded with a great deal of suspicion by the church establishment. Gradually, and particularly as a result of the

---

1. Stock, vol. 1, pp. 69-71. The point Stock is making is that evangelical ("serious") clergy were discriminated against and few had a secure place in the structures of the Church of England.

1

work of Josiah Pratt (honorary[2] clerical secretary from 1802 to 1824) and of John Venn's son, Henry Venn (secretary from 1841 to 1872), the society gained a secure and valued place within the life of the church. The existence of the CMS helped revivify the older Anglican mission societies and was crucial in the global spread of an Anglican communion. By 1899 the CMS had become one of the largest Protestant missions in terms of resources, personnel, and influence.

A century later, the Church Mission Society (so renamed in 1995) is again a small society, with limited resources and personnel at its disposal.[3] All mission agencies in the second half of the twentieth century have had to face a certain amount of suspicion about their goals and methods. Even within the churches, there has been increasing doubt about whether mission is really an important or even a legitimate task for the church; a suspicion that the whole project is bound up with Western superiority and colonial arrogance; and a loss of confidence in the sovereign and universal claims of the Christian gospel. As Graham Kings shows in chapter 11, it was part of the genius of Max Warren, a missionary statesman as important for the twentieth century as Henry Venn had been for the last, that he prepared missionary societies to address these issues with self-critical realism and yet with a sanguine confidence in God and in the *missio Dei*. Warren rightly discerned that the missionary imperative was not a temporary, aberrant phase of the life of the Christianity of the West, but was inherent in the nature of the Christian message, and something to which all Christians were called. The best impulse of the founders of the CMS was to proclaim a gospel of liberation from sin and social oppression, which deform both human beings and societies. Certainly missionary activity had accrued many unedifying and unhelpful associations, rightly rejected not least by those who had been the "objects" of such activity. Christians in Asia and Africa and indeed in all parts of the world that had been subject to

---

2. The organization and strategic planning of the society were directed by a group of secretaries with different area or functional responsibilities, presided over, as *primus inter pares*, by the "honorary clerical secretary." Throughout the nineteenth century, and in fact until 1922, this was a clergyman of independent financial means. "Honorary" referred to the fact that the position was unpaid, not that it was a sinecure or involved only nominal responsibilities. It was in fact a complex executive position.

3. The change in nomenclature was not intended to signify a weakening of commitment to send missionaries, but to emphasize the multidirectional nature of the sending and the importance of the fact that those sent are engaged "in mission."

colonial conquest, now demanded that the equality that was implicit in the missionary message be given practical reality. They demanded that parity of esteem be accorded not only in words but in reality. For the gospel was not the possession of the missionaries, nor could they dictate how the gospel be received and understood.

Werner Ustorf, in his inaugural lecture as professor of mission at Birmingham University,[4] has commented on the irony of the fact that "mission" has taken on an importance in business, commerce, and academic life — secular discourse generally — just at the time when the Christian churches seemed in danger of dropping it from their vocabulary as an outmoded concept of a colonial age. But far from being irredeemably imperialist, it can be argued that "mission" is essential to the self-understanding and self-critique of religion in its willingness to engage with others, to witness, to be vulnerable. For too long, perhaps especially during the unreflective self-confidence of "the great age of mission," mission was seen as something done "out there," on the fringes of Christian society, without a great deal of impact on the central core of beliefs and practices that make up Christian societies and individuals. Even to talk in these terms — about center and periphery — is to mistake what it is to be Christian. Paul's presentation of the gospel for the Gentiles was not simply the repackaging of an old tradition for Greek consumption, but was, rather, a radical transformation of the nature of religion in the process of reaching out with the gospel of the life, death, resurrection, and lordship of Jesus Christ. Christianity was and is being created and re-created on the margins, the boundary, the periphery, and in so doing challenges the validity of all boundaries and peripheries. This, among many other things, is the burden of Lamin Sanneh in a number of stimulating books, such as *Translating the Message* and *Encountering the West*,[5] that call for a radical reassessment of what is often regarded as the "strangeness," the foreign provenance, of Christianity to Africa.

Indeed, in the last decade or so, there has been a general reassessment of the importance of the missionary testimony as an historical resource. Mission archives are some of the most frequently consulted collections in many repositories. Historians of the non-Western world,

4. Werner Ustorf, *Mission to Mission? — Rethinking the Agenda* (Birmingham: Selly Oak Colleges Occasional Paper, no. 9, 1991).

5. Lamin Sanneh, *Translating the Message: The Missionary Impact on Culture* (Maryknoll, N.Y.: Orbis, 1989), and Lamin Sanneh, *Encountering the West: Christianity and the Global Cultural Process: The African Dimension* (London: Marshall Pickering, 1993).

with a wide range of interests, are attracted by the wealth and detail of this material on a vast range of topics: political and economic as well as cultural and religious. The biases and preconceptions with which the missionary was likely to approach other societies and cultures can be openly examined and taken into account from the different perspectives and biases of modern scholarship. But this does not detract from the tremendous value of missionaries as historical witnesses, men and women who often came to know a people and their language with an intimacy almost impossible for other outsiders to equal.[6] For example, the archive of the London Missionary Society for the nineteenth century is central to Jean and John Comaroff's pioneering study of Tswana society in southern Africa. The work might well be regarded as a radical deconstruction of missionary perspectives — but one that fully acknowledges the importance both of the missionary impact and of the creative appropriation and reconstruction of missionary Christianity by the Tswana themselves, in the formation of a modern Tswana consciousness.[7] Even the life stories of African converts as transmitted by missionaries, which certainly have to be used critically, should not be undervalued. Catherine Coquery-Vidrovitch points to their importance for the reconstruction of women's history in Africa. Even where women's accounts do survive, she says, either in literary or oral forms, it is still not easy to get beyond "the prevailing tradition of male dominance" that may be implicit even in those accounts. "More revealing," she continues, "are the life stories collected by missionaries in the past or from women born within the century, within which the impact of the interviewer/interviewee relationship has yet to be decoded."[8]

The CMS archives, now deposited at Birmingham University, are one of the richest and best ordered of all mission resources. Their historical value varies according to place and time, and the acuity or lack

6. See J. D. Y. Peel, "Problems and Opportunities in an Anthropologist's Use of a Missionary Archive," in *Missionary Encounters: Sources and Issues,* ed. Robert A. Bickers and Rosemary Seton (London: Curzon Press, 1996), pp. 70-94.

7. Jean Comaroff and John Comaroff, *Of Revelation and Revolution,* vol. 1, *Christianity, Colonialism, and Consciousness in South Africa* (Chicago: University of Chicago Press, 1991), and vol. 2, *The Dialectics of Modernity on a South African Frontier* (Chicago: University of Chicago Press, 1997).

8. Catherine Coquery-Vidrovitch, *African Women: A Modern History* (London: Westview, 1997), p. 4. Coquery-Vidrovitch refers to Kirk Hoppe's "Whose Life Is It, Anyway? Issues of Representation in Life Narrative Texts of African Women," *International Journal of African Historical Studies* 26, no. 3 (1993): 623-26.

of acuity of the individual missionary correspondent. But, overall, they have a value that goes far beyond the affairs of the specific religious community that came into being as a result of the missionary activity. As a source for the political, economic, social, and cultural history of countries such as Nigeria, Kenya, and Uganda, the CMS archives can hardly be overestimated.[9] What is increasingly recognized is that one cannot come to adequate understandings of whole areas of the historical experience of many people and cultures, not only in Africa, but in many other parts of the world, without addressing the issue of the impact of Christian missionary activity.

Yet, this still leaves questions about the value of a history of a mission institution. Something of the importance of mission societies for the general history of Christian faith, as well as for the reciprocal relations of cultures on a worldwide basis, is expressed by W. R. Ward, in connection with the eighteenth century:

> [M]issions are not just a function of the virility of churches, nor even of private enterprise. They require not only a particular state of mind in individuals and groups — the ability to mobilise resources of cash and manpower for new purposes, and some ability, however minimal, to think about the presentation of the gospel in unfamiliar circumstances — but also opportunities to get at what are regarded as "the heathen," which ensure that Christian missions can never be isolated either from the great game of European politics, or from the political systems local to the area where they are to operate. The modern process of transforming Christianity from a European to a worldwide religion raises questions therefore not only about almost every aspect of the societies from which missions are sent, but also about those to which they go.[10]

The success of missionary societies in nineteenth-century Britain in mobilizing congregations to active interest and participation is itself

---

9. Rosemary Keen was archivist for many years, and, with her colleague, the society's librarian, Jean Woods, became a familiar and helpful figure to generations of researchers at 157 Waterloo Road. Rosemary Keen supervised the transfer of the CMS archives to the Heslop Room of Birmingham University, where they form part of the special collections, under the care of Christine Penney. Parts of the CMS archives remain in London. The current archivist is Kenneth Osborne.

10. W. R. Ward, "Missions in Their Global Context in the Eighteenth Century," in *A Global Faith: Essays on Evangelicalism and Globalization*, ed. M. Hutchinson and O. Kalu (New South Wales: The Centre for the Study of Australian Christianity, Macquarie University, 1998), p. 108.

an important theme in British social history, as well as for the internal histories of the churches so involved. Among other things, the mission societies played an important role in encouraging and esteeming the role of women, of the laity and working class people, and, not least, of children, as active agents in the life of the church. And these developments had implications for society as a whole.[11]

In the light of the churches' renewed recognition of mission as vital to Christian faith, a study of the CMS ought also to have importance for a theological critique and appraisal of the missionary task. John V. Taylor has recently used the phrase "the Uncancelled Mandate" to speak of the task for the next millennium of the Christian era, the third century of CMS existence. As Diana Witts, the current general secretary of the CMS, has pointed out, for the Church Mission Society this will often now be primarily participation in the mission of the partner churches, rather than one in which the driving force, the power, and direction come from the North. This is because it is in the churches of the South and East that so often the vitality and inspiration and taking of creative opportunities will come:

> Both partner Churches and mission agencies have been trying hard to overcome patterns of paternalism and dependency inherited from the past. Much progress has been made, and relationships are transformed whenever a genuine, two-way sharing of gifts in mission becomes a reality. However, economic imbalances continue to distort many relationships. While mission agencies are trying to ensure that their involvement is focused on mission priorities, some economically dependent Churches still look to their "parent" agency as the one who will come to their rescue in order to help to maintain the structures of the Church. This is at the root of continuing tension, and represents a dilemma from which all parties long to be freed.[12]

---

11. This whole dimension of nineteenth-century church life has only fairly recently begun to receive the attention it deserves. Notoriously, it is virtually omitted from the great work by Owen Chadwick, *The Victorian Church,* 2 vols. (London: Adam & Charles Black, 1966, 1970). The only indexed reference to the CMS refers to John Henry Newman's criticism of the Oxford CMS association (of which he was secretary) for "leaning to friendliness with dissenters"! He resigned in 1830 (vol. 1, pp. 68-69).

12. Diana Witts, "The Future of the Mission Agency," in *Anglicanism: A Global Communion,* ed. A. Wingate, K. Ward, C. Pemberton, and W. Sitshebo (London: Mowbray, 1998), pp. 399-407.

Though at times this has been lost sight of, from the very beginning the expansion of Christianity has indeed been about such a shared enterprise. Thus, the "planting" of churches in various parts of the world from the beginning of the nineteenth century could never have been accomplished without the active initiatives of local people, who freely appropriated the Christian message for themselves and commended that message both within their own societies and beyond. Thus local people were as much missionaries as were members of the mission society. They were often the driving force in the work of evangelization, Bible translation, creating education and health facilities, and building up and providing pastoral care for the community.

To elucidate this movement, inherent in the work of the CMS from its inception, is one of the chief purposes of this book. It is intended, not as an account primarily of the institution or the missionaries who were sent from Europe to other parts of the world, but as an historical appraisal of the meaning of Christian mission and of the appropriation of Christianity in such varied contexts and for more than two hundred years in areas where the CMS has worked. In many cases that contact was indirect, in that for many, the gospel came to them not through the agency of a foreign missionary but through the preaching of evangelists from a neighboring community, or indeed from one of their own children who, through contacts outside their own society, had come to a faith that they now wished to communicate and share.

The awareness of diversity and complexity, and the multidirectional nature of mission, meant that in planning to commemorate the bicentenary it was decided not to ask a single person to write a general account of the society, but to ask scholars from all over the world to make contributions. Theirs would not be an exhaustive account, but would rather reflect the historical importance of mission through a discussion of particular peoples, places, and times. We were greatly assisted in giving coherence and unity to this project by obtaining a grant from the Research Enablement Program of The Pew Charitable Trusts to hold a "missiological consultation."

This consultation was held from 27 July 1997 to 1 August 1997 at Bishop Tucker Theological College, Mukono, the main ministerial training institution of the Church of Uganda. The contributors were asked to reflect critically on the history, missiological experience and practice, and theological understanding of the CMS as an important participant in the modern missionary movement. The consultation also aimed to help the society, and churches that have been involved in partnership with the society, to gain insights into the direction of their mission for the future. The papers were circulated and read in advance by each participant and the author briefly introduced the issues. Two people were asked to respond, and a lively conversation usually ensued. The process produced animated sessions and a strong engagement with the themes. The presence of the local Ugandan academic and church community also contributed to the liveliness of debate. A wide range of topics were touched upon: missionary motivation, freedom and antislavery, understandings of gender, relations with traditional religions and with Islam, political involvement, secularism as a world phenomenon, and mission to Britain and countries of the North. The majority of the essays included in this volume were given at this consultation and revised in the light of those discussions. But, in addition to the contributions included here, there were fascinating presentations from others. Yidan Shao from China spoke about the way in which Chinese Christian communities have survived and grown since 1949 and of the importance of the "Three-Selves" concept for their own self-understanding. Sarojini Henry gave a moving personal account of the immense importance of Christianity and the educational institutions founded by the CMS in the development of women in India. Alex Kagume presented a paper on spiritual developments in the Church in Uganda, noting in particular the growth of the Pentecostal movement.[13]

The group were guests of the Church of Uganda, one of the most important and dynamic churches to have resulted from CMS work. From its inception in 1877, the CMS Uganda mission was overwhelmed by the response of intelligent inquiry and committed faith. Baganda young people responded enthusiastically to the message they heard and in those early years suffered persecution during the purges at the court of the Kabaka (the ruler of Buganda) in 1885 and 1886, when many, both Catholic and Protestant, died together for their faith. Those who survived subsequently worked to create a new society in Buganda, based on the incorporation of Christian values into the fabric and institutions of the state. They became evangelists to the other peoples of Uganda and East Africa. Moreover, in the 1930s there began a remarkable revival that cut

---

13. It has not been possible to include these papers in the final collection, but I am very grateful for the insights and breadth of perspective that these contributions gave to the conference as a whole. I would also like to express our gratitude to E. C. John of United Theological College, Bangalore, who later prepared a paper on the CMS and the Syrian Christians of South India, which we have also not been able to include.

across the rigid racial demarcations engendered by colonialism, creating a realization of sin and of a broken humanity and a fellowship united by the common purpose of a saved people with a strong sense of mission. And yet, Uganda's Christian history also has its examples of narrowness of spirit rather than liberation, complacency rather than vitality — and in that, it shares the experience of all Christian communities. In 1977, Janani Luwum, archbishop of Uganda, became a modern Christian martyr, killed for his opposition to the tyranny of the Amin regime, at a time when all Uganda's people, Muslim as well as Christian, were suffering.[14] This is an immensely rich history, and it was an appropriate place in which to make some assessments of the role of mission, the contribution of the CMS, and the creation of a global Christianity.

The book contains three sections. Part 1 explores a number of historical and theological themes in the development of the society's understanding and practice. There is an examination of previous historians of the society, in particular Eugene Stock, the author of the great 1899 centenary history, one of the most impressive histories of a mission society ever written, and of Gordon Hewitt, who wrote about the work of the society in the first part of the twentieth century and who died just as this book was being produced.[15] Paul Jenkins examines the enormous importance of the work of continental men and women connected with the Basel Mission in facilitating the work of the CMS in its early years. Indeed without the Basel Mission, it might well have been difficult for the CMS to establish itself as a credible agency for mission at all. This cooperation was part of a European-wide evangelical "international." Jocelyn Murray examines the missionary calling of women in the nineteenth century, the new opportunities it gave for women's ministry and professional fulfillment, and the frustrations they experienced when their work was not valued or esteemed. Guli Francis-Dehqani's chapter examines the particular importance of women, both married and single, in the development of CMS work in Persia from its inception to 1934. Bishop Kenneth Cragg reflects on the particular dif-

14. On 9 July 1998 a series of sculptures was unveiled on the west front of Westminster Abbey in London, commemorating Christian martyrs of the twentieth century. Janani Luwum is one of those commemorated, along with Martin Luther King; Archbishop Oscar Romero; Dietrich Bonhoeffer; the young South African Anglican catechumen, Manche Masemola; and the Presbyterian evangelist from Pakistan, Esther John; Maximilian Kolbe; Grand Duchess Elizabeth of Russia; and Wang Zhiming, a Chinese pastor and evangelist.

15. Canon Gordon Hewitt died in July 1998.

ficulties and challenges for Christian mission working in the Muslim environment of the Middle East and on the importance of this witness for understanding the nature of the missionary task.

The second section looks at the relation between the missionary society and the indigenous church. For CMS any discussion of this issue finds its source and inspiration in the pioneering vision of Henry Venn in articulating a strategy for encouraging the creation of self-supporting, self-financing, and self-propagating churches. Peter Williams's chapter examines the importance for Venn of creating culturally adapted and authentically local church structures and of the struggle that he maintained to safeguard the native church against missionary or settler domination and Anglicization. West Africa was of particular significance for defining and shaping the general mission priorities of CMS, and Venn's understanding in particular. Lamin Sanneh's chapter focuses on the work of the African freed slaves and their Creole[16] descendants who became missionaries and were the basis of Venn's vision in West Africa for the organic growth of autonomous and indigenous, missionary-orientated local churches. Sanneh reflects on the importance of Christianity for the freed slave and Creole community and the value that they placed on what he calls "antistructure," a stance of radical criticism of all structures of authority that claimed, either through sacred authority or colonial force, an absolute obedience militating against the human dignity and freedom that the Christian message had restored to them. The chapter offers new reflections on Bishop Samuel Ajayi Crowther's understandings of African culture and its relation to the gospel. Crowther's long friendship with Henry Venn was of the utmost importance in helping to shape Venn's own mission thinking.

Allan Davidson's chapter is, in a sense, an extended commentary covering two hundred years on Venn's indigenous church ideal and its varied fortunes among the Maori community. It delineates the CMS's changing perceptions of its role with regard to Maori culture in the face of an increasingly settler-dominated New Zealand and the reassertion and reaffirmation of that culture by Maori Christians in this century. Geoffrey Oddie presents a comparative study of three types of conversion movements in areas of North and South India where the CMS was active, exploring the different appeal of the gospel for the different

16. In Sierra Leone "Creole" referred in a narrow sense to the children of freed slaves. It came to refer generally to the Sierra Leone immigrant Christian community.

communities and the differing dynamics of conversion that were entailed. John Karanja explores in detail the motivation and meaning of conversion for the pioneering group of Kikuyu Christians in central Kenya at the beginning of the twentieth century.

The third section looks at changing perspectives on mission in Britain. The CMS began as a movement outward — into all the world. But that movement itself has not left the church in Britain unchanged: there has been a movement inward. Graham Kings's chapter explores the theological thinking about mission of two important twentieth-century leaders of the CMS, Max Warren and John V. Taylor. They engaged profoundly with the theological and existential issues of what it means to be a Christian in the modern world and to be a worldwide church amidst the diversity of competing religious and secular values. Their thinking and statesmanship helped to transform Anglicanism into a truly global communion and had a powerful impact on the Church of England itself. John Clark looks at how the Church of England has been challenged in the last thirty years to be less insular and less self-sufficient and more open and responsive to the message of the churches outside Britain. It has also been challenged to utilize expertise of personnel from Christians outside Britain, not least in addressing the missionary situation in Britain. Brian Stanley writes a conclusion, reflecting on the contribution of the CMS to the emergence of "Anglicanism" as a global communion that is no longer definable by its "Englishness."

In a recent series of Bible studies entitled *The Uncancelled Mandate*, John Taylor reflects on the future of mission:

> It seems certain that the next few decades will bring more rapid and more far-reaching change to the whole world than anyone can remember or visualize. Yet Christ's mandate to his followers still stands, whatever the circumstances. It is, in fact, a mandate which changing conditions, resources and techniques can do little to alter, since the mission to which it commits us is primarily to be the human presence of Jesus Christ who is the same yesterday, today and forever. Our vocation is corporately to make visible his total response to God's love and truth in the terms of each distinct culture, old or new, so as to affirm, challenge, redeem and fulfil it from within, and to take the consequence of doing so with him.[17]

17. John V. Taylor, *The Uncancelled Mandate: Four Bible Studies on Christian Mission for the Approaching Millennium* (London: Church House Publishing, 1998), p. 41.

It is the hope of the authors of these essays that their work will contribute in a small way to that reappraisal process by which the Church Mission Society works out how it can most appropriately participate in the continuing mission of Jesus Christ and the Spirit of God in the world.

PART 1

THE CMS: HISTORICAL AND THEOLOGICAL THEMES

1. "Taking Stock": The Church Missionary Society and Its Historians

KEVIN WARD

Introduction

When Eugene Stock came to write his great history of the Church Missionary Society in 1899, he was faced with an arduous task, but one that did not seem to offer insuperable problems of organization or presentation. The internal structures and procedures of the society, with which Stock, as editorial secretary, had been intimately involved for a quarter of a century, provided the work with a unified, coherent, and satisfying structure. The issues do not seem as straightforward a hundred years later. There is no longer much taste for multivolume histories of institutions. More seriously, there is suspicion of unified and centralizing structures in historical writing as in life, and a much greater awareness of the necessity of diversity of perspective and multiplicity of voices. The very idea of mission history as a respectable branch of historical inquiry became rather suspect in the era of decolonization after 1945 and especially in the 1960s and 1970s (the era of independence for most of Africa). Was not mission history primarily an account of the expansion of Europe, which must now cede priority to the histories of Asian, African, and Latin American peoples and cultures, including the history of local Christian communities in their various expressions? In the light of this, what value does a history of a mission society have?

15

In examining this issue, this chapter will examine the two major histories of the CMS as an institution: that written by Stock at the turn of the nineteenth century and that by Hewitt in the 1970s. Gordon Hewitt continued the history from more or less where Stock had ended, down to 1942, when Max Warren became general secretary. The chapter will conclude by examining what shape a history of the CMS might take for the period from 1942 up to the bicentenary in 1999.

Eugene Stock's *History of the* CMS

Writing from his Tegel prison cell in 1944, Dietrich Bonhoeffer reflected on the fragmentariness of life in his day, compared to the lives of those who lived and worked just a generation before his own at the end of the nineteenth century:

> The portraits of the great savants in Harnack's *History of the Academy* make me acutely aware of that, and almost saddens me a little. Where is there an intellectual *magnum opus* today? Where are the collecting, assimilating, and sorting of material necessary for producing such a work? Where is there today the combination of fine *abandon* and large scale planning that goes with such a life?[1]

The great work of mission history that Eugene Stock produced to commemorate the first centenary of the Church Missionary Society in 1899 — with its portraits of great nineteenth-century missionaries and its tremendous industry of collecting, assimilating, and sorting — provokes a similar sense of awe, not to mention a little sadness at the loss of such solidity and security. *The History of the Church Missionary Society: Its Environment, Its Men and Its Work in Three Volumes* is nothing if not solid: volume 1 covers the first fifty years, 1799-1849, in 504 pages; volume 2, 1849-72 (the death of Henry Venn), in 659 pages; volume 3, 1872-99, in 832 pages. Then there was the *Centenary Volume of the Church Missionary Society,* published in 1902, containing the speeches and sermons surrounding the centenary celebrations, statistics, and useful directories of the 1,602 men (clerical and lay) who had gone out with the society, the 584 women (not including wives), and the 623 "native" clergy connected to the society between 1799 and 1900.

---

1. Dietrich Bonhoeffer, *Letters and Papers from Prison*, enl. ed. (London: SCM Press, 1971), p. 219.

Fig. 1. Eugene Stock (1836-1928), author of the
centenary history of the CMS.
Church Mission Society, London

Finally, Stock wrote a "Supplementary Volume the Fourth," taking the
story up to 1916.[2] Ironically, the work had originally been entrusted to
Charles Hole, who produced a first volume that covered only the first
fifteen years. He then abandoned the project, and it was decided to
start again "though on a smaller scale"![3]

Despite the solidity of this great project, something of the vulnerability and fragmentariness that one might say is the nature of mission-

2. The details are: Eugene Stock, *The History of the Church Missionary Society,* vols. 1-3 (London: CMS, 1899); vol. 4 (London: CMS, 1916); *The Centenary
Volume of the Church Missionary Society for Africa and the East* (London: CMS,
1902).

3. Stock, vol. 1, p. vii.

ary work, does come through again and again in Stock's narrative. The project was conceived by Stock as an institutional history, the history of a great institution, an institution whose very existence for its first forty years was precarious, but which had become a force to be reckoned with in the life of the Church of England. As one of Stock's sternest modern critics puts it:

> His great History is the story of English missionary structures at work at home and abroad. The non-English elements emerge only occasionally from the shadows and then to illustrate the work of English missionaries.[4]

In spite of this, the work remains a very great achievement. It is encyclopedic as a work of reference to the activities of the society, its missions, and its personnel. Yet Stock had the ability to present his material in a coherent and interesting way so that the text does not become a tedious list of forgotten names and places about which we know little. He has a particular skill in putting the life of the society in the context of English church politics and theological disputes. His style is precise and unfussy, a model of clarity. Stock once wrote of Philip O'Flaherty, one of the first missionaries to Uganda, that "his pen was the pen of a *too* ready writer." O'Flaherty was a man whose incautious utterances, both spoken and written, made him a difficult colleague to work with.[5] Stock's own fluency with the pen was legendary — he is said to have had only once to write out a page a second time.[6] On the other hand, Stock was as diplomatic as O'Flaherty was indiscreet. In the earlier part of the work, the pen of the historian is most in evidence, sifting and exercising his considerable critical faculties in a judicious way. But in the later part of the book Stock is an actual player. He began his editorial duties (the task of preparing the letters from missionaries overseas for various forms of wider circulation and publication) in 1873 and became a full secretary of the society in 1881. His social background was somewhat humbler than those of the honorary clerical secretaries (Henry Venn, 1841-72; Henry Wright, 1872-80; and Frederic Wigram, 1880-95) whose personalities and ideas often dominated the policy

4. Peter Williams, *The Ideal of the Self-Governing Church: A Study of Victorian Missionary Strategy* (Leiden: E. J. Brill, 1990), p. 170.

5. Stock, vol. 3, p. 414.

6. Georgina Gollock, *Eugene Stock: A Biographical Study, 1836 to 1928* (London: CMS, 1929), p. 128.

making of the society. Nevertheless, Stock's influence was increasingly felt. The son of a failed business man, he did not attend a university. He was a lay person who reflected the ethos of a successful institution in a period of sustained growth. In some ways he created, or helped to create, that ethos. This needs to be borne in mind when considering Stock's account of the last years of the nineteenth century, years of profound crisis for the society's work in West Africa, which are severely glossed over and skewed in Stock's narrative. The metropolitan, institutionally oriented point of view is paramount from the beginning of the work. But it is my contention that something of the significance and consequence of world mission from the perspective of the subjects of mission does emerge from Stock's pages.

Moreover, in defense of Stock, in almost every case he is scrupulous in honoring the leaders of the local church by recording their names and activities. The story never reads as simply, or indeed primarily, the activities of foreign missionaries. Philip O'Flaherty, the missionary reprimanded by Stock for his lack of reserve and diplomacy, can serve as a way into this theme. O'Flaherty was in no way typical of nineteenth-century missionaries, although, as an army man, he does represent a steady number of CMS recruits throughout the period. The "typical" missionary in the first period would perhaps be the German Lutheran from Württemberg, trained at the Basel missionary institute;[7] in the middle years of the century, he would be the product of England's homegrown missionary college in London, the Islington Institute.[8] At the end of the century, he would be the Cambridge upper-middle-class graduate, imbued with Keswick zeal. O'Flaherty was none of these. But his life does in several strange ways symbolize the experience of many of the subjects of mission in the nineteenth century.[9] First of all, O'Flaherty must have been one of the few CMS missionaries who had experienced both sides of missionary work — the giving as well as the

---

7. See chap. 2 below.

8. This was a missionary training college started in the early years of the nineteenth century specifically to train missionaries who did not have a university degree. Some of its graduates were subsequently ordained for ministry overseas by the bishop of London or by a bishop in the mission where they worked. But the institute was not primarily intended for ordination training.

9. For O'Flaherty's early life, see Thomas Simpson, "Rev. Philip O'Flaherty of Ballaghadallagh, Co. Mayo and of Uganda," *The Bulletin of the Presbyterian Historical Society of Ireland* 11 (Nov. 1981). Correspondence relating to his activities in Uganda is found in the CMS archives (Birmingham): G3/A60.

receiving. Born into a Roman Catholic family in County Mayo, Ireland, in the 1830s, he grew up in a society about to be disrupted by the impact of the outside world. In the aftermath of the Great Famine (when Roman Catholic pastoral support in the countryside had to some extent broken down), he attended the cabin school of a Presbyterian organization working among the Irish-speaking community of western Ireland, a movement that aimed at the conversion of Irish "Romanists" to the evangelical faith and their civilization by introducing them to English education and values. Marrying the daughter of the Presbyterian minister who had brought him to the faith, he took the middle passage to Liverpool, to work as a teacher. Enlisting as a soldier in the Tenth Hussars, he went to the Crimea, becoming proficient in Turkish and French and later Arabic. He became a sergeant interpreter for the British army. After the war he did some medical studies in Edinburgh, before being sent by the Free Church of Scotland to work as a missionary in Constantinople. It was here that he was engaged as an assistant to the great CMS missionary and expert on Islam, C. G. Pfander, until the mission was closed down by the Turkish authorities in 1864. Back in England, O'Flaherty was ordained into the Church of England, though he never quite felt at ease in the role of an English curate. In 1880 he was called to Uganda. He always claimed (though his own volatile nature makes this difficult to credit) that he was asked to sort out the interpersonal difficulties faced by the beleaguered mission community at the court of the Kabaka (king of Buganda). In reality he exacerbated the problems, but he was able to exercise his linguistic skills, demonstrate his knowledge of Islam and the Muslim world to the Swahili traders who were an important faction at the court, make his contribution to Catholic-Protestant diatribe, and (as a clergyman) to baptize the first Ugandan converts to Protestant Christianity. After five years of separation from his wife and children, he retraced his steps to the coast and boarded a boat at Mombasa in order to return home. He died of fever, however, on 21 July 1886, just before the ship entered the Suez Canal, and he was buried at sea.

The experience of O'Flaherty's own Irish community bears some resemblance to that of the Maori communities who were the object of one of the earliest CMS missions. The flight of Irish emigrants to America after the famine would resonate with the returnees and recaptives of Sierra Leone. In their different ways, both Irish peasants and enslaved Africans were the victims of an international economy impacting small-scale rural communities, causing disruption and the uprooting of individuals. Both O'Flaherty and the freed slaves had to learn a new language, a new culture, and a new religion. The missionary attitudes to Islam that O'Flaherty encountered in Turkey and in Uganda were in many ways a reflection of the prevalent attitudes of British Protestants to Roman Catholics: students at the Islington Institute in the 1850s were expected to try out their missionary vocation among the Catholic Irish community at the "Irish Courts" of the Angel Islington.[10] O'Flaherty's experience of fragmentation and reconstruction, of encounter and polemic, of participation in a complex world of conflicts and interconnections, must have been the experience of many, missionary and convert alike, in the nineteenth-century world in which the CMS operated.

The Origins and Motivation of the Church Missionary Society

As noted in the introduction, the formal inauguration of the society dates from the meeting in Aldersgate Street under John Venn's chairmanship, on 12 April 1799.[11] The society sprang out of the evangelical awakening and identified itself wholeheartedly with the distinctive emphases of this movement:[12] the sinfulness of human beings and their justification by faith in the work of Christ on the cross; the need for conversion of each individual; the supreme authority of the Bible as God's word; and an activism based on optimism about what converted men and women can achieve when inspired by God's Spirit. It was this activism that had such particular consequences for mission. The founders of the society shared with the Baptist William Carey the urgency of the Great Commission (Matthew 28:19) to make disciples of all na-

10. Stock, vol. 2, p. 80: "The late Graham Wilmot Brooke used to say that the best training the men could get for foreign work, particularly among Mohammedans, would be by joining the evangelists of the Irish Church Missions in Dublin and Cork. But the Islington students for many years had a precisely similar sphere of labour. The College definitely undertook the charge of one of the worst districts in London, known as the Irish Courts. . . . These courts were crowded with the lowest class of Roman Catholic Irish, a lawless, drunken, and quarrelsome population, among whom no policeman used to go alone."

11. See p. 1 above.

12. For the most sensitive theological treatment of evangelicalism from an historical point of view see D. W. Bebbington, *Evangelicalism in Modern Britain* (London: Unwin Hyman, 1989).

tions. "This Gospel of the Kingdom shall be preached in all the world for a witness unto all nations" (Matt. 24:14). The evangelization of the world was a spur to mission from the beginning. It achieved renewed prominence as "the evangelization of the world in this generation" at the end of the nineteenth century. The urgency of mission was intimately connected with the hope of a coming millennial age. In those early years this was mainly understood in terms of the gradual diffusion of the knowledge of Christ throughout the world and the amelioration of the injustices inherent in systems of world power as a prelude to the inauguration of God's kingdom. This harmonized well with the activism of early evangelicalism, with its sense of power to change the world through mission. It remained an important spur to mission. But increasingly a darker, more pessimistic note seemed to many evangelicals to fit better the experience of a world rushing to destruction, a world under judgment, crying out for the return of Christ as judge.

The overwhelming and decisive experience for evangelicals of liberation from sin and the enjoyment of freedom as children of God gave shape to their understanding of the worldwide missionary task. In 1799 that task seemed to be seriously vitiated in a number of areas:

- *the transatlantic slave trade,* with its degrading of humanity, rendering all talk of the common human need for God inane and ineffectual;
- *the active hostility of the East India Company* to missionary work among Hindus and Muslims; evangelicals saw this as a form of enslavement to English godlessness and rationalism;
- *the captivity of the Church of England itself to an antiquated state machinery* that confined its work and restricted its missionary vision.[13]
- *the lack of missionary vision in the Eastern churches;* particularly in Muslim lands, the CMS hoped to revitalize the ancient Orthodox churches and equip them for active mission to Islam.

The abolition of the British slave trade in 1807 and the renegotiation of the charter of the East India Company in 1813 (both steered

---

13. Anglican evangelicals, unlike the Methodist movement, were dedicated to working within the system of the established church. They had no proposals as such for radical constitutional change in the state church, but they did hope that a spiritual transformation would overcome the rigidities of state control.

through the House of Commons by Wilberforce) were hailed by evangelicals not only as humanitarian pieces of legislation but as the means by which the gospel could penetrate areas of darkness whose suffering had been caused at least in part, by a so-called Christian nation. Evangelicals remained committed to the struggle against slavery, which went on throughout the century. In India there remained an undercurrent of hostility to the work of missions: this sprang partly from a reluctance among company administrators to disturb unnecessarily the existing society and religions of India. Partly it was due to a strain of rationalism and libertarian thinking in many officials. For Stock the great exception was the work of Sir John Lawrence and his colleagues in Punjab of the 1850s, an example of what civil and religious cooperation could attain.[14]

An important task was to free the Church of England from the restricted vision of itself as a department of the state with a mission to English people alone. The Society for the Propagation of the Gospel in Foreign Parts (SPG) had been founded in 1701, but it was limited by its charter to ministering to English settlers in the colonies and to native people subject to the British Crown. At the beginning the CMS looked for work outside this British colonial structure — British India, which was a major focus of mission for the CMS, was not technically a British colony. Quite apart from the practical desire not to compete with the SPG, was the theological concern for universality in mission, a desire not to be inhibited to areas of British control. One of the problems for the CMS throughout the nineteenth century was that it found itself constantly overtaken by the advance of British colonialism, to which it responded in a variety of ways. CMS work turned out to be primarily in areas of British colonial power; indeed often their very presence was instrumental in making those areas British. But that was certainly not the intention in the early years of the nineteenth century. By the end of the century, the most important areas of CMS activity outside the British Empire were China and Japan, where the CMS's presence was just one of a number of Anglican missionary efforts from Britain and America.[15]

The ponderous structures of the state church also proved difficult to penetrate. The social, professional, and financial expectations and constraints of the clergy meant that few felt able to offer for mission

14. Stock, vol. 2, chap. 44.
15. See G. F. S. Gray, *Anglicans in China: A History of the Zhonghua Shenggong Hui* (The Episcopal China Mission History Project, 1996).

work in the early part of the century. In default, the CMS looked to the Basel Mission Institute and similar bodies in Germany to supply the mission field with Lutheran pastors (many coming from the strongly pietist Lutheran *Landeskirche* of Württemberg). This connection, a continuation of links established between Lutherans and Anglicans in the eighteenth century, remained a fruitful form of European cooperation for more than fifty years.[16] The expectations concerning assistance to the Orthodox churches also proved somewhat over-sanguine, not to say naive.[17] There was often some response from church leaders — in Egypt, Ethiopia, and the churches of St. Thomas in India — but political realities and natural ecclesiastical defensiveness made these links difficult to sustain. The CMS also came to realize that missionary work in Muslim lands required tact and patience.[18]

Eugene Stock and the Legacy of Henry Venn

The CMS, like practically all the mission societies created at the turn of the century, saw itself as having a home base that sent out (the CMS used the quaint term "dismissed") missionaries, who in turn reported and were answerable to the home secretariat. After the visit of Edward Bickersteth to Sierra Leone in 1814, no secretary of the society visited the "mission field" until Wigram's world tour in 1886.[19] Henry Venn (1797-1873) never left Europe, but there was a personal interaction with Christians from all over the world and especially with Africans. In his youth at Clapham Rectory in the early years of the century, he had played with West African boys sent over for education in London. And with the establishment in 1825 of the training institute at Islington, there was, throughout Venn's life, a stream of students from overseas, particularly from areas where the CMS had established work. The majority of students were British nongraduates, who were getting basic theological training before ordination by the bishop of London. There were also, in the first half of the century, many German Lutherans, improving their English language and, in some cases, preparing for Anglican ordination. Stock takes particular care to mention the non-

16. See chap. 2 below.
17. See chap. 5 below.
18. See chap. 5 below.
19. Stock, vol. 3, p. 337.

Europeans who passed through the Islington Institute, a list that included the future bishop, Samuel Crowther, as well as his son, Dandeson, later to be an archdeacon, and other Creole Christians from West Africa. The Maori chiefs, Tamihana and Hoani Wiremu [John Williams] lived at Islington in 1852 during their diplomatic mission to Queen Victoria. Wiremu wanted ordination, but in New Zealand "his industry in studying by dim candle-light [had] affected his eyes, and he had, to his great sorrow, to forgo his wish." (Possibly he was also victim of Bishop Selwyn's insistence on rigid academic standards.)[20] Chun de Quang (a youth attached to the Chinese court in the Great Exhibition of 1851, and afterward tutor at St. Paul's College, Hong Kong), William Sandys, a Burmese from Calcutta (later a catechist in North India), and the Indian Nehemiah Goreh, who came in the entourage of Maharajah Dhuleep Singh,[21] — are what Stock calls "irregulars" — that is, they spent some time at the institute but were not taking specific courses. The first Native American to be ordained in connection with CMS work, Henry Budd, studied at Islington and was ordained in Canada in 1850. An Indian, Vera Swami, training for the bar in London, stayed at Islington, became a Christian, was ordained, and returned to India as the Revd Arthur Theophilus Vera Swami, pastor of a Tamil congregation in Madras.[22] Stock does not mention foreign students at Islington in the third volume, which implies that with the expansion of the episcopate abroad and the development of local seminaries, the need for this kind of training in England diminished. For trainee missionaries the syllabus was reformed in 1868 to become directed more toward missionary training, including courses in apologetics ("Christian Evidences"), practical subjects such as agriculture and gardening, and some elementary medicine, botany, and chemistry, as well as "the Theological section . . . to be directed specifically to the requirements of Hindu and Mohammedan controversy."[23]

It was as a result of Venn's advocacy that the CMS, which had been viewed with considerable suspicion as a loose cannon by the es-

---

20. Stock, vol. 2, p. 638.
21. For a brief account of Goreh's life see M. E. Gibbs, *The Anglican Church in India, 1600-1970* (Delhi: ISPCK, 1972), pp. 181-85, 298-300. Goreh had been converted in the 1840s and baptized by a CMS missionary. He was ordained deacon in 1868 and priest in 1870 in Calcutta. He later became attracted to the community religious life associated with the Cowley Fathers but was not professed.
22. Stock, vol. 2, p. 396.
23. Stock, vol. 2, p. 397.

tablishment of the church of England in its early years, became acceptable to the hierarchy, with the archbishop of Canterbury and eight English bishops becoming members of the society in 1841. Venn was equally determined that episcopal patronage would not compromise the "voluntary principle" of the society — that the mission be distinguished from the church as a separate corporate body. For Venn the defense of the autonomy of the society was also the best guarantee for the integrity of the native church that would result from mission activity. But increasingly these views came under critical scrutiny from the revived Anglican consciousness of the church itself as an autonomous institution incorporated and commissioned by God, clearly separate from the state in Britain — with which, from the 1830s, the Catholic revival connected with the Oxford Movement was particularly associated. The CMS had itself been keenly involved in the establishment of the episcopate in India, for example. But in the face of calls (associated in Britain particularly with Samuel Wilberforce, bishop of Oxford) for missionary bishops, justified in some cases by somewhat exaggerated theological interpretations about missionary work being impossible without a bishop, Venn tended to become suspicious of an extension of the episcopate that obviated the Crown with the checks and balances to "autocracy" that the English system of establishment supposedly gave. The bishop of Oxford, as son of William Wilberforce, had known Venn since childhood (he was seven years younger than Venn). In 1853, Wilberforce wrote a letter to Venn's brother-in-law, James Stephen, who was opposing the bishop's proposal for an act enabling bishops to be appointed outside the queen's dominions, in which he spoke of Venn as "the autocrat of the Church Missionary Society. He fears that missionary Bishops would supersede Church missionary committees." This comment has often been misunderstood — it was a deliberate caricature of Venn by Wilberforce. What he was saying was, in effect: "You, [James Stephen] and Venn, are opposing this bill on the grounds of the dangers of episcopal autocracy. I could equally well, and with equal calumnious insinuation, make the same charge against the secretary of the CMS."[24] Venn was in reality strongly in favor of the extension of the episcopate but was very much aware that bishops must not be permit-

24. See T. E. Yates, *Venn and Victorian Bishops Abroad: The Missionary Policies of Henry Venn and Their Repercussions upon the Anglican Episcopate of the Colonial Period, 1841-1872* (Uppsala: Swedish Institute of Missionary Research; London: SPCK, 1978), p. 102.

ted to stifle the native church. He saw dangers, not only in the kind of monarchical bishops that were, rightly or wrongly, associated in evangelical minds with "missionary bishops" but equally in the development of colonial bishops who would be primarily concerned with the church as an English institution, and in which the culture of the native Christian community would not be able to develop. Famously, he saw the church being built up from its local roots in "native pastorates" (West Africa) or *panjayat* councils (India) with the episcopate as "the crown of the church." He did not want the multiplication of European bishops to retard the development of a native episcopate, and the complex negotiations about the best way forward for episcopal supervision in South India delayed the appointment of Edward Sargeant and Robert Caldwell as bishops of respectively the CMS and SPG areas of the Tirunelveli church.[25]

In his 1862 biography of the great Jesuit missionary, Francis Xavier, Venn believed that the example of Xavier cast doubts on the efficacy of "the notion that an autocratic power is wanted in a mission, such as a missionary bishop might exercise." But equally, his own willingness to sanction bishops representing one distinctive tradition in the church, to the exclusion of the broader theological and spiritual spectrum, could be, and was, accused of reinforcing a missionary paternalism, a virtual ecclesiastical *apartheid* (to use a twentieth-century term). But it is ironic that the group that Venn is most closely identified with, the West African Creoles, represented precisely the kind of Westernized culture that apologists for "indirect rule" and "separate development" in the colonial period particularly disparaged. The fact is that Venn's theories of the separation of church and mission, the euthanasia of a mission, and the development of the native church have been appropriated by his successors in a number of contradictory directions, as Peter Williams's study has shown.

It is one of the major contentions of Peter Williams's thorough and illuminating analysis of Venn's missionary theory and how that theory suffered at the hands of Venn's successors, that by the end of the century the CMS had become over-centralized, too concerned with its institutional identity and satisfying its constituency at home.[26] Stock is not, of

25. These two were consecrated bishops in Calcutta in 1877, many years after the proposal for suffragan bishops in the Tirunelveli church had first been mooted and some time after Venn's death in 1872.

26. Williams, *The Ideal of the Self-Governing Church*, p. 145: "[Venn's] theory had become more and more controlled by the interests of the institution rather than by its declared end — the independent native church."

course, the "successor" of Venn — he was never the complete authority as director of the CMS that Venn had been. But Stock, the lay secretary, was in close accord with the two clerical successors of Venn: Henry Wright (1872-80) and Wright's brother-in-law, Frederic Wigram (1880-95). His *History* faithfully reflects the changed priorities of that age. Positively, it was an age when the rather narrow and negative reaction to the internal revival of Anglicanism (seen as hostile to evangelical principles) was replaced by a much greater readiness to cooperate and work with diocesan structures overseas. For example, Stock was embarrassed by the conflicts the CMS had with Bishop Copleston of Ceylon in the 1870s and underplays the issues at stake,[27] in the interests of emphasizing the readiness of the CMS to play its part within the Anglican communion. By and large this was, in fact, a positive development; during the colonial period, refusal to accept "diocesanization," while theoretically true to Venn's mission strategy, could be the recipe for the missionary paternalism that Venn opposed. Stock's *History* comes after a generation of increasingly confident, not to say jingoistic, imperialism.[28] Sir John Seeley's *The Expansion of England,* with its bombastic talk of dominion and mastery as the destiny of the Anglo-Saxon race, was published in 1882, during the decade when Britain took over control in Egypt, and Gordon was killed at Khartoum. The Hulsean lectures of 1894-95, by Bishop Barry, were titled significantly enough *The Ecclesiastical Expansion of England;* "Without doubt," wrote Stock, "the best summary of the colonial and missionary work of the Church of England which has yet appeared."[29] There was little of popular jingoism in Stock, but he was not out of tune with the imperialist spirit of the age. To take just one example, the campaign launched in the 1890s by Bishop Tucker and given tacit support by the CMS for the British government to assume direct responsibility from the Imperial British East Africa Company, is presented by Stock as unambiguously a blessing for Uganda: "Thus Uganda was saved. . . . It may be truly said to-day, as Bishop Tucker has often said, that England owes the great empire she now rules over in Central Africa to the memorable meeting of the Gleaners' Union in Exeter Hall on October 30th, 1891."[30]

This confidence in the role of the English as colonial rulers became

27. Williams, *The Ideal of the Self-Governing Church,* chaps. 2, 3.
28. The Boer War began in October 1899, some six months after the end of the CMS centenary.
29. Stock, vol. 3, p. 685.
30. Stock, vol. 3, p. 439. The Gleaners' Union refers to one of the CMS countrywide networks for local support in England.

part of the assumption for understanding of leadership in the church overseas. Despite the enlightened nature of Tucker's proposed constitution for the Church of Uganda, Tucker found it hard to envisage a Ugandan priest as his successor or even as an assistant bishop — his actual successor, Bishop Willis, was even more dismissive of the idea. Apart from the belated appointment of an Indian, V. S. Azariah, as bishop of Dornakal in 1912, there was no appointment of a native diocesan bishop anywhere in CMS areas until the 1950s, and most had to wait until the 1960s.

Stock's promotion of Keswick spirituality was in part a response to this new climate of imperialism, which certainly had an impact on university students' enthusiasm for missionary work, especially in Cambridge in the 1880s. It culminated in the great student conference of 1896 in Liverpool, with its watchword "The evangelisation of the world in this generation" and the promotion of the Student Missionary Volunteer Union. But the Keswick movement should not be simply typecast as part of the new imperialism. It may have produced the conditions for the open display of racism on the Niger,[31] but it also produced Pilkington and Baskerville in Uganda. In the next generation some of the great missionary practitioners of the colonial period emerged from the Keswick movement, for example, Temple Gairdner for the CMS in Egypt and Donald Fraser for the Free Church of Scotland in Malawi. It is also to Stock's credit that he strongly supported the admission of women to missionary work. Stock believed rightly that the CMS, which had in some ways been at the forefront of encouraging women to a missionary vocation in the very early years of the century, had fallen far behind. The revivals of mid-century and the Mildmay movement in London had begun to provide opportunities for evangelistic and social work in home mission. After the death of his first wife, Stock lived with two of his unmarried sisters and two of his wife's unmarried sisters, and their mission activities in the East End of London were a constant reminder on this point.[32] Between 1820 and 1885, 99 women missionaries were sent out by the CMS (apart from wives) compared to 1,018 men. In the last fifteen years of the century, 485 women were sent (again not including wives) compared to 581 men.[33] The downside of this great upsurge of numbers, which naturally

---

31. See chap. 7 below.
32. Gollock, *Eugene Stock*.
33. *The Centenary Volume*, Lists of Missionaries 1 and 2, pp. 617-63.

seemed so heartening to those who attended the centenary celebrations, was the effect on the self-confidence and freedom of maneuver of the local churches. The missionary and evangelistic spirit were hardly abated in the age of colonialism — this was to be the age of Sundar Singh in India and Apolo Kivebulaya in Uganda and Congo, to name two men who became internationally famous and whose ability not to be repressed by the "missionary captivity" of the church can stand for the faithful ministry of countless native catechists and evangelists who preached the gospel and planted churches and established the church at a village level as never before. But, in terms of the strategy and self-understanding of the CMS, a radical rethinking of the priorities of mission had to wait until the secretaryship of Max Warren.

Gordon Hewitt's *The Problems of Success*

In the 1960s Max Warren commissioned a second official history of the society from Gordon Hewitt, a residentiary canon of Chelmsford Cathedral. Hewitt was a member of the Evangelical Fellowship for Theological Literature, a group that included Max Warren and Stephen Neill and whose purpose was to encourage a high intellectual standard of evangelical Anglican writing.[34] Hewitt had not been a missionary himself and unlike Stock had not been intimately involved in the administration of the society. The first volume, entitled *In Tropical Africa, The Middle East, At Home,* was published in 1971. Volume 2, *Asia, and Overseas Partners,* appeared in 1977. The term "Overseas Partners" signified sister mission agencies of the CMS in Canada, Australia, and New Zealand and in Ireland, where the Hibernian CMS had been founded as early as 1814.[35] In many ways Hewitt closely followed the format that Stock had made his own. The two volumes cover only thirty-two years (1910-42) — equivalent to two of the fifteen-year periods into which Stock divided his material — and the work has a similar broadly geographical basis for the arrangement of the material. But if Stock was the impassioned commentator on the society from the inside, Hewitt's work deliberately adopted a more distanced point of view, ap-

34. I am indebted to Bishop John V. Taylor for this information.
35. Gordon Hewitt, *The Problems of Success: A History of the Church Missionary Society, 1910-1942.* Vol. 1, *In Tropical Africa, The Middle East, At Home* (London: SCM, 1971), p. 506. Vol. 2, *Asia and Overseas Partners* (London: SCM, 1977), p. 424.

propriate to a detached observer. This is not to say that the author was not committed to mission or to the society but that he conceived his task as that of providing a dispassionate account that would finally be the more intellectually defensible and creditable apologetic for mission to skeptical secular historians.

Stock had looked back on a century of missionary endeavor with a certain sense of achievement and satisfaction and thanksgiving to God. This was an attitude shared by the missionaries at the Edinburgh World Missionary Conference of 1910 who reflected on a century of engagement in mission, of struggle, setback, and triumph. For Hewitt, as his title indicates, the success itself had become problematic. This was not because the aspirations of the missionary enterprise had not been accomplished. Indeed they had frequently been far beyond the dreams of the pioneers. Rather, for the period with which Hewitt deals, the very nature of mission, its relationship with colonialism, and the religious and cultural implications were becoming problematic, not least for the more perceptive missionaries themselves during the period under review, and even more so for the historian looking back in the aftermath of rapid worldwide decolonization. Hewitt had read Ayandele and Ajayi about Nigeria — with the devastating critique of the Niger diocese — which Stock of course had been concerned to underplay. In fact Hewitt is deeply critical of two interrelated aspects of the legacy of Stock and of his age: "the doubling of the CMS missionary strength in the decade 1890-1900 (1889-90: 630; 1899-1900: 1,238) was for Stock a glorious achievement in missionary obedience. For the contemporary historian, whose concern is primarily with the development of African churches as a social phenomenon, this flood of missionaries was nothing short of a disaster."[36]

The consequences were disastrous not only in inhibiting the development of an independent indigenous church. Hewitt was also concerned to point out the negative consequences for the self-respect of the society and of trying to sustain an increasingly burdensome level of operation in the twentieth century. The retrenchment of the interwar years, which was a drain in effort and morale, was in itself nothing new — Stock referred to these problems time and again in the nineteenth century and spoke of the society's determination, in faith, not to let finance dominate its response to missionary need. In 1910 there were 1,360 CMS missionaries, in 1942, 1,088. In fact, the decline in person-

36. Hewitt, vol. 1, pp. xiv-xv.

nel during this period was not as drastic as it would otherwise have been, largely because of the increasing reliance on grants-in-aid, especially for educational work, from colonial governments. The number working in Africa actually increased from 253 to 450 — made possible because of government funding of educational missionaries.[37] But the reliance on government had ambiguous consequences.

Education paid an increasingly central role in the mission work of the CMS. Some of its most imaginative and creative missionaries were engaged chiefly in this work. Take for example a series of important men and women who worked in Ceylon: A. G. Fraser, L. J. Gasler, Lilian Nixon and Gwen Opie, Paul Gibson, and John Macleod Campbell. They demonstrated a commitment to developing indigenous leadership, both clerical and lay. They made considerable efforts to appreciate the riches of Sinhalese culture and to encourage the church to respond to those riches. Gibson was important as an ecumenist, participating fully in the Peradeniya Training Colony, a teacher training college that was run jointly with the Methodists. These were people with openness and sympathy, operating in an environment that often contrasted with the colonial and ecclesiastical overcorrectness that sometimes seemed to characterize the period. Fraser and Gasler went on to important posts in mission education in Africa (Ghana and Uganda), where they were influential in establishing the basis of government-mission cooperation in the interwar period that J. H. Oldham of the International Missionary Council (established as a follow-up to Edinburgh 1910) was instrumental in setting up.[38]

In Africa education was considered unambiguously good — it obviously served both society and the church and had important evangelistic potential. This was not so obvious in Asia, where the Christian school and college tradition (inspired by the Scottish missionary Alexander Duff) aimed to influence an elite that was sympathetic to Christian values, even if they did not convert to Christianity. Missionaries had always agonized about whether this was a true fulfillment of the missionary vocation or a distraction from it. This dilemma continued in the twentieth century, not so much as a choice between education and evangelism as between, on the one hand, educating a high-class elite that, although not Christian, might exercise a general influence for Christian values broadly conceived and, on the other hand, a concep-

37. Hewitt, vol. 1, p. xiv.
38. Hewitt, vol. 2, pp. 181-95.

tion of the missionary task as primarily relating to the local Christian church, often poor and underprivileged, and assisting its needs.[39]

Another theme that Hewitt addressed was the increasing commitment to diocesanization, that is, the handing over of authority to the local diocese. Missionaries rarely had a problem with this in principle, though issues of race (especially in areas with settler populations) and a concern for the evangelical distinctiveness of the church, often meant that this was not an easy progression to negotiate. In Asia in particular, dioceses were rarely evangelized solely or even predominantly by the CMS, so other Anglican influences were often as assertive as those of the CMS in the creation of the diocese. Nevertheless, the society still frequently appeared to be the power behind the throne, even when responsibility had devolved to the local church. But increasingly the CMS was not, in fact, the paymaster — much greater responsibility was in the hands of the church. Government grants-in-aid tended to become increasingly important for maintaining mission budgets — but in this case, the fact that the government gave its grants directly to the mission society rather than to the native church could be seen as undermining the responsibility and autonomy of the local church. Moreover, the fact that government grants were not available for specifically clerical training created ongoing problems for the life of the church — many strong and vibrant churches had educated, literate, and articulate lay members, and a relatively inarticulate, underpaid, and undervalued native clergy.[40] This is one reason, apart from the racial expectations of colonial society, for the continued absence of native bishops. However, in the period of Hewitt's study, in India and West Africa and especially in China (where the church was especially vulnerable and sensitive about the need for an indigenous Christian leadership) assistant bishops were increasingly being appointed. But there undoubtedly was what J. V. Taylor has called a "disengagement" of the missionary from the life of the local community, which too easily in the colonial period expressed itself in "paternalism, clericalism, centralization, specialization" and "a

39. For a statement of the similar dilemma confronting CMS medical policy in the twentieth century, see M. A. Collins in Hewitt, vol. 2, p. 151.

40. Hewitt, vol. 2, p. 253. Hewitt quotes a CMS Newsletter for 1968 (written by J. V. Taylor) to emphasize this point: "The cause of the apparent neglect of theological training lay not in the indifference of mission boards, but in the harsh economic fact that the ministry was the only modern profession in the developing countries which was not artificially subsidized by local governments and international aid."

loss of contact with the world and the sense of responsibility for the world." Taylor (speaking specifically of Uganda but in terms that could be applied much more widely) saw this development as stemming from changes in the nature of the missionary vocation in the early part of the century, engendering attitudes that became "projected into the thinking of the church" and resulted in "a falling apart within the Body of the Church, so that each part no longer feels deeply its responsibility for all the other parts."[41]

All of these issues Hewitt picked up and dealt with sensitively in his regional studies of the different areas. Hewitt wanted his work to be judged as a "constitutional" history of the society. Yet, he was weaker than Stock about the place of the mission in British church life. The CMS now had a more secure place in British ecclesiastical life — its existence was no longer controversial or a threat to the establishment in the way it had been perceived at its beginning. But also one gets the sense that it had less obvious impact on the life of the church than it had had in the nineteenth century. Andrew Walls, drawing attention to the glaring lack of discussion of mission and missionary societies in Owen Chadwick's *The Victorian Church,* concludes that this shows how peripheral the missionary movement was in England even at the height of its influence. But I am not sure that this was not a blind spot in Chadwick's conception of his great theme, despite his understanding of missionary themes in other contexts.[42] Certainly Hewitt does not spend the same amount of time as Stock in putting the society in the context of the church issues of the time. The missionary societies were now part of the Anglican establishment, but marginal to the existence of the church in England. And yet, this period saw the increasing promotion of CMS personnel to positions of some responsibility within the Church of England. Cyril Bardsley was the first clerical secretary (the position Venn had held) to become an English diocesan bishop.[43] Wilson Cash (general secretary 1926-42) in turn became a diocesan bishop.

41. J. V. Taylor, *Processes of Growth in an African Church,* IMC Research Pamphlet, no. 6 (London: SCM, 1958), p. 12.

42. Andrew Walls, "Structural Problems in Mission Studies," in *The Missionary Movement in Christian History: Studies in the Transmission of Faith* (Maryknoll, N.Y.: Orbis Books; Edinburgh: T. & T. Clark, 1996), p. 144.

43. When Bardsley resigned in 1922, his place was taken by Herbert Lankester, the first lay person to take the equivalent position of honorary clerical secretary — which then became known as general secretary and for the first time was salaried.

A number of bishops from the mission field also became assistant bishops in English dioceses on retirement.[44] This fertilization of mission field, society, and church in England was certainly a fruitful development, but the extent of its impact on the life of the church is debatable.

The most controversial event of Hewitt's period was undoubtedly the crisis that came to a head in 1922 and split the society, dividing Anglican evangelical endeavor and producing the Bible Churchmen's Missionary Society. This was a conflict over definitions of biblical and theological correctness, with clear repercussions from the conflicts within student circles that culminated in the separation of the Inter-Varsity Fellowship from the Student Christian Movement in 1927-28. Hewitt rightly wished to stress the continuity of the majority opinion within the CMS with the original evangelical breadth of the society: a church society but not a High Church society, but equally one that did not define its evangelicalism too precisely. This was still a painful and sensitive issue, even fifty years later when Hewitt was writing, and he was reluctant to give the conflict prominence in his narrative. The conflict had repercussions that Hewitt understated, both in dividing evangelical mission endeavor in England and in producing some considerable and persistent acrimony in the mission field, especially in East Africa. Fortunately the CMS continued to find room within its membership for the distinctively robust conservative evangelical witness of Joe Church and other members of the Ruanda Mission of CMS. This was to be important for the development of the East African revival movement (the "Balokole") — though the roots of that movement must be looked for essentially in the development of an indigenous Ugandan spirituality rather than in the theological disputes of English evangelicalism.

Hewitt was strongly aware of the fact that it is the local churches that are the prime focus of historical and theological interest:

> A concentration upon "the mission" rather than "the church" in no way implies that what the missionaries were busily doing between 1910 and 1942 was *more important* for the reign of Christ than the things the local clergy or catechists or congregations were doing in the same period. In some cases it will be suggested that some of the things the missionaries were doing ought not to have been done by them at all

---

44. For example, two Uganda bishops, Willis and Stuart, each became active as assistants. Archbishop Leslie Brown (archbishop of Uganda) became a diocesan bishop when he retired from Uganda in 1962.

at that time and in that place. But it is still possible, and perhaps important, to write of these things from within the missionary fellowship when so many are writing about them from outside it.[45]

According to this analysis, before 1942 the mission still operated as a distinct entity — it was not simply a part of the local church, and therefore it was a proper object of study. In fact, Hewitt's study leads one to wonder about the extent to which this is true. Hewitt provided very good summaries of what Stock had called "the environment"; in this case the environment being the Chinese, Indian, or African political and social situation. To take Nigeria as an example, Hewitt began with a nuanced survey of the country and people and the impact of colonial rule. He examined the missionary legacy before describing the African church and its growth and the social problems it faced and tried to address (polygamy, domestic slavery, liquor). He then discussed diocesan constitutional developments in three separate chapters before exploring in detail the work of the CMS in western, northern, and eastern Nigeria.[46] The problem with this approach is that many of the more interesting and historically significant issues are touched on primarily in the initial chapter, perceptively but all too sketchily. The subsequent three chapters then strike the reader as rather an anticlimax: the mission, studied for its own sake or in isolation from these larger issues, seems rather inconsequential in comparison. Hewitt was not unaware of this problem and was concerned to relate the work of the church to these wider movements. For example, he offered a perceptive critique of the mission constitution in western Nigeria, a document that paid lip service to diocesanization while keeping the mission and its power over the purse largely intact. The result was a hybrid organization that had unfortunate consequences for the healthy development of the church.[47]

An awareness of issues like this, along with the legitimate desire to avoid any whiff of hagiography or romantic escapism, may have resulted in a restraint in recounting missionary life stories. The delightful vignettes of missionaries and indigenous Christians that enlivened Stock's account were largely absent from Hewitt. All in all, *The Problems of Success* poses very starkly the questions of how possible a history of a missionary institution is in the twentieth century. The historian of society or the church in Nigeria or Uganda, India or China is not

---

45. Hewitt, vol. 1, p. xvii.
46. Hewitt, vol. 1, pp. 27-114.
47. Hewitt, vol. 1, p. 60.

likely to be satisfied by the inevitably cursory treatment of his or her area of specialization. On the other hand, the volumes fail to examine the society rigorously as a social phenomenon to throw light on its place in British Christian life. In light of this, it is hard to dissent from Brian Stanley's assessment that the volumes were "perhaps the final specimens of an exhausted and dying breed, and attracted little notice outside the immediate constituency of the Society."[48]

A History of CMS in the Latter Half of the Twentieth Century: Is It Possible and/or Desirable?

Ironically, Hewitt would have had less of a problem in writing an institutional history of the society if he had also covered the next thirty years of its life. This period, the time when Max Warren (1942-63) and John V. Taylor (1963-75) were general secretaries, was a highly creative one for the CMS. Jocelyn Murray has a useful summary of this period in her general history of the society, *Proclaim the Good News*. Published in 1985, this attempts, in one volume and at a popular level, to tell the story of the society from its beginnings to the time of writing.[49] Her title for chapter 12 is "Max Warren's Prophetic Vision." Not since the time of Venn had there been such inspiring leadership. Warren combined the genius of Venn as an administrator with the sensitivity to other cultures of someone who had done missionary service. This had been, in Warren's case, brief, but intense. Warren, himself the son of an Irish CMS missionary to India, had been one of a group of young Cambridge graduates who formed the "Hausa Band" in the 1920s to work with the CMS in northern Nigeria. Warren's own brother, Jack, went to Uganda with the Ruanda Mission of the CMS, which similarly had a strong Cambridge base and whose members represented in many ways a similar spiritual and missionary vision to that which inspired the Hausa Band. Max Warren's serious illness and repatriation to Britain after only a year, in 1928, cut off a promising missionary career but reinforced his commitment to mission. This found its culmination when

48. Brian Stanley, "Some Problems in Writing a Missionary Society History Today: The Example of the Baptist Missionary Society," in *Missionary Encounters: Sources and Issues,* ed. Robert A. Bickers and Rosemary Seton (London: Curzon Press, 1996).

49. Jocelyn Murray, *Proclaim the Good News: A Short History of the Church Missionary Society* (London: Hodder & Stoughton, 1985).

he was called to be general secretary at the age of thirty-eight, in 1942. This was the year that William Temple became archbishop of Canterbury, and one can see a similar breadth of interests and enthusiasm for the world church and for the mission of the church in the world in both these great Christian figures. In his 1944 memorandum, setting out mission priorities for the society, Warren pointed out the importance of the growing power of the state in Western countries, the burgeoning nationalism and the demand for the end of colonialism in many parts of the world, and the growing vitality of the indigenous church in the non-Western world. Mission societies needed to have an adequate response to these developments, within a well-developed theology of mission and the outworking of God's Spirit in history.[50] During this period, the CMS took on a vital role, both in interpreting this "world revolution" and its consequences for the end of British imperialism to British society and the church. Warren was an important advisor, perhaps the most important, for Archbishop Fisher (who succeeded Temple in 1944) in relation to the development of the sense of a worldwide Anglican communion of sister churches, and the role of Lambeth in this.[51] In East Africa, in both Kenya and Uganda, the CMS had important mediatorial roles in negotiating the end of empire. Warren advised Fisher on issues connected with the deportation of the Kabaka and helped to secure a climate by which the British government was able to allow the return of the Kabaka and the constitutional development of Uganda toward independence in 1962.[52] In Kenya, the society also had a role in interpreting the aspirations of Kenyans during the freedom struggle of the Mau Mau period. It would be untrue to say that CMS has always identified with progressive forces or has consistently done so in nonpaternalist ways, but a critical examination of the role of the CMS in decolonization will be of great value historically.

Warren's successor, John Taylor, like Warren a Cambridge man with a sound evangelical pedigree, has had a profound importance in contributing to African theology and the writing of a history of the African church and in encouraging Africans to undertake the task of articulating their spirituality and history. Sent out by CMS in 1944 to

50. F. W. Dillistone, *Into All the World: A Biography of Max Warren* (London: Hodder & Stoughton, 1980), pp. 84-88.

51. See Edward Carpenter, *Archbishop Fisher: His Life and Times* (Norwich: Canterbury Press, 1991).

52. See Kevin Ward, "The Church of Uganda and the Exile of Kabaka Muteesa II, 1953-55," *Journal of Religion in Africa* 28, no. 4 (1998), pp. 411-49.

Uganda as warden of Bishop Tucker College in Mukono, as a conservative influence in the aftermath of the problems faced in the college as a result of the revival movement, Taylor soon demonstrated, again like Warren, that the evangelical tradition, of which the CMS has been such an important part, can be constructive and original and have a profound openness to the world and to culture without losing its vitality and evangelistic verve.[53] It was during Taylor's time as general secretary that the relationship between mission and the overseas churches that it had helped bring to birth profoundly changed — that the "euthanasia of a mission" that Venn had talked of in the mid-nineteenth century finally became a reality for the life of the majority of the Anglican churches with which CMS was in relationship. By the end of Taylor's secretaryship in 1975, the transition had been accomplished.

The history of the last twenty-five years has been a search to find a new role for mission. Like the empire, this has not been easy. It takes the form of the continued activism — involvement in social and political affairs, in advocacy and protest — that characterized the pioneers of the society. It is also characterized by "Christian presence," a way of embodying mission that has a long history in the Middle East and other Islamic lands.[54] One of the chief functions of CMS mission partners in Uganda in the Amin and Obote years was to provide a tangible presence, a symbol of universality for a struggling church and people. It was perhaps not historically significant in any obvious sense, but it was a participation in what was a devastatingly important historical period in the life of Uganda and of its church. In Sudan the contribution of CMS as presence and as partners has been of perhaps even greater significance. Whereas in Uganda it had been a matter of being alongside a strong and well-organized church with its own deep spirituality and the strong indigenous revival tradition of the Balokole movement, in Sudan it has been a question of being present at a great period of primary evangelization in the southern Sudan, in which people have found new resources and a transformed life in the Christian faith. These developments have been sensitively described by two CMS mission partners: in the theologically profound and lyrical treatment of Marc Nikkel and a historically precise and nuanced treatment by Andrew Wheeler, who,

53. For the Mukono crisis, see K. Ward, "Obedient Rebels," *Journal of Religion in Africa* 19, no. 3 (1989), pp. 194-227; and K. Ward, *Called to Serve: A History of Bishop Tucker Theological College* (Kampala, 1989).

54. See Michael Nazir-Ali, *From Everywhere to Everywhere: A World View of Christian Mission* (London: Collins, 1991), chap. 8.

together with Bill Anderson, an American Presbyterian missionary born in Africa, has well served the Sudan church as inspirer and organizer of the Sudan History Project. This is a fully ecumenical project involving Sudanese scholars and pastors, Catholic and Protestant, as well as missionaries, and which is publishing its researches in the Faith in Sudan series.[55] The titles of the first five volumes demonstrate the breadth of mission concern, a mission in which foreign missionaries have a part to play but in which the direction and impetus come from the missionary awareness of the local Christian community:

- *Land of Promise: Church Growth in a Sudan at War*
- *Seeking an Open Society: Interfaith Relations and Dialogue in Sudan Today*
- *In Our Own Languages: The Story of Bible Translation in Sudan*
- *Struggling to Be Heard: Christian Presence in Sudanese Politics, 1956-96*
- *Gateway to the Heart of Africa: Missionary Pioneers in Sudan*

The crucial importance that the CMS has at times had in the history of so many parts of Africa during the last two hundred years should not lead one to neglect the significant insights on Asian Christianity that have occurred through CMS involvement. In chapter 11 of this volume, Graham Kings examines the important correspondence between Pat and Roger Hooker (working in India) and Max Warren. The insights into race relations and interfaith issues that mission partners have gained in Asia have in the last twenty-five years been of very great value for the development of British Christianity's response to these issues. As well as the Hookers, there has been the work of Christopher and Tina Lamb, Colin and Anne Chapman, Andrew and Angela Wingate. They have had important roles in bringing their insights from the world church back to Britain, as well as contributing significantly to the self-understandings of the churches in which they worked.[56] One

---

55. The first five volumes of this series, edited by Andrew Wheeler and William Anderson, were published in 1997 by the Paulines Press in Nairobi, established by a Catholic order, the Daughters of St. Paul.

56. Roger Hooker and Christopher Lamb, *Love the Stranger: Ministry in Multifaith Areas* (London: SPCK, 1986); Andrew Wingate, *Encounter in the Spirit: Muslim-Christian Dialogue in Birmingham* (Geneva: WCC, 1988); Andrew Wingate, *The Church and Conversion: A Study of Recent Conversions to and from Christianity in the Tamil Area of South India* (Delhi: ISPCK, 1997).

could also mention the important work in relation to refugees and asylum seekers that Louise Pirouet (a CMS missionary in Kenya and Uganda) has conducted with single-mindedness and written about with passion and clarity.[57]

These sketches, arbitrary in picking out some people with which this writer has been personally acquainted and who have been active in writing and leaving others of perhaps equal or greater significance, demonstrate something of the continuing vitality of CMS as a society. Any history of this activity is bound to face the problems of coherence and unity implicit in an organization with worldwide ramifications and whose prime object is to reach beyond itself. The biblical text "Unless a grain of wheat falls into the ground and dies, it remains that and nothing more; but if it dies, it bears a rich harvest" (John 12:24) always seems peculiarly relevant to a mission society and must have been in Venn's mind when he talked of euthanasia of a mission. What is certain is that any history of the fascinating period in the life of the society since 1942 cannot be primarily a "constitutional" history but must be one that adequately reflects reaching out, crossing of frontiers, local participation, and global horizons.

Max Warren expressed the importance of history for the CMS in this way:

> I am deeply convinced that only a right attitude to the past provides me with any possibility whatever of a right attitude to the future. And by a right attitude to the past I mean a genuine conviction that the Holy Spirit was operating in the past, that he guided our fathers before us, and that he was all the while at work taking up the cross-threads of human ignorance and failure and sin and using them to weave a pattern whose full revealing awaits the future. This does not mean that we treat the past as sacred, that we must not pass judgment upon it. Far from that I believe we only do justice to the past when we lift it up into our belief that God was in it both creatively and redemptively, creating all that was good in it and redeeming all that was evil and mistaken. A belief in the God of history is a positive invitation to the passing of judgments upon history. But our judgments will be passed with due humility for we will remember that we are ourselves in history and that God is at work today, the creative agent

57. See, for example, Louise Pirouet, "Refugees and Worldwide Anglicanism," in *Anglicanism: A Global Communion*, ed. A. Wingate, K. Ward, C. Pemberton, and W. Sitshebo (London: Mowbray, 1998), pp. 252-58.

in anything good that we do and the Redeemer of that which is wrong.

I believe that history matters tremendously and that we must take the past as seriously as we hope the future will take us. There is an attitude of mind involved that is not easy to compass. I am not advocating the approach of the traditionalist. I do not idolise the past. I am not a conservative in the common meaning of that term. I am deeply convinced that we sometimes keep faith with the past best by making some new departure that will, in fact, fulfil what in the past was being attempted in other ways. But I make this departure in fellowship-with-the-past and not in any sort of contemptuous antagonism for it. As it were, I try and enter into conversation with the past, make it my contemporary, argue with it and treat it as a living companion. I do not believe we can understand the present and plan for the future unless we see clearly how continuous the present is with the past and how all-pervading is the influence of past patterns upon present behaviour.[58]

This bicentenary volume is an attempt to relate past, present, and future in the way that Warren advocated.

58. Dillistone, *Into All the World,* p. 80.

42

2. The Church Missionary Society and the Basel Mission: An Early Experiment in Inter-European Cooperation

PAUL JENKINS

Introduction: CMS Missionaries from the European Mainland

During the Church Missionary Society's first half-century, it was able to send many more missionaries abroad than it proved able to recruit in Great Britain. Its non-British missionaries did not come from other parts of the English-speaking world as would be the case later, but from mainland Europe. In retrospect one can see that this was a major project in intercultural Christian cooperation. It deserves careful analysis by modern Christians concerned about intercultural partnership in mission — and about the parameters of sustainable international cooperation.

The number of missionaries from mainland Europe entering CMS service until 1860 is surprisingly large to any who think of the CMS and Anglicanism in the nineteenth century as quintessentially English. According to the statistics in Stock's centenary history, by 1824 the society had sent one hundred men overseas — of whom more than one-third were from the European mainland. Moreover, of the seventy key, long-serving missionaries from the period 1824-40, almost half of them were not British by origin.[1]

Thus, when one surveys the areas in which the CMS was active in these pioneer decades, one repeatedly comes across people with European names playing major roles. In Sierra Leone, for example, German missionaries must have provided much of the continuity for the society in a land noted for its high death rate — Friedrich Bultmann[2] and Johann Ulrich Graf[3] (in Sierra Leone 1837-60 and 1836-55 respectively) are two examples. Farther east, David Hinderer lived through years of isolation and threat during the Yoruba wars in Ibadan.[4] The famous names in early CMS history in East Africa are from the European mainland too: Johann Ludwig Krapf[5] and Johannes Rebmann.[6] And so it goes on from region to region. Indeed, a systematic presentation of Basel Mission trainees in CMS service (see Table 1, p. 45) indicates that the CMS used this source of manpower to develop new emphases and strategies.

In the late 1820s missionaries from continental Europe played an important part in developing work in the Mediterranean region. Johann Rudolf Gottlieb Lieder, who worked for the CMS in Egypt from 1826 to 1865, is reputed to have had a high reputation among

1. Stock, vol. 1, pp. 243, 263-64. Late nineteenth-century statistics tend to emphasize the male side of CMS history — this chapter attempts to redress the balance to some extent. See also the contributions of Jocelyn Murray and Guli Francis-Dehqani.

2. Friedrich Bultmann, b. Bremen 1812, d. Oldenburg 1884, married (1) Henrietta Kaufmann from Lahr, (2) Lina Wilkens of Bremen, and (3) Elisa Ramsauer of Oldenburg. Data on persons in this chapter have been taken from the *Brüderverzeichnis* — the List of the Brethren — maintained by the Basel Mission with basic data on all men who entered the Mission Seminary in Basel. Its accuracy for missionaries and their wives once they had joined CMS is not guaranteed.

3. Johann Ulrich Graf, b. Grub (Canton Appenzell/Switzerland) 1812, d. London 1887, married (1) Mary Taylor, (2) Lucy Paris.

4. David Hinderer, b. Birkenwiesbuch/Württemberg 1819, d. Bournemouth 1890; CMS, Yoruba Mission 1849-77. Married Anna Martin from Lowestoft.

5. Johann Ludwig Krapf, b. Derendingen/Württemberg 1810, d. Kornthal/Württemberg 1881. CMS missionary in Ethiopia and East Africa 1837-55. Married (1) Rosine Dietrich of Kornthal, (2) Charlotte Pelargus, and (3) Nanette Schmid of Cannstadt/Württemberg.

6. Johannes Rebmann, b. Gerlingen/Württemberg 1829, d. Kornthal 1876. In East Africa with CMS 1846-75. Married (1) Emma Tyler, (2) Luise Finkh née Däuble.

Table 1. Destinations of CMS Basel-trained Missionaries, 1819-58

	India	Sierra Leone	Mediter-ranean	Caribbean	Ethiopia, East Africa	Australia, New Zealand	Nigeria	Died, resigned	Totals
to 1825	5	4	1						10
1825-30	3	1	8						12
1831-35	8	4	1	2	1	1		1	18
1836-40	11	3	1	2	2	1		3	23
1841-45	3	4			2				9
1846-50	7	2		1	2		1	1	14
1851 on	5	3			2		6		16
Totals	42	21	11	5	9	2	7	5	102
	*4	*1	*4	*2	*2	*1	*2		

Notes:

1. Figures are based on records in Basel.

2. Each missionary's first arrival overseas has been registered. Some missionaries worked in more than one overseas region. The figures marked with an asterisk (*) indicate how many Basel-trained missionaries were sent to a specific region after having already worked for the CMS elsewhere.

3. "Died, resigned" indicates Basel-trained missionaries taken over by the CMS who died or resigned before reaching an overseas place of assignment.

45

Fig. 2. David Hinderer (1820-1890) and
Anna Hinderer (née Martin; 1827-1870),
CMS missionaries in Yorubaland.

Church Mission Society, London

leaders of the Coptic church.[7] Friedrich August Hildner worked in
Greece from 1827 to 1875, running a *Pädagogien* (teachers' training

7. Johann Rudolf Gottlieb Lieder, b. Erfurt 1798, d. Cairo 1865 (of chol-
era). Married to Alice Holiday from Scarborough. Confusion can arise because
some German names are Anglicized in the CMS records. One notorious case is
"Gottlieb," which became "Theophilus," as here with Lieder, but also with the
Basel Mission's first *Inspektor*. "Who was *Theophilus* Blumhardt?" people asked
when the CMS message to the Basel Mission's 175th anniversary was read out.
Another case is the Basel-trained missionary Dürr, who appears as "Deerr" in
some CMS records.

Fig. 3. Johann Ludwig Krapf (1810-1881),
CMS missionary in East Africa.

Church Mission Society, London

college).[8] In the 1830s the attempt to initiate mission in Ethiopia was largely staffed from the Continent and included Samuel Gobat, later second Anglo-Prussian bishop of Jerusalem.[9] Quite apart from Hinderer, Basel-trained personnel bore the burden of much of the early work in Nigeria. And right through the period, CMS work in the Ganges Valley was staffed with people of non-British origins, including, after 1838-39, a number of former Basel missionaries from the Caucasus, forced to leave Russia by the government's withdrawal

8. Friedrich August Hildner, b. Querfurt/Saxony 1800, d. Hermupolis/Syra 1883. Married (1) Caroline Damm of Querfurt, (2) Angelica Georgiadu.
9. Samuel Gobat, b. Cremine, Canton Bern/Switzerland 1799, d. Jerusalem 1879. Married Maria Zeller from Beuggen/Baden.

of permission for their work. Perhaps the most distinguished of these was C. G. Pfander, whose skills in Urdu and Persian as a Christian propagandist provoked the important public debate staged with Rahmat Allah al-Kairanawi in Agra in 1854.[10]

It is correct to describe these men as having been recruited from the European mainland, but this assertion needs to be made more precise. The great majority spoke German as their mother tongue and came from the regions that were to be pulled together into the German Empire by Bismarck. Indeed, many of them came from one German state, Württemberg.[11] Exceptions to this rule were Samuel Gobat, who was from the French-speaking region of Canton Bern, and Peter Fjellstedt from Sweden, who became a key initiator of Swedish Protestant mission work after his CMS service.[12] Secondly, almost all those entering CMS service from mainland Europe had been trained in one of two German-speaking mission seminaries: the short-lived institute run by Johannes Jänicke in Berlin, which supplied the first CMS missionaries, and the missionary college that was founded as a major part of the activities of the Basel Mission in 1815.[13] It was Basel-trained men who provided the great bulk of missionaries from the European mainland recruited by the CMS — one hundred of them by the time recruitment faded away in the 1850s.

Another important consideration in the relationship between the CMS and the Basel Mission is the fact that about half of the marriages of their missionaries from the European mainland were concluded with English women and half with women from the German-speaking

10. Carl Gottlob Pfander, b. Waiblingen/Württemberg 1803, d. Richmond, England 1865. Basel Mission (Caucasus) 1825-38, CMS (North India and Mediterranean region) 1840-65. Married (1) Sophie Reuss from Moscow, (2) Emily Swinborne. See Avril A. Powell, *Muslims and Missionaries in Pre-Mutiny India* (London: Curzon Press, 1993).

11. Württemberg is, roughly speaking, the region around Stuttgart, its capital city, in southwestern Germany. Since the Second World War, it has been half of the modern province of Baden-Württemberg. Württemberg is the traditional heart of the Basel Mission — as many as 50 percent of Basel missionaries came from there in the nineteenth century; as did, until 1939, the great majority of the full-time staff in the Mission House in Basel.

12. Peter Fjellstedt, b. Sillerud/Sweden 1802, d. Uppsala 1881. CMS missionary in India and the Mediterranean region 1831-40. Married Christiane Schweizerbarth from Stuttgart.

13. Johannes Jänicke's Mission College in Berlin was opened in 1800 and closed on its founder's death in 1827. Jänicke had close Moravian connections. Why the CMS gave up this source of recruitment after taking more than sixteen of Jänicke's graduates by 1817 was also unclear to Stock — *History,* vol. 1, p. 124.

world.[14] Hinderer's wife Anna, who was an important presence in Iba-dan, grew up in a parsonage in Lowestoft. Her foster-mother was a sis-ter of Elizabeth Fry.[15] On the other hand, some marriages with Ger-man-speaking women linked the CMS with important missionary and pietist dynasties on the European mainland. Maria Gobat was a Zeller,[16] for example, and Emilie Hörnle a woman from the redoubt-able Weigle-Moegling clan, closely linked by friendship to the Gunderts and the Hesses.[17]

Why did the German-speaking world play such an important role in supplying missionaries for the early CMS? It would perhaps be tempting to answer this question at a superficial level and point to eighteenth-century precedents in missionary connections between the English- and German-speaking worlds. That Zinzendorf and his Moravian followers played an important part in stimulating revival and mission in Britain through their influence on John Wesley is well known. It is also well

14. Background information on women and marriage in the history of the Basel Mission is available in English: *Mission History from the Woman's Point of View* (Basel: Basel Mission, 1989), for the nineteenth century, and *Women Carry More Than Half the Burden* (Basel: Basel Mission, 1996), for the twentieth century. These pamphlets offer a summary of the results of a Basel Mission project on women's history presented by Waltraud Haas, *Erlitten und Erstritten, der Befreiungsweg von Frauen in der Basler Mission, 1816-1960* (Basel: Basel Mission, 1994). The Tübingen anthropologist Dagmar Konrad is currently writing a doc-toral thesis on marriage in the Basel Mission, using especially the private correspon-dence still held by many German-speaking missionary families in Württemberg.

15. See note 4 above. Anna Hinderer was a woman of many parts; sketches she made of Ibadan were published as engravings in CMS periodicals.

16. As a family, the Zellers played a central part in the life of two major pietist centers in the nineteenth century: Schloss Beuggen, on the German side of the Rhine upstream from Basel, in which there was a training college for primary-school teachers, and Männedorf in Canton Zurich/Switzerland.

17. Gottlieb Hörnle, b. Ludwigsburg/Württemberg 1804, d. Cannstatt/Württemberg 1882. With the Basel Mission in the Caucasus 1832-38, and with CMS in North India 1838-80. He married Emilie Moegling from Mössingen/Württemberg in March 1838. She was a sister of Herrmann Moegling and step-sis-ter of Gottfried Weigle, both key figures in the establishment of Basel Mission work in the Kannada language of Karnataka, South India. Moegling was a close friend and colleague of the Basel Mission's Malayalam linguist Hermann Gundert of Kerala, South India, later editor of the Calw Mission Press and maternal grandfa-ther of the German writer Hermann Hesse. Gottlieb Hörnle's lightning missionary courtship of Emilie Moegling is described in Hermann Gundert, *Hermann Moegling* (Kottayam: DC Books, 1997), p. 101. This is a modern English transla-tion of the German original biography of 1882.

known that the SPCK supported and even virtually directed German and Danish missionaries in South India, in what is now Tamil Nadu.[18] But taking this approach to English-language literature on the eighteenth-century church takes the risk of trivializing something extremely important. Revival was occurring all over Protestant Europe (including Britain) in the decades either side of 1800. Something like an *International* of Protestant activists developed, people who looked for concrete and innovative ways of carrying out what they saw as the will of God in the face of the evil existing in the world. They knew about each other's efforts through international networks of communication and the ties of friendship and family. One of the increasing priorities in this *International,* alongside the antislavery movement, was missions to the non-Western world that were motivated by a concern to show the love of God to all humanity, even — or especially — where that contact had been degraded by slavery.[19]

The difficulties of following up this *International* are, however, considerable. First, studying an international movement cuts across the boundaries of national and national-confessional history writing — the mode of discourse about the past that still comprises much of the writing about the church.[20] Secondly, the Europe of the period under discussion was multifocal. Only France resembled Britain by its focus on a single dominating metropolis — Paris. The German-speaking world before 1871 was bewilderingly diffuse. Someone wanting to follow up the whole picture of the German-speaking contacts with the Protestant *International* would have to study not only major urban centers like Frankfurt, Berlin, Bremen, and Hamburg but also less famous yet nevertheless proud and self-conscious communities like Calw.[21] Beyond the German-

18. Stock, vol. 1, pp. 23, 90.

19. The international aspects of the religious revival in the Protestant world in the early and mid eighteenth century, involving continental Europe, Britain, and North America is superbly conveyed in W. R. Ward, *The Protestant Evangelical Awakening* (Cambridge: Cambridge University Press, 1992).

20. The brevity of the modern bibliography, which could be taken as a background to this essay, is an eloquent testimony to the accuracy of this observation. See Martin Brecht, "The Relationship between Established Protestant Church and Free Church: Hermann Gundert and Britain," in *Protestant Evangelicalism: Britain, Ireland, Germany and America, c. 1750–c. 1950 — Essays in Honour of W. R. Ward,* ed. Keith Robbins, Studies in Church History, Subsidia 7 (Oxford: Blackwell, 1990), pp. 135-51.

21. Calw is a small manufacturing town in the northern Schwarzwald in which a *Missionsverein* and a Mission Press grew up in the 1820s. The directors

speaking world there were Protestant activists in France, Holland, Denmark, Scandinavia, and eastern Europe. Concentrating on relations between the CMS and what became its main European partner, the Basel Mission, is thus not only intended to recall a forgotten aspect of CMS history. It is also an attempt to show in depth something of the nature of the diffuse intercultural cooperation that developed at the beginning of the nineteenth century among evangelicals in Europe, which was in some measure the heir to the partnership established in the previous century between the Halle pietist mission at Tranquebar and the SPCK in Britain. The nature of Basel as a center of Protestantism in the early nineteenth century also helps to indicate both the range of Protestant action in these years and the breadth of international contact.

The Basel Mission:
The Main European Partner of the CMS, 1815-60

The Basel Mission is part of an extended family of organizations founded in connection with the Basel *Deutsche Christentumsgesellschaft,* literally the "German Christianity Society." This was started as a focus of pietist thought and activity in Basel in 1780. The standard collection of historical documents to illustrate its history lists no fewer than thirty-seven other organizations in or linked to Basel whose foundation can be traced back to this prolific "mother," including the Basel Mission and the Pilgrim Mission St. Chrischona, a society to support development in Greece, a trading company in Jerusalem, three publishing projects, a Bible society, a teacher training college, four orphanages, three specialist hospitals, an order of deaconesses, and two organizations for the conversion of Jewish people. The wide energies of Protestant activism were clearly not confined to Britain at this time. The *Deutsche Christentumsgesellschaft* was led and supported by a varied group of people in the Basel region attempting to carry out what they believed was the will of God in many fields of activity.[22] It was not, however, simply an organization fo-

---

were, in turn, Christian Gottlieb Barth (well-known as the compiler of *Dr. Barth's Bible Stories*), Hermann Gundert, and Gundert's son-in-law, Johannes Hesse.

22. The Basel *Deutsche Christentumsgesellschaft* is the theme of two bulky volumes of documents from the society's archives which contain excellent indexes: Ernst Staehelin, *Die Christentumsgesellschaft in der Zeit der Aufklärung und der beginnenden Erweckung* (Basel: Friedrich Reinhardt Verlag, 1970), and Ernst

cused on Basel. Its name implied a major geographical program. Its declared aim was to network existing groups of pietist activists in centers great and small over the whole of Europe, partly through the production of a periodical devoted to pietist spirituality and action,[23] and partly through encouraging people to establish "particular societies" to promote contact and local action. Its links with major non-German cities like Rotterdam, Paris, Stockholm, Geneva, and London also gave it an important international dimension.

The Basel Mission was an integral part of the network built up by the *Deutsche Christentumsgesellschaft*. The early and very rapid expansion of the mission's circle of supporters can be traced back to the way the *Christentumsgesellschaft's* periodical printed German translations of reports from Anglo-Saxon missionary activities in the early years of the nineteenth century, preparing the broad German-speaking pietist movement for the idea of a missionary center in Basel. And the early centers that committed themselves to support the Basel Mission included not only groups in what became that mission's heartland (Württemberg, Baden, Hessen, the Palatinate, and German-speaking Switzerland) but also communities that later developed independent missionary societies of their own: Wuppertal/Barmen, Hamburg, Bremen, Dresden, and Leipzig were oriented toward the Basel Mission in the years immediately after 1815.

Especially important were the links between Basel and London created by the *Deutsche Christentumsgesellschaft* that began with its foundation. In 1779-80 a German pietist named J. A. Urlsperger[24] traveled widely to consult with interested groups on the foundation of a society to increase fellowship and strengthen witness. His last port of call was the German-Lutheran congregation named after the Savoy Chapel

Staehelin, *Die Christentumsgesellschaft in der Zeit von der Erweckung bis zur Gegenwart* (Basel: Friedrich Reinhardt Verlag, 1974). The list of *Christentumsgesellschaft* foundations is in *Erweckung bis zur Gegenwart*, pp. 735-37. The "Address Book" of the society for the years 1818-36 (i.e., its list of chief local contacts in Europe) is also highly suggestive: *Erweckung bis zur Gegenwart*, pp. 341-55.

23. *Sammlungen für Liebhaber christlicher Wahrheit und Gottseligkeit*, first published in 1786. The title could be translated as, "Collected Texts for Those Who Love Christian Truth and Holiness."

24. Johann August Urlsperger, b. Augsburg 1728, pastor of the Protestant Church in Bavaria, d. Hamburg 1806. Urlsperger's visit to London is discussed (though without reference to the Basel Mission) in Eamon Duffy, "The Society of Promoting Christian Knowledge and Europe: The Background to the Founding of the Christentumsgesellschaft," *Pietismus und Neuzeit* 7 (1981), pp. 28-42.

in London. It was there that the decision to found the *Christentumsge-sellschaft* took final shape. Indeed, those interested in London formed the first Particular Society of the Basel *Deutsche Christentumsgesell-schaft* in 1779.[25]

A more permanent role as coordinator and contact-person for London, the European mainland, and Basel was played by the German Lutheran pastor C. F. A. Steinkopf, who was secretary of the *Christen-tumsgesellschaft* in Basel from 1795 to 1801, chaplain of the Savoy Chapel congregation from 1801 until his death in 1859, and from 1804 foreign secretary of the British and Foreign Bible Society.[26] If Url-sperger's visit to London helped consolidate the decision to found the *Deutsche Christentumsgesellschaft,* Steinkopf's interventions from London helped to confirm the determination of the Basel Mission Com-mittee to start a missionary society in 1815. There was concern in Basel as to whether local support would be strong enough in the initial stages to sustain both a missionary society and a missionary college. These in-hibitions were partly overcome by Steinkopf's assurances of a keen En-glish interest in this development. Basel Mission tradition says that in 1815 concrete offers of financial help were made from London, should difficulties arise. The earliest message of this kind seems to have come from the London Missionary Society. But Steinkopf soon mediated a CMS link. In 1817 the first request was received in Basel to supply mis-sionaries for the CMS. A relationship started that was to be important for both societies for the next fifty years.[27]

25. Ernst Staehelin, *Aufklärung und der beginnenden Erweckung,* summarizes these developments on pp. 3-13 (see especially p. 7). It was on Christmas Day 1799 that the pastor of the Savoy congregation announced to his flock that "die Gesellschaft da sei" ("the society was there") thus establishing the London "Particu-lar Society" *before* the main society in Basel had been formally constituted. Susanne Steinmetz, *Deutsche Gemeinden in Großbritannien und Irland: Geschichte und Archivbestände* (1988), p. 237, reports that hardly any archival material exists on the involvement of this congregation or Pastor Steinkopf himself with missions. She does indicate that key people in the congregation were skilled German workers and that its prevailing theology and spirituality was pietist (pp. 14-16). See also, Susanne Stein-metz, *Deutsche Evangelisch-Lutherische St.-Marienkirche London, 1694-1994/St. Mary's German Lutheran Church in London* (London: St. Mary's German Lutheran Church, 1994). Texts in German and English.

26. Carl Friedrich Adolf Steinkopf, b. Ludwigsburg/Württemberg 1773, d. London 1859.

27. The most modern discussion of this episode is in Andreas Waldburger, *Missionare und Moslems, die Basler Mission in Persien, 1833-1837* (Basel: Basileia,

The Basel Mission thus came to be the main focus of CMS contact with the European mainland in the first half of the nineteenth century. It came to this prominence partly because of certain unique aspects of the situation of Basel at the end of the Napoleonic Wars but partly because the *Christentumsgesellschaft's* initiatives corresponded to what was becoming a broad, although not yet well-articulated movement. Basel was a city-state in Switzerland, and its republican-oligarchic politics gave its leading citizens maneuverability to start new forms of activity and found new organizations. Many people living in kingdoms and principalities in other parts of Europe had less freedom in this area. Furthermore a good proportion of Basel's leading citizens, with their concrete organizational skills in banking and trade, were serious Christians of a pietist character and already had wide trading connections that ran parallel to, and no doubt interacted with, the *Christentumsgesellschaft's* growing network. Basel, as a border city, evidently also had wider and more dynamic links to France and Germany than locations like Bern and Zurich at this time. Indeed Basel played a key mediatory role between France and Switzerland during the revolutionary and Napoleonic periods.[28] All of these points help answer the question of why a *Basel* mission should have taken on the role it did vis-à-vis the CMS and not an organization in Stuttgart, Frankfurt, or Zurich.

In addition, the Basel Mission, representative as it was of the new evangelical activism spreading in Europe, could and did canalize the growing popular concern with mission in wide areas of mainland Europe. Indeed, by the middle of the nineteenth century, when links between the CMS and the Basel Mission were loosening, Basel's role as pacemaker of mission development in the German-speaking world was also dissolving, giving way to a situation in which approximately ten centers that had previously supported the Basel Mission were building up their own independent missionary societies.[29]

1984). In spite of its title, this dissertation concerned itself, inter alia, with the history of the founding and early development of the mission. See section 2.1, specifically p. 35. The old official history of the Basel Mission, Wilhelm Schlatter, *Geschichte der Basler Mission, 1815-1915,* 3 vols. (Basel: Basel Mission, 1916), confirms the point (cf. vol. 1, pp. 61-62).

28. For the international significance of Basel in relations between Switzerland and France in this period, see Beat von Wartburg, *Basel 1798 — vive la République Helvetique* (Basel: Museum der Kulturen, 1998). Main texts in German.

29. The best, if somewhat biased, description of this process is still Wilhelm Schlatter, *Geschichte der Basler Mission,* vol. 1, chaps. 3.3, 3.4, and 4.5.

The Distinctive Contribution of Missionaries from the European Mainland to the CMS

Continental missionaries joining the CMS in this period had undergone a long period of training in a German mission seminary before they crossed the Channel to receive further education with an English tutor or, after 1825, at Islington College. Their main formation, therefore, was not English, and one might ask what their German-language background brought to the CMS. This is an extremely difficult question to answer at the moment. There is, for example, no modern intellectual history of the nineteenth-century Basel Mission.[30] It would be difficult to describe how a Basel trainee differed from his English colleagues in his thinking about mission. In this essay I can only raise the question and rehearse one or two examples of the way it could prove to be important.

One starting point is the assertion made in 1854 by S. W. Koelle,[31] one of the great Basel-trained CMS linguist-missionaries, that African languages are fully human and capable of expressing as great a range of differentiated thought and emotion as European languages. Taken in isolation this opinion might seem puzzling, suggesting that Koelle had traveled to Sierra Leone with a paternalistic attitude that he had subsequently rejected only as a result of his studies in Kanuri language and literature. Recent publications on German nineteenth-century academic linguistics point out, however, how deeply racist these were: African languages, like African cultures, were regarded as primitive.[32] Koelle's testimony as to the quality of African languages is almost certainly to be understood as addressed to this German discourse. This is one case

30. Though one should note Jon Miller, *The Social Control of Religious Zeal: A Study of Institutional Contradictions* (New Brunswick, N.J.: Rutgers University Press, 1994).

31. S. W. Koelle, b. Kleebronn/Württemberg 1823, d. Fulham 1902. Worked for CMS in Sierra Leone 1845-53 and in the Mediterranean region 1855-77. Married Charlotte Elisabeth Philpot. Compiler of the *Polyglotta Africana*. His own main work was on the Kanuri language of West Africa. The statement referred to here is in *African Native Literature, or Proverbs, Tales, Fables and Historical Fragments in the Kanuri or Bornu Language* (London: CMS, 1854), pp. vi-vii.

32. For a recent discussion of this topic with a strong mission orientation see Thomas Bearth, "J. G. Christaller. A Holistic View of Language and Culture and C. C. Reindorf's History," in *The Recovery of the West African Past: African Pastors and African History in the Nineteenth Century — C. C. Reindorf and Samuel Johnson,* ed. Paul Jenkins (Basel: Baseler Afrika Bibliographien, 1998), pp. 83-101.

for which a knowledge of the German-language context of a CMS missionary's thinking helps us to understand more clearly what he was doing and how he expressed himself.[33]

More than one historian has observed, in recent years, that some Basel-trained missionaries seem to have exhibited a quality in their approach to evangelization and pastoral care that differed from that of their British colleagues in that it was at once more robust and energetic and yet more intimate. Recent writing has identified two such examples of Basel-trained missionaries who illustrated this through their involvement in important episodes of indigenous intellectual ferment. In this volume, Allan Davidson mentions the role of the Basel-trained missionary Georg Adam Kissling in the early years of theological training among Maoris.[34] John Peel suspects that Kissling's Abeokuta colleague Gottlieb Friedrich Bühler played a major role in inspiring the Christian Yoruba intellectual renaissance during his years in the Pastors' Seminary in Abeokuta (1858-64), though it is not easy to identify with any precision how this took place. J. F. A. Ajayi has pointed out that Bühler believed a broad general education was central to good mission practice. But initially this was not a Basel concern, though it may have become part of the Basel identity by the time Bühler was a student there.[35] We must, in any case, beware lest the search for differences between German and British missionaries in the CMS, impelled by romantic assumptions about a peculiarly German intellectualism, blind us to the evangelical, pietist activist heritage that they had in common.

33. See also Adam Jones, "Reindorf the Historian" in *The Recovery of the West African Past,* ed. Paul Jenkins, pp. 118-19. Jones uses Koelle and the mid-nineteenth-century Bremen missionary Bernhard Schlegel, who was trained in Basel, to define what he calls a distinctively "Enlightened-Protestant tradition" in attitudes to African culture in the mid-nineteenth century.

34. See below, p. 214; Georg Adam Kissling, b. Murr/Württemberg 1805, d. Auckland 1865. Worked for the Basel Mission in Liberia 1828-31, with CMS in Sierra Leone 1833-37(?) and New Zealand from 1842. Married (1) Caroline Tanner of Ludwigsburg/Württemberg, (2) Margaret Moxon.

35. Gottlieb Friedrich Bühler, b. Adelberg/Württemberg 1829, d. Untertürkheim/Württemberg 1865. Worked with CMS in Nigeria 1854-65. Married (1) Sophia Mary Jay, (2) Anna Norris. See John D. Y. Peel, "Two Pastors and Their Histories: Samuel Johnson and C. C. Reindorf," in *The Recovery of the West African Past,* ed. Paul Jenkins, p. 71; and, in the same publication, J. F. A. Ajayi, "Samuel Johnson and Yoruba Historiography," p. 58. Avril Powell's assessment of C. G. Pfander also suggests one or two distinctively Basel features of the seminary training and its missionaries' approach to evangelization. See Powell, *Muslims and Missionaries,* pp. 133-38.

Organization, Church Order, Culture, and Conflict

If it is difficult to compare the work and impact of British missionaries with that of their colleagues from the European mainland, we can look at organizational aspects of the relations between the CMS and the Basel Mission in some detail to uncover the potential for conflict that was undoubtedly present. The level of mutual organization attempted by the two sides deserves careful attention and reflection.[36] Basel and London are a long way apart. It is at least eight hundred kilometers from Basel to the nearest channel port, and fast methods of transport by rail and steamboat only became available towards the end of the period of active cooperation between the societies. Yet between 1818 and 1850, at least five official visits were made by delegates from the CMS to Basel and at least four took place in the opposite direction. In 1835, delegations from both sides met in Paris. Thus, key figures visited the other's headquarters: Bickersteth, Coates, Jowett, and Venn visited Basel, and the first two Basel Mission *Inspektoren*, Blumhardt and Hoffmann, visited London.[37]

The basic structure of the agreement established in 1818 between the two sides, frequently updated, confirmed as late as 1861 and apparently never formally revoked, was that the Basel Mission would provide the CMS with an agreed number of missionaries, and the CMS would contribute an agreed amount to the costs of their education. In 1818 this was twenty-five pounds per head per year.[38] If this agreement secured for the CMS a supply of missionaries prepared to die for the gospel, its implications for the Basel Mission were more than merely orga-

---

36. The material in this section is largely taken from Wilhelm Schlatter, *Geschichte der Basler Mission*, vol. 1. For the Basel Mission, the history of their cooperation with the CMS was still, at the beginning of the twentieth century, much more important than was the case in reverse. At least that is the conclusion one is likely to come to by comparing the amount of attention given to it by Schlatter and Eugene Stock.

37. It is a sad comment on a current unawareness of the importance of this kind of connection that we have no reliable list of journeys between Britain and the European mainland concerned with mission in the period discussed here. Martin Brecht in "Hermann Gundert and Britain" indicates how important the British connection was for Gundert and how he visited Britain from Calw in 1860 and 1862. In 1846 the foundation of the Evangelical Alliance in London occurred, and German-speaking delegates included Hermann Moegling and Christian Gottlieb Barth. There must have been many more such mutual visits.

38. Schlatter, *Geschichte der Basler Mission*, vol. 1, p. 64.

nizational and financial. It gave the organization a purpose and an international credibility that apparently appealed to its potential circles of supporters on the Continent.[39] Furthermore, the sources and secondary literature on the Basel Mission are unanimous in presenting the influence of the CMS as important in the evolution of the famous Basel five-year mission seminary program, which was, in fact, ended only in the 1950s.[40] The CMS asked in the early 1820s for a stronger general, literary, and theological education (including Latin, Greek, and Hebrew!) than the Basel Mission had originally intended. This demanded extreme measures in Basel, since the great majority of the Basel Mission trainees had completed only primary school before learning a craft or working on the land. After a short period in which a two-tier education was attempted in Basel, it was decided that all trainees should take the whole course, designed in the 1820s to meet the wishes of the British partners.[41]

The contacts between the CMS and the Basel Mission were neither distant nor superficial, but close, vital to both sides, and remarkably intimate, given the communications of the time. When, in 1835, William Jowett, secretary to the CMS Committee, drafted instructions for a CMS delegation to meet representatives of the Basel Mission in Paris, he described Inspector Blumhardt[42] as "that aged and experienced friend of our common cause," and referred to "that affectionate relation which has so long and so happily subsisted be-

---

39. Schlatter, *Geschichte der Basler Mission,* vol. 1, p. 65. Of the first fifty-three young men admitted to the Basel Missionary College for training between 1816 and 1821, five never worked for a mission. Of the remaining forty-eight who entered missionary service 1818-26, no fewer than twenty-one joined CMS. The Basel Mission itself employed a further eleven, other missionary societies eight, and eight entered the service of the Russian government as pastors for German congregations in Russia.

40. Schlatter, *Geschichte der Basler Mission,* vol. 1, chaps. 2.3, 3.2, 4.3, and 5.2. For the seminary in the period from the First World War to 1940 see Hermann Witschi, *Geschichte der Basler Mission, 1920-1940* (Basel: Baeileia, 1970), chap. 1. The implications of the CMS requirements were wide reaching: the *other* Basel Mission — the Pilgrim Mission St. Chrischona — was founded, not least, to offer training in mission for simple tent-making ministries and was thus a reaction against the more rigorous academic expectations of the Basel Mission.

41. Schlatter, *Geschichte der Basler Mission,* vol. 1, chap. 2.3, esp. pp. 72-74.

42. Christian Gottlieb [CMS: Theophilus] Blumhardt, b. Stuttgart 1779. Pastor of the Protestant Church in Württemberg, theological secretary of the *Deutsche Christentumsgesellschaft* 1803-7, *Inspektor* of the Basel Mission 1815-38, d. Basel 1838.

tween the two Societies." His words seem to have been more than mere rhetoric.[43]

The "relation between the two societies" may have been often "affectionate," but it was not entirely trouble-free. The cause célèbre of Anglo-German conflict in the CMS in these years was probably the case of the Berlin-trained missionary Karl Rhenius in the South Indian mission station of Tirunelveli, whose confrontation with Anglican authority in 1835-38 became so acute that his church was boarded up to prevent his using it.[44] But other instances of tension and dispute concerning Basel-trained missionaries were a continuing concern for CMS leaders in the 1820s. There is also the remarkable case of the informal theological examination to which Wilhelm Hoffmann, then *Inspektor* of the Basel Mission, was subjected in 1846 while on a visit to London, to ensure that his views on the incarnation were orthodox.[45]

Conflict is a subject seldom touched on in conventional mission history. Missions rarely tackled the issue of conflict systematically as something likely to be faced, and still more rarely did reports about conflict within the organization find their way into the public record. In the case of the CMS and its missionaries from mainland Europe, one type of conflict has, however, been discussed publicly *in extenso* — the ecclesiological questions about the enforcement of Anglican discipline on people with a non-Anglican background, especially in relation to ordination. But one must also look at the cultural roots if one is to understand adequately the nature of these conflicts. Both themes — the ecclesiological and the cultural — need to be examined in order to do justice to this experiment in intercultural cooperation and to sense what lessons it may have today.

It is evident that ecclesiastical difficulties were likely to come up

---

43. Basel Mission Archives, QK/GB/CMS, MS copy of the "Instructions of the Committee of the Church Missionary Society to Col. Phipps and the Lay Secretary, Preparatory to Meeting the Revd T. Blumhardt at Paris. Delivered April 3. 1835" and signed by W. Jowett.

44. Karl Rhenius, b. 1790, graduate of Jänicke's Mission Seminary. Worked for the CMS from 1814 in Tamil Nadu, India. Left CMS 1835, d. 1838. Rhenius has a long bibliography in English and German. An interesting German-language assessment is given by Hermann Gundert in *Hermann Gundert: Quellen zu seinem Leben und Werk*, ed. Albrecht Frenz (Ulm: Süddeutsche Verlagsgesellschaft, 1991), pp. 321-36.

45. Schlatter, *Geschichte der Basler Mission*, vol. 1, pp. 82-85.

when the CMS employed missionaries with a German background.[46] Neither Anglican ordination nor the Thirty-Nine Articles nor the Book of Common Prayer were automatic foci of loyalty or enthusiasm among Lutherans. Moreover, the enforcement of Anglican orthodoxy seems to have been consistent in neither the CMS nor among the ecclesiastical authorities overseas. The impact of the Tractarian movement meant that there was a general tightening-up in the field of church order that gave much less latitude to a generous acceptance of Lutheran ordination or of forms of service and liturgy independent of the Prayer Book. But even before this, these were potential areas of conflict, as the Rhenius case that led to his severing his connection with the CMS in 1835 shows.

On the CMS side there was also a recognition of the cultural basis of difficulties. After some years characterized by tensions in differing parts of the mission field involving missionaries of mainland European origins, the society in 1828 proposed to concentrate its continental personnel in one region, and the North India mission was earmarked for this.[47] William Jowett drafted a magisterial comment on conflict in the early 1830s that reflects this philosophy of developing separate spheres:

> One chief principle, concerning which the [CMS] Com[mitt]ee trust you will find the deputation from Basel fully disposed to concur, is the importance of establishing Missionary Stations not so near to one another as to endanger collision or interference. Fellow-labourers in the same vineyard, are found to work most harmoniously and most effectively, when they are placed at such a distance as not to interfere with one another, and consequently so as not to draw out differences of opinion, or cause collision in their measures. The Lord has, in His infinite Wisdom, condescended to commit the most precious of all trusts, that namely, of bringing wandering souls to Christ, to men who are naturally prone to err, and encompassed with infirmities; and although by His Spirit, He is ever ready to endow them with that measure of kind and forbearing love, which may suffice for their harmoniously performing His work, still, in labouring for His Church, He would have us to select the most prudent and orderly methods.[48]

46. Stock, vol. 1. See index references to Bishops and Bishoprics, Ordination, Tractarian Movement.
47. Schlatter, *Geschichte der Basler Mission*, vol. 1, p. 78.
48. Basel Mission Archives, QK/GB/CMS.

In short, Jowett's principle was to keep people of differing views and backgrounds as far apart as possible.

One area that evidently caused frequent difficulties was the Basel-trained missionaries' English-language skills — or their lack of them. More than once between 1818 and 1850, questions were raised in London about the theological orthodoxy of the teaching in the Mission College in Basel. In each case the problems were partly rooted in the young foreigners' difficulties in expressing themselves simply and accurately. This situation was a recipe for increasing mutual misunderstanding — the more complicated the theological questions the British asked in order to understand where a young man really stood, the more likely his floundering replies were to add to the confusion.

In a recent study of the organizational sociology of the nineteenth-century Basel Mission, Jon Miller has pointed to another specifically cultural issue that caused difficulties among Basel-trained missionaries and between them and the CMS.[49] Miller investigated the question that, in principle, must have been important for the nineteenth-century CMS, too: namely, how a mission committee in a European city could control and direct the activities of missionaries in fields none of its members had visited and that were weeks and indeed months away by post. Miller spotted the use by the Basel Mission leadership of mutual surveillance in this connection. The directing committee of the Basel Mission expected its men in the field to keep an eye on each other and report on their brothers' deviant behavior so that they could be checked and then put firmly under the center's authority once more. Furthermore, they had been expected to practice this form of "fellowship" while in training in Basel. In consequence, Basel-trained missionaries often had a record of mutual tension and mistrust when they were taken up by the CMS. The CMS leadership found this philosophy strange and dysfunctional, but when they approached Basel about it, the Basel leadership was far from feeling that this policy needed to be reconsidered. Rather Inspector Blumhardt reiterated the fundamental Basel attitude in formulations that, according to Miller, remained authoritative in the Mission until 1914. These procedures were presumably adhered to because they were culturally acceptable in the German-speaking world. They can perhaps stand here as a symbol of the minefield intercultural cooperation can become when one side is unaware of specific cultural mechanisms at work on the other and lacks

49. Miller, *The Social Control of Religious Zeal*, pp. 150-52.

Fig. 4. A German CMS missionary setting out at sunset in mid-19th-century north India to journey to an outstation. Engraving, first published in the *Calwer Missionsblatt* in September 1861.
The article accompanying this ironic German comment on national stereotypes in mission starts (in English translation): "'That can't be a missionary.' Actually, yes, it is a missionary. 'Well, it can't be a German missionary.' Actually, it is a German missionary, in the service of an English society. 'Then he can't be a humble one.' Why not? He is giving his utmost, even if it may not look like that at first sight. He is going to an outstation. The railway hasn't been built. There is no post or omnibus. If he is carried in a hammock he needs 8 trained carriers. So he asked himself how he could save money, uses an old buggy, and spends far less money employing four unskilled coolies."

knowledge of the foreign vocabulary or chains of thought that would create some degree of sensitivity to what is going on.

Conclusion

We could, of course, argue that the conflicts recorded in the history of the cooperation between the CMS and the Basel Mission were due to the inherent tension in mission between the claim to be representing a higher, better, more accurate truth, and the difficulty, in the hurly-burly of everyday intercultural and interconfessional relations, to recognize that one's own — or even one's church's — grasp of the truth is conditional and imperfect. Unfortunately, it was a lesson that was not adequately learnt by either side as their relationship matured.

This is a hard judgment, perhaps, but it can be illustrated from the comment of Inspector Josenhans at the dedication of the new Mission House in Basel in 1860. Joseph Josenhans was Hoffmann's successor as *Inspektor*.[50] He was a famous disciplinarian and the systematizer of the Basel Mission's hierarchical organization. A number of Basel Mission supporters reproached him that his organization was no longer sending missionaries to work with the CMS in spite of the fact that the cooperation agreement was still in force: the mission might be opening a larger Mission House, they quipped, but its spirit had become narrower. Josenhans replied, "When the English come to us, study here and enter our service, then limitations [on Basel people going into service with English missionary societies] will be broken down. But as long as the English are too proud to come to us, we will be too proud to go to them."[51]

His language was hard and perhaps unnecessarily abrasive. But his demands were justified; no English men or women joined the Basel Mission until the 1940s, though German emigrants to Australia, and others with German background but British passports, did join the Basel Mission in the decades before the First World War. Josenhans was demanding partnership and two-way cooperation from the CMS, and the English generally, and felt aggrieved that this reciprocity did not occur.

50. Friedrich Joseph Josenhans, b. Stuttgart 1812. Pastor of the Protestant Church in Württemberg, Basel Mission *Inspektor* 1850-79, d. Leonberg/Württemberg 1884.
51. Schlatter, *Geschichte der Basler Mission*, vol. 1, pp. 86, 282-83.

CMS-Basel Mission cooperation began to end as the beginnings of Anglo-German nationalistic rivalry and tension became more pronounced. It is true that by 1860 the CMS was evidently able to recruit enough missionaries from within Britain, and this could be plausibly argued as an explanation for the decline in numbers of Basel recruits becoming CMS missionaries. Equally we should not try to soften the assertion that nationalism played a role in the quiet death of the relationship between the two organizations. It is not only that Josenhans's resentments can undoubtedly be matched by English ecclesiastical and political arrogance. The career of Inspector Hoffmann also illustrates the gradual drifting apart, a progress from a commitment to Protestant internationalism to a much more narrowly focused national calling. Inspector Hoffmann was a son of the founder of the archetypal southern German pietist village Kornthal, near Stuttgart. It is highly indicative of the reality of the *International* I am describing that, when he became Basel Mission *Inspektor* in 1840, Hoffmann had two important liberal and Anglophile reforms in mind (one of them the building up of women's mission to women). Ten years later he moved from Basel to be one of the leading ecclesiastical civil servants of Brandenburg, Prussia, and chaplain at the court of King Frederick William IV. As such he was intimately linked with the reactionary restoration of monarchic rule in Central Europe after the revolutions of 1848. It is highly unlikely that he promoted Anglophile reforms in this function or felt a strong supranational Protestant identity.[52]

The experience of the 1848 Revolution in the German-speaking world, which carried waves of refugees over the Swiss border from the German state of Baden, is likely to have had a major influence on his new orientation. But it is hard to believe that Hoffmann's experience in England in 1846 had nothing to do with the turn from internationalism that his move to Berlin implies. This gives another dimension to the picture of Henry Venn as a tragic figure. His attempts to maintain open and cooperative fellowship with Hoffmann and the Basel Mission during and after Hoffmann's visit to London in 1846 failed in spite of the sincere signals of friendship he regularly sent to Basel in the name of CMS. Even before Venn's retirement, Josenhans's comment on the En-

52. Wilhelm Hoffmann, b. 1806 in Leonberg/Württemberg. Pastor of the Protestant Church in Württemberg. Basel Mission *Inspektor* 1839-50. From 1853, chaplain to the court in Potsdam and senior official of the Ecclesiastical Department of the Government of Brandenburg-Prussia.

glish in 1860 signaled the end of cooperation between the Basel Mission and CMS. It was a very different spirit from that which had imbued Jowett's instructions to the CMS delegates to the Paris meeting with Basel missionaries in 1835, which ended with this prayer:

> May our Lord Jesus Christ be with your spirits, while you are visiting places, where in former years there has been manifested great enmity to His saving name, and where, consequently, scenes have been witnessed of such profligacy, wretchedness and confusion as might be expected to characterize the enemies of the cross of Christ. Incidentally you may be the means of doing some great good, far beyond what is contemplated in the present specific mission: — for the heart and eye, and voice of Christian men, are ever directed to the greatest possible good; and the God of all grace hears their prayers, and blesses their exertions to a degree far beyond the reach of our present views.[53]

By the 1860s the British missionary movement was entering a period of self-confidence, in which British recruitment to missionary work was much easier and the necessity of employing missionaries from the Continent much less urgent. The heightened confessional consciousness in both Anglican and Lutheran communions made cooperation more problematic and the awareness of a common Protestant identity less easy to take for granted. Growing nationalism on the Continent was impacting on religious identity and self-definition, with an effect on missionary societies. Nevertheless, in 1865, the CMS did send a jubilee greeting to the Basel Mission that spoke warmly of the relationship of fifty years: "Our link to one another has been a witness for the power . . . of evangelical truth and life which enables Protestant churches, although different in the organisations of their churches, to unite in the work of the extension of the Kingdom of Christ."[54]

It had indeed been a most fruitful experiment in inter-European missionary cooperation.

---

53. Basel Mission Archives, QK/GB/CMS.
54. Schlatter, *Geschichte der Basler Mission*, vol. 1, p. 84.

3. The Role of Women in the Church Missionary Society, 1799-1917

JOCELYN MURRAY

Women in Mission in the Nineteenth Century: The Background

It is increasingly recognized that women were of fundamental importance in defining, developing, and shaping the course of the modern missionary movement and that women missionaries working abroad served as a catalyst that opened opportunities for women denied them in their country of origin. This development was noted first in North America, reflecting to some extent the greater opportunities for women from early days in contributing to the American missionary movement. Older missionary publications were slow to take into account the role of women. A discussion of any kind on women missionaries is conspicuously absent from what remains a standard text on the history of Christian mission by Stephen Neill.[1] Perhaps more surprisingly, a reflective work such as Max Warren's *Social History and Christian Mission*[2] failed to record anything substantial on women, even though there

---

1. Stephen Neill, *A History of Christian Missions* (London: Hodder & Stoughton, 1964).

2. M. A. C. Warren, *Social History and Christian Mission* (London: SCM Press, 1967).

were chapters relating mission to social service, education, and creating a bourgeoisie — all areas in which the role of women was central. Only one woman appears in the index — Anna Hinderer, who worked in Ibadan, in the Yoruba country of West Africa. However, Warren does speak highly of her journal and letters for giving insights both into the nature of missionary work and the vitality of the Yoruba culture in which she had become immersed.[3] Warren was writing in the mid-1960s at a time when, by many indicators, women had attained parity with men; numerically they far outnumbered men in mission. The acknowledgment of their work, let alone a recognition of their power and their status, still lagged behind, but this was not often seen as a particularly pressing issue. In such a climate, to focus on specifically gender issues was not a priority; indeed, it might be seen as remarginalizing women. The climate has since changed dramatically, and "women no longer want simply to adopt the same aims and values as male culture 'patriarchy' but desire to discover and postulate their own scale of values, identity and culture."[4] The time has come for a reassessment of women's role from the beginning of the modern missionary movement. It is in the United States, appropriately, in view of its pioneering role, that this neglect is being most adequately addressed — as Dana Robert's recent book on American women missionaries powerfully illustrates.[5] In Britain, an important collection of essays titled *Women and Missions: Past and Present* was published in 1993.[6]

In 1977 Ann Douglas published a book titled *The Feminization of American Culture.*[7] One of her major theses was that, with the decline of the old intellectual orthodoxies (in New England this was predominantly Calvinism) and their status as public truth, there grew up a "softer" theology in which Christianity was seen to have influence rather than authority and power. The evangelical revival further as-

3. Warren, *Social History,* p. 157.

4. Barbara von Wartenberg-Potter, "Women," in *Dictionary of Mission,* ed. Karl Müller et al., Engl. ed. (Maryknoll, N.Y.: Maryknoll Publications, 1997), p. 488.

5. Dana L. Robert, *American Women in Mission: A Social History of Their Thought and Practice* (Macon, Ga.: Mercer University Press, 1996).

6. Fiona Bowie, Deborah Kirkwood, and Shirley Ardener, eds., *Women and Missions: Past and Present. Anthropological and Historical Perspectives* (Providence: Berg Publishers, 1993).

7. Ann Douglas, *The Feminization of American Culture* (New York: Knopf, 1977).

sisted this process by its emphasis, in response to the gospel, on the affective rather than the intellectual arena — a domain seen as particularly congenial to the sensibilities of women. Certainly, the public role for women was extremely circumscribed in 1799 when the CMS was founded. Not only were no women present at the meeting in the Castle and Falcon hostelry, but initially women did not attend the public meetings of the society.[8] Evangelical religion mitigated some of the implications of this domestic ideal. It put value on women's religious experience and gave a sense of worth. Moreover, the one area in which middle-class women were encouraged to exercise a role outside the home — in voluntary good works, "the practice of benevolence"[9] — was precisely where a voluntary society such as the CMS could make its appeal and use women's energies and talents. Women became essential for the local organization of "auxiliaries," which were to provide the core of the society's support and strength throughout the nineteenth century. Missionary magazines equally played an important part in fostering and sustaining interest in missionary work, and the target readership was increasingly directed at, and written by, women.[10] By the mid-nineteenth century, outlets were becoming available outside the home for active work for religiously committed women. The work of W. E. Pennefather and the Mildmay Mission was important in providing opportunities for women to exercise an active ministry, particularly in what was called "home mission" — in particular among the poor in the slums of Victorian industrial cities.[11]

But missionary work itself was still considered the province of men. It had an essentially virile profile rather than the "soft" (feminine) one of which Douglas speaks. And yet there was the necessary emphasis on self-sacrifice and on compassion for the less fortunate, those denied access to

8. See Stock, vol. 1, p. 68; also Brian Stanley, *The History of the Baptist Missionary Society, 1712-1992* (Edinburgh: T. & T. Clark, 1992), p. 228.

9. Cf. F. K. Prochaska, *Women and Philanthropy in Nineteenth-Century England* (Oxford: Clarendon Press, 1980). Prochaska also emphasizes that the mission societies were early in focusing their publicity on children, a focus that was also seen as particularly involving women's skills as writers and Sunday school teachers.

10. At the end of the century, Georgina Gollock was an important figure as editor of CMS publications.

11. See " 'Open doors for female labourers' ": Women Candidates of the London Missionary Society, 1875-1914," in *Missionary Encounters: Sources and Issues,* ed. Robert Bickers and Rosemary Seton (Richmond: Curzon Press, 1996), p. 53. See also Stock, vol. 2, p. 357.

physical, moral, and spiritual well-being: areas in which women were perceived to have a special sensibility. Moreover, the missionary project could never have been an exclusively male sphere. Women were needed as spouses and helpmates for men. Single men and husbands separated for long periods from their wives presented a moral dilemma for a missionary society. Missionaries did not have the option of other male colonialists who availed themselves of sexual encounters (both casual and more sustained) with women from the indigenous community. Even marriage to a local woman, which was never common, was completely unacceptable behavior for society members by the end of the nineteenth century.[12] Although it is not inconceivable that many women simply joined their husbands in mission as an expression of loyalty that one would expect in regard to missionary service, the man had an obligation to consult his spouse and be assured of her wholehearted commitment. Moreover, many single women deliberately chose to offer themselves as partners to single men preparing to leave for or already in the field.[13] But there was a deeper reason for the indispensability of women in mission: without them it was impossible to model the Christian monogamous family life that it was hoped could bring about a transformation of societies not yet influenced by the gospel. If that was unlikely, the possibility of engendering a native Christian community in which these ideals could take form also existed. This placed an even greater weight of domesticity on the mission field and allowed it to be expressed in a wider range of situations than might be expected at home. Thus, missionary wives became teachers of the local Christian community, from the mission house or its environs, conducting classes for inquirers and full baptized members, inculcating the domestic skills of cooking, sewing, tailoring, laundry, and kitchen gardening: what has been called the "reshaping and reclothing" of indigenous society.[14] Moreover, missionary wives soon found that the distinc-

12. The most notorious example of this was perhaps Charles Stokes, an Irish CMS missionary in East Africa in the 1880s and 1890s. He first married outside the society, a woman missionary of the UMCA. When she died, he married a Gogo woman. His connection with the society was discontinued. He became an arms dealer and was eventually hanged by the Belgians in 1897 for gunrunning in what was to become the Belgian Congo.

13. An example is Rosina Dietrich who answered Ludwig Krapf's call for a wife while he was in Ethiopia. She traveled from Egypt to meet him there. They married in 1844 and went together to Mombasa to pioneer CMS work in East Africa. Rosina died there in childbirth in 1846.

14. Adrian Hastings, "Were Women a Special Case?" in *Women and Missions,* ed. Bowie et al., p. 155. For issues of the construction and transformation of

tions between the (male) world of work and of female domesticity, which so circumscribed their lives in Britain, were of little account in most missionary situations. They soon became fully involved in teaching and evangelism, in translation work and medical work, a public role in the life of the church that would have been frowned upon in England.

In Britain in the second half of the nineteenth century, women were becoming more insistent on their right to education and to entry into the male professions. Society was sensitive to the fact that there was a growing body of women who did not marry and who were not content to be dependents of their families all their lives. Some professions, such as teaching, recognized the need for women without much protest; others, such as medicine (not to mention the ordained ministry), put up strong resistance. It has been noted that women were still largely excluded from entering the medical profession except as nurses even after winning the right to train in the field. Missionary service was one way of obviating these restrictions. The development of *zenana* work in Asia made missions much more sensitive to the need for qualified women doctors.[15] As the great ecumenical pioneer, Kathleen Bliss, put it,

> Foreign missionary work gave women their first chance of seeing what services they could render to the church, and in spite of the opening of many doors for full time work for the churches at home, it is still true in very many churches that the woman with gifts, vision and a great will for service finds all her powers more fully exercised abroad than at home.[16]

---

society as part of the missionary project see Jean Comaroff and John Comaroff, *Of Revelation and Revolution*, vol. 1, *Christianity, Colonialism and Consciousness in South Africa* (Chicago: University of Chicago Press, 1991).

15. See Rosemary Fitzgerald, "A 'Peculiar and Exceptional Measure': The Call for Women Medical Missionaries for India in the Late Nineteenth Century," in *Missionary Encounters*, ed. Bickers and Seton, pp. 174-96. The *zenana* was the curtain behind which the high-caste and high-status Indian women were secluded, and by extension enclosure for all women. *Zenana* missions worked within the social system with regard to women, providing home education and developing concern for women's issues from within that environment and using these as evangelistic opportunities to influence women, to the extent that this was possible without compromising the trust that permitted entry to the *zenana*.

16. Kathleen Bliss, *The Service and Status of Women in the Churches* (London: SCM Press, 1952), quoted in Lavinia Byrne, *The Hidden Journey* (London: SPCK, 1993), p. 9.

Women in the CMS

The first three women to offer their services to the CMS did so in 1815.[17] The offers were taken seriously and discussed, but perhaps not surprisingly, they were refused. At first only clergy and catechists were recognized as missionaries; all other men were only lay agents who were listed in separate registers. Whether clergy or lay, all were male. They were going out into almost completely unknown situations, and the complications of having female agents to settle could not be thought of. What is surprising is not that the early offers were refused but that as early as 1820 some were accepted, and another register became necessary, listing the names of "the Female European Teachers sent from Europe or adopted in the Missions."[18] It seems to be from the time that the CMS started to work in India (1814) that attitudes began to change, as it belatedly became clear that in India only women could speak to women. Two societies were founded to specialize in this work: the Ladies' Female Education Society (Calcutta, 1824) and the Society for Promoting Female Education in the East (1834). Even earlier the British and Foreign Schools Society sent a woman to work in Calcutta. When its funds failed in 1822, the woman, Mary Ann Cooke, was "taken up" by the CMS and continued her work. She stands as fourth on the CMS List, but in the length and significance of her service she is first.[19] (The first three women listed had died or married by 1823.) Cooke herself married a CMS missionary in 1823 but was soon widowed. As spinster, wife, and widow Mary Anne (Cooke) Wilson continued her work, as will be seen later in this chapter.

Unrecognized, Unknown: Missionary Wives and Their Unmarried Assistants

What was initially not clear (partly because of the way it was recorded) is the fact that, long before any women were officially accepted, unmarried women, as well as wives, were serving abroad. From the beginning it was the policy of the CMS to encourage its agents to go abroad as

17. Stock, vol. 1, pp. 124-25.

18. Church Missionary Society, *Register of Missionaries (Clerical, Lay, and Female) and Native Clergy. From 1804 to 1904* (London: Church Missionary Society: printed for private circulation, 1905).

19. See *CMS Register*, List 2, Female Missionaries, no. 4.

married men, with their families. And many of the wives at once began to teach women and girls. The first men to go overseas — German Lutherans — took their English wives to Sierra Leone in 1804. In 1826, a widowed missionary was described as marrying "Mary Hickson, who for ten years resided with Mrs Renner [first wife of the missionary] and assisted her in her school."[20] Clearly Hickson was in Sierra Leone by 1816, but this fact is only accidentally recorded. Other wives found single women — in some cases a sister — to assist them, for they soon saw that there was work to do with and for women and girls, but they had their own children to care for and teach. The first officially designated "Female Missionaries" did not sail until 1820.

Death (for married women, often in childbirth) or marriage to a fellow missionary was frequent. Of the first fifty women listed in "Female Missionaries" (1820 to 1857) twenty-six married, usually within two or three years of arrival. Among the first fifty men (1804-17), at least thirteen were widowed while in service. Those wives who survived accomplished a great deal. We find notes (under the entry for the husband) of women such as Elizabeth Bailey, in Kottayam, 1816: "the first who received Native Syrian Christian females for education,"[21] and Eliza Perowne in Burdwan, who from 1820 "super-intended the various girls' schools."[22] After 1820, the names of single women who traveled overseas to help wives or unmarried brothers are recorded — Jane Knight to Ceylon in 1821; Mary Anne Stratford also to Ceylon in 1827; and Maria Coldham to New Zealand in 1832.[23] Clearly the wives, with their own large families, or men who had no female help at all, had requested assistance.

Widows at Work

Further confirmation comes from the number of widows taken up by the society after a husband's death. "Taking up" was the term used when an individual was accepted as a missionary when already overseas, and most often referred to nationals or to the widow, sister, or daughter of a male missionary. Clearly such women wished to continue work already begun

20. See CMS Register, List 1, Clerical and Lay Missionaries, no. 77.
21. See CMS Register, List 1, Clerical and Lay Missionaries, no. 30.
22. See CMS Register, List 1, Clerical and Lay Missionaries, no. 61.
23. See CMS Register, List 2, Female Missionaries, nos. 3, 7, 12.

in their relative's lifetime and were placed on the Register of Female Missionaries, receiving directly the allowance that had previously come through the male kinsman. The CMS *Register of Missionaries and Native Clergy* contains information up to 1904, and in that time 743 women were listed — less than half the number of men. But this is to ignore the wives. Of those 743 at least 31 were the widows or daughters of deceased male missionaries. The earliest wife to be taken up as a widow was Mary Beale, married in 1840. Her husband died in Sierra Leone in 1856, but she worked on until her own death in 1866.[24]

Similar examples are numerous. Sabina Peter Clemens served in Sierra Leone for almost nineteen years after her husband's death; Sarah Jerrom stayed in Bombay for eleven years. Amelia Sharkey, a Eurasian like the husband she married in 1847, continued her successful girls' school in Masulipatam for eleven years after her husband's death in 1866, until her own death in 1878.[25]

Women in Families

Women played an important part in sustaining the interdependence of family members, in families that were much larger social units than is common in Western society today. The sister who had gone out to live with a single or widowed brother often found mission work to do and stayed on even after the brother married. Thus Henrietta Neale went to Bengal with her widowed brother in 1864; he remarried in 1866 but as late as 1892 she, with a niece, was still active in girls' education in Calcutta.[26]

Even more striking was the frequent phenomenon of a family serving in the same area over several generations — something rather different from a son returning after education and training in the home country. It generally involved women and usually occurred in situations where the climate was friendly enough to enable daughters to be educated at home by a mother or governess. One of the most remarkable of such families was that of Henry Baker of Essex (1793-1866), who was posted to Kottayam, South India, in 1817.[27] He revised the Malayalam

24. See *CMS Register*, List 2, Female Missionaries, no. 22.
25. See in *CMS Register*, List 2, Female Missionaries, nos. 38, 43, 67.
26. *CMS Register*, List 2, Female Missionaries, no. 60.
27. *CMS Register*, List 1, Clerical and Lay Missionaries, no. 38.

Bible and wrote books and tracts in the language, but perhaps his greatest contribution came through his marriage, in 1818, to Amelia Kohlhoff.

Only seventeen at the time of her marriage, Amelia (1801-88) was already of the third generation of her family in South India.[28] Her grandfather, father, and uncle belonged to that group of German Lutherans originally sent out and supported by the King of Denmark, who eventually became linked with the SPCK and later the SPG. The first of her eleven children, Henry Baker Jr., born in 1819, returned to India from education in England in 1843 to work with his father. The daughters, who had never left India, were soon helping their mother in the Girls' School; three married CMS missionaries and in their turn were taken up when widowed to continue their work. Amelia herself, taken up in 1866, died in 1888 at Kottayam. Her son's wife, Frances, widowed in 1878, had commenced a school for girls after her marriage in 1843 and is recorded as being present at its jubilee in 1899. Her own three daughters all worked as teachers for many years before they were recognized as missionaries. Isobel Amelia Baker lived and taught at Kottayam till her death in 1939 at the age of ninety-two. She and her sister Annie assisted a third sister, Mary Frances, in the Baker Memorial School, which still flourished in the 1960s, with the help of other family members. The school celebrated its official jubilee in the 1930s, but in fact it was the same school started by the young Amelia Baker, assisted by another missionary wife, in her bungalow, with "twelve Syrian girls" (i.e., members of the South Indian Orthodox Christian community), in 1820. A similar story, likewise from South India, is told of Mary and John Thomas, from Wales, and their family, in Mengnanapuram, a Tamil-speaking area, and among Tamils in Ceylon.[29] Daughters-in-law, daughters, and granddaughters worked before and during marriage and as widows, over three generations.

New Zealand, the second CMS field (1809), where the missionaries were pioneers, was eventually to become a British colony, and it becomes hard to know whether and when the missionaries became settlers. Like South India, this was another area where families could live happily all the year round. For the first two generations the sons were usually sent back to England for education, but the daughters, fluent in

---

28. *CMS Register,* List 2, Female Missionaries, no. 65.

29. *CMS Register,* List 1, Clerical and Lay Missionaries, no. 229; List 2, Female Missionaries, no 63.

Maori from early childhood, were often taken up to become teachers of Maori children, often when they were not much more than children themselves. Two brothers, Henry Williams and William Williams, arrived in New Zealand in 1823 and 1826. Both came with their wives, and Henry with three small children.[30] Eventually there were to be twenty children in the two families, all but one reaching adulthood. Other missionaries already had older children, and Marianne Williams and her sister-in-law, Jane, commenced a school for English girls as early as 1827, while William Williams began to teach the boys. Marianne, just thirty when she sailed to New Zealand, had deliberately set about acquiring skills and knowledge, such as teaching and midwifery, that would be useful in the new life.

As their children grew up, many of them became involved in the work of the mission. Mary and Jane Williams married their cousins Samuel and Henry Williams Jr., sons of Henry and Marianne. Their sister, Catherine, married Octavius Hadfield, who was to become bishop of Wellington.[31] Her older sister, Marianne, began teaching in a CMS school in 1833, when she was only thirteen, together with other Maori-speaking daughters of missionaries.[32] A missionary visitor described "the plump jolly Maori children" whom she observed in Marianne's infant class. (Marianne taught for ten years before herself marrying a CMS missionary.) William Williams became the first bishop of Waiapu, the east central diocese of the emerging New Zealand church, and his oldest son, Leonard, became its third bishop. Leonard's son, Herbert William Williams, sixth bishop of Waiapu, did not die until 1937. In the nineteenth century, a secondary boarding school for Maori girls, Hukarere College, was founded in Napier, center of the diocese, and when Jane Williams was widowed in 1877 she lived on there with her three unmarried daughters, all fluent speakers of Maori, who taught in the school. Jane Williams died in 1896, in her ninety-fifth year; her daughters, Marianne and Catherine, were in their nineties when they died in Napier in the 1930s. That school continues today.

The second bishop of Waiapu, Edward Craig Stuart, was a Scot who had worked for more than twenty years in North India before becoming bishop in New Zealand in 1877.[33] In 1894 he resigned the see

---

30. *CMS Register,* List 1, Clerical and Lay Missionaries, nos. 75, 103.
31. *CMS Register,* List 1, Clerical and Lay Missionaries, no. 264.
32. *CMS Register,* List 2, Female Missionaries, no. 13.
33. *CMS Register,* List 1, Clerical and Lay Missionaries, no. 417.

and at his request, the CMS assigned him to the relatively new work in Persia. From the beginning he was accompanied by his daughter Anne, who was taken up by the society eight years later. Two nieces, Emmeline Stuart, a doctor, and Gertrude Stuart, a qualified nurse, also went to Persia.[34] (It may be noticed in passing that medical work, for which women were often needed, seems to have been particularly useful in Islamic areas, where the creation of girls' schools was often much less feasible. Two other female doctors offering before 1904 were assigned to the Persian mission.) Edward Stuart, who was now "a missionary in episcopal orders," continued the work in Persia until his death in 1911, at age eighty-four.

It is not hard to guess that the society sometimes took advantage of these missionary daughters, who were often happy to stay on in a place they knew, speaking a language they had heard since childhood, and continuing with work they had first seen done by their mother. In New Zealand, Bishop Selwyn pushed one missionary daughter, Elizabeth Fairburn, into what proved to be an unhappy marriage with a bachelor missionary, William Colenso, because he wanted her help, as a native speaker of Maori, in the revision of the Maori Bible.[35] Another unrecognized daughter was Maria Louise Hoernle, whose father, a German Lutheran, had first worked on the border between Russia and Persia under the Basel Mission. In 1838 he was taken into CMS connection in North India, where Maria, her sister, and four brothers were born. Each of her brothers became CMS missionaries after attending university in Switzerland or Germany, and her sister married a missionary. But of Maria we read: "For a considerable time [she] had sole charge of the Girls' Orphanage School at Benares without any remuneration from the Society." Not until 1873 was she taken up and granted a salary. For ten more years she worked for the CMS before moving to the Punjab under the Church of England Zenana Missionary Society (CEZMS).[36]

One final example of a missionary widow in India that caught the attention of supporters at home was that of Margaret Elmslie. Margaret Duncan was a young Scottish woman who in early 1872 married

34. *CMS Register,* List 2, Female Missionaries, nos. 411, 468, 653. On Emmeline Stuart, see chap. 4.

35. See entry on Elizabeth Colenso (1821-1904) by Patricia Sargison in *The Book of New Zealand Women,* ed. Charlotte Macdonald (Wellington: Bridget Williams Books, 1991), pp. 145-49.

36. *CMS Register,* List 2, Female Missionaries, no. 76; she was daughter of Christian Hörnle, List 1, no. 268.

William Elmslie, a doctor from Aberdeen. In 1864 he had been entrusted with the task of commencing medical work in Kashmir. Permission had been given only reluctantly by the Maharajah, on condition that all foreigners left before the winter. In October 1872 the Elmslies started too late on the journey through the mountain passes. Margaret gave up her litter to her ailing husband but Elmslie died in the Punjab. His young widow stayed on at Amritsar until 1878, working in the orphanages and among the women. In 1881 she remarried; her second husband, Francis Baring, was also working in the Punjab, and she returned there with him, but died one year later.[37]

Independent Single Women

Those in charge of evangelism within the CMS, even in India, were slow to realize that if women and girls were to be reached, the reaching must be done by women. But there were concerned Christian women among the families of British civilians and army officers in India, and it was in fact through them that the so-called zenana work was begun. Mary Anne Wilson (née Cooke) has been mentioned as the first single woman to serve for any period of time. She had gone to India "at the request of a local committee, to endeavour to commence a school for Hindu girls." By 1822, "funds failing," she had been taken up by the CMS, and in 1823 she married a widowed CMS missionary, Isaac Wilson, who died in 1828. Wilson continued her work for women and girls. Best known of the institutions she started was that at Agarpara, outside Calcutta, first described as an orphanage "out of which grew the Christian Girls' Boarding School."[38] After some twenty years of work under CMS auspices, she separated herself from the society, but not from her mission to Indian women and girls. In an article written during this period, she challenged Christian women to come independently to India and advised them how they might start schools for Indian girls.

This was not impossible, as it might sound. Most missionary work in India took place in cities and large towns where premises might be

37. *CMS Register*, List 2, Female Missionaries, no. 73; see also List 1, nos. 657, 755.

38. Jocelyn Murray, *Proclaim the Good News: A Short History of the Church Missionary Society* (London: Hodder & Stoughton, 1985), pp. 67, 109.

rented near other European men and women. A woman with a small income, if her school was for middle-class girls whose parents could pay fees, could live without difficulty. Work for the poorer classes, "ragged schools," needed the backing of a missionary society. The life and work of Mary Ann Aldersey, in Ningpo, China, offered a comparable situation. Sadly, she is better remembered for her eccentricities and for her opposition to the marriage of her protegée, Maria Dyer, to James Hudson Taylor, than for her valuable pioneering educational work. She was much assisted by the country-born daughters of missionaries, such as Maria Dyer and her sister Burella (who married John Burdon, a CMS missionary) and of other Europeans, like Mary Ann Leisk. These young women, born and brought up in Batavia among Chinese-speaking peoples, were able to communicate without difficulty. Aldersey's initial mission contacts had been with the London Missionary Society, but she was always an independent missionary, and when she left China, she passed her school over to the CMS.

Therefore, even without the support of a missionary society, it was possible for a few women to establish themselves as independent missionaries in certain environments. It would hardly have been possible in Africa.

Single and Recognized:
Single Women as Overseas Missionaries

Thus, beginning officially in 1820, but unofficially even earlier, single women went overseas or were taken up by the society when, as sisters, daughters, or widows, they had already been working with a male family member or helping a missionary wife in her work for women and girls. However, the extent of this work was very limited. By 1866, when one hundred women had been listed, the number of men sent overseas exceeded one thousand.

A number of features stand out in the list of female missionaries. Very many of the women were sisters or daughters of missionaries and went overseas to work with their male relation — almost one-third in the first hundred, though year by year this proportion decreased. A very high proportion married in the first two years they were overseas. The marriage was normally to a fellow missionary, and, as his wife, she stayed on in the same place. In the first twenty-three years, thirty-one women sent overseas married, some so soon that one wonders whether the couple were not already engaged. Since it was CMS policy to encourage its male missionaries to marry, it seems highly likely that the Home Committee knew an early marriage was a distinct possibility.

The number of marriages decreased year by year. Of the thirty-three women who went overseas between 1869 and 1886, only seven married; only three of those were married within two years after they arrived. It is also notable that the number of women serving for four years or more continued increasing. Until 1844 this was only nine; by 1886, when a hundred women had gone overseas, the total was forty-nine — almost 50 percent. Similarly, far fewer women had gone home within the first two years — which may be taken to indicate that there were fewer cases of break-down in health or inability to fit into the situation demanded of them. In the same period, fifteen widows were taken up to continue work in which they had already been involved.

However, although Eugene Stock refers favorably on many occasions in the CMS Centenary history to the work of these pioneering single women and widows, as well as that of the wives, a change occurred in 1885. He then spoke of "the new race of CMS women missionaries."[39] This was during what the historian described as "three memorable years" — 1885, 1886, 1887 — when there were a number of important political and ecclesiastical changes in the country and the society. The enlarged CMS House was reopened, and the "Cambridge Seven" — university-educated men of "good family" — went to China with the China Inland Mission. Other university men offered to the CMS, and some outstanding missionary meetings were arranged, which resulted in further offers as well as large contributions to funds.

Stock saw the earlier work by women as exceptional. He wrote:

> We have seen in former chapters how the Society resisted every suggestion that it should take up women's work systematically, and how it depended for such aid as single women could render, in the main, on the three Ladies' Societies, the F.E.S., the I.F.N.S. (or Z.B.M.M.) and the C.E.Z.M.S. But the Committee had always set a high value on the work and influence of missionaries' wives, and many of them had been in the fullest and highest sense missionaries themselves. . . . Moreover, the Society had from early days employed a few single women, principally in girls' schools, as at Sierra Leone; and several who had laboured faithfully and efficiently have been mentioned in this history. From time to time, also, the sisters and daughters of mis-

39. Stock, vol. 1, p. 367.

sionaries have done good service, and the widows of men who had died in the field.[40]

There was now a change, the beginning of a new era. A series of offers from women "led the Society, step by step, into a policy never formally or designedly entered upon." First, Mary Harvey, who had been working as a deaconess with Mildmay (in the East End of London), was accepted for work in East Africa in 1885; she completed almost seven years before marrying within the mission.[41] Then in 1887, several well-qualified and well-connected women also offered, and all were accepted for work in China. Meanwhile, a specific request came from Bishop Parker of Eastern Equatorial Africa for suitable women. An advertisement appeared in the *Church Missionary Intelligencer* of May 1887: "*Wanted immediately: three ladies for East Africa. Must be whole-hearted missionaries, physically strong, and thoroughly understanding the principle, 'In honour preferring one another.'*"[42]

Offers came in immediately, and one woman was accepted and left for East Africa as early as July of 1887. A number of others followed, and (what was undoubtedly helpful) many were able to offer as an "Honorary Missionary," not needing an allowance from the society. From 1879 to 1884, 27 women were accepted. From 1888 to 1892, the number rose to 132, an increase of almost nine-fold. But not until July 1895, when the number of women missionaries listed had reached 348, was a Women's Department, with its own "Lady Secretary," set up. This "lady," Georgina Gollock, the first woman to become a regular member of staff, had worked in the editorial department since 1890. In addition to her CMS achievements, in 1896 she was able to help five women graduates, who were members of the Student Volunteer Missionary Union, to set up a Missionary Settlement of University Women in Bombay, aimed at reaching in particular upper-class Indian women.

The changing situation of women within Britain had already begun to be reflected in the education and training of the women who were offering. Harvey, who had gone to Mombasa in 1885, had worked as a deaconess for Mildmay. William Pennefather of Mildmay founded the Training Home for Female Missionaries in 1860, with the

40. Stock refers to the Female Education Society, the Indian Female Normal School and Instruction Society (or Zenana Bible and Medical Mission), and the Church of England Zenana Missionary Society (vol. 1, p. 367).

41. *CMS Register,* List 2, Female Missionaries, no. 98.

42. Stock, vol. 3, p. 368; Murray, *Proclaim the Good News,* p. 112.

model of German deaconess orders in mind. A course at Mildmay could be followed by specialized training. It had been also in the 1860s that Florence Nightingale began to use trained women in hospital nursing, beginning with the needs of soldiers who had been wounded in the Crimean War. The Cambridge Seven and the China Inland Mission influenced other men but, even earlier, Hudson Taylor's employment of women had been noticed. Taylor assigned women to work as evangelists, not only as teachers and nurses; this began to change the climate of thinking about what women might and could do.

In the brief biographies inserted in the *CMS Register,* the training or education of women was now more often mentioned — "clerical training"; "engaged in education." In 1888 the first woman with a university degree was accepted. She was Katherine Tristram, with a degree in mathematics from London University. She was sent to Japan, where she became principal of the CMS School for Girls in Osaka.[43] Two other women sailed for Japan at the same time.

In 1887, the organizers of the Keswick Convention (established in 1875 and one of the major movements within evangelicalism at the time) permitted a missionary meeting during the convention. At that meeting a missionary in Palestine, J. R. Longley Hall, appealed for ten women to offer for Palestine, and the response was rapid. Three were accepted before the end of the year — all of whom were honorary or partly honorary. Of the seventeen women sent out from 1885 to 1887, ten were from sufficiently affluent backgrounds to enable them to go out at their own expense. But even more remarkable, perhaps, were the greatly increased numbers now offering. Year by year there were more women: seven in 1887, thirteen in 1888, eighteen in 1889, twenty-two in 1890, thirty-six in 1891, forty in 1892, forty-two in 1893. In 1895 the number of women missionaries accepted by the society since its inception stood at 348. This number had doubled by 1904.[44]

The importance of Mary Harvey's offer to the society focuses again on East Africa. The German missionaries, J. L. Krapf, and then J. Rebmann, worked in the Mombasa area from 1844 to 1875. Each was for part of the time accompanied by his wife, but no work with or for women seems to have been started. W. S. Price arrived in 1874

43. *CMS Register,* List 2, Female Missionaries, no. 120; see also Murray, *Proclaim the Good News,* p. 112.

44. See Stock, vol. 4, List 2, "Women Missionaries," pp. 650-63, for a year-by-year list to 1900.

and others followed him, but not until the late 1870s were any married couples living at Frere Town or Rabai. Mary Harvey and the other unmarried women who arrived in 1887 and 1888 were therefore much needed. Twenty-five had been assigned by 1894, including (in 1892), the three Bazett sisters, Louisa, Mary, and Sibella, who were all honorary missionaries.[45] Mary Bazett became the wife of Harry Leakey, a pioneer at Kabete, outside Nairobi. Sibella married George Burns, who initiated city work in Mombasa and then Nairobi. Both had daughters who later gave many years of service to the CMS in East Africa.

The first group of eight male missionaries designated for Uganda left Britain in 1876. By the end of 1877 only two of the party remained. Two had been invalided home; two had died en route; and of the four who reached Uganda, two were killed on Ukerewe island in Lake Victoria. The seventh, in ill health, returned to England after three years. Only Alexander Mackay remained, and he worked for twelve years before his own premature death. Two of these eight men were married but all went out alone. Uganda seems to be the only CMS mission where wives did not accompany husbands initially. This later gave concern to Bishop Tucker (bishop from 1890 to 1911), who recognized the need for women missionaries. He wrote of his approaches to the CMS: "Before leaving England in 1894 I represented the changed condition of things in Uganda, the fact that the country was now under British protection, . . . its comparatively settled conditions — and the possibility of passing through the healthy countries of British East Africa with little or no risk of a breakdown in health."[46]

There were those who doubted "whether a journey of some eight hundred miles into the interior of Africa would not be too great a tax upon ladies' powers of endurance."[47] But the bishop convinced the committee, and the first women to reach Uganda were five single women. Edith Furley, Eleanor Browne, Jane Chadwick, Louie Pilgrim, and Mary Thomsett walked up from the coast in 1895, with the possibility of a litter when necessary. Edith Furley was a woman of forty who had already spent two years in Mombasa (1892-94). The other

45. *CMS Register,* List 2, Female Missionaries, nos. 215, 216, 217.

46. Alfred Tucker, *Eighteen Years in Uganda & East Africa* (London: Edward Arnold, 1911; new ed., Westport, Conn.: Negro Universities Press, 1970), p. 157. Ironically, Bishop Tucker's own wife, for health reasons, was never able to accompany her husband to East Africa.

47. Tucker, *Eighteen Years,* p. 15.

Fig. 5. Bishop Alfred Tucker of Uganda with the first five CMS women missionaries to Uganda, *c.* 1896. From *l.* to *r.:* (back row) Eliza L. [Louie] Pilgrim, Eleanor E. W. Browne; (front row) Mary S. Thomsett, Edith M. Furley, Bishop Tucker, Jane E. Chadwick.

Church Mission Society, London

four, aged between twenty-six and thirty-four, were making their first journey to Africa. They traveled from Mombasa with a party that included the bishop as well as six male missionaries. Leaving in mid-July they arrived in Kampala in early October.

Bishop Tucker described their reception.

> The welcome accorded to the ladies by the Baganda women at Ngogwe was well nigh overwhelming. They ran along by the sides of the ladies' chairs grasping their hands and uttering all manner of joyful and loving greetings. . . . When the ladies alighted to climb the hill on which the Mission-house stood, they were embraced by the Baganda women in all the fulness of their hearts' joy.[48]

48. Tucker, *Eighteen Years*, p. 177.

Fig. 6. From *l.* to *r.*: Katherine Timpson, Jane Chadwick, Edith Furley, with group of readers, Uganda, late 1890s.

Church Mission Society archives, University of Birmingham

One would love to know what the Baganda women made of these five white women in their late-Victorian apparel — the first they had ever seen.

Eleanor Browne married a fellow missionary in 1898. All five gave long service to the CMS. John Cook, who married in March 1899 just before sailing for Uganda, appears to have been the first missionary to take his wife with him to Uganda, and it was to be several years more before this became customary. A number of married men (including the bishop) served many years while their families remained in England, but a large number went out unmarried. One result of this was that an unusually large number of the single women who went to Uganda from 1895 onward married fellow missionaries. Of the twenty-one women who had arrived by 1903, no fewer than ten married, and in every case but one, the couples remained in Uganda. In other important respects, these women were typical of those going overseas at the time. Training, education, and work experience is frequently noted. We find words and phrases such as "governess," "trained nurse," "Lady Superintendent,"

Fig. 7. Katherine Timpson, the first CMS nurse in Uganda
(and later the wife of Dr Albert Cook), administering
pill-box medicine, Uganda, late 1890s.

Church Mission Society archives, University of Birmingham

YWCA," "Mildmay Hospital," or "Lady Travelling Secretary, SVMU"
(referring to a woman who had studied at Cambridge).[49] All these are
applied to women who went to Uganda. Others are listed with "M.A.
degree," "stenographer," or "chemical demonstrator." By the end of
1904, twelve women with medical degrees had gone abroad, four to
China and seven to hospitals in Islamic areas, where medical work was
often the only means of making contact with the people.

For many areas of CMS work, very little is known about the work
of the missionary women, whether wives or single, and this is especially
true for those in pastoral work. More is known about medical and educational initiatives. Even less is known about the national women
workers whom they trained. For Uganda, fortunately, much can be
learned through the work of Louise Pirouet, who in her study, *Black
Evangelists,* wrote about the pioneering work of Ugandan Christians
taking the gospel to other parts of the protectorate. When a female mis-

49. SVMU stands for Student Volunteer Missionary Union.

Fig. 8. Katherine Timpson boarding a canoe on the
Semliki River, Uganda, 1901.
Church Mission Society archives, University of Birmingham

sionary was well educated and performed evangelistic work, she provided a powerful role model for her national colleagues. By 1895 missionaries and Baganda evangelists in Uganda had begun work in the western kingdom of Toro. In 1901, two of the single women who had followed the pioneering party, Edith Pike and Ruth Hurditch, were assigned to work in Kabarole, Toro.[50] They began teaching and training women church workers in a program that was required to include literacy as well as study of the Old and New Testaments. Early in 1902, twelve women — some of them wives of national workers, others the wives of chiefs — were licensed and sent out.[51] Some were still active as church teachers twenty years later. Pike herself was still active. In 1902 Ruth Hurditch had married one of the first men to work in Toro, A. B. Fisher. She also was to give many more years of work to Uganda.

The End of an Era

According to the invaluable *Register,* by the end of its first century the CMS had sent 1,556 men overseas and 550 women. By 1899 the num-

50. M. Louise Pirouet, *Black Evangelists: The Spread of Christianity in Uganda, 1891-1914* (London: Rex Collings, 1978), pp. 60, 64-65.
51. Pirouet, *Black Evangelists*, pp. 60-61.

ber of women was consistently high and in some years exceeded the number of men. When it is remembered that most of the men were married, it is clear that overall more women than men must have gone out. But how many women had there been overall? It is difficult to estimate this. Many of the single women became wives; many of the wives, when widowed, were considered women missionaries; many of the men were married two, three, or even four times.

By the beginning of the new century, in most of the CMS fields, there were various institutions where women workers were essential: a national church was also developing. Hospitals were especially important in Islamic areas, and here female doctors were doubly needed. Women were needed for the girls' boarding schools that were being set up in Africa as they had been in India, China, Japan, and New Zealand. In Africa, the village primary schools quickly became a major feature, and qualified women teachers were needed to train women — and men — for that task. And women were needed to work with and for women — to train women evangelists, to visit in the villages and homesteads, to teach and encourage. The missionary who undertook this work became known as "the lady worker." In many cases, she had traveled overseas after completing her education and training, still a young woman, who then spent thirty, thirty-five, forty years in the same general area, perhaps in the same place. She had observed two or three generations of Christian women as they grew up and married. Because of the way in which the church was structured, she never received much official recognition for the pastoral and evangelistic work she did. The ordination of women, and their consequent place in local and diocesan leadership, was something not even to be thought of.

Nevertheless it is worth remembering that it was in a diocese founded through the work of CMS missionaries and still in close touch with the society that the first ordination of a woman to the Anglican priesthood took place. This was in China, in a time of crisis in 1944, when Bishop Ronald Hall of Victoria Diocese, Hong Kong, ordained Deaconess Florence Tim-Oi Li to the priesthood "to serve the Anglican congregation in Macao isolated by the Japanese occupation of south China."[52] Acceptance of this major innovation may have been assisted by the fact that, in the Fukien Diocese (southeast China), an order of women deacons had been set up in 1922 and six women missionaries ordained as deacons. Other dioceses followed, including the diocese of

52. Hewitt, vol. 2, p. 223.

South China. There in 1931, Lucy Vincent, a CMS missionary, was ordained deacon. Attending that service was Florence Tim-Oi Li, who received her call by responding to Archdeacon Mok's plea for a Chinese girl to follow Lucy Vincent's example. Within a few years other Chinese women had joined them.

Conclusion

What can we conclude about the place of women missionaries in the Church Missionary Society? They do seem to have been accepted, and employed, both earlier and more extensively, than in many other societies founded at the same period. This is, of course, with the exception of the specific women's societies, but even these, in their home administration, were dominated by men. It may be helpful to look at what happened in another of the early Protestant missionary societies founded at the end of the eighteenth century. The London Missionary Society was begun in 1795, four years earlier than the CMS, and sent workers overseas eight years earlier. They were Englishmen, and they went to Tahiti, in the south Pacific; by 1797, twenty-three had begun work there, and all but two or three were married. As was the case with the CMS, many of the wives were active as missionaries, but no unmarried woman was appointed until 1827. That was Maria Newell, born of a missionary family, and she was sent to commence education for Chinese girls in Malacca. This she did until the end of 1829, when she resigned to marry a German missionary, Karl Gützlaff, but she died in 1831. No other single woman was appointed by the LMS until 1864, when an unmarried woman was sent to South Africa. In the next year several single women were sent to Madagascar and to India.[53]

By 1864, 620 men had proceeded overseas under the LMS, very close to the number of CMS male workers (672). But the number of women sent out with the CMS had reached 60 by the time that the LMS appointed only its second single woman. By 1895 the LMS had sent 136 women overseas, 97 to India and 39 to China, at a time when some 1,000 men had proceeded overseas. CMS figures at the end of 1895

---

53. The information and statistical details about the LMS come from Richard Lovett, *The History of the London Missionary Society*, 2 vols. (London: Henry Frowde, 1899). See the entry for Maria Newell in *Biographical Dictionary of Christian Missions*, ed. Gerald H. Anderson (New York: Macmillan, 1998), p. 492.

were 1,377 men and 743 women. At a time when the number of single women appointed under the CMS had reached just over a quarter (26 percent) of the males, only slightly more than 13 percent of those appointed under the LMS were women. Is it possible to explain these very different figures? In both cases, the greater number of women were working in India, and it must have been clear that any mission working in India required women to reach Indian women and their families. Again, the great surge in numbers, with CMS, occurred in the 1880s, and a very high proportion of the women offering arrived as honorary missionaries, which tells us a great deal about their backgrounds. Many were sisters — or kin — of the men who had offered to the China Inland Mission and other societies after the Moody and Sankey campaigns of the early 1880s. It was not until the late 1890s that women began to be accepted in any number by the LMS. Although, in both societies the education and training of the women varied, the CMS was supported by more women from the upper and upper-middle classes, who were more easily able to offer for overseas work and who had the appropriate background for it.

It was certainly not until the last decades of the nineteenth century that the service of women overseas began to become commonplace, and in earlier studies of mission (like Stephen Neill's) their contribution is almost totally ignored. Even Stock's comments on the CMS change of policy, from 1885, are patronizing, at the very least. Women were accepted reluctantly, and their work inadequately recognized, whether they had been wives or female missionaries. Where their assignments were to hospitals or schools, their tasks were easier. The increase in the number of women since the 1880s had been rapid. In the centenary year (1899), there were 1,134 missionaries working with CMS. Single women accounted for 281, and 323 were wives, together making slightly more than half of the total (53 percent). Wives accounted for more than 53 percent of those women. Single women accounted for 46 percent.[54] It was only in 1917 that women were admitted as voting members of the General Committee of the CMS.[55] It took even longer

54. Figures abstracted from Louise Pirouet, "Women Missionaries in Uganda, 1894-1904," in *Missionary Ideologies in the Imperialist Era: 1880-1920*, ed. Torben Christensen and William Hutchinson (Århus: Aros Publishers, 1982), pp. 231-32.

55. Cf. Peter Williams, "'The Missing Link': The Recruitment of Women Missionaries in Some English Evangelical Missionary Societies in the Nineteenth Century," in *Women and Missions*, ed. Bowie et al., p. 65.

for women to have adequate representation in the missionary councils in the field. In Kenya a gathering of women missionaries had been in operation for a number of years, but it could only give recommendations to the governing board of the mission and had no executive power of its own. In 1919 a dispute broke out between the women and the governing council of the Kenya mission over the location of one of the women. The women believed that her health demanded that she be relocated; the men felt that she was indispensable in the hospital where she was working. The women decided to stand up for their point of view. As the women's secretary, M. L. Mason, wrote to the general secretary in London: "We have always tried to come to an agreement with the men all these 20 years and more when we have differed from them, although time and time again our recommendations have been sent back to us — this is the first time we have insisted on their going home."[56]

Partly as a result of this altercation, women began to receive representation on the district committees of the mission: the "lady missionaries" elected two of their number to sit on a committee of which all the male missionaries were automatically members.[57] There was still a long way to go in according women the equality of esteem that they deserved.

56. CMSA, G3 A5/0 1920 Secretary of Women's Conference to Manley (7 August 1920).
57. CMSA, G3 A5/0 1922 Reorganization of the Kenya Mission.

4. CMS Women Missionaries in Persia: Perceptions of Muslim Women and Islam, 1884-1934

GULI FRANCIS-DEHQANI

Establishing a Mission in Iran

Christianity has existed in Iran since its earliest days.[1] Traditionally, the three magi are from "Persian lands afar" and St. Luke writes in the book of Acts (2:9) that on the day of Pentecost, Parthians, Medes, and Elamites (inhabitants of Persia) were present among the disciples. Later legends suggest that St. Thomas visited Persia on his way to India while others claim that Simon the Zealot brought Christianity to Iran. One way or another, by the end of the fifth century there was an organized form of Christianity in the region. The ancient Assyrian and Armenian Orthodox churches have continued as established communities maintaining their own religious, linguistic, and cultural identities. During

---

1. The word "Persia" is linguistically related to *Fars,* a region in southeast Iran, whose language — Persian — is dominant in the country. In the Persian language, the country has always been known as Iran — derived from the ancient Persian meaning "land of the Aryans" and signifying the early migrations of the Indo-Aryan people to the region. However, outside its borders it was commonly referred to as Persia until 1935 when Reza Shah ordered that the name Iran should be used throughout the world. During the period covered in this chapter, "Persia" was used to describe the country; however, the terms "Iran" and "Persia," "Iranian" and "Persian" will be used interchangeably.

91

the nineteenth and twentieth centuries, however, many new churches and Christian groups mushroomed across Iran. The period witnessed the arrival of several foreign individuals and missionary organizations eager to embark on evangelistic activity.[2]

The work of the CMS in Iran began almost by accident during the latter part of the nineteenth century. Henry Martyn had already translated the Bible for Persian speakers in India and had spent some time in Iran improving his knowledge of the language. Some years later, in 1869, a CMS missionary by the name of Robert Bruce likewise interrupted his journey to India in order to learn Persian. At that time foreigners were not permitted to reside in Muslim towns, so Bruce and his wife, Emily, settled in Julfa — an Armenian district in the city of Isfahan. While he was preparing to leave for India in April 1871, several Muslims requested baptism, and Bruce took this as a sign from God that he should remain in Iran. The CMS was initially opposed to the idea, and it took Bruce considerable time and effort to persuade his society that Persia was fertile ground for missionary work. The station was finally given official recognition by the CMS on 14 June 1875, and the mission slowly began to establish itself.[3]

During the early years, access to Muslims was extremely difficult and the small band of missionaries directed most of their educational and medical efforts toward the Armenian people of Julfa. However, the socio-political environment in Iran at the time meant that as the mission became known, its philanthropic endeavors were increasingly welcomed by the people. Furthermore, burgeoning British cultural, political, and economic influence assured the missionaries a certain status, leaving them relatively free to carry out their activities. Nevertheless, apostasy for Muslims remained officially punishable by death, and the work of the CMS proceeded with caution. The extent of the restrictions imposed on the missionaries varied according to the socio-political climate at any given time.

Until 1891 the work of CMS in Iran was, by and large, carried out

2. Very little published material is available on the beginnings of Christianity and its subsequent history in Iran. For more details, see Robin Waterfield, *Christians in Persia* (London: George Allen & Unwin, 1973); and Hassan Dehqani-Tafti, *Masih va Masihiyyat Nazd-e Iraniyan, II: Dar She'r-e Farsi, Douran-e Sabk-e Kohan (Klasik)* (Christ and Christianity Amongst the Iranians, vol. 2, In the Classical Period of Persian Poetry) (London: Sohrab Books, 1993).

3. For more on Robert Bruce and his early years in Persia, see Stock, vol. 3, pp. 123-24.

by male missionaries with the unofficial and ad hoc assistance of their wives.[4] This seriously hampered efforts, for strict segregation laws meant the male missionaries soon discovered that if access to Muslim men was difficult, contact with Muslim women was virtually impossible. Once CMS began accepting single women as missionaries, a steady stream began arriving in Iran and through their contribution considerably expanded the mission's scope and influence.

The Role of Women and Their Significance for the Persia Mission

The early CMS single women and missionary wives in Iran were not officially involved in any policy matters or decision-making processes. Without them, however, it is unlikely that the mission could have established itself as a viable organization in Persia. The presence of women missionaries was vital to the enterprise and, though denied official power within the organizational structures, they formed a large and potent part of the workforce. Much of the day-to-day running of the mission fell upon their shoulders and in practical terms they enjoyed a significant share of responsibility in the life of the small community and its growing institutions.[5]

A cursory glance at the statistical information exposes an extraordinary array of data with regard to the CMS women in Iran. From 1891 (when the first female CMS missionary arrived in Iran), until 1980 when all missionaries left the country, there were more women than men working on behalf of the CMS in the Persia mission. Moreover, from 1903, even after wives were excluded from the calculation,

---

4. The one exception to this was the contribution of Isabella Read, who arrived in Iran during 1882. Under the auspices of the Society for Promoting Female Education in the East (or Female Education Society), Read worked in the CMS Persia mission for many years.

5. Hassan Dehqani-Tafti (the first convert to become the Anglican bishop in Iran) was a young boy during the latter part of the period. During school terms he lived with the missionaries, because his family were too far away for him to be at home. While acknowledging that in some ways it was "very unsatisfactory for a young person to grow up like that," he recalls with fondness the enormous effect some of the women had upon his life. (Information obtained during an interview conducted on 22 February 1995 in Basingstoke, Hampshire.)

there was still a significantly larger number of single women than all male missionaries added together.

The average number of years served by the seventy-eight single women recorded as CMS missionaries in Iran during the period between 1891 and 1934 was 15.8. Of these:

- forty-eight (61.5 percent) stayed for ten years or more;
- twenty-six (33.3 percent) stayed for twenty years or more;
- sixteen (20.5 percent) stayed for thirty years or more;
- ten (12.8 percent) married missionary husbands and, though taken off the CMS records, continued working in Persia;
- ten (12.8 percent) died in Persia or on the way home to Britain.

These figures bear witness to a remarkably high level of commitment shown by women toward their work among the people of Iran. It is more than mere hypothesis, therefore, to maintain that the current church in Iran owes much to the presence of such dedicated women. Undoubtedly, from a late twentieth-century perspective, mistakes were made, and their working style, together with many of their methods, seem incomprehensible. Nevertheless, in forging a way for themselves and participating as active agents to improve the position of women in Britain, these missionaries also played a major part in the establishment of a mission and the formation of an indigenous church in Iran.

Preparation for Missionary Work

Little biographical information is available about the women before their arrival in Iran, for application forms and candidates' papers housed at CMS headquarters did not survive the bombing of London during the Second World War. However, it is clear that in common with most CMS single women missionaries of the time, those representing Iran came, on the whole, from middle-class families.[6] Indeed, missionary women in the late nineteenth century were generally expected to be "ladies of some education, culture and refinement."[7] Most of the

6. See John Isherwood, "An Analysis of the Role of Single Women in the Work of the Church Missionary Society, 1804-1904, in West Africa, India and China" (Master's thesis, University of Manchester, 1979), p. 5.

7. Rosemary Seton, "'Open Doors for Female Labourers': Women Candi-

women in Iran were well educated, though few, other than the doctors, had university degrees. Many were comfortably secure financially, often partly or even fully supporting themselves. Several women worked as honorary missionaries without receiving any stipend from the society during their entire career in Persia, while others paid for the training and expenses of colleagues. The majority were English, although an increasing number were attracted through local CMS associations, from countries such as Ireland, Canada, and Australia.[8]

Throughout the period, the CMS trained few of the single women to work as missionaries. Prior to 1891 approximately one-third of the society's female candidates received some training at The Willows, a private foundation established in 1888, and from the 1890s onward, several other institutions were also developed.[9] As time progressed there was growing realization of the need to improve the quality of training provided for missionary women.[10] The CMS continued, however, to rely on women's experience of Sunday school teaching and more general charitable activities. Professional training in typically "feminine" areas such as nursing or teaching was especially useful for female candidates. All philanthropic work was regarded as a valuable prelude for the missionary vocation of women, which was justified as a further extension of their "natural" private sphere into the public arena.

Arguments promoting benevolent maternalism, allowing women in Britain to expand their activities beyond the home, were inevitably based upon a class-based ideology that perceived middle-class women as striving to ameliorate the circumstances of their working-class sisters. By relying to such an extent on experience of welfare work in England instead of providing more relevant missionary training for single women, organizations such as the CMS colluded with the transferal of

---

dates of the London Missionary Society, 1875-1914," in *Missionary Encounters: Sources and Issues*, ed. Robert Bickers and Rosemary Seton (Richmond: Curzon Press, 1996), p. 58.

8. For a historical account of CMS in Ireland, for example, see Jack Hodgins, *Sister Island: A History of the Church Missionary Society in Ireland, 1814-1994* (Dunmurry: Transmission Publication, 1994).

9. For more on the history of women's training in CMS during this period see, for example, Isherwood, p. 6; and Stock, vol. 3, pp. 672, 703-4, and vol. 4, p. 467.

10. See H. Weitbrecht, "The Training of Women Missionaries," *Church Missionary Review* 44 (May 1913), pp. 298-302.

this class-based superiority into a racial one on the mission field. Used to regarding themselves as social workers and improving the position of less fortunate women in Britain, missionary women required only a subtle shift in emphasis in order to interpret their role on the mission field as "savior" to the less fortunate "heathen" women of the East.

Many women, therefore, arrived in Iran with very basic missionary instruction, in no way geared toward the specific needs of Persian people. Having been informed of their destination toward the end of their training, they were then commissioned by CMS officials before leaving Britain. On arrival in Iran they immediately began learning the language in which they would later be examined for proficiency. Other necessary skills were learned through trial and error and with advice from experienced or senior colleagues. Those who remained long enough were permitted furlough — home leave — up to two years, at approximately five-year intervals. For the remainder of the time, their life changed dramatically as they began mediating a new and diverse religious and cultural environment.

The Threefold Classification of "Women's Work"

Early CMS missionaries in Persia were not exceptional in recognizing the advantages of female workers. The notion that a nation could only be changed through its women, who carried the greater burden of rearing and influencing the next generation, was prevalent in the late nineteenth century. Views such as those expressed in 1883 by Allan Becher Webb — bishop of Grahamstown — were commonplace: "We know that home is the centre and foundation of social life; and woman is the centre of home. Such as the women are, such are the homes, and such the civilization and the Christianity of society."[11]

Keen to promote Christianity in Persian society, the CMS mission soon understood the need for women missionaries to partake in its Christianizing program. Female workers were necessary in order to gain easier access to Iranian women who lived largely in seclusion. As the number of women missionaries began to increase, the tasks they carried out were divided into three distinct categories: education, medicine, and evangelism.

11. Allan Becher Webb, *Sisterhood Life and Woman's Work in the Mission-Field of the Church* (London: Skeffington & Son, 1883), p. 3.

Protestant missionaries had long emphasized the importance of education as part of mission strategy. Literacy was regarded as essential, for it provided converts with the capacity to read the Bible. Moreover, during the nineteenth and early twentieth centuries, educating local women was regarded as the key to elevating their position in society and thereby advancing the entire nation.[12] In Iran there was general awareness within the mission that, ultimately, the country could only be evangelized through the work of indigenous Christians. Therefore, great emphasis was placed on the need to educate converts to work among their compatriots and prepare future leaders for the indigenous church community. Accordingly, many of the CMS women were educationalists who worked as teachers in the developing network of schools and other learning establishments. Work among Muslim girls and women was especially significant because a high percentage of the female population in Iran was illiterate. Apart from a handful of schools set up by religious minorities — such as the Armenians and Zoroastrian communities — for their own girls, and the efforts of the American Presbyterians in the north of Iran, there were no government establishments providing female education until well into the period covered in this chapter. Therefore, the CMS missionaries were involved in a new and ground-breaking movement: assisting Persia's women to improve their own condition. In the early years, when work among Muslims was not yet possible, CMS concentrated its efforts in Julfa. Isabella Read was the first unmarried female missionary sent to work as a teacher in the Armenian Girls' School set up in 1871 by Robert Bruce.[13]

Although education was important, the CMS missionaries soon discovered that medical efforts were a more efficient means of gaining contact with Iranian women. Moreover, on witnessing the suffering caused by a lack of adequate skills and provisions, they were keen to provide physical aid wherever possible. During the period between 1891 and 1934 many women worked as missionary nurses and doctors in Iran. For almost forty years, however, the women's side of CMS med-

12. See Eleanor Jackson, "*A True Mother in Israel*": *The Role of the Christian Mother as Evangelist in Nineteenth-Century India*. NAMP Position Paper 30. (Cambridge: University of Cambridge, North Atlantic Missiology Project, 1997), p. 11.

13. Soon after the period under study, in the second half of the 1930s, several prominent CMS women missionaries became conspicuously involved in education among Muslim girls in Iran. For details see Guli Francis-Dehqani, "British Schools in Iran," in *Encyclopaedia Iranica* (forthcoming publication).

Fig. 9. Mary Bird (1859-1914),
CMS missionary in Persia (Iran).
Church Mission Society, London

ical work was under the supervision of Dr. Emmeline Stuart. From her
arrival in 1897 Stuart, together with fifteen other female doctors, offered medical care and assistance to the people among whom they lived.
During that time several hospitals were developed and a model of medical work established that set the pattern for future efforts.

Education and medical care were regarded as valuable tasks in
helping to alleviate the suffering and hardship endured by many Iranians. However, they also served a crucial purpose in creating easier opportunities for contact with the local people, because the missionary

Fig. 10. Dr. Emmeline Stuart (1866-1946), with group of women
converts at Isfahan, on the occasion of her retirement, 1934.
Church Mission Society archives, University of Birmingham

aim was primarily religious and all activities were carried out within
the spiritual context. Philanthropic enterprises, while important, were
considered worthless without specific efforts to evangelize. For it was
evangelism that defined the missionary task as separate from secular
welfare work. In theory the medical and educational missionaries
were expected to operate as evangelists also. In practice, however,
busy schedules allowed them little time for this basic form of outreach. To assuage the tension caused by this problem, other missionaries were set aside as "pure" evangelists. These women spent their
days visiting, teaching Bible classes, and preaching the gospel whenever opportunities arose. Mary Bird was undoubtedly the most prominent of the early women evangelists to serve in Iran. She was remembered fondly by many, long after her untimely death in Iran during a
typhoid epidemic in 1914. Though well known for the basic medical
skills she practiced with considerable skill, she thought of herself
above all as an evangelist. Bird's style and approach set the pattern
for much of the women's work in the Persia mission and her influence
was deep and long-lasting.

The CMS women participating in these three areas of missionary
work were part of the ongoing evangelical tradition of social action
rooted in an individualistic understanding of spirituality dependent

upon personal salvation. Religious transformation was regarded as the ultimate solution for the problems in society. However, it was also necessary for the love of God to be shown through benevolent action in order for people to experience and understand the need for change. Today this may be viewed as a patronizing assumption at best or an insuperable deadlock at worst. Contemporary efforts to improve social conditions are usually considered entirely detachable from evangelistic work leading to religious conversion. Within the Victorian context, however, the interdependence between these elements was taken for granted and seldom questioned. Both components — the spiritual and the physical — were regarded as necessary for the missionary task in its fullness. The source of missionary motivation was undoubtedly spiritual and was expressed as a desire for the personal salvation of converts. However, this did not represent a disingenuous approach to welfare work. The majority of CMS women in Iran could not have conceived of working for social improvement or the conversion of individuals without balancing one with the other.

Married Women

Mission researchers often raise the problem of the invisibility of missionary wives in the archives and other historical sources.[14] The records of CMS activity in Iran likewise present a paucity of information on married women. Nevertheless, their tacit participation does provide a great deal of material for interpretation. Although that task falls beyond the scope of this chapter, the project would be incomplete if there were no acknowledgment of the role played by the many married women present during the early years of the Persia mission.

In countries where missionary societies were active for many years before the advent of single women workers, pioneering wives usually established a large and significant field of work.[15] In Iran, however,

14. See, for example, Deborah Kirkwood, "Protestant Missionary Women: Wives and Spinsters," in *Women and Missions: Past and Present: Anthropological and Historical Perceptions,* ed. Fiona Bowie et al. (Oxford: Berg, 1993), p. 28.

15. Writing about the South Travancore District in southern India, for example, Jane Haggis notes that by the time single women arrived in the 1880s and 1890s, a sphere of work had already been developed with thousands of pupils attending the missionary schools and other educational establishments. See Jane Haggis, "Professional Ladies and Working Wives: Female Missionaries in the London

numbers were too small and time too short for progress of any consequence to take place prior to the arrival of single women. Emily Bruce
worked virtually single-handed for almost ten years before Isabella
Read joined the station in Julfa.[16] She taught in the Armenian Girls'
School and did some district visiting. However, her solitary efforts were
insufficient for establishing women's work in Iran. Recognizing this
herself, Emily Bruce wrote several articles entreating British women to
join the missionary enterprise in Persia.[17]

According to Jane Haggis's analysis, missionary wives created a
significant sphere of work that soon demanded the more specialized efforts of single women.[18] She argues that within the missionary movement in southern India, women's work was initially demarcated by
wives who defined and provided the appropriate parameters. Though
these did not change with the arrival of single women, the importance
attached to them shifted significantly as the enterprise was profes-
sionalized under the efforts of single women's specialization. Haggis's
data about changes in the understanding of women's work carried out
by wives and undertaken by single women do not apply directly to the
circumstances in Iran. Nevertheless, many of her insights about the difference in perception of the two are highly pertinent.

Throughout the years that CMS was active in Iran, wives labored
alongside unmarried women missionaries. They were the silent partners
in work that was, for the most part, indistinguishable from that carried
out by single female colleagues. While many were extremely influential
in significant ways, they were not accorded the official status of a missionary according to CMS records. Margaret Thompson (née Carr), for
example, was born in Iran in 1897 to missionary parents and later married William Thompson (in Persia from 1914 and bishop in Iran from

Missionary Society and Its South Travancore District, South India in the Nineteenth
Century" (Ph.D. thesis, University of Manchester, 1991), p. 236.

16. Bruce's two daughters also lived in Iran and participated in the early years
of CMS's work. One of them married Edward Hörnle, another early CMS missionary, in 1885 but died in childbirth the following year.

17. The FES primarily sponsored single-women missionaries but also represented a number of wives by including information about them in its journals and
providing them with opportunities to write about their work. Several articles by
Emily Bruce, describing her work and the position of the mission in Julfa, provide
the only written sources about her. See *Female Missionary Intelligencer (FMI)*,
1879, pp. 161-62; *FMI*, 1881, pp. 170-73; and *FMI*, vol. 2, 1882, pp. 1-2.

18. For an excellent discussion concerning the distinction between single and
married women missionaries see Haggis, "Professional Ladies," pp. 234-80.

1935). She worked tirelessly for the cause of the CMS in Persia until her husband's retirement in 1961. Never, however, was she formally recognized by the society as an active participant in her own right. She referred to herself as "just a little *m*," explaining that the only proof of her existence in many CMS documents was a letter *"m"* printed next to her husband's name, indicating that he was married.[19] Likewise, women who arrived in Iran as single missionaries and later married colleagues were required immediately to resign their post. Though they continued with much of the work they had previously been doing, their salary was withdrawn and their name wiped out of the record books.

The problem was that formal recognition of married women's contributions would cause an ideological difficulty. Indeed, the justification for permitting single women to work as missionaries would have been seriously undermined, because "The raison d'être behind the women's missionary movement of the late nineteenth century was that single women, without the encumbrances of husband and children, would be able to devote their entire lives to missionary work."[20]

For the most part, the two groups of women — married and single — did similar work and their involvement in committees and decision-making bodies was largely the same. Nevertheless, there they were perceived differently. This ideological distinction was expressed through the relative invisibility of wives in official documents, the title of "missionary wife" (compared to that of "lady missionary" used for single women), and their lack of financial remuneration.

This last was a particularly significant factor affecting the position of wives. By virtue of their salary (albeit smaller than that of their male colleagues), single women were regarded as professionals, qualified to do their job and accorded their worth through financial reward. Married women, meanwhile, though embarked upon similar tasks, experienced a qualitative reduction in the value placed upon them. Wives did not receive any financial benefits and single missionaries who married while in Persia were subject to an immediate loss of earnings. Indeed, those married within their first two or three years were required to recompense the CMS for the cost of their training and travel even if, as wives, they intended to continue working for the mission. This meant that the CMS could effectively ignore their presence, thereby stripping them of any identity other than a male missionary's

19. Author's recollection.
20. Seton, "Open Doors," p. 66.

wife. Agnes Carr, for example, was in Iran for thirty-six years with her husband, Donald. On their retirement, the CMS recorded their grate-fulness to Donald Carr for his services to the mission in Persia. In a long account of his career no mention of Agnes is made until near the end where there is a brief reference to "the wife" who shared his career.[21]

In short, married missionary women were taken for granted by the CMS. Had they not been there, or simply refused to participate in the work, their absence would have been keenly felt. Their involve-ment, however, at minimum cost to the society, was an unspoken expec-tation, implicit within the missionary code of practice.[22] If a wife was believed to be opting out of her duties, it was a matter for comment by other missionaries. In 1899, for example, Charles Stileman wrote to the CMS complaining that one of the missionary wives in Kerman — Flora Blackett — was not doing the work expected of her:

> Complaints here [have been] made to me . . . that Mrs Blackett re-fused to see the Persian ladies when they sent to ask if they might visit her, and she has not of course qualified herself in the language for much active work. I mention this because the usual idea in this mis-sion is that when a married couple occupy a station, the wife does some pioneer work amongst the women, thus preparing the way for single ladies, this pioneer work is not being done and the sooner the single ladies go there the better it will be for the work.[23]

Other than the benefits provided by wives through the activities in which they participated, married women also accorded missionary soci-eties with the ideological and theological justification for the presence of single women workers. An apology for women's involvement in the workforce during late Victorianism was provided by a particular inter-pretation of the separate-spheres philosophy in which public work was regarded as an extension of the domestic realm. If this logic was to con-tinue operating, the domestic world needed to remain intact as a dis-cernible reality supported by part of the female population. Missionary wives, therefore, completed the equation of Victorian womanhood by ensuring that the private world of domesticity was maintained. They filled the role of homemaker, providing comfort and stability for the

21. CMSA, G2/PE/P4 1930: 64.
22. Married men were given a "married man's allowance" that increased their salary by a small amount.
23. CMSA, G2/PE/O 1899: 56.

family and wider society. They represented the essence of Christian morality, based on monogamous marriage, Christian motherhood, and womanly self-sacrifice, which was an essential component of the missionary education. Meanwhile, the single women were liberated to reinterpret the private world, moving it beyond the safe domain of domesticity into the public world of work. The result for married women was dualistic. On the one hand, their role gave them a kind of status as upholders of the basic Christian virtue at the heart of stable society. On the other hand, however, it restricted them professionally and limited them financially.

Within the CMS Persia mission there were, of course, disagreements and controversies resulting from the relationships among wives, single women, and male missionaries. The ambiguous role played by married women inevitably meant that the stronger personalities wielded greater power. Equally, they were easier targets of personal attacks by other missionaries, especially men, who felt freer to remark on the contribution of wives because they were not officially regarded as colleagues. For example, soon after his arrival in Persia in 1893, William St. Clair Tisdall wrote to the CMS offering some general opinions on the state of the mission. Among other things, he commented on Emily Bruce, describing her as "a most unpleasant woman, miserly in the extreme among her other bad qualities."[24] She had, he believed, "much influence on her husband and biase[d] his mind against people. . . . I can understand how troubles have arisen in the past. A great many of them have been due to Mrs B. doubtless."[25] For the most part, however, the various constituencies within the mission circle worked alongside each other peaceably. The single and married women, in particular, provided the ideological justification for one another's presence and between them depicted the ideal of Christian womanhood, fulfilling responsibilities both at home and in the public domain.

The Paradoxical Nature of Women's Involvement in the CMS Persia Mission

In order to appreciate the lives of past women more fully, it is necessary to observe them from the point of view of their times rather than

24. CMSA, G2/PE/O 1893: 36.
25. CMSA, G2/PE/O 1893: 36.

merely judge them by alien late twentieth-century standards. This necessitates a dual perspective approach, requiring respect for historical context as well as presenting the challenge of contemporary priorities. Indeed, the subjects of any historical study such as this are best understood within the interpretative spectrum of "responsibility" and "usability" as depicted by Eleanor McLaughlin.[26] While a critical inquiry should be based on present-day assumptions, women of previous ages should also be understood and evaluated according to the context in which they lived and worked. This creates a tension within the research process, best resolved by an interpretation based on a paradoxical approach rather than one searching for straightforward simplicity. Accordingly, if the CMS women are to be credited with a distinct, but no less significant, part in the development of the women's movement, it is necessary to reiterate several contradictory elements within their gender, theological, and imperialist perceptions.

First, their professional careers and also their self-understanding were limited by clear Victorian gender boundaries. They viewed the world in terms of separate spheres for men and women and did not conceive of breaking down these barriers or moving beyond them. What they achieved, rather, was to use the restrictions to their advantage, ingeniously finding ways to expand the customs deemed acceptable for women. The legitimacy of their part in the women's movement is based on an astute interpretation of a conservative and potentially limiting ideology rather than an attempt to destroy that ideology. Though involved in activities few women had previously experienced, they preempted the risk of full-scale opposition by men (which may have curtailed their opportunities) by ensuring that the ideology itself remained in place. For this reason it is important to judge them more by their actions than their words. They were not interested in shifting the philosophical ground under the prevalent gender assumptions by arguing for equality with men. However, they were able to participate in the move toward change through their work, which took them beyond the physical confines of home life.

Second, the CMS women in Persia embody the paradoxical nature of religion in the lives of Victorian women. Most feminist historiography still refuses to acknowledge the potency of religious faith and its

26. Eleanor McLaughlin, "The Christian Past: Does It Hold a Future for Women?" in *Womanspirit Rising: A Feminist Reader in Religion,* ed. Carol Christ and Judith Plaskow (New York: Harper & Row, 1992), pp. 93-106.

potential for motivating women, regarding it instead as an entirely re-
strictive force. For the CMS missionaries, however, the capacity to face
the struggles and dangers came from a spirituality that gave them hope
for the future and belief in their own abilities. To be sure, the prevalent
evangelicalism of late nineteenth- and early twentieth-century Britain
tried to restrict women through its insistence on an ideology that connected them irrevocably with the home. At the same time, however, it
promoted the spiritual and domestic superiority of women, thus providing the impetus many needed in order to work for change.

Finally, one of the most common paradoxes at the heart of the imperialist agenda was at play for the CMS women in Iran. It enabled
them to retain an overall attitude of superiority toward the country
while at the same time building close ties of friendship based on genuine mutuality with individual Iranians. Edward Said has written extensively about the orientalist mind-set, especially during the age of empire, and its ability to incorporate generally accepted negative views
about Islam and the East with a more positive personal encounter with
it.[27] He evinces that there is a distinction between the "particular" and
the "general" in a Western approach to the East, arguing that people
learn "to separate a general apprehension of the Orient from a specific
experience of it," while allowing them to coexist.[28] Accordingly, the
CMS women were, on the whole, willing to criticize the entire nation or
pronounce judgment upon Islam generally. At the same time, however,
their encounters with individuals brought them close to a real understanding of Persian people in their own right and not as potential converts. By operating according to this paradox, the CMS women remained within the linguistic and ideological boundaries expected by
their supporters in England. In reality, however, their attitudes were often changing, even if subconsciously, through their personal experiences with the people among whom they lived and worked.

Muslims and Islam, or the Particular versus the General

It is important to probe more deeply into the paradox unfolded by Edward Said's theory, with specific reference to the CMS women mission-

27. Edward Said, *Orientalism: Western Conceptions of the Orient* (London:
Penguin, 1995), pp. 95-103.
28. Said, *Orientalism*, p. 101.

aries in Iran, distinguishing between their general approach toward Islam that fulfilled the ideological and linguistic expectations at the heart of empire, and their shifting attitude toward Muslims as people whom they encountered and came to know. This requires a close exploration of the CMS archives and a careful investigation of the views expressed. There are no lengthy treatises or systematically developed arguments for interpretative dissection. Rather, one must scrutinize the material for first- and second-hand references, searching for passing remarks and occasional comments relevant to the topic. In this way, a picture can be painted, depicting the views of the women, that can be analyzed as a means of better understanding them within their particular context.

In order to provide a suitable structural framework for the task in hand, an insight from Kenneth Cracknell's book *Justice, Courtesy and Love* has been modified and used as an appropriate model. Prior to the World Missionary Conference (WMC) held in Edinburgh in 1910, questionnaires were sent to 149 active missionaries representing different denominations and geographical regions in order to assess their attitude and approach toward other religions and their adherents. A report was prepared in time for the conference, largely reflecting the views expressed in the responses. Entitled *The Missionary Message in Relation to Non-Christian Religions,* its perhaps surprisingly positive tone concerning the world faiths was presented as an indication of the prevalent mood among missionaries at the time. In the course of a thorough examination of the report, Cracknell suggests various explanations for the fact that some missionaries were able to express more charitable sentiments about their encounter with other religions than might be expected.[29]

Two of these prove especially useful as a means of structuring the disseminated data about the women in Iran. First, Cracknell argues, the more positive replies were couched in terms of people rather than whole religious systems.[30] Many showed an instinct for the personal — the individuals they knew — rather than the abstract. For example, Anna Smith, who worked in Bangalore, demonstrated remarkably progressive thinking and clearly had her eyes on the people rather than

29. Kenneth Cracknell, *Justice, Courtesy and Love: Theologians and Missionaries Encountering World Religions, 1846-1914* (London: Epworth Press, 1995), pp. 202, 219, 285.
30. Cracknell, *Justice,* p. 202.

their beliefs and was therefore able to recognize in them the presence of God.[31] This approach relied on an assessment of non-Christian religions in their present form — according to the here and now — rather than judging them on their past history. Second, most generous contributors were unwilling to judge other faiths on the basis of unacceptable social manifestations, though these were acknowledged and frequently criticized.

With this critical framework now in place, it is possible to negotiate Said's theory of Western schizophrenia regarding the East and its people and apply it to the CMS women in Iran. Cracknell's observations show how the paradox of relating to the particular in a positive way while judging the general negatively is highly pertinent to the study of missionaries, particularly during the age of empire. For it was a subtle emphasis of one over the other that differentiated the views of various missionaries. Generous respondents to the WMC questionnaire stressed individual relationships (i.e., the particular) and concentrated less on criticizing the entire religious system (i.e., the general). In contrast, an inspection of the CMS papers reveals that the women missionaries in Persia wrote more in terms of Islam as an institution rather than Muslims as people with whom they were in relationship. Accordingly, it was much easier for them to denounce the whole nation without the need for personal criticism of particular individuals.

Two themes emerge within the context of their general reproaches: namely, "the land" en masse, that they considered to be in darkness; and "the people" as a unit, whom they believed to be lost. In 1892, for example, Mary Bird wrote of her hopes to build up house visiting in order that she should be used for God's service "in this dark land."[32] Out of this developed a call for "the evangelization of the land"[33] as the means by which God's Spirit could become active in Iran. This rather abstract idea of "the land" found its reflection in the notion of a "thirsty perishing *people*"[34] (my emphasis), which in turn, required missionary commitment to "gather many souls out of the darkness into His marvellous light."[35] Occasionally, the land and the people were combined, or ambiguously united, in references such as the "evange-

31. Cracknell, *Justice*, p. 219.
32. CMSA, G2/PE/O 1892: 53.
33. Bird — G2/PE/O 1898: 28.
34. Bird — G2/PE/O 1893: 87.
35. Ethel Stuart — G2/PE/O 1903: 36.

Fig. 11. Persian women in purdah, no date.
Church Mission Society archives, University of Birmingham

lization of *Persia*"[36] or "the salvation of this erring *nation*"[37] (both emphases mine). In either case — land or people — both were regarded as residing in darkness, and the missionary hope and belief was that the Lord would "answer the many prayers for these lands *speedily*."[38]

Though "land" and "people" formed the most comprehensive units, the work of the female missionaries directed their attention more toward the women of Persia. It is perhaps not surprising that they too were usually mentioned in terms of a distinct, definable category, often referred to simply as "Muhammedan women." Three themes in particular run through the CMS women's attitude toward this unified group. First, they had to be *reached* if the missionary endeavor was to be successful. Second, they were, on the whole, regarded as uninformed and ig-

---

36. Included in a joint letter from "the missionaries of the C.M.S. labouring in Persia" to the Home Committee in London registering a complaint at their decision not to "occupy Isfahan" but to continue "concentrating their forces in Julfa." Laura Stubbs and Mary Bird were among the five to sign. CMSA, G2/PE/O 1893: 105.

37. London Partnership House Library, Mary Bird, *Annual Letters*, 1895, pp. 10-12.

38. Wilkes — CMSA, G2/PE/O 1895: 57.

Fig. 12. Persian village women,
near Isfahan, no date.
Church Mission Society archives,
University of Birmingham

norant. Finally, the missionaries expressed pity toward Persian women, believing that they could be helped only by means of the gospel message.

According to the prevailing belief that to change a nation, its women needed to be reached, from the earliest days of female presence in the Persia mission, contact with indigenous women was regarded as essential. Soon after her arrival in 1891, Mary Bird wrote that her time was occupied in learning Persian so she could take best advantage of any opening among the Muslim women.[39] The following year she af-

39. CMSA, G2/PE/0 1891: 85.

firmed the importance of visiting women "where ever I can gain admittance, so as to win their confidence, and get opportunities of hearing and speaking, and thus paving the way for future work."[40] Prior to the growth in educational and medical work, visiting them in their homes was regarded as "the only way . . . possible to get at the *women*."[41]

Having made contact with Muslim women, the missionaries were quick to express generalized opinions about them as a group, regarding them, on the whole, as ignorant and uninformed. However, during the early years when Iran was part of the Turkish-Arabia mission, an interesting distinction appeared between views postulated by the CMS women in Iran compared with those in Iraq.[42] For the former, the ignorance they perceived as a trait of Persian women was usually considered an attribute caused by their environment in which the education of girls was not encouraged. Whereas for the latter, the Arabian women of Baghdad were criticized due to their apparently inherent limitations from a very young age. In other words, comments about Persian women's ignorance were due more to sociological observations about the condition of women, whereas in Baghdad unqualified remarks were presented as physiological truths.[43]

Emmeline Stuart, for example, commenting on the high levels of female illiteracy and the unavailability of educational opportunities, held that this was due to mistaken assumptions within Iranian thinking that women lacked the capacity for learning.[44] However, Arabella Wilson writing from Baghdad was much more critical of Arabian women

40. CMSA, G2/PE/O 1892: 53.
41. Arabella Wilson — G2/PE/O 1890: 84.
42. When Persia was formally recognized by CMS as a field in which they would operate, it was coupled with the CMS station in Baghdad under the general heading of the Turkish-Arabia mission. For several years, these two areas coexisted as one administrative unit. However, it soon became apparent that, though both were Muslim countries, the distinction between an Arabic and a Persian environment was too great to sustain an identical strategy. Furthermore, the geographical distances were too large to sustain reasonable contact and communication between the two regions. In 1897, therefore, the decision was taken by CMS to separate the two stations, henceforth leaving the Persia mission to operate independently.
43. The actual and perceived distinctions between Arab and Persian Muslims is a complex and convoluted subject that falls beyond the scope of this chapter. It is a topic I cover in some depth in my "Religious Feminism in an Age of Empire: CMS Women Missionaries in Iran, 1869-1934" (Ph.D. thesis, University of Bristol, 1999).
44. "The Social Conditions of Women in Muslim Lands," *Church Missionary Review* (August 1909), p. 462.

and girls: "I have begun an infants class on Sunday afternoon just to teach them to repeat and, as far as I can, to understand verses of the Bible. It is work I dearly love, but they need an immense amount of patience for *thinking* is not in them and you may tell them a thing again and again without their taking it in, even the simplest thing."[45]

The missionaries in Iran were equally fond of generalizations, many of which were far from flattering. However, their comments about the aptitude for learning of Muslim women in Iran were usually more generous and gracious. Emily Skirrow, for example, considered Parsi (or Zoroastrian) women somewhat stupid and dull, but remarked upon the intelligence of the Muslim women in Kerman.[46]

By far the most common feeling expressed by the CMS women toward Iranians was one of pity. This is distinguishable from sympathy or compassion, which were also typical missionary responses but ones that usually developed over a longer period of time and grew from personal contact. In contrast, pity was a sentiment that many expressed in broad terms and with little knowledge of particular circumstances. Alongside it, there was an unequivocal assurance that the missionaries themselves, as channels for the Christian message, could help relieve the misery of Persian life. Thus, assertions of pathetic, pitiable lifestyles were often imposed upon the people even by the newest missionary recruits hoping for opportunities to aid the suffering they perceived. Laura Stubbs, for example, soon after reaching Julfa, recalled her land journey across Persia: "As we passed through the villages one felt so sorry for the people. We longed to be able to speak to them and to tell them the 'Old, old Story.' They looked so like 'sheep having no Shepherd.'"[47]

Ten years later her sentiments had barely changed. Writing of her visit to Dehbala — a village near Yezd — she recalled her sadness at passing through the mountain villages, knowing that they were in utter darkness without a single missionary: "Oh that God may make us [Mary Bird and herself] channels of life to these dying souls."[48] Not surprisingly, comments like these were often directed more specifically toward Iranian women. Philippa Braine-Hartnell first went to Persia in 1892 as a child-care helper for William St. Clair Tisdall and his wife,

45. CMSA, G2/PE/O 1890: 136.
46. CMSA, G2/PE/O 1910: 135.
47. CMSA, G2/PE/O 1891: 90.
48. CMSA, G2/PE/O 1901: 143.

while also doing missionary work in an unofficial capacity. Approximately three years later she applied to be taken on as a full missionary by the CMS. Employing typical missionary language, her letter of application expressed her desire to work "among the poor downtrodden women of Persia."[49]

This emphasis on the need for missionary help to compensate the supposedly lamentable circumstances of Persian lives was essentially an expression of theological significance. Clearly, the tiny CMS mission was in no position to solve the problems arising from the socio-political and economic structures of late nineteenth- and early twentieth-century Iran. Although they recognized their human restrictions, most missionaries still held to the belief that religious conversion on the part of individuals and the Iranian nation as a whole could serve to alleviate much of the suffering. This hypothesis was based on the commonly held evangelical belief in the need for personal salvation as the antidote for all societal problems. Ultimately it provided the CMS women with a resolute motivation to work for the achievement of their goals.

Inevitably, the desire to palliate the ills of society by redemption through personal conversion was accompanied by a condescending demeanor that, at its worst, intimated arrogance. The patronizing approach from which so many missionaries suffered was also a typical feature of contemporary evangelicalism that Elisabeth Jay has referred to in terms of the paradox of "wholescale commitment."[50] It originated from a deeply held belief in Christian superiority that placed a burden of responsibility upon all who accepted it. In militaristic terms common at the time, the gospel was used as a weapon in the battle to win souls. For it was believed that conversion, followed by personal salvation, would lay the foundations for the formation of a new spiritual and physical community. As providers of the Christian message, the missionaries were convinced that they possessed the solutions necessary to ensure a positive future for the people of Iran. Their motivation was, by and large, genuine, as was their desire to alleviate suffering. However, the figurative generalizations to which they clung in order to express their ideas, together with the deeply embedded assumptions of superiority, meant that a patronizing tone remained inescapable.

It should also be noted that the close contact the women mission-

---

49. CMSA, G2/PE/O 1895: 77.
50. Elisabeth Jay, *Faith and Doubt in Victorian Britain* (Basingstoke: Macmillan, 1986), p. 19.

aries had with the ordinary people of Iran was a rare experience for Europeans at the turn of the century. They are, therefore, among the most reliable social commentators from that period, and it is incumbent upon us to take their comments seriously. They witnessed extraordinary levels of hardship and suffering in the lives of Persian people that they elucidated by means of the familiar linguistic framework of Victorian evangelicalism. The oppressive structures that persistently limited their use of the English language should not, however, diminish the underlying reality of their words. To acknowledge the poor condition of Iranian society, especially with regard to the position of women, is not to discriminate against Islam or condemn all that is Persian. It is rather a rejection of that particular brand of distorted orientalism that, refusing ever to criticize the Orient, loses the impetus in the search for truth and fails to understand the nineteenth century within its true context.[51]

Two exceptions should be noted to the CMS women's widespread classification of Persian Muslim women as a single homogenous group. The first was the distinction often made between rich and poor. The second concerns those occasions when the missionaries were able to move beyond generalizations and relate to individual Persian women.

From the earliest days, the missionaries were aware of the profound implications that the social chasm between rich and poor had upon their work. They soon discovered that access to wealthy women was usually much more difficult. This meant fewer opportunities were available for conversing with and influencing this group. The reasons for this were twofold. First, the conventions of the Islamic separate-spheres philosophy were normally adhered to much more strictly for wealthy urban women whose seclusion was closely guarded in comparison to their poorer rural counterparts. Second, the rich townswomen were not required to work but had regular staff to carry out all household duties. This, according to Mary Bird, created a superficiality among wealthy Persian women that resulted in their being "so frivolous, so taken up with their gorgeous dresses and ornaments, their endless cups of tea and pipes, and so self-satisfied."[52]

This difference between rich and poor was frequently expressed in terms of a typically English fascination with class distinction. Before

51. For a fuller discussion concerning the dangers of distorted orientalism see Maxime Rodinson, *Europe and the Mystique of Islam* (Seattle: University of Washington Press, 1991), p. 127.

52. London Partnership House Library, Mary Bird, *Annual Letters*, 1895, pp. 10-12.

Emmeline Stuart arrived in Persia, the mission was already aware of the need for a medically qualified woman who could enable them to reach women of all classes, including the relatively inaccessible wealthy women.[53] This desire to influence the upper echelons of Iranian society grew from a belief that only they could forge real change within the country. The theory was based upon a transferal of the British class-based ideology (in which middle- and upper-class women were regarded as affecting change for their supposedly helpless working-class sisters) to a Persian context.

This did not mean the social and religious concerns of poorer women were neglected, but simply that they were considered entirely differently. The missionaries always remained aware of the divergent needs of women and children according to their social ranking. Jessie Biggs, for example, wrote about the desirability of educating various classes of women separately so that each could be taught according to their needs. English, French, and science may not be of much use to the poorer girls who needed to be "taught to earn their own living . . . according to the customs of the country."[54] Although this may have been based on a form of class-based superiority, it did in fact respond to practical requirements. Poorer women who had no other means of income were taught skills in order to earn money at a time when Persian society would have had little use for developing intellectuals among such women.

In contrast to the more general remarks about the women of Iran and the distinction recognized between rich and poor, there are also countless examples of detailed narratives concerning the lives of individuals.[55] What these accounts have in common is that the majority refer to people who, under the influence of the mission, were either showing keen interest in Christianity or had already been baptized. There are, for example, detailed descriptions of the faithfulness and courage displayed by a number of female converts, while inquirers not yet willing to commit themselves to the Christian way of life are entrusted to the prayers of readers at home in the hope that conversion may soon follow.[56]

53. Tisdall in CMSA, G2/PE/O 1893: 75.
54. CMSA, G2/PE/O 1919: 67.
55. This is particularly true of the printed Annual Letter extracts and articles written for CMS journals rather than the ordinary letters.
56. See, for example, London Partnership House Library, Emmeline Stuart, *Annual Letters*, 1899, pp. 77-78 and 1900, pp. 262-63; Mary Bird, *Annual Letters*, 1895, pp. 10-12; 1896, pp. 20-24.

The willingness of the CMS women to refer to individual Persians who were of professional interest to them while continuing in their disposition to generalize about the people as a whole may be interpreted in a variety of ways. It is possible, for example, to argue that they were willing to develop relationships only with those from whom they had something to gain. Accordingly, their association with most Persian women was always based on a power balance in which they were offering something but had nothing to acquire in return. On the other hand, the women they met through work were obviously those with whom they formed relationships. It was natural, therefore, that these should be the people about whom they wrote as individuals. The pertinent point is, rather, that the development of personal friendships did not eliminate the generalizations but simply coexisted alongside them. While an attitude of superiority seeps through the missionary letters, it is balanced by genuine warmth and friendship. This is once more an element of the paradoxical nature of the missionary presence in Iran.

To be sure, the letters they wrote were aimed at a specific audience eager to hear positive results about the work of the CMS in Iran. The language and tone of much of the material is designed to satisfy these requirements and, moreover, adumbrates a pattern within which the CMS women felt secure. However, the archives also include authentic expressions of humility and admiration for the strength and courage shown by converts experiencing persecution. While the language is often restricted, there remains a real sense in which the missionaries regarded Persian Christians as fellow pilgrims along the same journey. For many years they continued to insist that the growing indigenous church needed to be nurtured and developed through seasoned missionary expertise. However, they also acknowledged their own need to learn from the Persian experience in particular with regard to accepting the burden of suffering.

The CMS women in Iran are typical of Said's orientalists whose individual and general approach to the East and its people coexisted, each apparently unencumbered by the other. Inevitably, this resulted in a complex relationship between the missionary women and the Persian people. An inability to recognize the inappropriate use of universalized assumptions resulted in an air of superiority running throughout the mission during its formative years in Iran. Moreover, it means that the appropriation of the early stages of a positive theology of religions, in the way expressed by some missionary responses to the questionnaire prepared for the 1910 World Missionary Conference, was not possible.

The generalized approach employed by the CMS women persistently suggested that the mission had something to offer the people of Iran for which nothing could be gained in return.

Nevertheless, analyzing their attitude toward individuals introduces a variant approach indicating the composite nature of their relationship with Iranians. Friendships undoubtedly developed and many were profoundly influenced through the Persians whom they knew. To be sure, they remained unwilling or unable to supersede the theological framework in which they operated, never displaying radical change from the traditional CMS approach. However, this in itself should not lead to the assumption that their relationships were all one way. In reality, many of the women were aware of gaining more than they had given and learning more than they had taught. The majority developed a deep love for the people of Iran and this grew primarily from their experience of those with whom they became friends. Their weakness lay in an inability to recognize the paralyzing effect of assumptions based on generalizations with regard to both the people of Iran and the indigenous church community.

Despite all this, their writings act as a kind of counterbalance to much contemporary postimperialist literature which, with its fiercely antimission stance, refuses to concede the right of non-Western individuals to choose Christianity for themselves.[57] There is a tendency to assume that all who converted as a consequence of missionary efforts did so merely in the face of coercion and intimidation, and that subsequent generations have followed suit because of the overwhelming power of Western cultural imperialism. This patronizing hypothesis betrays an equally arrogant neopaternalism akin to the orientalist attitude of nineteenth-century missionaries in which Westerners declare what they believe to be best for the people of the East.

In contrast, through genuine admiration for the courage of those who converted, the CMS women in Iran reveal their faith in a Christianity that transcends cultural and national boundaries and adapts to its new environment. Despite the contours of their orientalist mind-set and the limitations of its accompanying vocabulary, in essence they did not want to Westernize Persian society but to Christianize it. For the missionaries the distinction was self-evident. The benefits of Christian-

---

57. See Frances Hiebert, "Beyond a Post-Modern Critique of Modern Missions: The Nineteenth Century Revisited," *Missiology* 25, no. 3 (July 1997), pp. 259-77.

ity may, for some, have been inexplicably linked with the influence of Western civilization. However, from a relatively early stage in the Persia mission, a conscious effort was made to separate the two dimensions. The missionaries believed that this was both possible and desirable. Annie Gauntlett, for example, argued that "the need for the Gospel and *the Gospel only* in Persia, has grown with the facilities for preaching it" (my emphasis).[58] Yet, as explained by Dr. Winifred Westlake in 1903, this was not synonymous with a case for Westernization: "We don't want to Anglicise the Persian women, do we? No, if we may be used to set them free from the trammels of Mohammedanism, placing them in the light of the Gospel of Christ, they will develop as God wills, and who can tell what they may do in His honour and glory."[59]

The experience of the CMS women in Iran challenges the theological assumption that to be a Christian is to side with power and hierarchy, to become part of an institution based on gender imbalance and inappropriate clericalism. Theirs was a faith that encompassed something of the richness of human experience.

Conclusion

It remains impossible to judge the efforts of the CMS women missionaries in Iran objectively as either entirely beneficial or harmful.[60] For such a conclusion would either undermine the context in which they

58. CMSA, G2/PE/O 1916: 72.
59. Westlake — CMSA, G2/PE/O 1903: 140.
60. From an Iranian perspective it is also difficult to determine the impact of the missionary movement in Persia. Converts remained few and the Anglican Church that has survived the Islamic Revolution of 1979 is small and vulnerable. Little has been written on the influence of missionaries in any depth. Existing publications, including novels and autobiographies, present a variety of views — many of them as passing references — which vary from severe criticism to warm gratitude. For positive impressions see, for example, Sattareh Farman Farmaian, *Daughter of Persia: A Woman's Journey from Her Father's Harem Through the Islamic Revolution* (London: Bantam Press, 1992), pp. 56-60, 73-75; and Rouhi Shafii, *Scent of Saffron: Three Generations of an Iranian Family* (London: Scarlet Press, 1997), pp. 8, 32; and Hassan Dehqani-Tafti, *Design of My World* (London: Lutterworth Press, 1959). For critical interpretations see, for example, Gohar Kord, *An Iranian Odyssey* (London: Serpent's Tail, 1991), especially pp. 97-106; and Simin Daneshvar, *Persian Requiem*, tr. Roxane Zand (New York: George Braziller, 1992 edition).

lived through an obsessive present-mindedness or it would neglect the serious challenges of late twentieth-century theological and cultural insights. Their consistent use of dominant ideologies upheld the tenets of empire and their strict adherence to the recognizable codes of contemporary evangelical and orientalist language often restricted their vision. The harsh tone of their words, however, should be set against the example of many lives spent in the service of others and in an effort to improve the position of women. For the majority of the CMS women in Iran, their inherent sense of superiority was balanced by a genuine love for and commitment to the women of Persia.

Their part in the religious strand of the Western women's movement is also assured through their commitment to work for new opportunities. Despite the weight of both actual and ideological restrictions encumbering their efforts, the CMS women in Iran forged a new path by participating in activities hitherto confined to men. While complying with many Victorian assumptions about gender distinctions, their example began the process of blurring the boundaries that separated masculine and feminine behavior. The early endeavors of the CMS Persia women together with those of many other female missionaries, paved the way for following generations to develop new methods in the struggle for a future based on mutual cooperation between the whole people of God.

5. Being Made Disciples — The Middle East

KENNETH CRAGG

I

There has always been something odd about the title "The Church Missionary Society" (as indeed of the more recent change to "The Church Mission Society"), in the sense that the word "Church" made the others unnecessary. For they simply repeat its meaning, as one might think to say "The automobile self-propulsive car." A "society in mission" was the very nature of the church. Were not "Catholic, Apostolic" in the Creed precisely, in words of Greek origin, what "universal, missionary" were in Latin?

The point was not lost on the first founders, nor — indeed — on Max Warren who was, nevertheless, sturdy to the point of doggedness in the belief that only a society, organized and committed for action, could in fact be the church in all that mission demanded. Without the vision and the impetus which a society could generate, the church in toto — certainly not the Church of England — would never achieve its true missionary vocation.

That issue of "the part for the whole," with all its implications for diocesanization and global interdependence, is dealt with elsewhere in this book. Its relevance in this chapter is simply that it underlines what is implicit in all other themes, namely that mission is a learning process. Hence the play on words in the chapter title. Matthew 28:19 uses the imperative word *matheteusate* (noun into verb), which could be anglicized into "disciple all nations." Though not strictly permissible in grammar, is there not a true sense in which "discipling" is a reflexive verb? It is not quite as with the ten lepers in Luke's Gospel: "As they went they were cleansed," but certainly mission understands only as it goes. There is a learning process in that the very effort to tell and translate, to mean and serve, becomes an education. The pitfalls are many, the tuition taxing, the lessons often rooted in enigmas.

It is intriguing to realize that the Great Commission itself in Matthew 28:18-20 could have been formulated in its trinitarian shape only in the sequel of obeying it instinctively already. Its origins lay in the significance of Christ, crucified and risen for humanity, read and loved in terms inclusively redemptive. The intention for the world was explicit in the very nature of the cross, the sign of a boundless embrace and of its cost. But reading it so was the "learning" of an implementing society that only in the going reached the credal language in which Matthew's Gospel enshrined it. Action itself enabled them to formulate what it was that they were doing and to realize that they were partnering the mind of Christ preceding them — but only with the knowing in the going.

We may be sure that the paradigm persists and in few places more searchingly than in the Middle East. It might be wise to ask where the Middle East begins. At the outset in 1799, the emphasis for the CMS was on Africa, where its most evident achievements have been. West Asia certainly did not come into the society's range until 1815 when a Mediterranean Mission was set up in Malta, which, though strategic to the Middle Sea, was hardly Middle East. The locale was significant, however, for a reason that in various ways has waited on its story. Malta was British territory, as — much later — India, Egypt, and, more briefly, Palestine (in Mandate terms) were to become. Foreigners might go briefly to the Ottoman Middle East as pilgrims but could trade and reside only by permits (known as "capitulations") regulating their activities. Hence the necessity of Malta as a base. Hence, too, the diplomatic measures and political persuasion necessary to secure the *firman*, or authority, from the Ottoman caliph to admit a Jerusalem bishopric in 1841.

That situation must be kept in mind throughout in the story of the CMS as a symbol of the paradox and ambiguity which were always prominent in the thinking of Max Warren.[1] A Muslim educationalist

---

1. These themes preoccupied him as an historian. See his *The Missionary Movement from Britain in Modern History* (London: SCM Press, 1965), and a sober apologia for empire in *Caesar, the Beloved Enemy* (London: Highway Press, 1955).

and civil servant during the Palestine Mandate, A. L. Tibawi, could title a meticulous, well-documented survey of missions, including the CMS, as: *British Interests in the Middle East, 1800-1901.*[2] The aegis of mission in the context of empire could be read both as a destiny and a guilt complex. His East India Company chaplaincy had been both embarrassing and enabling for Henry Martyn in India, the sweetest and worthiest icon of the CMS–Charles Simeon tradition.

This ambivalence around the auspices of English mission, with urgent issues for theology, accompanies the historian at every point. It meant that CMS missionaries were always cheek by jowl with other presences, political and ecclesiastical, with whom relationships were crucial. All Saints' Church (later Cathedral), Cairo, through and beyond the Cromer years in Egypt,[3] was to be symbolically read in different terms from CMS ministries in Old Cairo and the Harpur Hospital. Similarly, its counterpart in Jerusalem (St. George's Collegiate Church) served the Mandatory power for more that a quarter century and thus related ambiguously to the inclusive dimensions of a diocese-in-mission. The realm of the political being always relevant, these problematics were inescapable. Mission is never pursued *in vacuo*. Thus the significance of that first locale in Malta attaches to the whole story through the heyday and the eclipse, the waxing and the waning, of British *imperium*, political and developmental. What a missionary society could venture has always been in fee to the waters it must navigate. More recent incidence of this condition must concern us later.

II

The Malta location of the Mediterranean Mission of 1815 was significant in another radical particular. The mission established a printing press and, in cooperation with the Religious Tract Society and the Brit-

2. A. L. Tibawi, *British Interests in the Middle East, 1800-1901: A Study of Religious and Educational Enterprise* (Oxford: Oxford University Press, 1961). "British Interests" was misleading, if not mischievous, and had reviewers assuming that it was a political study. It also implied that "mission" was a front for imperial interests. Tibawi later wrote a companion volume, similarly titled and subtitled, about American interests in Syria-Lebanon. His research in mission archives was, however, thorough and meticulous.

3. Evelyn Baring, Lord Cromer, the British Resident and virtual sovereign in Egypt, 1884-1907.

ish and Foreign Bible Society,[4] planned to print and stock Christian Scriptures in the liturgical languages of the Eastern churches and in Arabic, which could be streamed into Ottoman territory by steady distribution. In first charge at Malta were William Jowett, the brother-in-law of CMS secretary, Josiah Pratt, and James Connor, who moved to Constantinople in 1816. Christopher Burckhardt of the Basel Mission was their colleague. A decade earlier, Henry Martyn had concentrated his whole effort into New Testament translation — though in his case a tragic tubercular condition had precluded vocal ministry. He was confident that the availability of the hallowed text would be the open sesame to evangelism.[5]

A certain theology of inspiration may have underwritten this confidence, though a careful attention to the experience of Philip and the Ethiopian in Acts 8 might have given it pause. "How can I (understand) unless some man guide me?" the latter had asked. Incomprehension, if not prejudice, would always put the discipling of nations far beyond the capacity of the printed text alone. Exegesis always claims the personal rapport of scholarship and witness — a perception that vastly deepens the problems. Moreover, where Muslims are involved, there is entrenched another sacred textuality with which mere invitation into another readership does not wrestle. Furthermore, as Henry Martyn heroically found, translation itself falters unless it engages creatively with what has prior pride of place.[6]

It would seem, then, that the earliest years of the CMS in an Ottoman East disclosed to the leadership and the field-servants of the society the three dominant themes that have remained constant elements in its history. They fit neatly into the three words "church," "society," and "mission," if read as together constituting a vocation

---

4. The title was sharply indicative of how the world was seen with that ambiguous "and."

5. See *Journals and Letters of Henry Martyn*, 2 vols. (London: Seeley & Burnside, 1837) and Kenneth Cragg, *Troubled by Truth: Life Studies in Inter-Faith Concern* (Edinburgh: Pentland Press, 1992), pp. 15-31. Martyn sailed directly to India and was not part of the Malta project.

6. The task of translation brought this home when *munshis* — necessary local consultants — were either unable or unwilling to suggest equivalents. They fully knew the receiving language: only the Christian knew the nuances of the giving one. The burden is perennial and belongs inside even Arabic, quranic, and — by translation — biblical literature.

(1) Moving with human history,
(2) Attaining to be the church,
(3) Undertaking — in this context — the onus of Islam.

For two centuries these have intertwined. Separately and together, they have been a discipling in the double sense of taking the mind of Christ to be the school of the world, and, so doing, coming painfully into what only the will to teach could begin to learn. There has been great irony in the story of Christian mission in that it has often seemed to fail in what it purposed while reaping harvests it had not foreseen. In that sense it belongs inside the paradox of Jesus' own cross.

III

The art of navigation is an exacting realm for those who think themselves straightforward. The wily Palmerston, as well as Samuel Gobat, has to figure at the junctures of history in the tally of the Ottoman decades throughout the nineteenth century and into the twentieth. Declining from its high zenith under the "magnificent" Sulayman (1520-66), vexed by the long defection of Muhammad Ali in Egypt (1806-41), pressured by Western trade and consular interests to grant extraterritorial rights, the Ottoman caliphate was a tense and suspicious sovereignty, jealous for its Islamic prestige and compromised by massacres that outraged the conscience of Gladstone and by the tyranny of Sultan Abd al-Hamid II (1876-1909). Christian mission had to proceed in a context always laden with political overtones and dependent on political factors.

All was drastically transformed by the issue of World War I (as it had been in Egypt from the onset of British power in the 1880s). Britain's moment in the Middle East (as it has been called)[7] during the Palestine Mandate was beset by bitter stresses, but mission was by then in circumstances for which tenure posed no great problems. It was free to pursue its traditional pattern of hospital and school, ministering in kind to human need, enjoying the avidity for the English language on every hand and untroubled by the feasibility — for the most part — of visas to reside. Its will to evangelize was heavily in debt to its ability to serve,

7. For example, Elizabeth Monroe's study had the title *Britain's Moment in the Middle East* (London: Chatto & Windus, 1964).

patients and pupils yielding a ready, if not perhaps questionably captive, audience for verbal ministry. Even in Persia, never colonized politically, relatively favorable regimes allowed a widespread implanting of Christian action.[8]

The balance sheet between imperialism and mission has been hard to draw and accountants have their prejudices.[9] But none doubt that the vocation to Christian mission has undergone radical education by the recession of empire and the nearly universal emergence of the nation-state. With rare exceptions hospitals and schools have been absorbed into state medicine and state education, their proxy for evangelism sharply elided. Onus for communication is thrown back onto Christians present in lay and professional capacities. The pastoral and sacramental ministries of chaplaincies to these "present folk" are often pledged to nonproselytism or otherwise circumscribed in their relevance to local culture and faith patterns.

That there has ensued a crisis in mission is clear, as the will to be Christian interrogates itself about the meaning of how and where it now finds itself incarnationally by these national constraints. For a time, or in specific places, there might be factors offsetting, or delaying, these developments, such as diversion into specialist fields, for example, mental health care, public health consultancy, the ministry of bookshops, or initiatives in technological servicing for which local agencies were not yet competent. But these left untouched the basic issue of adjustment to an increasing "laicization" of the Christian presence and the abeyance of long traditional patterns.

This mind searching was necessarily accompanied by signal changes in the mind-set of Islam, moving from the nadir of the termination of the caliphate in 1924 and a seeming disintegration,[10] into the new self-confidence that accompanied the — as it seemed — God-sent boon of oil and the stimulus of nascent nationalism. The consequent interior debate of Islam with itself had profound consequences for the Christian appraisal of what business Christian mission had with it and for it. These belong later with our third category.

8. See chapter 4 above; and Robin Waterfield, *Christians in Persia* (London: George Allen & Unwin, 1973), pp. 133-76, for the CMS story there.

9. For the most sharp indictment see Omar Farrukh, *Al Tabshir wa-l-Isti'mar* [Eng. trans. Evangelism and Imperialism in Arab Lands] (Beirut, n.d.).

10. The word that often came to mind in Western musing on the forceful secularism of Ataturk in Turkey and the querying of, for example, H. A. R. Gibb, *Whither Islam?* (London: Victor Gollanz, 1932).

The sundry junctures in the flux of history and negotiation with their meaning entailed a steady realization of vast social and economic factors bearing on Christian liability both of mind and hand — the heavy growth in population, the disequilibrium of wealth and poverty, the continuing incidence of illiteracy, the sheer speed of social transition between immediate generations, and the astounding juvenization of the populace.[11]

IV

Attaining to be the church was thus bewildering enough in the external Middle Eastern scene. It was no less perplexing in the education of events. The CMS understood itself as committed to the world of Islam. The early origins of the Jerusalem bishopric, it is true, had to do with Jewry and Judaism, the first bishop, Michael Solomon Alexander, being a former rabbi. Four years later, in 1846, he was succeeded by Samuel Gobat, a Swiss Lutheran, whose episcopate lasted until 1879. An indefatigable traveler and a paragon of energy, he proceeded, at the outset, on a simple ecclesiology, or concept of "churchness," that saw in the (non-Uniate) churches[12] of Eastern Christendom, both Chalcedonian and Monophysite, ready partners in his evangelical vision for Islam. Working through them would be the means, even the raison d'être, of reaching Muslims.

He sadly miscalculated their amenability to such a role, a miscalculation that revealed a sharp ambiguity in what "churchness" was or could ever be. A naive assumption of feasible unison passed into an ambiguous venture of confusion. One might have said that, from the viewpoint of the Eastern patriarchates, the CMS was, indeed, a society, and no proven church, possessing as such, no authentic mission. There were those in England who, from the outset, had thought that Anglicans-in-mission had no place, no true "churchness," in Eastern

11. In numerous Middle East countries, there is a steady lowering of the average age of the population and a consequent acceleration of the surrender of the past.

12. The Uniates being those elements that withdrew from Eastern loyalties and turned to papal adherence and submission, thanks to the blandishments and pressures of the Jesuits and others, and in the light of Roman interpretation of who were the Schismatics after the great Schism of 1054. The Maronite Church in Lebanon was always a special case.

Christendom.[13] The two English archbishops had not thought so, but when they proceeded and the Gobat period ensued, the practicalities proved how disparate "churchness" — claimed, offered, denied — would be. Interpretations of what it could mean to be the body of Christ in the world differed markedly.

It was only in the sixth decade (1851) that the CMS entered Palestine, though pioneers had earlier been sent to Egypt and Ethiopia. Very soon Gobat's evangelical labors collided with the ethos of the churches he had hoped to recruit to his mind and purpose. Though he had written in 1848, "I could not countenance them in forsaking their church," that is precisely what he soon found himself obliged to do. Freedom of lay access to Scriptures, personal faith, piety, and perceptions of grace all combined to make relations tense, and, when pressures against would-be adherents developed into threats of expulsion from the original fold, Gobat argued that he could not abandon his own human fruits of "the true Word." He wrote in 1850:

> And now, what am I to do? I have never wished to make converts from the old Churches, but only to lead to the Lord and to the knowledge of His truth as many as possible. From henceforth, however, I shall be obliged to receive into our Communion such as are excluded for Bible truth's sake from other churches and I trust that in doing so, the Lord will grant His blessing upon the proceeding.[14]

Beginning in Nablus, he established schools that sharpened the issue and an Industrial Home for Converts in Tiberias that signified no retreat. The four archbishops in Britain and Ireland supported Gobat when representations were made to them about the shape of events.

In default of his own original, if naively held, purpose, Gobat's tireless episcopate brought a Palestinian Anglicanism into being that formed the substance of its perpetuation when, after an intermission of the bishopric in the 1860s, its new incarnation under Bishop G. F. P.

13. Indeed, the Jerusalem bishopric project was one factor in John Henry Newman's secession from the Church of England to Rome. Anglicans could never have invaded a Christian jurisdiction if they had understood a true ecclesiology. There was also a certain naiveté about Gobat's expectation of an Eastern Orthodox amenability to evangelical ministries of enlightenment and friendship. They had a quite different theology of *theopoiesis,* or "partaking of divine nature," in their understanding of redemption from sin.

14. *Samuel Gobat, Bishop of Jerusalem: His Life and Work* (London: James Nisbet, 1884), p. 265, quoting his journal.

Fig. 13. Samuel Gobat (1799-1879), CMS missionary
in Ethiopia and bishop of Jerusalem, 1846-1879.
Church Mission Society, London

Blyth expressly repudiated the patterns of its genesis. The Church Mission as understood in Salisbury Square (its London headquarters) was being discipled into learning that the very nature of the church was at issue in the very mission it undertook. Mission could not yet, perhaps never, be ecumenical on its own ecclesial terms. Yet it could not fulfill mission without the church dimension. That might not matter in "pagan" Africa where no church existed save the one that mission established. It could not fail to matter in the core of the original Christian East. All was a deep education into irony. The gospel might be meant for the whole ecumene — but how was the ecumene to comprehend the gospel? Meanwhile, within this irony, lay the sharper mystery of the mosque.

When, by the last decade of the nineteenth century, the Jerusalem

Fig. 14. W. H. Temple Gairdner (1873-1928),
CMS missionary in Egypt, 1899-1928.

Frontispiece to Constance E. Padwick,
Temple Gairdner of Cairo, SPCK, 1929.

bishopric was reconstituted, the CMS entered into a new and exacting version of the church-society equation. On the one hand there was the anomaly of a sizeable, irreversible local Anglican-Arab community, widely dispersed in towns and villages on either side of the Jordan, using its Arabic liturgy, spiritually and pastorally nurtured by CMS personnel relating to a Palestinian Native Church Council (as the usage had it). On the other there was a bishopric pledged by its new Canterbury mandate to a firm policy of nonrecruitment from local communions. The Church of England, guided by Archbishop Edward Benson (unlike Archbishops Howley and Sumner in the 1840s), was now resolved to heed the misgivings that had been originally ignored or discounted, and to proceed only in amity with the local patriarchates that excluded the patterns which, albeit reluctantly, Gobat had felt compelled to countenance.[15]

Inside this anomaly came a further ironical tension in that the new bishop, chosen for the new policy, was minded to pursue it in terms with which CMS personnel found themselves administratively and theologically ill at ease. They had, of course, no quarrel with the focus on Islam (the relations with Jewry being in the purview of the Church's Mission to [later Ministry among] the Jews). That society remit had to be squared with the diocesan dimension that Bishop Blyth, under his own remit, was resolute to pursue. It was an issue that had never arisen under Gobat, when episcopate and society were virtually synonymous.

Qua society, CMS personnel — one Charles Wilson in particular — assumed a directing aegis over Palestinian clergy. When friction arose, Blyth sustained the latter against the former within his due episcopal right and authority. The old theme of "the part within the whole" came home to roost. Asserting the society autonomy, with some asperity vis-à-vis both the bishop and their native colleagues, CMS personnel went so far as to claim they were a lay society and, as such, external to the bishop's jurisdiction insofar as it trespassed on their mission autonomy.[16]

Not himself a society man, Blyth, while operating with firm gentleness and restraint in a locale into which he had been drawn without prior experience of it, built up the diocesan concept, sponsoring a new collegiate church, St. George's, alongside the Palestinian St. Paul's, and moving the episcopal seat there from the original Christ Church, in old Jerusalem. He brought into being the Jerusalem and the East Association for the financing and recruitment of diocesan ventures. His leadership proved a lively succor for the local clergy and congregations in their uneven relations with the society that was their primary mentor and sustenance.

There was a further turn to the irony when, on the eve of the First World War, Bishop Blyth was succeeded by a CMS field leader in the person of Rennie MacInnes. Thereafter the society had digested its

15. See the careful analysis in Tibawi, *British Interests.*

16. This was a curious argument in that Wilson and Theodore Wolters (who was Gobat's son-in-law) were clergy and could have no grounds for an extra-episcopal tenure. They were, in fact, proposing to elide the word "church" from the society's name. The part might be the galvanizing "part for the whole" in England (the terms in which Max Warren later championed its indispensability): it could not constitute the whole on terms unique to itself.

learning experience and there was no recurrence of the earlier tension, or need for it. Slowly too, there came a new quality of rapport between local clergy and CMS personnel. Zealous among the latter for the due esteem of each for all, of all for each, was the Revd Eric F. F. Bishop serving 1921-48, a noted Arabist and an ecumenical enthusiast.[17] He might justly be seen as a representative pioneer, now that the wheel has come full circle, the Middle East dioceses these twenty years being in fully local control and the society sustaining exchange of workers, in both directions, entirely within the jurisdictions in place.

The society principle that had done so much to educate and stir the church to fulfill itself in mission was given to learn, in sometimes bitter retrospect, that all true mission becomes a lesson in humility. Negotiating with the vagaries of political history was one thing; digesting the stresses of an evangelical intent within an ecumenical scene quite another. The Eastern and Coptic churches could not be ignored, nor could they be partnered on unilateral terms. The Western Reformation had been, almost exclusively, a Western experience.[18] It could not be merely assumed germane to where those churches found themselves. What Christians might express in witness to Islam, they could not attain authentically except within an ecumenical Christianity striving to know and tell itself by all the clues it could discern from and for the world of the Qur'an — a world partly parallel and partly sharply at odds. The society had to learn to be theologically less self-sufficient than the early pioneers thought themselves to be when they turned to add Islam to Africa as their God-given mandate. The part-for-the-whole principle was both a proud confidence and a precarious venture, being discipled both ways. As John Bunyan observed: "The valley of humiliation is a fruitful place."

<h1 style="text-align:center">V</h1>

It was a valley that encounter with Islam in the familiar terms of mission only deepened and shadowed. It is invidious to those who pre-

---

17. He served in Egypt and Palestine from 1917 to 1948.

18. Much turns theologically and ecumenically on that fact. See also the significance of the career of Cyril Lucar (1572-1638), patriarch first of Alexandria, then of Constantinople, and his ill-starred efforts to introduce "reformed" thinking into Orthodoxy, Eastern style. See G. A. Hadziantonian, *Protestant Patriarch* (London: Lucan, 1961).

ceded and to those who followed through some eighteen decades to single out Douglas Thornton and Temple Gairdner as symbols of the CMS in its relation with Islam (the one recruited in 1898, the other dying in 1928), in thirty years of talented, high-minded, vigorous evangelism, briefly in tandem (Thornton died in 1907) and then in bereavement. They had been fired by the stirring romance of General Gordon. They coincided with the heyday of the British presence. They were strong in their conviction that Cairo was the strategic center of Islam rightly commanding their utmost devotion. They were ideally equipped with resources of spiritual stamina and lively imagination. Their story owes much of its inspiring legacy to *Temple Gairdner of Cairo,* a biography ardently written by that other exemplar of a Christian Islamics, Constance Padwick.[19]

Yet, for all its being discipled in intensity and zeal, their mission married into sorrow. At an early point, explaining the return of a convert back to Islam, Gairdner wrote to his fiancée, still in England:

> I seem to have left the uncloudedness . . . behind me for ever and have entered into what I feel to be a sadder life. . . . I see the same thing in front of me — this apparently hopeless effort to cope with Islam . . .

19. London: SPCK, 1929. It was written in the bright afterglow of his passing. Constance Padwick, after rejection by the CMS, made her way — and career — in the Middle East under her own steam. See Cragg, *Troubled by Truth,* pp. 52-73. Padwick's *Muslim Devotions* (London: SPCK, 1961; reprint, Oxford: One World, 1996), is a shining example of imaginative Christian penetration of the soul of Islam and of the vocation mooted here in closing this chapter. Her associations with the CMS were, of course, very close, despite her independence, when she fulfilled her role as mainspring of the Central Committee on Literature for Muslims of the Near East Council of Churches and when she undertook the Gairdner biography. It was the imaginative quality of her love to Islam that set her in ardent pursuit of the manuals of private devotion available for discreet purchase from tiny book stalls at mosque doors. These she assiduously gathered through gentle converse with their vendors. After careful and prolonged study, tabulation, and musing on their contents, she distilled their piety, their penitence, and petitionary prayer, into a forum for Christian understanding and mediation. Her aim was to appreciate in Islam the dimensions of spirit that might enable Christian ministry to its mind. One notable area lay in *Tasliyah* — the "calling down of blessing" on Muhammad, which Surah 33.56 required Muslims to say in response to Allah's doing so. How might divine satisfaction in human agency on the divine behalf relate to the New Testament theme of God in the Christ — "with whom He was well-pleased"? To perceive a clue was also to realize disparity. Dialogue may at first only discover its real problems, but at least it breaks free of the aridity of sheer contention. As the Latin runs: *Manet amor, manet spes* (where love remains, hope remains also).

and above all these terrible disappointments. That's the life I have chosen . . . sordid miseries, unheroic and uninteresting. . . . This is a call to enter into a very inner chamber of the sufferings of Christ. The danger is that one should remain in the ante-room of mere disappointment and grow hard and cold in it.[20]

Within betrothal his words had a strange frankness of which his betrothed was worthy. As a missionary's prospect it rings with sincerity. Reproduced variously elsewhere in and beyond the CMS, if with less eloquent introspection, it lends itself to the parting words of Hamlet:

. . . "and in this harsh world draw thy breath in pain to tell my story." If there is, indeed, for mission, an "inner chamber of the sufferings of Christ," then what is there beyond that "ante-room"?

All the traditionally identified ingredients were present. These were first-class minds and gifted characters. They were free to pursue all the proven methods of public discussions among mullahs and students. They could deploy musical skills that reached into Coptic patterns. Gairdner was competent to compose commentaries on New Testament books in the quranic style of the great Al-Baidawi.[21] A lively journal, *Orient and Occident,* was produced and widely circulated. Tracts were written and debated in open forum. There was a lively pastoral nurture of Egyptian congregations. It was possible to envisage and anticipate recruitment into Christ in a society — thanks to the opening of the Suez Canal and orientation westward of which their contemporary Taha Husain became the spokesman[22] — arguably moving away from static modes of mind and culture.

Yet how long could they continue seeing disappointment as "the ante-room"? To be sure, Gairdner was left to deplore the loneliness of his vocation in that his fostering society burdened him with administrative duties that clogged his true genius. It proved unable to send him the recruits he yearned for to share his load. Yet was that circumstance index to a vision sore beset? At the approximate middle of his career, he

20. Padwick, p. 95.
21. The most renowned of Muslim exegetes (d. 1286). Gairdner's New Testament commentaries in Arabic concerned Galatians, Philippians, and Hebrews.
22. The blind essayist and thinker (1889-1973), whose Arabic work (Eng. trans. *The Future of Culture in Egypt* [Washington: American Council of Learned Societies, 1956]) firmly insisted that Egypt belonged to the Mediterranean and the West.

did enjoy an interlude of academic respite at Hartford Seminary in Connecticut and as a visiting scholar in Europe. Here he savored the stimulus of erudite orientalists, especially Duncan Black Macdonald and Ignaz Goldziher.[23] It would seem that the experience moved him away somewhat from the direct evangelism he had saluted in his biography of his colleague Douglas Thornton, in broadly common mind with whom he had also penned *The Reproach of Islam,* as a manual of study toward mission.

While that title, with its accent both on debt and Christian delinquency, closely represented and conveyed contemporary thinking in the Christian West, it was subtly different from the perspectives of the academics. Steeped as the two professors were in things Islamic, they had settled into academies. Their researches and animadversions were relieved of missionary intent. At once Gairdner was faced with what could be read as an invitation only if it were not perceived as a temptation. In particular, his studies in Al-Ghazali, the renowned Islamic divine of the eleventh century,[24] revealed to him themes and accents within Islam that could well temper the bluntness of the evangelical mind and deepen the bearings of the gospel upon the practice of Islam.

Yet such was Gairdner's quality that he would not substitute for being discipled to Christ the discipline of separate academic pursuit. Moreover, the society that had approved his loved *Wanderjahr* (1910-11) brought him back remorselessly to the treadmill of Cairo. That the vision nevertheless remained with him to his premature death in 1928 makes him the very epitome of an abiding tension in mission to Islam between the tasks of the scholar and the claim of an evangelist. It was at this time that Gairdner made the acquaintance, in correspondence, of Louis Massignon, the French Christian scholar of Islamic Sufism who, in his own highly idiosyncratic way, wrestled with the same dilemma. There were missionaries whose careers in Islam were transmuted — or diverted — into abstract scholarship. The problem Gairdner exempli-

23. MacDonald, a Scot by birth, was the famed pioneer of Arabic studies in New England, while Goldziher gained eminence as an Islamicist with his researches into Tradition and Shari'ah. Together they kindled in Gairdner a deep sense of the role of scholarship and inspired his translation of Al-Ghazali's *Mishkat al-Anwar* (1914).

24. Born in 1058, dying in 1111, Al-Ghazali renounced a career in Baghdad to become an intellectual Sufi and to contribute massively to Islamic religious and ethical thought with his celebrated *Ihya 'Ulum al-Din,* the much translated *Reviving of the Knowledge and Practice of Religion.*

fied, and carried as part of his "sorrows," was how feasibly to marry into one unity the claims of study and the demands of witness. Was there a theology that could honestly reconcile them, even supposing that the exigencies of ordination, the pastoral office, and the cares of a secretariat could admit of their practicality?

Vocation allowed Temple Gairdner no answer. The issue could be seen as the legacy of his generation. The problem has been in no way mitigated since his day. Rather the fundamental matter of mission to Islam has accentuated. Apart from the erosion of liberties via the rise of the nation-state and the end of medical ministries that afforded windows of interpretation, there has come a genuine crisis of confidence as to the viability of mission in traditional terms. How, for example, do we respond now to reading words used by Stanley Morrison in *The Way of Partnership* (1936)? "This evangelising aim is to be its distinguishing mark both now and for all the years of the future, generation after generation, until this land becomes Christ's."[25]

If we are seeing an education in the very will to mission as suggested at the outset — an education that the mission needs — what is the tuition saying? The intended engagement with Islam, it might be said, is always eluding us. How many loyal servants of the CMS have found themselves involved in what might be honestly acknowledged to be proximate things? Eric Bishop was among the most gifted of Arabists, as his translation of Al-Baidawi's Commentary on Surah Yusuf proved. Yet his major energies were devoted through long years to the training of new recruits at the Newman School of Missions (until 1948). When injury withdrew him to a professorship at Glasgow, his deep compassion passed into a Palestinian advocacy, signaled in his trilogy: *Jesus of Palestine, Apostles of Palestine,* and *Prophets of Palestine,* and his unremitting concern for refugees.[26] All was within authentic vocation, yet on the margins of the other mission.

Parenthetically, it has to be noted that the multiple issues stemming from Zionism have profoundly affected the themes — even the very possibility — of Christian mediation of Christ to Muslims. If, as

25. S. E. Morrison, *The Way of Partnership* (London: Highway Press, 1936), p. 72. Morrison, a layman, was an esteemed missionary statesman in mid-century. He was writing six years after a National Church Council had taken over direction of the Anglican Church in Egypt from CMS. See also his *Mid-East Survey* (London: SCM Press, 1954), for the feel of the time prior to the Suez crisis of 1956.

26. London, 1955, 1956, and 1962 respectively. They were a loving celebration of a Palestinian ethos discernible in the biblical text and personalities.

was said, the Balfour Declaration had "planted the hatred of England in every Arab heart," what ensued from it was highly prejudicial to open, frank, and truly deliberative engagement of Christians, local or European, with Muslims. Palestinian Christians have long felt that to behave as if things spiritual were conversible, as long as basic injustices festered and rankled, conversation about God-in-Islam and God-in-Christ was either a trap or a delusion, implying all was fair when all was foul. Eric Bishop was deeply right in finding himself constrained by refugees to read his priorities concerning mission in terms more chastened than those his CMS contemporary, Morrison, used about "all the years of the future." Something had supervened that spelled a different generation, the more so when an amoral Christian Zionism, blandly assuming no injustice done, bitterly accentuated the burden.

When not thus heavily embittered, Christian missionary encounter with Islam has been contrived (we might say paradoxically) by abeyance, in that personnel have been engaged in pastoralia warranting their presence but absorbing their relevance. Deprived of the more traditional facility to be the Douglas Thorntons of their day by the changing of the scene, they were taken up into more domestic Christian ministry. Two CMS men of honored memory were provosts of All Saints' Cathedral, Cairo. In the dark post-Suez days of 1957, Archbishop MacInnes turned to Donald Blackburn, well loved in Jordan, to renew its life out of the disaster. Similarly, Archbishop Appleton appointed Brian de Saram of the Sudan in the early 1970s. Vital as their functions were, they were ancillary to the kind of mission Temple Gairdner had followed in Old Cairo, when the métier of cathedrals was more imperial. Now across the whole Middle East the society is liable to find itself servicing chaplaincies so that direct mediation of Christ to Islam may appear somewhat far removed.

Musing in this way is in no sense to decry such ministry. It chimes with local diocesanization and belongs with "the servant church." But the question persists — how bent is it toward Islam? Is there a de facto forfeiture of intent? Or perhaps a tacit recognition of new appraisals of vocation emerging from the throes of a long crisis, a deep perplexity of soul? The pattern, arguably right as it is, of short-term service contributes to the same abeyance of soul and mind investment in a full caring for Islam. To what, then, are we being discipled in the society's two-century experience of the Middle East? If mission, in and since the New Testament, has learned only itself in its honest practice, what is the logic now?

Fig. 15. CMS Jerusalem missionary conference, 1910.
Church Mission Society archives, University of Birmingham

VI

Citing earlier the plea of Hamlet and applying it to the storytelling for Christ that mission is — "In this harsh world draw thy breath in pain to tell my story" — we omitted earlier words. Hamlet pleaded with his friend, Horatio: "Absent thee from felicity awhile. . . ." By "felicity" he meant death. "Stay alive to clear my name: do not take an easy exit by suicide."

Honored Christian missionary tradition has long found nothing more felicitous than the enlisting of recruits, the making of converts. That seemed the only loyal thing. The commission of Matthew 28:19 was about baptism. "Confessing by mouth Jesus as Lord" (Romans 10:9) was Paul's formula, though he also said cryptically: "Christ sent me not to baptize but to preach the Gospel" (1 Corinthians 1:17), not staying to explain the distinction. The conversion of the individual in register of his or her avowal of faith has been classically the goal and end of evangelism.

Was the ready assumption of individual liability right? Was it fair to make it in indifference to the mental and social regime that Islam

137

magisterially set for its pursuit — namely a legal and spiritual ethos in which individuality was inexorably bound into a religious citizenship for which alternative faith-cognizance meant political treachery? Ought there not to be a mission toward authentic religious freedom, not merely to facilitate Christian hopes but for its own validity per se? Would not that mean, in some sense, mission to Islam rather than to this or that Muslim? Were not cultures fit for baptism in the sense of being invited into acceptance of a different liability for themselves and for how they handled the humanity they purported to organize?

Questions that are phrased to expect the answer "Yes!" are always likely to provoke the answer "No!" This one surely will. There is a long tradition of belief that the Christian church is fulfilling its mission only when it is adding to its ranks. The answering souls must become immediately and forthwith responsible in and for the institutionalized fabric of the Christian faith. But may there not be around that instinctive duty a measure of self-esteem, the satisfaction of trophy taking, the better confirmation of the faith itself, the further sanction of a gained allegiance? The historian, Arnold Toynbee, wanted to apply to the institutional faith the dictum of John 12:24: "Except a corn of wheat fall into the ground and die it abides alone. . . ." It had to be ready only for Gethsemane. For he did not believe in Easter except as something premature.[27]

Here we are in deep waters. But the thought persists that a rudely self-seeking church might be a contradiction in terms. Since, unlike the days of the New Testament, it monumentally exists, the faith is in long historic care. Need it then recruit as if it could afford no confidence about its continuity and have no courage in its vulnerability, unless solicitous about its own aggrandizement?

They are hard queries, but we cannot well elude them. That the church truly lives only when it lives for those who do not belong, who will never adhere, is explicit from the start, as Temple Gairdner once wrote: "If Jesus prayed those prayers [in Gethsemane] then of course the world must know." The gospel is never fit for privatization. "Whosoever will may come." There is nowhere in the world, after Galilee, to which the Word was not brought. Not Paul, not Patrick, not Augustine, not Boniface, not Francis, not Loyola, not William Carey, were origi-

27. See Kenneth Cragg, *Troubled by Truth*, pp. 222-41, with an extensive bibliography, for a study of this deeply significant figure in twentieth-century Middle Eastern issues.

nals. All had nothing they had not received. The New Testament itself, as a document of epistles and gospels, owes itself to its own "going into the world." There can never be a legitimate abeyance of this sentness. For it arises from, and belongs with, the very hospitality of God. The question about mission can never be "whether": it can only be "how." The "ifs" that have to do with it do not concern its mandate, only its method. The raw material of the kingdom of heaven has always been the personal disciple alert to the world. The making of Christians will always be the onus in being one. "To be and to bring to be" are one.

That heart conviction, however, only returns us to the interrogatives that have led us back to it, about "the corn of wheat" and a community *qua* truth-trustee that might have longer patience — or perhaps even a right indifference — about its own institutional size. It is surely experience within the Muslim realm that suggests this thought. Is there not, in some sense, a Christian relevance to Islam as distinct from private Muslims? Could Paul in Corinth have thought that possible conversion in the singular might disserve mediation of meaning to the whole? Or was he merely having others do the baptizing — in which case he was implying options of mission that would rightly forbear from that satisfaction?

It is clear that transfer of faith-community (on all present and foreseeable Islamic principles) is precluded.[28] A Christian quest for it is thus directly confrontational. There will always be a Christian instinct to see this as ineluctable. Need that be our only conclusion? That which Christians most dearly seek, namely personal Christ-confession in baptism, is that which collides most squarely with what Islam most characteristically repudiates, while being in no way impervious to the meanings, the criteria, the perceptions that — short of such action — could find some blessed register.

It has long been realized that polemic only breeds polemic. Rebuttal of items of dogma required their reassertion with the compound interest of greater obfuscation and/or bigotry. In its different way, allegiance fronts against allegiance, identity counters identity, loyalty sanctioning loyalty forbids disloyalty. Always the odds multiply in favor of enmity and tension. It may be heroic to defy the odds but, even then, there will remain the ethical duty to lessen, if not obviate, them by

---

28. By the law of apostasy. Though some Muslim states have adopted UNO human rights principles, there are great obstacles to their effective application. Muslims tolerate wide discrepancies in personal Islamic living but explicit departings are anathema.

ministering in the patience that sees itself relating to a continuing ethos. When Bishop Blyth appealed to Canterbury in the issues he faced because of tension between himself and the CMS as earlier noted, the four English bishops to whom the matter was referred supported him. In doing so they wrote of: "recognisable merits in the system [Islam] which has to be displaced and of the high character of many who sincerely live in its obedience."[29]

That was almost exactly a century ago. The current archbishop of Canterbury echoes the appreciation yet finds "has to be displaced" a thoroughly obsolete stance.[30]

It belongs with conceded diversity that plurality is a fact of the situation and that, in measure, facts of belief *are* facts. Not that profound issues do not persist, but that even these are only to be joined by the sanctions that arouse them. Hence the inevitability of converse about meanings and of "dialogue" with all the liabilities of that vogue word. In that we are required to coexist, we had better proexist. Without patronage or pretension — as the Holy Spirit enables us to forgo institutional self-will or dogmatic aggression — we must covet to share in the interior travail of alert Muslims with the present meaning and application of their self-understanding and their structure of belief and practice. The factors that necessitate such travail are broadly common already in global terms and many are the direct sequel to the bearings of the West, whether in political or economic or technological power, on Muslim society and intellectual quest. That fact alone constitutes a certain Christian indebtedness, all spiritual mission apart.

The degree to which Muslims might be suspicious of, or receptive to, such Christian rapport with their own searchings, must turn on the degree to which they perceive it to be genuine and disinterested. Dialogue is still suspect in many quarters as being no more than disguise for ulterior designs or former postures more cunningly contrived.[31] Such misgivings may best be allayed and authentic good faith exchanged if interfaith negotiation, using the term advisedly,[32] avoids the

29. Tibawi, *British Interests,* p. 257.

30. See Archbishop George Carey's Younghusband Lecture for the World Congress of Faiths at Lambeth Palace, 18 November 1996, "Journeying Together."

31. See the forward-looking but cautious study by Ataullah Siddiqui, *Christian-Muslim Dialogue in the Twentieth Century* (Leicester: Macmillan, 1997).

32. In the sense for which I tried to argue in *Faith and Life Negotiate: A Christian Story-Study* (Norwich: Canterbury Press, 1994). It is a thoroughly right word, not bargaining but — as the Latin implies — taking mutual pains.

old formulae that ensnared and clogged Muslim-Christian discourse down the centuries from John of Damascus to C. G. Pfander. Christian custody of the inner meanings of divine Trinity, the Sonship of Christ, the incarnation, and the cross has too long been trapped into credal or verbal minutiae that have "darkened counsel" and ill-served the meanings they handled in the Graeco-Roman, Latin, context far from the rigorous Semitism of quranic norms.

We need a search for mutual discourse that can faithfully take its departure from where Muslims are by dint of how their Qur'an has given them to be. This does not involve any final Christian compromise, seeing that a common, if also disparate, theism belongs with us all in our convergences and our contrasts. Faith is fulfilled rather than compromised in caring, like good handwriting, for its legibility. Interpretation is where truth keeps faith.

Let the Qur'an afford the vocabulary. We might take four basic term-concepts — *Shirk, Zulm, Fitrah,* and *Fitnah* — among many, from which to explore the ultimate meanings of Islam and — in their context — express a Christ-faith in their light. *Shirk* tells the urgent Islamic intolerance of all idolatry, the vital message in Muhammad's Arabia. "Let God alone be God." All association of deities with the One Allah, whether *qua* trust, worship, petition, or representation, must be anathema. This, however, must not be thought to dissociate Allah from the human realm whence such false associations arise by dint of pagan folly, frailty, or fear. On the contrary, that very natural sphere is where belong the Creatorship of God and the reciprocal creaturehood of humans, the "dominion status" or *khilafah,* the consequent guidance and the mission of prophethood. All this enshrines a divine association with us in earth-dwellingness and obligation. There remains the possibility that this deep association — for reasons close to its very transcendence — might venture further than guidance into redemption, given the significance of *zulm.*

Meanwhile *shirk* has another bearing on Christian meaning. In "letting God be God" there are other idols than the pagan sort — idols of the state, the nation, profit, science, indeed religion itself — absolutes we falsely erect to the exclusion of Allah.[33] These are more culpable and more heinous in that they usurp to human hands what belongs to God alone and is safe only in so belonging. The concepts of *Tawhid*

---

33. A recurrent quranic phrase, it makes an exact definition of bland secularity oblivious of things divine.

and *Takbir,* of divine unity and divine "Magnificat," must be seen to be inclusive of some divine mastery over all that defies or distorts the Godness of God. These acts of *shirk* are not subdued by merely affirming that God is One but proving how he is, a need that takes the Christian into Christology and the cross.

It does so because of *zulm* — the fundamental quranic term for human wrong — a perversity of the self against its own truth, against its neighbor, and against Allah. Its frequency in the text is eloquent of its centrality. The panorama of human history in the Qur'an is evidence of how aberrant humanity has been and remains. The seriousness of evil, which is at the heart of the gospel, is also deep in the Islamic text. It ministers to a common realism about the mischief of religions themselves in the modern world.

It is balanced, however, by the concept of *fitrah,* a human nature meant for a conformity to divine will and wonder. Islam identifies what makes man man, the human human, with what makes the Muslim Muslim. Nature and religion are seen as one equation, once *zulm* has been groomed and muted by submission. The gospel reads our human nature in more radical terms, and so, in turn, perceives a more costly claim on the divine liability toward our waywardness since our creaturehood is owed to him. Yet the kinship of significance is unmistakable.

The theme of *fitnah* brings together *zulm* and *fitrah,* in that our perceived recalcitrance, lapsing from a given divine intention in our quality as human, necessitates the structure of the guarding, ensuring Islamic state. *Fitnah* means, in origin, what tries or tests, and so attests. When Muslims were a small, oppressed minority it meant "persecution." When they became a dominant success, it meant "sedition." The crux either way was a cause in crucial encounter with what disallows its claim. It captures conceptually the entire politicization of Islam in that "war is a lesser evil than *fitnah*" (Surah 2:191, 217), confirming the rubric that "*fitnah* is a greater wrong than killing." Islam trusts characteristically in the feasible and imperative fusion of *din* and *dawlah,* of religious faith and, in some sense, political sanction. Hence many of the issues that dog liberty of movement of belief.

Here the Christian mind, for all the vagaries of Christendom in emulation of Islam, will always be at odds. The *fitnah* concept risks muting the entirely necessary criticism of religion itself, absolving it from its own temptations or perceiving its trials only in terms of an external *Dar al-Harb.* Yet, in this day, many significant Muslim populations are out from under, as minorities, the aegis of Islamic power — ir-

142

reversibly so.[34] It follows then that the *fitnah* they face can find no escape in armed belligerence but stands only in the quality of their own spirituality. But by the same token, the surrounding world, insofar as it can be discerningly Christian, may be a very different trial of spiritual integrity in honest relation.

VII

"Absent thee from felicity awhile." The foregoing leaves many issues of mission aside. It presupposes numerous forms of sheer interhumanity on which we all depend. It is not meant to trespass on how other minds, in the liberty of their own duty to God in Christ, perceive and pursue their mandate in the gospel. Concerning the continuity of mission at the turn of a third century of the CMS it must be said that "we see through a glass darkly." Where sight fails us, we walk by faith. We have a brighter "lantern on the stern" than on the prow. That we have a task that must incarnate us into where Islam now is and into its own inner tensions and decisions, as far as may fall to us, cannot be in doubt. What our "absence from felicity" will never mean is any dimming of the felicity ever to be known in and from "the light of the knowledge of the glory of God in the face of Jesus as the Christ."

It may be fair to ask whether mission should not always be musing on what it is that obliges it to be present in the traffic of religions, what it is that must not be allowed to perish from the earth, what it is for which sake the church as its trustee and servant must never abandon humankind. If time and place are the subjunctive and the gospel the affirmative in our soul's grammar, what is the imperative? It is that "face," "the countenance lifted upon us," the vision of the love that comes and bears and suffers, the vicarious dimension of "God in Christ" — not inscrutable in enigmatic serenity but rather crowned in the paradox of thorns. It is the gospel of a God "absent from felicity" in the very credentials of sovereignty. Only when we perceive this treasure do we understand how earthen, "mere pots of clay," are the concepts and the means that serve it.

34. For twenty years or more, the interior thinking of Muslims about minority circumstance and response has been ably ventilated in the journal of The Institute for Muslim Minority Affairs. Where the rubric "Muslims must always be ruled by Muslims" can no longer obtain, how does Islam resolve itself into being (as the West would say) "just a religion"? — a notion and a condition traditionally unthinkable.

PART 2

MISSION AND THE INDIGENOUS CHURCH

6. "Not Transplanting": Henry Venn's Strategic Vision

PETER WILLIAMS

A mature appreciation of history and tradition enables Christians to stand on the shoulders of the giants who have preceded them.[1] Theoretically this should mean that every generation of Christians sees with greater clarity than the one before. Often this is not so because too often the past is either ignored or misunderstood. And consequently, instead of standing on the shoulders of the giants, we fumble and struggle as if the issues we face had never been faced before. A good example of this is the general neglecting of the theological depth, ecclesiological creativity, and cultural humility of mid-Victorian missiology. This is at least partly because it is too easily assumed that the theological shallowness, ecclesiological unimaginativeness, and cultural arrogance of much late nineteenth- and early twentieth-century missionary thinking is a reflection of what preceded it. It is anything but. The third quarter of the nineteenth century provides a particularly rich seam. And at its apex stands the great CMS secretary, Henry Venn. If his importance is now well-enough recognized by historians who are specialists in missionary history, he and the ideas he stood for have yet to be appreciated even by historians of nineteenth-century religion, and that inevitably

---

1. Note how so evangelical a theologian as J. I. Packer is committed to this high view of history and tradition. See Alister McGrath, "The Importance of Traditions for Modern Evangelicalism," in *Doing Theology for the People of God: Studies in Honour of J. I. Packer,* ed. Donald Lewis and Alister McGrath (Downers Grove, Ill.: InterVarsity Press, 1996), p. 172.

means that he is largely unappreciated by the more general reader. What is aimed at in this chapter is an assessment of some of his key ideas, placing them in the context of current missiological thinking, and unpacking some of the most radical, controversial, and little-known directions in which his thinking drew him.

What Venn did in essence was to wrestle with the reality of cultural distinctiveness and to map out a missionary strategy that both took this seriously and sought to extrapolate and implement biblical and historical principles of church growth. And in doing this he was no lonely beacon seeking to spread light amid the darkness of his generation. He was rather the most articulate and systematic exponent of ideas that had a very wide currency in missionary circles and even beyond those. It is often said or implied that nineteenth-century missionaries sought to propagate little replicas of their own church systems with strict instructions that dress, architecture, and worship should deviate at no point from the norms expected in London, Edinburgh, New York, or Berlin and with the expectation that European bishops and clergy had a natural right to rule over inferior but happily compliant "natives." One reason this is said or implied is that it was often true. What is not true is that missionaries went abroad with instructions to act in this manner. The reality that was ringing in their ears as they embarked on their often hazardous journeys from Tilbury or Liverpool was the echo of an altogether different message. Certainly they should be concerned with passing on sound doctrine but the expectation was that the churches they established would quite naturally "adopt various modes of worship, various systems of Church order, and different principles of fraternal association." The aim of missionaries was to create independent churches and to this end they were "to take advantage of such national customs, notions, and tendencies" as they could.[2] So said the representative Conference on Missions at Liverpool in 1860, and that was the prevailing orthodoxy for the next thirty years or so. And some of the leading representatives who attended it were as witheringly scornful of gothic churches planted in India, or transportation to far-distant countries of interchurch British controversies, or the tendency to teach not merely Christianity "but an English form of that Christianity"[3] as any twentieth-

2. *Conference on Missions Held in 1860 at Liverpool* (London: James Nisbet, 1860), p. 310.

3. These three points were all criticized in a speech to the Liverpool Conference by the Revd J. Mullens, leading LMS missionary and soon to be the secretary of that society (*Conference on Missions,* pp. 284-86).

century critic of missionary paternalism. The question of why most missionaries went about their designated business as if such ideas had no relevance to their particular situation is beyond the scope of this chapter. What is central to its scope is the part Henry Venn had in developing, articulating, and turning into the accepted wisdom of missionary administrators ideas that strike many in the twentieth century as audaciously radical.

Henry Venn was born in 1796 of a distinguished evangelical pedigree. His direct lineage contained two of the most able and influential evangelical Anglican leaders of their respective generations, his grandfather Henry Venn of Huddersfield and his father John Venn of Clapham. His background was that of evangelical philanthropy.[4] In other words his desire to bring the message of freedom from the spiritual shackles of sin through Christ's redemption was held in easy harmony with his conviction that every fiber of energy should be bent to ensure that people were delivered from the physical shackles of slavery both through government action and through the opening up of new horizons by means of education, commerce, and the life-changing impact of the Christian gospel.

Underlining such evangelical philanthropy was the conviction that people were equal in their capacity to hear and respond to the challenge of Christ and equal, too, in their fundamental capacities. Nobody was to be treated as a subspecies of the human race. Such views were grounded both in Venn's theology and in his philanthropic humanism — each in any event inextricably intertwined. Among his earliest memories, he recalled as an old man writing in 1871, was that of being a playmate with African youths sent to England for education.[5] It consequently pained him greatly to discover that "even Missionary societies suffer from the tendency to underrate the social and intellectual capabilities of the native races."[6] He had a high respect for people of other races, who were often deemed to be inferior and treated as such. He cited the story of meeting an African merchant who said to him, "Treat us like men, and we will behave like men . . . treat us as children and we

---

4. The nickname Clapham Sect was used of those who lived in Clapham, attended his father's church, and bent all their energies toward the reconversion of England and the application of Christian principles to some of the most pressing social problems of the day — most notably slavery.

5. Church Missionary Society Archives (hereafter CMSA), CA1/L8, p. 347, 22 September 1871, Venn to J. B. Pinney, New York.

6. CMSA, CA2/L3, 391-92, 22 September 1964, Venn to D. Hinderer.

shall behave like children."[7] In a sense, that simple story illustrates the heart of his missionary strategy, but of that more presently. He admired the great Jesuit missionary Francis Xavier because he maintained the rights of the native races against the "oppression and injustice of his own fellow countrymen, and treating them as possessing the same feelings and capacities as their more civilized fellow-men."[8] He argued, in relation to the many Africans he had met and instructed, that he had "never been able to detect any inferiority of natural ability in my Negro pupils." They had "all exhibited an intellectual ability fully equal to that of Englishmen of a similar amount of education, while some of them rank with the ablest European Missionaries, in grasp of mind, vigour of thought, and force of expression." Indeed one of them had been commended by the bishop of London, the formidable Blomfield, for producing "as striking a paper on the evidences of the Christian religion as he had received in a very long course of examining for holy orders."[9]

Now if, as Venn conceded, such convictions marked him off from many missionaries, they did not mark him off from many of the leading administrators and civil servants of the day — for a significant number of them had been shaped by precisely the same religious and intellectual traditions as Venn.[10] His sister married the famous Sir James Stephen, himself the son of a notable Claphamite. Stephen did much to form the

7. *Church Missionary Intelligencer* (hereafter *CMI*), 1873, p. 141. The *Intelligencer* was the flagship of CMS productions and provided an always extensive and sometimes remarkably in-depth account and analysis of missionary work. When Venn used the childhood analogy, it was to illustrate the need for independence as one entered adulthood (CMSA, C I2/L6, 149-150, p. 149, 10 April 1862, Venn and Knight to Royston) and not, as often when used by missionaries, to justify dependence. See H. A. C. Cairns, *Prelude to Imperialism: British Reactions to Central African Society, 1840-1890* (London: Routledge & Kegan Paul, 1965), pp. 94-96.

8. Henry Venn, *The Missionary Life and Labours of Francis Xavier* (London: Longmans, Green, 1862), p. 252.

9. CMSA, G/AC 1/16, 55-56, p. 56, 28 November 1863, Venn to W. Fawcett. Though the point was made in relation to Africans with whom Venn had most personal contact, it manifestly holds in the logic and action of Venn's life in relation to all other races.

10. Annan calls such people the "intellectual aristocracy." "Philanthropy was the magnet which drew them together." See N. G. Annan, "The Intellectual Aristocracy," in *Studies in Social History: A Tribute to G. M. Trevelyan,* ed. J. H. Plumb (London: Longmans, Green, 1955), p. 244. The intellectual aristocracy was shaped by evangelicalism.

British colonial policy of the time, first as under-secretary at the Colonial Office and then as an extremely knowledgeable colonial expert and Privy Councilor. He belonged "by birth, upbringing, family and social connections to the coterie of English people who in the first half of the nineteenth century strove to rid the British Empire of the blot of human slavery and sought to bring the Christian evangel of the fatherhood of God and the brotherhood of man to the farthest corners of the earth."[11] Venn, then, was formed in and remained close to a rich seam of evangelicalism that held together concern for the whole person in a remarkably balanced way. It is a major factor in understanding his thinking.[12]

After a period tutoring at Queens' College Cambridge and a couple of incumbencies, Venn became honorary[13] secretary of the CMS in 1841 and continued as the dominant influence in the society until his retirement in 1872 and for many more years posthumously, as the revered architect of sound missionary policy. It was in some ways surprising that Venn should attain such authority. He was not an accomplished orator and seldom spoke in public.[14] He seems to have genuinely believed his own self-description as a man who put aside "all private feelings" and became "the pen of the Committee."[15] He was evidently hurt by the accusation that he was "the great man and doer of everything." Any influence he had depended rather, in his estimation, on his "consulting and anticipating their [the committee members] minds in everything, upon sinking my identity and being merely their

11. P. Knaplund, "Sir James Stephen: The Friend of the Negroes," *Journal of Negro History* 35 (1950), p. 370. Knaplund also speaks of him as being committed to "the establishment of racial equality and social justice in the British Empire beyond the sea" (p. 407).

12. Wilbert Shenk, *Henry Venn — Missionary Statesman* (Maryknoll, N.Y.: Orbis Books, 1983), p. 60.

13. It was accepted at that time and for many years afterward that the occupant of such an important position should be financially independent. When in 1881, Venn's successor, Henry Wright, was drowned, a contributing factor in the appointment of his replacement was whether the candidate had real financial independence. One possible candidate, William Hagger, was ruled out because he had not. See Margaret Barlow, *The Life of William Hagger Barlow* (London: George Allen & Sons, 1910), p. 101. Stock pointedly draws attention to the fact that Frederick Wigram who was appointed was "a man of private fortune" (Stock, vol. 3, p. 260). It was part of the same philosophy that dictated until the early 1950s that the captain of the English cricket team should be an amateur.

14. William Knight, *Memoir of Henry Venn, BD* (London: Seeley, Jackson, & Halliday, 1882), pp. 182-83.

15. CMSA, CA1/L8, 5, 24 April 1865, Venn to bishop of Sierra Leone.

mouthpiece as well as their thinker."[16] And perhaps that was true — up to a point. But the anticipator of minds and the careful presenter of very well-marshaled thoughts can easily become the controller of minds. There seems no doubt that Venn became the master of CMS committees because he was better briefed than anybody else; because he had talked more widely, read more deeply, thought more profoundly than anybody else; because he could express himself more forcibly than anybody else and because the structures of the society at that time gave the secretary great powers.[17]

Venn became chief executive of a society in crisis — partly financial and partly personnel and driven particularly by the savage mortality rate that in turn produced something of a recruitment problem.[18] Driven by these realities the society was obliged to retrench radically — effectively withdrawing its West Indies operation. And Venn was obliged to think radically if the yet tender missionary plant was not to be fatally damaged. He did so modestly and cautiously because, throughout his life, he was very aware that principles of missionary work were only just beginning to develop; that there was much "incompetent theorizing" often tinged by romantic notions that Venn, ever the realist, implied were unhelpful;[19] that the Bible was "for missionary purposes a sealed book," and that much work had to be done to relate modern missionary work to that of the New Testament, always bearing in mind the difference because "ours is not a miraculous dispensation."[20] Thus he expected that "the main

16. CMSA, CA1/L3, 74, 23 March 1853, Venn to Grapf.

17. At that stage in the procedures of the society, there were no agenda papers and most communications from missionaries went through the secretarial sieve before being presented to the committee. For procedures, see R. N. Cust, *Essay on the Prevailing Methods of the Evangelization of the Non-Christian World* (London: Luzac, 1894), p. 132. Cust, a doughty and plainspoken critic of almost everything about the missionary operation, is of course a prejudiced source but the view that Venn was an "autocrat" within the society recurs. See A. R. Ashwell and R. G. Wilberforce, *Life of the Right Reverend Samuel Wilberforce, DD: Lord Bishop of Oxford and afterwards of Winchester,* 3 vols. (London: John Murray, 1880-82), vol. 2, pp. 201-3. When he died he was referred to as "our revered and beloved Chief." CMSA, CA1/L8, 440, 16 January 1873, Hutchinson to Lamb.

18. Of the twenty-six missionaries who went to West Africa between 1825 and 1834, eighteen had died (CMSA, C A1/L3, 441, 16 October 1843, Venn, Dawes, and Coates, Instructions to Crowther, Cheesman, and Denton). The point was reinforced by the Niger expedition of 1841. Of its 150-strong European crew, forty-two died within two months (Stock, vol. 1, p. 455).

19. CMSA, G/AC 17/2, 442, 6 September 1854, Venn to Rufus Anderson.

20. CMSA, CI1/L6, 13-14, 27 January 1862, Venn to Barton.

truths and principles" relating to missionary work would "be gradually unfolded in the progress of the work," would "be thought out in secret communion with Christ," and would "be carefully gathered from the general tenor of prophecy, from the example of Christ, from the acts and writings of the Apostles."[21]

Though he proceeded with caution, he did proceed, and soon two key ideas had emerged. First, the aim should be to develop native pastors under European superintendence and thus prepare the way "eventually to leave the work in their hands."[22] And in those last few words was the germ of the second aim — the so-called "euthanasia" of "missionary operations." As early as 1844, while reassuring the bishop of Madras that the CMS would not abandon its South India mission and while acknowledging that the CMS committee might be over-optimistic about the time-scale of a "euthanasia," he was very explicit that its members desired "to shape their course from the first with a view to it."[23] And these core ideas were developed in a series of minutes in the late 1840s and early 1850s. These need not detain us here, for what they did was flesh out the central thinking. What they did not do was point in the direction of a "native bishop," which was soon to become central in Venn's thinking.[24]

We have already noted the strength of evangelical-leaning humanitarianism. Some of its most influential figures spoke with high confidence of the "native" capacity to rule in secular positions.[25] They were in part prompted by exactly the same unacceptable mortality rates among their own European personnel as had been experienced by missionaries. But, if the point could be made of the business and political world, why not of the ecclesiastical? It was out of this milieu that the idea of an African bishop was first suggested as early as 1851 by Hugh Stowell,[26] a very influential evangelical preacher of

21. CMSA, CN L/6, 380, 8 June 1860, Instructions to the Revd and Mrs. J. W. Gedge.
22. CMSA, C I2/L4, 196, 18 July 1846, Venn to J. Tucker.
23. CMSA, C I2/L4, 75, 1 August 1844, Venn to Bishop G. T. Spencer (Madras).
24. Peter Williams, *The Ideal of the Self-Governing Church: A Study of Victorian Missionary Strategy* (Leiden: E. J. Brill, 1990), pp. 5-9.
25. Williams, *The Ideal*, p. 10.
26. T. E. Yates, *Venn and Victorian Bishops Abroad: The Missionary Policies of Henry Venn and Their Repercussions upon the Anglican Episcopate of the Colonial Period, 1841-1872* (Uppsala: Swedish Institute of Missionary Research; London: SPCK, 1978), p. 145.

the period.[27] He continued to press the case for native bishops and never more clearly than in 1860 in Liverpool at a conference on missions when he criticized the tendency of missions "to keep the native converts in a state of pupilage, and not to let them walk independently and alone" and when he rounded on those Europeans who "would not bear to be under a black Bishop," maintaining that for his part he "should rejoice to be under a black bishop" and putting his finger of blame for such attitudes firmly on "a little of the taint of our former slave-trading and slave-holding amongst us."[28] And such strong views from within his own circle were pressed on Venn by a whole host of influential figures, including the archbishop of Canterbury, the secretary of state for the colonies, and the influential evangelical Anglican magazine the *Record*.[29]

Pressure also came from a source with which Venn had no natural sympathy. High Anglicans of the time were increasingly drawn to the idea of the missionary bishop. This was in large part a reaction to the perceived excesses of erastianism in England. The missionary bishop with no state connection was idealized. For some it seemed as if, in Gavin White's words, "the undefiled wilderness could allow the undefiled bishop to exist." Whether or not it is true to say, as he goes on to suggest, that this was "almost the only idea which the Tractarians held on the subject of missions,"[30] it was a very influential one and not least because of the directions in which it prodded Venn. And that direction was negative in respect to missionary bishops but increasingly positive in respect to "native bishops."

His negativity came in part because the whole tenor of his thinking was toward an increase in indigenous independence rather than the creation of a new sort of dependence. It came in part because of his dislike of Tractarian theology. It came in very large part because he feared unfettered prelatical authority in a context where the young church would simply not have the strength, experience, confidence, or legal ba-

27. Ian Scott Rennie, "Evangelicalism and English Public Life, 1823-1850" (Ph.D. thesis, University of Toronto, 1962), p. 79. Rennie regards Stowell as one of the three most influential evangelical clergyman of the time (the others being Francis Close and Hugh McNeile).

28. *Conference on Missions,* p. 356.

29. Williams, *The Ideal,* p. 11.

30. G. White, "The Idea of the Missionary Bishop in Mid-Nineteenth Century Anglicanism" (M.S.T. thesis, General Theological Seminary, New York, 1968), pp. 22-23.

sis to provide the necessary checks and balances there should be to prevent the misuse of the office of a bishop. He pointed to a "fatal" fault in Xavier's strategy, namely his encouragement of "absolute power" in a context where there were no canons to restrain its abuse.[31] Venn's defense against the missionary bishop proposals came, then, from two overlapping convictions. First he argued that the Church of England practice made it clear that though the laity were debarred from discharging "spiritual functions," "their co-operation is often necessary for the accomplishment of ecclesiastical actions." This cooperation was reflected in the constitution of the CMS, according to which bishops were involved with, but did not control, the "temporal affairs" of the mission.[32] Venn, then, shared the Protestant conviction that the state and lay participation, for example in patronage, was a healthy counterbalance to episcopal and clerical dominance. Missionary bishops would be inappropriate because they would operate in a context where there were no such checks. Second, he believed that a bishop was unnecessary at the beginning of a missionary operation as there were no strictly episcopal functions for him to perform. If, at that stage, he acts as a bishop "he will expect deference to his views" and the mission will "be thus cast into the mould of his idiosyncrasy."[33] When the time comes for a bishop, he continued, the most appropriate person will be someone "who is familiar with the language and habits of the native Christian Church, and who fully enjoys its confidence. But the question will then arise whether a *native* will not be the proper person."[34] And that flowed from his fundamental conviction that a far more important question than that of the extension of the episcopate was how to find the best system "to prepare the Native Converts, in their transition from heathenism to Christianity, for the euthanasia of the Mission in the establishment of a Native Church under Native Pastors and a Native Episcopate."[35]

The movement of his thinking toward the rejection of missionary

31. Venn, *The Missionary Life and Labours of Francis Xavier,* p. 146.

32. CMSA, G/AC5, 131-32, 5 June 1846, Venn to Chevalier Bunsen.

33. "The Memorandum of the Church Missionary Society on the Extension of the Episcopate," *CMI,* 1858, p. 163. This article is probably not by Venn (Stock attributes it to the *CMI* editor, Ridgeway [*CMI,* 1901, p. 261]) but it echoes Venn's views.

34. CMSA, G/AZ1/1, no. 93, "Memorial of the Church Missionary Society upon the Extension of the Episcopate in India," 13 April 1857.

35. CMSA, G/AZ 1/1, no. 98, "Letter to a Friend," 12 April 1858.

bishops and the embracing of the idea of native episcopacy was further strengthened by his analysis of the natural movement from mission to church. It was analogous to human growth. Behavior that is entirely appropriate in "childhood is fraught with mischief in manhood." Thus as the indigenous churches emerged into manhood they must be released from "leading strings." If this does not happen, there will be failure and indeed, the "infantile feebleness" that could be observed in many missions was often because they were "not trusted to go alone." Missionaries must be relaxed about the mistakes of the young church. These are part of the process of growth. Attempting to avoid them is "a contravention of Divine Providence" and will result only in "a pupillage which destroys character."[36] The missionary was, then, like the parent learning to let go, or like the elder brother finding that his younger brothers had suddenly emerged into equality,[37] or like the incumbent wisely giving his curate more responsibility.[38] And all that meant that the "the great Missionary problem of the day" was the relationship of native ministry to European missionaries. It had once been possible to proclaim the slogans "Native agency under European superintendence" and "Native ministry the crown of the Native agency." But now, Venn declared, another maxim needed to be added, "a Native Church the soul of a Mission." Here he drew from Paul the idea of the indigenous church as the holy temple and the missionaries as the master builders and then, warming to the analogy, he continued:

> the Mission, speaking of its machinery, is the scaffolding, the master builder is the chief actor, and all the poles and platforms which he creates are the chief objects; but as the building rises the builders occupy less and less attention — the scaffolding becomes unsightly and when the building is completed it is taken to pieces.

With such thinking it was fitting to think in terms of "association" rather than "superintendence," and Venn was encouraged because this also had Pauline precedent — "not as lords over God's heritage, but as helpers over your faith."[39]

His so-called Second Paper on the Native Church was issued in

---

36. CMSA, C I2/L6, 149-50, 10 April 1860, Venn and Knight to Royston.
37. CMSA, C I2/L6, 149-50, 10 April 1860, Venn and Knight to Royston.
38. CMSA, C I1/L6, 128, 2 June 1859, Venn to Mrs. Lamb.
39. CMSA, CN/L6, 384-87, 8 June 1860, Instructions to the Revd and Mrs. J. W. Gedge.

1861. It provided a structure by which a mission might move to a church stage when it would have no further need of "foreign agency" and when it would be "fully prepared for a native Episcopate." It brought his thinking together. Missionary work involved two tasks — bringing people to Christ and the forming of a church. The missionary was essentially the evangelist and the native leaders would be increasingly the pastors within the newly formed church. Unfortunately this is not what generally happened. Rather the missionary became increasingly responsible for the pastoring and upbuilding of the converts. This had three unfortunate results. First, the missionary finds that he is working "in a continually decreasing ratio" and involved in ever more secular activities, looking after the operation he has set up. Second, the converts become dependent and they do not get the vision of a church aiming to be self-supporting, self-governing, and self-extending. Third, the missionary society is unable to press on to "the regions beyond."[40] The paper had many echoes of the Liverpool conference of the previous year. There the conclusion was also that the European missionary ought not, "except in their mere infancy," to be the pastor of the new converts.[41] Nonetheless, it may be judged that Venn took his, the conference's, and the accepted wisdom of the day to a more developed and worked-out stage than anyone else had achieved hitherto. The last decade of his life was devoted both to attempts at implementation and to a drawing out of the implications of the theory — sometimes in radical and controversial ways.

Insofar as the implementation was concerned, Venn was the inspiration behind the setting up of the Sierra Leone Pastorate in 1861 that gave the local church a substantial degree of independence from the CMS; the consecration in 1864 of Samuel Crowther as bishop of "the countries of Western Africa beyond the limits of our [i.e., Her Majesty's] dominions" — the first black bishop of modern times; the laying down of a basis for Native Church Councils; and the appointment of a European missionary bishop for Ningpo (Hong Kong) in 1872. As these have been extensively covered elsewhere it is not necessary to examine them in detail. It is, however, necessary to trace developments in Venn's understanding of the relationship of the indigenous church and missionaries and in his acceptance of missionary bishops, albeit in a radically redefined way, and the starting place for both of these is the appointment of Crowther.

40. CMSA, G/AZ 1/1, no. 116, 9 July 1861; Knight, *Memoir*, pp. 414-20.
41. *Conference on Missions*, p. 310.

Many have concluded that Venn was being highly inconsistent to his own theory in allowing Crowther to become a bishop for a loosely defined area where there was no developed ecclesiastical organization.[42] But that was certainly not Venn's intention. He believed that the church on the Niger was sufficiently established to have a native bishop over it.[43] More significantly he wanted Crowther to have an episcopal role in the whole of West Africa, including Sierra Leone and the Yoruba states, where there had been a missionary presence for some time and where church organization was quite advanced. In keeping with this vision, he contended that Crowther's appointment would provide "the native African Church . . . with the means of its complete organization and self-extension."[44] Though he agreed that the missionaries and their congregations among the Yoruba could continue to be under the authority of the bishop of Sierra Leone, he did so reluctantly and on the understanding that this would be temporary — "until they may be desirous of placing themselves under his [Bishop Crowther's] authority."[45] Thus he pressed missionaries to accept Crowther's episcopal oversight.[46] He of course knew all about the long-standing opposition to such a proposal. It was based then, as it was in the middle of the twentieth century, on the contention that the time was not ripe.[47] Occa-

42. J. F. A. Ajayi, *Christian Missions in Nigeria, 1841-1891: The Making of a New Elite* (London: Longman, 1965), pp. 185-86; E. A. Ayandele, *The Missionary Impact on Modern Nigeria, 1842-1914: A Political and Social Analysis* (London: Longman, 1966), p. 182; Peter Beyerhaus and Henry Lefever, *The Responsible Church and the Foreign Mission* (London: World Dominion Press, 1964), p. 65; W. R. Shenk, "Henry Venn as Missionary Theorist and Administrator" (Ph.D. thesis, University of Aberdeen, 1978), p. 276; Max Warren, *To Apply the Gospel: Selections from the Writings of Henry Venn* (Grand Rapids: Eerdmans, 1971), pp. 29-30; Yates, *Venn and Victorian Bishops Abroad,* p. 153.

43. CMSA, C A2/L3, 340, 23 January 1864, Venn to Lamb.

44. CMSA, G/AC 1/16, 122, 28 April 1864, Earl of Chichester, Henry Venn, and C. C. Fenn to Earl Russell.

45. CMSA, C A2/L3, 370, 23 July 1864, Venn to the missionaries of the Yoruba Mission. Crowther himself was not prepared to be placed over European missionaries against their will (Venn to Lamb, 352, 23 March 1864).

46. CMSA, C A2/L3, 378, 22 September 1864, Venn to Hinderer.

47. See, for example, the strong rejection of the idea by one of the leading West African missionaries, Henry Townsend, on the grounds that the introduction of Christianity was a revolution "of the most extensive kind and the commanding minds that introduce those changes must and do become leaders; it is a law of nature and not contrary to the law of God, and efforts to subvert such laws must produce extensive evils" (C A2/85/62, 18 October 1858, Townsend to CMS).

sionally, but rarely, more blatantly racist views surfaced as when Venn reported with some evident disgust, that he had received a communication from West Africa arguing that to place a "white man" "under a black man as bishop" would be to degrade the European.[48]

Despite such opposition, Venn felt with the greatest of passion that this was the right step. But he did not believe it merely because he wanted a black bishop at any cost. Indeed, when there had a few years earlier been very great pressure from the highest quarters to appoint Crowther as bishop of Sierra Leone he had resisted this "with difficulty" "on the grounds that it was too much of an English colony." By the same token if a genuinely "native" church could be found and there was a suitable indigenous candidate for the episcopate, then he should be consecrated and as quickly as possible. Because a missionary is, said Venn using a favorite and vivid metaphor, "an exotic amidst native congregations," and because "all attempts to regulate the relations between him and native clergymen have hitherto failed," the "true remedy" must be a "native bishop." Once that had happened then the relationships between the native bishop and European missionaries "would be capable of more easy adjustment."[49] Such adjustment would come about as genuinely self-governing churches were established outside the colony, for example in the Yoruba area. In such churches Crowther would exercise "Episcopal functions *if the clergy and congregations are willing to receive them.*"[50] Clearly Venn expected that many would choose in this way and it seems, even with the hindsight of more than 130 years, a not unreasonable assumption.[51] Nonetheless it can be argued that Venn was unwise to believe that this solution would solve such an intractable problem, and the argument has additional force because manifestly it did not provide the solution he expected. It can also be argued that the arrangement that placed the decision whether or not they received Crowther's ministrations into the hands of the missionaries and the European bishop of Sierra Leone,[52] gave them the whip hand. Given the known opinions of most missionaries, this was more than likely to exclude Crowther from having an effective role in the existing native church. What is unfair to Venn's actions is to argue that he

48. CMSA, C A2/L3, 340, 23 January 1864, Venn to Lamb.
49. CMSA, C A2/L3, 341, 23 January 1864, Venn to Lamb.
50. CMSA C A1/L7, 466, 20 September 1864, Venn to Bishop Beckles of Sierra Leone (emphasis mine).
51. Ajayi, *Christian Missions in Nigeria,* p. 207.
52. CMSA, C A2/L3, 352, 23 March 1864, Venn to Lamb.

acquiesced in a plan that was entirely inconsistent with his own beliefs. He enthusiastically supported Crowther's elevation, which he regarded as a step forward of immense importance for the whole missionary operation, precisely because it was, in his judgment, key to the full development of the "Native African Church." As such it would signify "a great palpable triumph of Christianity."[53] Quite self-consciously, and indeed in revealingly emotional language, Venn drew on his own heritage in his description of Crowther's consecration. It fulfilled the dreams of what he called the "great philanthropists" who had desired to see the establishment of a native church in West Africa but had seen it not "ere they rested from their labours." But those dreams, he continued, had been fulfilled at the very moment when "the hands of the Primate of all England and of his suffragans rested upon the woolly head of the Negro, and gave him the full commission to constitute a native church in West Africa and to ordain elders amongst his sable countrymen."[54]

Venn's critics, most notably some of his more High Church contemporary adversaries and the CMS's own historian, Stock,[55] have also charged him with inconsistency because he came to think of "missionary bishops" in a much more positive way than he had done just a few years before. Thus he sometimes spoke of Crowther as a "missionary bishop,"[56] and thus he argued for a European missionary bishop in Ningpo. In part, he used the phrase as a simple and accurate way of describing a bishop who was not appointed by the state, but it went deeper than that. In response to the charge that he had changed his views, Venn replied that what he had in mind was an altogether different sort of missionary bishop than that he had criticized earlier — not a bishop appointed at the beginning of the missionary process and responsible for missionaries, but one coming after the native church had been formed and precisely in order to reduce the probability of its being shaped overmuch by a Western, European model. His preference remained for a native bishop of "an independent native church, however small" but, if one was not forthcoming, a European missionary bishop thoroughly familiar with the people and their language was the next

53. CMSA, C A2/L3, 340, 23 January 1864, Venn to Lamb.
54. Venn, "The Negro Bishop," *Christian Observer* 69, no. 381, 1869, p. 642.
55. CMSA, G/C 8/2, 8 March 1900, "A Brief Historical Sketch of the Society's Views and Actions in Regard to Native Christians."
56. CMSA, C A3/L1, 196, 23 December 1863, Venn to Wilmot.

Fig. 16. Consecration of Samuel Crowther as bishop on the Niger,
Canterbury Cathedral, June 1864.

Church Missionary Juvenile Instructor, September 1864.

best thing. Such a bishop, he was at pains to stress, would differ from
the High Church vision of a missionary bishop in the sense that his responsibility would be for "an organized native church" and not for
"European Missionaries."[57]

In this distinction between the "native church" and European missionary leaders, there is a clue to the later Venn. In the last seven or
eight years of his life, he moved from cajoling European missionaries
out of their reluctance to allow sufficient independence to their converts, to looking for organizational and institutional ways of by-passing
this reluctance. One of Venn's characteristics was a capacity to learn
from failure, including his own. One area of weakness that fascinated
him was the church in Jamaica. It had not prospered as had been expected when the CMS withdrew its missionaries in 1842.[58] Venn, writ-

57. CMSA, G/AC 1/17, 261, 26 August 1869, Venn to W. M. Fallows.
58. The CMS had withdrawn from Jamaica in 1842 partly because of its own
financial crisis but partly also because the parochial system appeared to be more developed there (Stock, vol. 1, p. 347).

Fig. 17. Henry Venn (1796-1873), honorary
clerical secretary of the CMS, 1841-1872.

Church Mission Society, London

ing in 1867, traced this to the fact that there were not enough "Negro teachers" and to the mistaken belief of the CMS that black Christians would "fall naturally into the ecclesiastical establishment of the island." Such a view, he contended, took no note of the importance of "race distinctions." What Venn had in mind was of course the difference between the black converts of CMS and the white-dominated church. Because these were ignored, "the best hopes of the Society" foundered. Only the establishment of a "Native Church Organization" would turn back the tide of failure.[59]

A much more recent and more bruising failure was the resistance of the European missionaries in West Africa to his proposals that they should serve under an indigenous bishop. But critical reflection on

59. CMSA, G/AZ 1/2, no. 152, January 1867, Venn to bishop of Kingston (Jamaica), paragraphs 13, 27.

that drove him to conclude that the objective of insisting that missionaries serve under a native bishop might not only be unrealistic but also inappropriate. Indeed, having discussed the matter further with Bishop Crowther, he had soon begun to conclude that the presence of European missionaries under an indigenous bishop might place such a bishop "in a false position" and "might have a bad effect on the native Church." It was far better for the health of the indigenous church, he now began to contend, to allow Europeans involved in a diocese where there was a native bishop, as in West Africa, "to be regarded as separate from the Native Church." The problem was easily stated, "The European element in a Native Church is the great snare and hindrance to its growth." The solution flowed from this: keep the indigenous church separate "with a complete organization of Bishop, priest and Deacon" and it "would exhibit a more firm and rapid development."[60]

And these pointers lead to the most interesting and least observed part of Venn's later years — not merely his advocacy of an independent native church on a much shorter time-scale than missionaries thought possible but his growing perception that it would only be accomplished if the realities of racial and cultural differences were faced. It was ludicrous to judge young churches established out of a pagan culture by "Anglo-Saxon ideas."[61] He constantly urged his missionaries to be balanced in their judgment of moral failure. It happened in the early church;[62] it happened even in England;[63] it was only to be expected where ministers were not operating in "privileged England" surrounded by "established Christian institutions and quickened continually by Christian influences, which keep us up to the mark."[64] In the light of this it was "a most unhappy and mistaken suggestion" to put indigenous clergy back under European superintendence because of a moral lapse or two.[65] Indeed, "far greater evils would arise" from such a course than ever were remedied. The whole

---

60. CMSA, C I1/L6, 430, 26 December 1864, Venn to bishop of Calcutta.
    61. Venn, *Retrospect and Prospect of the Operations of the Church Missionary Society,* 2d ed. (London: CMS, 1865), p. 17.
    62. CMSA, C A1/L7, 195, 20 November 1861, Venn to J. Hamilton; Venn, *Retrospect and Prospect;* 484, 22 December 1864, Venn to Hamilton.
    63. CMSA, Venn to Hamilton, 20 November 1861.
    64. CMSA, C A3/L1, 225, 23 January 1866, Venn to Crowther.
    65. CMSA, C A3/L1, 214, 30 January 1865, Venn to Crowther. This was being proposed by Bishop Beckles in Sierra Leone.

development of the independent church would "be frustrated."[66] Running through his writing of this period is a new stress on the inevitability of racial tension. Venn had moved from a place where he spoke of European superintendence, to one where primacy was given to European and "native" association and now he was moving beyond this to one where he both accepted the likelihood of racial conflict and had a marked preference for the separation of the "native" and European elements in the church.

The movement is discernible. In 1861 he was noting the problem of race division and commending it to Christ for wisdom.[67] By 1867 he was telling his missionaries that conflicts were inevitable at a time of "transition to independence." It is a "collision of races" that "meets an advancing Christianity in every mission field over the whole world."[68] It will lead to "a season of peril, of personal collisions, of outbursts of jealousies."[69] These must be patiently borne,[70] taking St. Paul's example in his dealing with the native Corinthians (1 Corinthians 4:8).[71] But such advice fell on unreceptive ground. Indeed Venn complained that the society's attempts "to inculcate upon their Missionaries the importance of conciliating the class of aspiring natives, who rise by education or by trade, to a position analogous to that of the wealthier class at home" had been largely "in vain."[72]

Venn became increasingly conscious that the preaching of the gospel would produce "national churches" and at this point his analysis became more profound and far-reaching than that of many of his contemporaries. It received its clearest expression in his paper "On Nationality" presented in 1868. There Venn argued that the "Great Commission" was to make disciples "of all nations." This was a calling "not only to induce a few individuals of every nation to flock into the Christian Church, but that all nations should gradually adopt the Christian religion as their national profession of faith, and thus fill the universal

66. CMSA, C A1/L7, 499-500, 20 January 1865, Venn to Beckles.
67. CMSA, CI1/L5, 437, 9 September 1861, Venn to Long.
68. CMSA, C A2/L3, 123, 4 February 1862, Venn to Townsend.
69. CMSA, C A1/L8, 148, 21 May 1867, Venn to Beckles.
70. CMSA, Venn to Hamilton, 20 November 1861; cf. CN L/6, 388, 8 June 1860, Venn and Knight, Instructions to Gedge, where he asks for patience with "the uppishness of a transition age."
71. CMSA, C A1/L7, 340, 16 October 1863, Venn, Long, and Davies, Instructions.
72. CMSA, C A1/L7, 155, 23 May 1861, Venn to Beckles.

Church by the accession of national churches."[73] But different national-
ities received the gospel in extremely varied ways and that meant that it
was of paramount importance that missionaries should "study the national character of the people" among whom they worked and should
show "the utmost respect for national peculiarities" and in that way
they will discover that their "modes of thought" will come to "sympa-
thise with their difficulties" and will "discover any common standing-
ground" that might form a base from which they might "start together
in the search of truth."[74] He warned his missionaries that the English
found it particularly difficult "to show respect to national peculiarities"
that differed from their own and this defect in their cultural lenses was
particularly "mischievous" when "exhibited in a Christian missionary
towards downtrodden or half-civilised nations." The best antidote to
this besetting sin was "to study and to *respect* the national habits and
conventionalities" until that became "second nature." He returned to
the theme of racial difference. There was a strong likelihood that "race
distinctions" would "rise in intensity with the progress of the Mission."
This was to be accepted as natural and inevitable.[75] Instead of railing
against this, missionaries should seek to work with it and above all seek
to see how the "native church" could be "organised as a national institution." To this end they were to avail themselves "of national habits"
and seek to ensure that every church member "feel himself doubly
bound to his country by this social as well as religious society."[76]

And this meant reiterating the point often made before that missionaries should not pastor because, quoting Mullens of the LMS, coming "from a much higher civilisation" they were "too strong for the
people" and had fostered an unfortunate spirit of "childlike dependence." However much we recoil from this typically Victorian assumption of superiority, the driving consequence, at any rate so far as Venn
was concerned, was to find ways of reducing an unhealthy dependence.
The logic, then, at this point was precisely in keeping with what we
have already noticed in the later Venn — *"the proper position of a missionary is one external to the native church."* He takes a place not
within the native community of Christians but *"ab extra."* But there

73. Henry Venn, "On Nationality," in *The Missionary Secretariat of Henry
Venn,* ed. William Knight (London: Longmans, Green, 1880), p. 282. (Instructions
given to missionaries 30 June 1868; hereafter known as "Nationality.")
74. "Nationality," p. 283.
75. "Nationality," p. 284.
76. "Nationality," p. 285.

was also an emphasis far more distinct than before on the rights of every national church "to change its ceremonies, and adapt itself to the national taste." This was a right given by the Prayer Book itself and, though Church of England missionaries were bound to train their converts "according to the discipline and worship" of that church, there was an implicit provisionality about its discipline and liturgy. This gave grounds both for creating the expectation that there would be differences from national church to national church and also for reaching a much more positive assessment of other denominational missionary work than was common in England.[77]

And the story of his last years in the CMS gives many examples of this thinking being articulated and worked out. These were most forcefully put in the *Intelligencer*.[78] It constantly returned to the dangers of creating a dependency relationship and in a more sloganized way than Venn would ever have allowed himself to use. The sole object, it stressed, was evangelization and not Europeanization.[79] The objective was not to allow Christianity to be part of a process of "denationalizing" converts so that they became "Anglicized," but rather for it to be "nationalized" and thus to be placed "in an advantageous position for permeating the whole race."[80] There was a real danger that Christianity would become "an alien element," productive only of "disorder and confusion" and, rather than bringing new national strengths, would encourage its converts to deny their national heritage. In particular Christianity could too easily be seen as furthering the interests of the evange-

77. "Nationality," pp. 286-87. These points were not new for Venn. There are echoes, for example, in 1861 (*Proceedings of the Church Missionary Society,* 1861, p. 224), but they are made with more sustained vigor here than ever before. See also *CMI,* 1869, p. 315.

78. See note 7 above.

79. *CMI,* 1858, p. 176. This was in contrast to a few years earlier where it had been happy to use the children/parent model and to see the current time as one of "tutelage" (1849, p. 150).

80. *CMI,* 1869, p. 98. It is of considerable interest that Karl Graul, the German missiologist, uses very similar language ("anglicize," christianize," "europeanize") in his critique of Anglo-American missionaries of a few years earlier. See Karl Graul, *Die Stellung der evangelisch-lutherischen Mission in Leipzig zur Ostindischen Katenfrage* (Leipzig, 1861). I am indebted to an as-yet unpublished paper by Jan Jongeneel ("European-Continental Perceptions and Critiques of British and American Protestant Missions," given at the North Atlantic Missiology Project Symposium at Boston University, June 1998) for the references to Graul. More work needs to be done on establishing whether Graul did influence Venn and his circle.

lizing nation "at the expense of the interests of the one which is being evangelized." But it ought not to be so, and great care should be taken "to eliminate from Christianity everything of mere national peculiarity which might excite prejudice and obstruct progress."

> The gospel is a seed sown in a different soil and that soil will modify the product, and a Christianity will be raised up which, in all that does not compromise essential principles, will be so modified as to be in sympathy with the national peculiarities. It is the homogeneousness of the leaven with the lump that facilitates its action. Were that homogeneousness to be interrupted, the influence of the leaven would be enfeebled, if not destroyed; and so, in organizing our first body of converts in a land, we must be very careful to avoid in anywise so dealing with them as to lead the people to think, that, in becoming Christian, they have become less native, and are not so entirely and identically national as they were.[81]

It follows that great care must be taken that a church does not become too "Anglican" so that its native leaders are never faced with a conflict between their loyalty to "an English authority" and "their own rulers."[82]

The writer boldly spelt out the implications for a place like India where there was "an Anglican church establishment, a branch of the parent church at home."[83] Precisely because the aim is the formation of an indigenous church and not the extension of a branch of an English church, the English bishop must be prepared "to relax his authority" and "to remit all jurisdiction over the native clergy" that might interfere with "the formation of a Native church, and the elimination of all incidentals which, however in usage by the English church, prove to be unsuitable to the position of a native church, and injurious to its nationality." And there is consequently the firm expectation that indigenous daughter churches will be "characterized," as is often true of mothers and daughters, "by many and by no means unpleasing variations" from the mother church.[84] And the conclusion is then bold and stark: "If we would propagate Christianity amongst the natives, we must be prepared to let them have it without its Anglicanism, which,

81. *CMI*, 1869, p. 99.
82. *CMI*, 1869, p. 100.
83. *CMI*, 1869, p. 101.
84. *CMI*, 1869, p. 104.

however valuable for us, is unsuitable for them. If we say that we cannot separate the essentials from what is adventitious and incidental, then do we obstruct the progress of the Gospel."[85]

These questions had been particularly brought center stage by Venn's strong advocacy of a missionary bishop for Ningpo on mainland China and attempts to separate it from the Crown bishopric of Victoria (Hong Kong) that had episcopal oversight of "all English clergy residing in China."[86] Venn, in keeping with the convictions I have noted, wanted to appoint a bishop on "racial" rather than territorial grounds. The CMS thus argued that "the division of the Bishoprics *by races* is the more expedient course." Yes, the memorandum continued, there was an ancient canon that prohibited two bishops exercising jurisdiction in the same area, but it was clear from ecclesiastical jurists such as Joseph Bingham that it applied "to persons and Churches of the same race and language." Where there were different races and languages, it was quite normal to have several different bishops — for example in Jerusalem there were currently Syrian, Armenian, and Greek bishops. "It would therefore be no violation of this Canon to have a Bishop in China exercising jurisdiction over the Chinese Native Church and another exercising jurisdiction over the English clergy and English congregations."[87] Venn pressed the archbishop of Canterbury (Tait) that the missionary bishop "should exercise his Episcopal Ministrations only over the native Ministers and native congregations."[88] In the end Venn had to accept that racial bishops would not be acceptable in the current ecclesiological climate, but he did so reluctantly. The letter from Christopher Fenn to the bishop-designate of Ningpo maintained the society's preference for the previous plan because it had recognized "that distinction between the European and the Chinese races which it is impossible to abolish, and therefore which it seems unwise to ignore."[89]

The *Intelligencer* wondered whether China had brought such issues to the fore for the first time.[90] For Venn it was merely a particular laboratory for convictions that had already been well-formed. "The eu-

85. *CMI*, 1869, p. 105.
86. CMSA, G/AZ 1/2, no. 306, 2, 10 November 1869, memorandum, unsigned.
87. Memorandum, 10 November 1869, p. 3.
88. Lambeth Palace Archives, Tait Papers, vol. 169, 303, 20 April 1870, memorandum from Venn.
89. CMSA, C CH/L2, 247-48, 10 February 1871, Fenn to Russell.
90. *CMI*, 1869, "Government of Native Churches," p. 316.

thanasia of Missions," he diplomatically instructed the archbishop of Canterbury in relation to China, "is when a Native Church is established under a Native Bishop. But the Native Church can scarcely be said to be in training for such a happy consummation" when the bishop is "a stranger speaking a strange tongue and paying occasional visits." Certainly China "peculiarly requires the early organizing of the Native Church as a self-supporting and self-governing Institution, for the peculiar jealousy of foreigners, for the threat of persecution, and for the precariousness of any lengthened European superintendence."[91]

But, if the context was a little less pressing in India because it was under British sovereignty, the principles were exactly the same as Venn had seen for at least the previous seven or eight years and which the *Intelligencer* began to trumpet forth to the CMS constituency. What missionaries were doing, it declared, was planting seed that was "in essentials identical with our own, but in form and discipline assimilating to us only so far as is consistent with the formation of a national and independent church, possessed of that freedom and elasticity which will enable it to adapt itself to the exigencies and circumstances of the new people amongst whom it is to grow."[92] The great danger was of producing native churches that were "nothing else than fac-similes of the mother church, and therefore disqualified from taking up a national position and exercising a national influence." Thinking men, it continued, are beginning to realize the importance of allowing the church to develop in a way that is appropriate to the Indian culture

> if, indeed, the native Christianity in that country is to be national and Missionary; otherwise we have to fear lest it degenerate into an excrescence, something growing on the living body, and not part of it, which assimilates to its own peculiarity of existence whatever it takes from the trunk to which it is attached, while the tree itself remains unchanged. Such has been the Syrian Church in Travancore. It never became national; never identified itself with the life-blood of the people. The ligaments which bound it to Antioch never were severed, and it never assumed an independent position, in which nurtured by the dews of heaven, it might grow and spread. We are not speaking of colonial churches. They are off-shoots of the English Church, and it is for their welfare that they retain that connexion; but we are speaking

91. CMSA, G/AC 1/17, 519, 11 December 1871, Venn to Tait.
92. *CMI*, 1869, p. 315.

of native churches, and they must be so planted out that they may have a separate existence.

It must be remembered that in Missionary work we are not transplanting . . . native Christians have been raised from seed — "the seed is the word of God." Now, seed sown in a new country and climate will not yield a produce precisely the same with the mother plant in the old country. It will be essentially, yet not identically, the same. There will be variations more or less pronounced, and we must conclude that it will be so in the propagation of Christianity.[93]

In this concern to develop churches that were genuinely national;[94] in this fear of "transplanting"; in this confidence in sowing for a "separate existence"; in this sharp awareness of the difference between the colonial church and the native church, we are close to the issues that dominated Venn's later thinking.

The year of Venn's death, 1873, saw the appearance of a remarkable article. It is so close to Venn's ideas that Max Warren thought it might have been a final memorandum from him.[95] Though this does not appear to be the case, it can be taken as working through his heritage in relation to a particular field — India. It pointed to the relationship difficulties that had gradually become evident between missionaries and indigenous clergy.[96] In misguided reaction, the missionaries had been inclined to retreat to the old catechetical system, but happily there were those in England and America who understood what was happening and sought rather to reconstitute the native church

---

93. *CMI*, 1869, p. 316.

94. A concern that may have been given added force because the process leading to the disestablishment of the Irish Church (1869) prompted CMS thinkers to analyze its weaknesses precisely in terms of its failure to become genuinely national. See C. Peter Williams, " 'Too Peculiarly Anglican': The Role of the Established Church in Ireland as a Negative Model in the Development of the Church Missionary Society, 1856-1872," in *Studies in Church History*, vol. 25, *The Churches, Ireland and the Irish*, ed. W. J. Sheils and Diana Wood (Oxford: Blackwell, 1989), pp. 299-310.

95. CMSA, "Pamphlets and Papers in India Educational," no. 13, p. 11; and "Native Church Organisation." Max Warren also speculates that this might be from an associate or disciple of Venn. Both of these possible explanations are in his house index at the CMS. It, in fact, appeared in the *Madras Church Missionary Record* in 1872 (cf. *Church Congress Report*, 1882, pp. 531-33, where Sir Bartle Frere quotes extensively from it). It may therefore not have had a London provenance at all. Even if this is so, its ideas converge remarkably with those of the home society.

96. CMSA, "Pamphlets and Papers," pp. 1-3.

on an independent organic basis of its own; a Church which, while it should be in the closest and most intimate relation with the mother Church which first gave it being, should nevertheless stand on its own bottom as the native Church of India, and not be merely a poor and feeble imitation of a far distant Church across the sea.

And this meant that the foreign missionary would be an "adviser and counsellor merely" and not an "office-bearer."[97] In all this process, the article continued, missionaries of the established church were at a disadvantage because questions relating to clergy remuneration, the up-keep of church fabric, and matters of church law had long since been laid down "by the law of the land." Nonconformist missionaries, con-versely, had a positive advantage because they were much more used to such questions having to be decided in particular localities. In conse-quence, little had been done and what little had been done had "been based on an unsuitable model, viz, the established endowed Churches of England and Germany, than which perhaps none could have been perhaps less adapted to the requirements of an infant church newly planted in the midst of heathenism." The result of all this was that in-digenous clergy were in a curate/rector relationship to the missionary, somewhat parallel to what might happen in a large town or rural parish in England.[98] Attractive as this might appear, it was in fact disastrous, because "We are compelled sadly to admit that most of the fabric, so fair to look upon, rests upon an unsound foundation, and that if once the foreign missionary were withdrawn, like an arch from which the keystone has been removed, the whole would soon fall to pieces."[99] In the light of this reality, the arguments for combining the emerging church with an established European church collapsed, to be replaced by the conclusion that the native church should look "to the establish-ment of a separate Church organization of its own."[100]

And that was Venn's heritage. Such convictions dominated the CMS and circles far beyond it for the next twenty years and more. He was acutely aware, as he wrote to Rufus Anderson, the American missiologist whose thinking he much admired, of living in an age "of incompetent theorizing and with it a tinge of Missionary romance." He was at bottom an evangelical clergyman of the established Church of

97. CMSA, "Pamphlets and Papers," p. 3.
98. CMSA, "Pamphlets and Papers," p. 8.
99. CMSA, "Pamphlets and Papers," p. 9.
100. CMSA, "Pamphlets and Papers," p. 11.

England strongly influenced by the Enlightenment, who regarded the interpretation of "the leading of Providence" as "a great science." As he followed "this guidance," he confessed that he was "better able to realize the presence with us of the great Prophet of his church — who has specially attached the promise of his presence to Missionary operations."[101] And his principles have the hard-edged realism about race, cross-cultural relationships, and the actual "success" that lay behind upbeat missionary rhetoric as might be thought to come naturally to a product of the Enlightenment; they are deeply rooted in his understanding of biblical developments as would be expected of an evangelical; they are worked through with an immense desire to appreciate and empathize with the representatives of the younger churches as is not surprising from a child of the antislavery movement, and yet they are always presented with a deep and humble awareness of the mysterious ways of providence in history as befitted one who allowed his understanding to roam far beyond his evangelicalism and indeed even his Anglicanism. And perhaps they are revisited today not on account of some antiquarian interest but because within them are thought to be some of the most important principles for the development of strong churches that are appropriately rooted in their cultural context. Venn's principles — above all the immensely strong conviction that culture and context matter and that paternalism is the enemy of the effective church — are admired at the end of the second century of the existence of the CMS as much as they were bypassed at the centenary. The reasons for this lie beyond the scope of this chapter, but they do represent the most significant missiological heritage that the CMS has been able to provide to the wider church.

101. CMSA, G/AC 17/2, 6 September 1854, Venn to Rufus Anderson.

7. The CMS and the African Transformation: Samuel Ajayi Crowther and the Opening of Nigeria

LAMIN SANNEH

Introduction

It was two Hausa Africans, themselves former slaves who had been emancipated in Trinidad and had decided to return to Nigeria, who took steps to take the antislavery movement beyond Sierra Leone to Nigeria. They arrived in Freetown in 1837 on their way to Badagry, a slave port in the Bight of Benin. While in Freetown they attracted considerable attention among the recaptive population, many of whom became very enthusiastic about joining them. For that purpose, three of the recaptives joined in 1839 to buy a ship, which they renamed *Queen Victoria*, furnished with trade goods, took on a restricted number of

---

This chapter is an adaptation of a section of the author's forthcoming book *The American Factor in West African Christianity: 1776-1892: A Study in Antislavery and Antistructure* (Cambridge, Mass.: Harvard University Press).

Editorial note: the term "antistructure" is developed as an important concept in this chapter. It conveys the idea that, in its close association with the campaign against slavery, West African Christianity espoused a culture of radical criticism of all power structures, a demystification of ideologies of absolute authority, and a dissemination of what are often regarded as "democratic" and "liberal" values.

passengers, only sixty-seven out of the more than two hundred who had applied, and set sail for Badagry.

The CMS was not much in the picture at this stage. Yet the 1839 voyage to Nigeria was in a profound sense the logical outcome of the CMS strategy of taking Christianity to former slaves and ex-captives. In the early nineteenth century in Freetown, Sierra Leone, the CMS had launched the Christian movement as an international, ecumenical, and cross-cultural force for antislavery and as the ally of the dispossessed and the outcast. Long before it was fashionable to speak about "the Africanization of Christianity," the CMS had advanced the much more radical concept of leadership by ex-slaves and ex-captives. If Africanization meant assimilation into the chiefly caste and political genealogy, with their norms of enslavement and suppression of women, then Christianity combining with antislavery was opposed to it. On their part, the chiefs were opposed to the religion, seeing that they could not reconcile it with the structural integration of the court. The Christian movement as antistructure would cut deep channels into hinterland Africa only by flushing out the old authority structures that produced and used slaves and thus precluded any second chance of human recycling for such victims. The ideology of indigenous innocence that fostered a climate of political tolerance for African chieftaincies and native authorities as the litmus test of colonial administrative wisdom had not at that time intervened to weaken the cause of antislavery and its decisive alliance with Christianity.

Thus the CMS fostered Africanization as the leadership of victim populations whose example of redemption and productive enterprise would generate new, alternative structures of agency and society to transform, and, if necessary, replace the slave-ridden structures. Mission, then was a human-rights imperative, based on the validation of those tainted by the slaver's shackle. It follows from that logic that the CMS had little choice but to be drawn into Nigeria. Thus, after the passengers returned to Freetown, they resolved to continue the mission and accordingly petitioned the government and, indirectly, the CMS to allow them to start a colony at Badagry under the British flag. Alone among Western nations, Britain, which had been carrying more than 40 percent of the slave trade, was now distinguished in shouldering the heavy cost of abolition and became identified as such with antislavery. It had spent 30 million pounds to underwrite abolition.[1] Thus the Brit-

1. Lord Rosebery (1847-1929), the liberal politician, had declared: "I believe

ish flag was perceived locally by victim populations as a symbol of antislavery rather than as a symbol of the classical empire of a later age. Accordingly, the settlers agreed to have a European missionary join them as a partner, not as an overlord.

In the intervening years when government and mission were still wary of any reckless scheme of territorial overreach, the recaptives bought ships and traveled up and down the coast, demonstrating that expansion beyond Sierra Leone was viable and a logical development of the antislavery cause. They had the resources to pursue the idea and to build on accumulating evidence of its viability. Growth in the standard of living in Freetown quickened the pace of expansion abroad. As a consequence the missionary societies of the Anglicans and the Methodists, with the Catholics soon to follow, experienced a revival of interest. Settler and recaptive churches were filled to overflowing, and the missionary societies rebuilt old abandoned chapels and staffed them with recaptive preachers. The school rolls swelled, new schools were opened, and still children had to be turned away. By 1840 more than eight thousand children, about a fifth of the population, were at school.

Such advances in the personal circumstances of the settlers and recaptives produced the educated and successful individuals who could plan and direct the antislavery outreach to Nigeria and elsewhere. Preachers, pastors, school teachers, traders, and clerical personnel composed the ranks of this buoyant cadre of modernizing agents, with their skills supporting their mobile lifestyle. Thus trained, equipped, and resolved, they formed the core of the repatriation movement to Nigeria, ready to establish there the cause of antislavery and antistructure.

Change in the Old Order

Yorubaland, their destination, was no stranger to change, and even before the outfitting of the dramatic Niger Expedition of 1841, there were straws in the wind. The old chieftaincy rule, upheld by slavery, had been in crisis in several respects, as Samuel Johnson (d. 1901), the renowned Yoruba historian who was born in Sierra Leone, amply docu-

---

that this country [Britain] when it stands before history, will stand, when all else has passed away, not by her fleets and her armies and her commerce, but by the heroic, self-denying exertions which she has made to put down this iniquitous traffic." Cited in J. Wesley Bready, *This Freedom — Whence?* (New York: American Tract Society, 1942), p. 224.

mented in his *History of the Yorubas*.[2] Oaths were no longer taken in the name of the gods, who were considered too lenient. "May the king's sword destroy me!" was the new oath, with its sharp self-imprecatory edge. The nation, warns Johnson darkly, was ripe for judgment.

The chief architect of the CMS plan to open up West Africa to antislavery was Samuel Ajayi Crowther. Born around 1806, the year before abolition, Crowther (the name was adopted from his missionary benefactor) came from the Yoruba town of Oshogun from where he was captured by invading Fulani (or Fulani-sponsored) Muslim forces from north Nigeria who sold him as a slave to a Portuguese slave ship in Lagos. By a series of remarkable coincidences, he was eventually rescued, in April 1822, by the British naval squadron and brought to Freetown where he came under missionary instruction.

After his enfranchisement he was taken to Bathurst village (one of the settlement villages established at Freetown), and in 1826 went to the Islington School in London. Then he returned as a teacher at Bathurst, moving subsequently to the village of Leicester, where a training school had been established for recaptives. Then, with his wife, he went in 1829 to Regent, followed with a stint at Wellington. Back in Freetown he preached to Yoruba recaptives at Kissy, attracting interested Muslim inquirers.

Crowther rose rapidly to positions of responsibility and influence, his relatively young age notwithstanding. His intellectual gifts and his flair for languages equipped him to lead the recaptives back to Nigeria. Faced with a growing population of Nigerian recaptives in Freetown and their remarkable talent for religion and commerce, Crowther and a few of his compatriots decided to pursue the idea of mounting a mission to the slave ports of Nigeria.

It was in the cause of that mission that Crowther's fate became intertwined with that of Henry Townsend, the CMS missionary pioneer of Abeokuta. Townsend arrived in Abeokuta on an exploratory visit for the CMS in 1842. He was only twenty-one and frail looking, but keen to run things. Townsend's Abeokuta visit was sponsored by Captain Harry Johnson, a Sierra Leonean trader who gave him free passage on his ship, the *Wilberforce,* together with fifty-nine other emigrants. The party arrived in Abeokuta on 4 January 1843. Townsend met King Sodeke, who received the recaptive party warmly and offered to coop-

---

2. Johnson's *History* was commenced in the 1880s and published in London in 1921 and subsequently.

erate with a mission there, giving up a whole quarter of the town for the purpose. Townsend declined to commit the CMS to that extent but was impressed enough with the positive response of Sodeke to return. He wrote a report on that visit and then went to London to prepare himself for ordination. At about the same time, Crowther, with the achievement of the 1841 Niger Expedition under his belt, was also called to London to be trained at the CMS Training College at Islington, London, and ordained in 1843, to return to Abeokuta.

As if sensing that trade, not Christianity, was their best ally, the chiefs came forward at this time to petition Queen Victoria to open the road to Lagos so they could go there to trade. Crowther received the testimony of the *alake,* the chief of Abeokuta, to the effect that in ten years the community had been transformed and the people changed from the pursuit of war to peace. The roads that had been controlled by armed brigands were now peaceful and everyone, including women and children, could venture out without fear of being seized and sold. The results of this transformation, the *alake* testified, were plain for all to see. Though he was not himself a Christian, the *alake* challenged that if Christianity was such a force for good, then he, for one, would wish more of it for his people. Before too long, however, circumstances would change and the *alake* would be singing a very different tune, indeed. That happened in 1867 when the *alake,* Chief Abokko, seized Crowther, who was then bishop, and his party and demanded a stiff ransom for their release. The *alake* asked for two hundred slaves as payment, but Crowther vowed he would rather die than pay. Mediation bought crucial time for a British trading vessel, the *Thomas Bagley,* to steam into port and rescue Crowther. But in the late 1840s no one foresaw that, and so the *alake's* resounding expression of confidence in Crowther's personal agency echoed far and wide, and, soon enough, word of it reached Lord Palmerston. Crowther's star was set to rise.

Crowther and the Niger Expedition

In 1841 with public support for the scheme, Lord John Russell, then colonial secretary, authorized an expedition to the River Niger in response to the ideas of Sir Thomas Fowell Buxton. Its purpose was to open up the riverain system to lawful commerce and to help put down the slave trade. The expedition was given power to enter into treaty agreements with the chiefs to suppress the slave trade and support commercial enterprise. Factories would be established at trading stations. With government plans set out thus, the CMS agreed to equip a missionary party to accompany the expedition, placing James Frederick Schön and Samuel Crowther in charge. It would prove a most hazardous enterprise, because, to begin with, without armed protection, the missionary party would be at the complete mercy of the well-armed and better equipped slave traders who controlled the riverain channels. Besides, the members of the expedition would be exposing themselves to the dreaded malaria fever, at that time understood only in folklore terms as a disease of contaminated vapors, hence its name "mal-aria," "bad air." It was not until 1897, the year of the scientific discovery of the malaria parasite, that those who for centuries had wistfully "questioned the winds and waters" could abandon their mute oracles and scatter.[3] Until that happened, the peril remained, thus concentrating Crowther's mind on thoughts for his wife and four children. In the event, the expedition of 145 Europeans proved a disaster. Three ships were fitted out for the voyage, named the *Albert,* the *Wilberforce,* and the *Soudan.* In charge was Captain Trotter. Of the members of the expedition only Schön and Crowther had any missionary experience.

Crowther and Schön kept a journal of the expedition, which, on 1 July 1841, left Sierra Leone, entering the marshy delta uneventfully in mid-August. However, within days the journals of Crowther and Schön began to make grim reading. The chief medical officer reported that by

3. In 1896 Dr. Patrick Manson of London advanced for the first time the theory of mosquitoes as carriers of malaria. In August 1897, Major Ronald Ross, working in India, independently discovered malarial parasites in the stomach of a female anopheles mosquito, a scientific breakthrough. The search for a cure then commenced in earnest. Ross came to Freetown in 1899. In 1900 the U.S. Army Medical Department in Cuba discovered yellow fever, another tropical scourge, to be mosquito-borne. Already quinine, an alkaloid, also known as the "bark," after the *cinchona* tree from which it is extracted, was used as a prophylactic. The 1853 expedition up the Niger, led by Dr. Baikie, were given daily quinine rations. They all returned alive. Robert Campbell, the companion of Martin Delany, said he used quinine as a prophylactic in 1859 and found it effective against bilious fever, but he continued to believe that the fever came from "marsh miasmata common to other tropical countries, as well as to the southern sections of the United States, as well as to the West Indies and Central America." R. Campbell, "A Pilgrimage to My Motherland: An Account of a Journey among the Egbas and Yorubas of Central Africa: 1859-60," in *Search for a Place: Black Separatism and Africa, 1860,* ed. M. R. Delany and Robert Campbell (Ann Arbor: The University of Michigan Press, 1969), pp. 245-46. But only after 1897 did such remedies receive more than anecdotal attention.

4 September, "Fever of a most malignant character broke out in the *Albert,* and almost immediately in the other vessels, and abated not until the whole expedition was paralysed." The *Soudan* was loaded with forty of the sick and dying and, like a scapegoat, was turned loose and made to turn around, to be grimly followed two days later for the same reason by the *Wilberforce.* Only the *Albert* forged on ahead, making encouraging progress among the chiefs. By 3 October, however, the malaria fever was carrying off so many of the survivors that Captain Trotter, by then three hundred miles up the Niger, contemplated abandoning the whole enterprise altogether and admitting defeat. The decision was taken to quit. It was a ragged retreat. No sooner had he turned round than Captain Trotter himself went down with the fever, followed by the three engineers, then by the navigator, who died soon after falling ill. Others followed him in rapid succession: three officers and a marine died and were buried at sea. Of the 145 Europeans, 130 had contracted malaria and 40 had died.[4] Many of the survivors, wracked with high fever and suffering aches and shivers, were delirious to the point of requiring restraints. Some flung themselves into the river only to be rescued by an alert African attendant. Rio Nun, where the expedition entered the delta, earned the nickname, the Gate of the Cemetery. Members of the expedition entering the river did so with the Nunc Dimittis on their lips.

Crowther survived along with Schön. In spite of the hazards and difficulties, Crowther accomplished a surprising amount of work on the Niger, making the most detailed observations and reports of his progress on the banks of the Niger. He was interested in the religious ideas and practices of Africans, and he inquired diligently, listened closely, and depicted as accurately as he could what he observed and heard for himself. He was eager to corroborate, test, and confirm for himself, leaving issues of dispute open to opinion. He avoided rushing to judgment.[5] Thus, although he noted somber aspects of their customs and traditional practices, Crowther was nevertheless enthusiastic about

---

4. Kenneth Dike says there were 162 whites of whom 54 died. *The Origins of the Niger Mission: 1841-1891* (a paper read at the Centenary of the Niger Mission at Christ Church, Onitsha, 13 November 1957) (Ibadan: Ibadan University Press for the CMS Niger Mission, 1962), p. 6.

5. To show his scrupulous method, Crowther rebuked himself often for writing down things he was told, only to find from later inquiry that he had been given false testimony. James Frederick Schön and Samuel Crowther, *Journals,* 2d ed. (London: Frank Cass, 1970), p. 144.

what he learnt of religion among the Ibo people, including their ideas about God (Chukwu, Chineke), ethics, and moral conduct. He said he had heard references to such things among the Sierra Leoneans of Ibo background but had refrained from stating them as facts "before I had satisfied myself by inquiring of such as had never had any intercourse with Christians. . . . Truly God has not left Himself without witness!"[6] The idea that premodern Africa had anticipated in several crucial respects Christian teaching was stated by Crowther with such spontaneous conviction that it marked him as a native mouthpiece, not just as a foreign agent. His eloquence on the matter had none of the collateral safeguards of planned economic development as a Christian prerequisite. Crowther credited the Ibos with crucial theological advantage. One cannot help comparing him on this point to Olaudah Equiano, the Ibo ex-slave who was prominent in the antislavery movement in England. Crowther wrote about Chukwu thus:

> The Ibos are in their way a religious people, the word "Tshuku" [Chukwu] God, is continually heard. Tshuku is supposed to do everything. When a few bananas fell out of the hands of one into the water, he comforted himself by saying, "God has done it." Their notions of some of the attributes of the Supreme Being are in many respects correct and their manner of expressing them striking. "God made everything. He made both white and black," is continually on their lips.
>
> It is their common belief that there is a certain place or town where Tshuku dwells, and where he delivers his oracles and answers inquiries. Any matter of importance is left to his decision, and people travel to the place from every part of the country.
>
> I was informed today that last year Tshuku had given sentence against the slave trade. . . . They sincerely believe all these things, and many others respecting Tshuku, and obey his orders implicitly; and if it should be correct that he has said that they should give up the slave trade, I have no doubt that they will do it at once.[7]

Crowther regarded traditional Africa as ripe for antislavery, and, as such, for the Christian movement too. He believed that Chukwu should be drafted into the ranks of antislavery and antistructure, the advantages of deference to him diverted into modernized paths of emancipation and productive enterprise. Furthermore, Chukwu could

6. Cited in Schön and Crowther, *Journals*, p. 5.
7. Schön and Crowther, *Journals*, pp. 50-53.

be used to justify depersonalizing authority, bypassing the chiefs or traditional title-holders who made and executed laws, and shifting attention instead to local ideas of the values of life, liberty, and productive enterprise.

However, Crowther was no mere romantic, bowing to native custom and practice. His natural habit of stringent scrutiny of the evidence he never abandoned to nativistic pride, and so he plunged into remote hinterland districts, grateful for what he discovered of encouragement there, certainly, but resolved also to confront what he judged harmful. On the Niger he found evidence of both. Chukwu belonged to the encouraging side. On the negative side, Crowther once met a crowd shouting and crying as people made their way to the river, "dragging a poor young girl, tied hand and foot, with her face on the ground . . . for they believe in making a sacrifice for their sins by beating out the life of a fellow-creature in this manner. As she is drawn along, the crowd cry, 'Aro ye, Aro, Aro!' i.e., 'Wickedness, wickedness!' and believe that the iniquities of the people are thus atoned for."[8]

Thus, he reported that on a pastoral visit to Obitsi in the Niger Delta and after taking the service there, he received word from the chief of Atta inviting him for a visit,

> to which I consented to go. After the accustomed etiquette of offering the kola nuts and palm wine as marks of friendship and kind reception, the subject was broached, namely, their wish to be correctly informed whether what the Onitsha converts had told them in their preaching was correct, that, when any of their chiefs or persons of rank die, they should not keep the body for many days, during which time they keep up firing guns, drumming, and dancing until they obtain a slave for human sacrifice to be buried with the dead. The Christians never did such things, but quietly bury their dead as soon as possible. I confirmed the teaching of the converts as being quite correct.[9]

Crowther's moral commitment to antislavery, sharpened by the events of his own personal history, sprang nevertheless from much

8. Jesse Page, *Samuel Crowther: The Slave Boy Who Became Bishop of the Niger* (New York: Fleming H. Revell, 1889), p. 106. See also, the London edition: Jesse Page, *Samuel Crowther: The Slave Boy of the Niger* (London: Pickering and Inglis, n.d.), p. 126.

9. Page, *Samuel Crowther: The Slave Boy of the Niger,* pp. 181-82.

Fig. 18. King Ockiya of Brass in the Niger Delta, presenting ancestral
idols to Bishop Samuel Crowther, *c.* 1877 or 1878.

Church Mission Society, London

wider principles. Africans were no exception to the rule of righteousness, a rule opposed to any compromise with slavery and its supporting
chiefly and priestly structures. Crowther would not denounce or ap-
plaud indigenous institutions and native authorities merely for their being African. Rather, he demanded of them an unyielding, stringent com-
pliance with the credo that slavery "is a great abomination in the sight
of God." Pledging his total commitment to the cause, he wrote, "For
Zion's sake will I not hold my peace, and for Jerusalem's sake will I not
rest, until the righteousness thereof go forth as brightness, and the salvation thereof as a lamp that burneth."[10] He would not spare tainted
institutions and customs or exempt them from the purifying pains of
critical historical scrutiny.

10. Samuel Crowther, 30 September 1851, citing Isaiah 62:1, in a personal
inscription in *CMI*, 1850. Isaiah 62:2 goes on to speak about God's righteousness
being extended to the Gentiles and rulers, a thought that would have been very
much in Crowther's own mind.

Fig. 19. Sierra Leone mission party, Christmas 1902.
Church Mission Society, London

The importance of making advances on that front urgently, and preferably with indigenous cooperation, was crucial to Crowther, and it modified his views on civilization. Emmanuel Ayandele, the Nigerian historian, has entered a stern and understandable judgment on Crowther's attitude to African culture, saying that Crowther disdained African culture, attacked polygamy, paraded about in English clothes, and abetted the British colonial takeover of Nigeria.[11] That is a serious charge, even though it preserves an important dimension of the complex story of Crowther. The evidence supports that view, but also supports, one has to say, a much more lenient view than that. Ayandele himself agrees that such a view was not the whole story, nor, in the final analysis, was it the most lasting aspect of Crowther's legacy.

For example, Crowther chafed under the CMS policy of transferring leadership of the Niger Mission to European missionaries. Second, Crowther was not a crusader against polygamy. Thus in fifty years of

11. E. A. Ayandele, *The Missionary Impact on Modern Nigeria, 1842-1914: A Political and Social Analysis* (London: Longman, 1966), p. 206.

missionary work in the Niger Delta he presided at not a single monogamous marriage, yielding on this matter to indigenous exigencies.[12] Third and most significantly, Crowther's pioneer linguistic and translation work in African languages, in particular his recognized contribution to Yoruba as a national language, formulated terms that became a permanent frame of reference for the Christian movement in its non-Western phase. His own testimony in relation to this matter is worth recalling. He was describing his experience at a Christian religious service in Freetown in January 1844, where Yoruba was used as the language of liturgy, the first such use.

> A large number of Africans crowded thither to hear the words of prayer and praise for the first time in their own tongue in an English church. "Although it was my own native language," says the Revd S. Crowther, "with which I am well acquainted, yet on this occasion it appeared as if I were a babe, just learning to utter my mother-tongue. The work in which I was engaged, the place where I stood, and the congregation before me, were altogether so new and strange, that the whole proceeding seemed to myself like a dream. . . . At the conclusion of the blessing, the whole church rang with *ke oh sheh* — so be it, so let it be!"[13]

With his linguistic and ethnographic inquiries, Crowther formulated terms for Christianity as an African religion, with the use of Afri-

---

12. Venn instructed the missionaries in Nigeria that, although they may baptize a slave-holder and do the same for the wives of polygamists, such a sacrament must be refused to polygamous men on the grounds that "polygamy is an offence against the law of God, and therefore is incapable of amelioration." Cited in J. F. A. Ajayi, *Christian Missions in Nigeria, 1841-1891: The Making of a New Elite* (London: Longman, 1965), p. 107. This ruling, however, was far from settling the matter, as Venn hinted with his concession to polygamous wives. Thus, if a determined polygamous husband accepted to divorce all his wives but one in order to receive baptism, he would confront Venn with the awkward theological problem of remedying the offense of polygamy with the sin of divorce. Polygamy was for that reason a prickly pear that most missionaries opted to leave well alone.

13. Modupe Oduyoye, "The Planting of Christianity in Yorubaland: 1842-1888," in *Christianity in West Africa: The Nigerian Story,* ed. Ogbu Kalu (Ibadan: Daystar Press, 1978), pp. 251-52. A similar contemporary story is told of an elderly Tartar who was given the first translation of the Scriptures in his own language. He "fell on his knees . . . and with tears in his eyes thanked God for having vouchsafed to him at least once in his life to pray as he should." James J. Stamoolis, *Eastern Orthodox Mission Theology Today* (Maryknoll, N.Y.: Orbis Books, 1986), p. 26.

can languages in Scripture, prayer, worship, and study to promote it. The clear implication of all that was, at the minimum, to raise obstacles for continued foreign control. Even on that limited ground, Crowther was not, then, as *deraciné* and *outré* as it might first appear.

Liberal historiography has not been kind to Crowther or, for that matter, to the CMS, and consequently Crowther has come under attack for being only a mouthpiece of the CMS and English establishment ideas.[14] Moorhouse, for instance, says that Crowther's journal was actually "the diary of a fellow who has acquired opinions of his own and the confidence to pronounce them with some authority; basically they are echoes of attitudes which Crowther must have heard expressed many times in the CMS headquarters in London and elsewhere in his widening experience."[15] Moorhouse takes particular issue with Crowther's implicit faith in the alliance of mission and colonialism, saying that by this stage of his career, Crowther was becoming steadily "less the pure African and more the hybrid Afro-European in outlook."[16]

However, Crowther maintained the native perspective and looked at the question of African agency in those terms. In contrast, Lord John Russell and Governor Doherty, for example, were inclined to view West Indian blacks as a more hopeful bridge between Europe and Africa than an indigenous recaptive population. That attitude of Russell and Doherty implied that the alienation of Africans from their culture was the most desirable way of going about the civilizing mission. In their view recaptive Africans were at a disadvantage from their very limited exposure to European values.

Crowther dissented. Russell and others had argued that West Indian blacks, long uprooted from Africa, would be less likely to harbor any lingering nostalgia for African traditions and thus be less likely to lapse into Africa's unredeemed past. As such, they were more likely to provide the civilized, intermediary threshold that Africans could cross

14. Sir Richard Burton aspersed Crowther and his fellow recaptives in Freetown as "half-reclaimed barbarians in dishclouts [sic] and palm oil," saying, "No one is more hopeless about the civilisation of Africa than the semi-civilised African returning, to the 'home of his fathers.' " Burton, *Wanderings in West Africa from Liverpool to Fernando Po,* 2 vols. (London, 1863; reprint, New York: Dover Publications, 1991), vol. 1, pp. 210, 217. Burton dedicated the book to "The True Friends of Africa — Not to the 'Philanthropist' or to Exeter Hall."

15. Geoffrey Moorhouse, *The Missionaries* (London: Eyre Methuen, 1973), p. 102.

16. Moorhouse, *The Missionaries,* p. 102.

without stumbling. When the issue is expressed in those terms, they reveal the implicit thesis that African culture, prone to proliferate in its natural setting, was best kept in the background where a transplant European civilization could smother it without costly contest or resistance. Crowther had some opinions of his own on that civilized plan, and so I will turn to that now.

Crowther observed that the authorities had contended that West Indians would "in many respects be better qualified than the liberated Africans at Sierra Leone: they have seen more of European habits; are better acquainted with agricultural labors; and have a much greater taste for European comforts, if that be considered an acquisition." Yet, he said, he was not moved by the merits of the argument. He suggested that the very reasoning the officials used to commend the West Indians, the reasoning, that is to say, of their alleged proximity to European culture and, correspondingly, their alienation from African culture, was a weakness, not an advantage. The one salient requirement, he insisted, that the West Indian argument had not satisfied is the commitment to antislavery for which a black skin was no automatic qualification. In the case of the West Indians, he said, we should remember that some of them could, in theory, "carry a recollection of the [slave] driver's lashes with them; and many more [may harbor] a disposition to inflict them on others," and thus by their conduct oppose the cause of antislavery and antistructure.[17] For that reason, recaptive Africans represented the best hope, and the last chance, of securing the future of the cause in Africa. Their closeness to their people, their natural connections to the culture, and the fact that they had never been socialized in Europe or in European establishments, qualified them for their pivotal role as agents of social change.

The Niger Mission Redefined

The CMS was impressed enough with Crowther's achievement in the otherwise disastrous 1841 expedition to decide to resume further exploration with his help and leadership. Crowther was the ideal "new man" in the new transitional order, deeply enough grounded in the old Africa to be in tune with its authentic values and yet sufficiently molded by the new forces to be a credible and effective guide. Accord-

17. Schön and Crowther, *Journals,* pp. 62-63.

ingly, he and Townsend were ordained the same year in London in 1843, and together they entered Abeokuta in 1846, Townsend based at Ake and Crowther at Igbein. Success soon followed the establishment of the mission in Abeokuta, and in 1848 the first baptisms were performed. In pursuit of the plan to promote Christianity and antislavery in hinterland Africa, Crowther encountered more militant alternatives to his gradualist policy. There was, first, the policy of those who may be called cultural prescriptivists who believed that a ready-made, one-size-fits-all imported template should be imposed on Africans, if need be at the unobtrusive hands of civilized West Indians. Another was the evangelical pietism which, with its "gnostic," individualist tendencies, eschewed having any truck with worldly arrangements, including indigenous cultures, and trusted instead in the preaching of the word to effect the wholesome moral and social transformation necessary for salvation.

The answer Crowther gave to the cultural prescriptivists, the answer, that is, of the need for receptivity to African culture, was similar to the answer he gave to evangelical pietism. Christianity, he said, did not come into the world to undertake to destroy national cultures. Even where it sought to correct false and oppressive ideas and structures, Christianity must still do so "with due caution and with all meekness of wisdom."[18] The system of mutual aid that might be found in African society should not be condemned or despised but appreciated for the example it offered Christians entering the culture for the first time. Even those aspects of traditional culture that might strike the foreigner as puerile amusements that excluded the ideas of the spiritual and eternal, such amusements as stories, fables, proverbs, and songs, said Crowther, were actually a storehouse of knowledge and original thinking.

Similarly, local religious terms and ceremonies should be carefully observed, because even where such things were improperly made use of, that "does not depreciate their real value, but renders them more valid when we adopt them in expressing Scriptural terms in their right senses and places from which they have been misapplied for want of better knowledge."[19] Although Crowther did not develop an African Christology, his theological method, based on the new anthropology of indigenous languages, local religions, and social custom, grasped the sources required for such a Christology.

18. Cited in Ajayi, *Christian Missions*, p. 224.
19. Cited in Ajayi, *Christian Missions*, p. 224.

The political implications of this policy of indigenous appropriation were obvious to Crowther's critics. Not only had he abandoned pure evangelical doctrine (one critic said he followed Crowther around closely to find when he preached that he made no mention of sin and the atoning sacrifice of Christ), but he was now contending that African culture, shorn of its political caste distinctions, must set the terms for Christianity. At the time Crowther made this address in 1869 at Lokoja as a public charge to the clergy under his episcopal jurisdiction, he was under a Townsend-inspired investigation from the CMS for compromising its missionary warrants. It shows how much Crowther's thinking was modeled on his African experience.

At this point Crowther paused to reflect on the methods and goals of the wider antislavery enterprise in which he was engaged. He said he and his agents must act

> as rough quarry men do who hew out blocks of marbles from the quarries, which are conveyed to the workshop to be shaped and finished into perfect figures by the hands of the skilful artists. In like manner, native teachers can do, having the facility of the language in their favour, to induce their heathen countrymen to come within reach of the means of Grace and hear the word of God. What is lacking in good training and sound Evangelical teaching [would be supplied by others more qualified].[20]

Crowther pursued this idea of conciliation and gradualism with wisdom and sensitivity. He was being dragged through a process of ecclesiastical inquiry, in fact through a humiliating public censure, which was nearing its end. What was at stake was the viability of Christianity's historic alliance with antislavery and their combined effect in Africa. Crowther had been accused by the Parent Committee of the CMS in London for not taking tough, punitive sanctions against those of his African assistants who had been charged with offenses. Where discipline was called for, Crowther offered solicitude. Crowther responded that he preferred trying first admonition, private counseling, temporary suspension, reprimand, and relocation before resorting to final expulsion.

Appearing in London before the Parent Committee to defend himself on 8 October 1889, Crowther repeated his general view with the aid of an arresting figure. He said a freshly made fire was bound to

20. Cited in Ajayi, *Christian Missions*, p. 97.

make a lot of smoke at first, but that if the cook at that early stage decided to search out and pull out all the logs that smoked, the food would never be cooked. Instead, an experienced cook would look for a fan to blow the fire and wait patiently. He continued: "We are all weak and imperfect agents, faulty in one way or another, which need be strengthened, supported, reproved and corrected, when not beyond amendment."[21] Those sentiments would be used against him as proof of indecisiveness and weak leadership.

The Native Pastorate and Its Nemesis

In any case, in 1851 Henry Venn at the CMS had decided to push ahead with the Africanization of the clergy to create a native pastorate. Venn instructed that two more Africans be ordained in Abeokuta as soon as the bishop arrived there from Sierra Leone. The two Africans were T. B. Macaulay, trained, like Townsend himself, at the Islington institution, and Thomas King. Townsend opposed this native policy, saying Africans lacked the stability of character to become anything except schoolmasters and catechists. Townsend reacted with indignation to the news that the CMS was proposing to elevate Abeokuta into an episcopal see and to appoint Crowther to it. Townsend drafted a petition to oppose it, obtaining signatories for the purpose. The petition argued that even if Crowther were fit and qualified, his being black tainted him: he would never have the respect and influence worthy of his high office. Native teachers had been received and respected by the chiefs and ordinary people, but the ordained office belonged only to the white man. The natives accepted Crowther as a priest only by treating him "as the white man's inferior. . . . This state of things is not the result of the white men's teaching but has existed for ages past. The superiority of the white over the black man, the Negro has been forward to acknowledge. The correctness of this belief no white man can deny," Townsend concluded triumphantly.[22]

Townsend then attacked the new conception of society in which a recaptive African like Crowther would emerge as leader. He said as long as Africa remained what it had always been, no native without a traditional title, rank, or pedigree could command respect and accep-

21. Cited in Ajayi, *Christian Missions*, p. 97.
22. Cited in Ajayi, *Christian Missions*, p. 181.

tance outside the protective custody of the mission stations, except, that is, as subordinate agents and servants of the white man. He said there was such endemic jealousy in the culture, such tribal malice and ethnic intolerance, that Crowther's ethnicity would be called into question and destroy all credibility for his leadership — an implied repudiation of the alliance of Christianity and antislavery. In any case, Townsend decided the lottery was worth a jackpot, and so he bargained his theological stock. "There is one other view," he said, "that we must not lose sight of, viz., that as the Negro feels a great respect for a white man, that God kindly gives a great talent to the white in trust to be used for the Negro's good. Shall we shift the responsibility? Can we do it without sin?"[23]

Venn sinned and had Macaulay and King ordained in 1854, to be followed in 1857 with three more ordinations. In Sierra Leone he went ahead with instituting the native pastorate and giving it control of the churches in the colony. The work was expanding, more qualified hands were needed and available, and so they were appointed. Townsend disapproved, in inflammatory language. The Parent Committee of the CMS felt compelled to admonish Townsend that the tone and manner of his letters were unworthy of his vocation. Townsend's only advantage, and a critical one at that, was his racial views being shared by all the white missionaries at the time, as the CMS found out when it asked directly which of them would be willing to serve under Crowther. It was a disconcerting discovery.

We may ask, had the CMS done right by Townsend? In answer, we may say that much could, in fact, be said in mitigation of him in recognition of his being the real architect of the Yoruba mission. He was compiler of the first hymn book in Yoruba, founder of a fortnightly Yoruba publication, and publisher of the Yoruba version of the Book of Common Prayer. Thus as the driving force of the Abeokuta mission[24] he was entitled at least to a share of the responsibility for directing CMS work in Nigeria. Venn's policy of native agency, Townsend would be right to feel, unjustly deprived him of the power to which in other circumstances he would have acceded quite naturally. But Townsend wanted all or nothing. That troubled Venn, and accordingly he wrote commending Crowther for keeping the peace, promoting harmony and

23. Cited in Ajayi, *Christian Missions*, p. 182.
24. Church Missionary Society, *Register of Missionaries (Clerical, Lay, and Female) and Native Clergy: From 1804 to 1904* (London: CMS, n.d.), pp. 41-42.

reconciliation, and showing real wisdom and humility amidst all the bickering, ugliness of spirit, and struggle for power.[25]

The recaptive population of Abeokuta, which included a significant and prosperous number of Muslim recaptives, was increasing in size and wealth at this time, and showing signs of independence. They could use their new-found social influence and economic power to challenge foreign control. The example of Captain Harry Johnson, a recaptive, still remembered for sponsoring Townsend's first visit to Abeokuta, showed recaptives in command of events. Townsend acted to forestall a likely recaptive bid for white acknowledgment. Accordingly, he decided to attack Crowther's flanks by taking on the recaptives. It led to open conflict, with the younger members of Crowther's own family drawn into the fray. The city of peace Abeokuta was not to be.

Crowther: Influence Without Power

Perhaps without realizing the full political implications for mission of the British annexation of Lagos, or what separatist twist that would give to Townsend's ambitions, Venn authorized the consecration of Crowther as bishop in June 1864, based in Lagos. Yet, bishop of what? That was never made clear, perhaps because the CMS was torn between the pressure of the traders and its own missionary concerns. Townsend remained unmoved in his opposition to Crowther's consecration. In January 1864, Townsend said the impending plans to consecrate Crowther were misguided and potentially divisive, an opinion expressed in a way calculated to carry a whiff of threat. He said so to Venn, too, even after the fact. Crowther, Townsend said with one part of his mouth, was too partisan and obnoxious, too deeply marked with the captive's chain, to be esteemed with respect in native society or to be acceptable to the chiefs and people. But, with the other part of his mouth, Townsend said he was unwilling to place himself under the episcopal rule of Crowther because Crowther "is too much a native."[26] Townsend suggested instead that they appoint a white missionary or a colonial bishop with jurisdiction over white religious personnel, in other words the containment of Crowther in hinterland native reservations.

25. Cited in Ajayi, *Christian Missions*, p. 183.
26. Ajayi, *Christian Missions*, p. 195.

Venn rejected that as totally unacceptable to the British government or to CMS's own recaptive policy.

Crowther's episcopacy, otherwise so pivotal to Christianity as an African movement, was compromised by the kind of ideological opposition Townsend mounted and by the halfhearted definition the CMS gave to the diocesan boundaries in question. In one regard and as Townsend intended, the CMS ruled that Crowther would not have jurisdiction over Abeokuta, Ibadan, or Lagos, the areas with white missionary concentration. Instead his diocese would include stations of the Yoruba mission outside the European sphere. This anomalous arrangement was made even more so with Crowther being headquartered in Lagos.

Under no circumstances was Townsend prepared to accept African leadership in church and mission. The importance of this view became clear when the missionaries insisted that Crowther could not be trusted to run a "purely native mission." As one white agent declared, "I feel more and more convinced that it will have to be a mixed Mission and that Europeans must lead if there is to be any genuine substantial Christianity in the Niger."[27]

The Debacle

The excuse to act on that policy presented itself after Crowther obtained possession of a steamer named the *Henry Venn*, donated by his admirers in England. Crowther decided to place the ship in the hands of an African merchant, with the idea of trading on the Niger and contributing its profits to mission work. However, the new secretary of the CMS, T. J. Hutchinson, reversed Crowther on the matter and gave control of the ship to J. H. Ashcroft, a layman, and one James Kirk. Hutchinson went further by asking Ashcroft and Kirk to assume authority for all the African agents of the Niger Mission, in effect demoting Bishop Crowther without his knowledge or consent.

In 1879 Hutchinson appointed a finance committee to take over the administrative affairs of the Niger Mission, followed in 1880 with the appointment of a Commission of Inquiry into the conduct of the mission. The commission, set up under J. B. Wood, was a response to complaints by European traders that Crowther's African assistants

27. J. H. Ashcroft in Ayandele, *The Missionary Impact*, p. 208.

were venturing out into commercial work and neglecting the spiritual concerns of their work. It did not take long for Wood to produce his report. It was a hatchet job, highly damaging to Crowther and the mission, and libelous to the extent that it was secreted out to London without Crowther or any of his assistants seeing it. Wood requested that Crowther not ever see it. Crowther learnt of the contents of the report only when acrid puffs of it drifted back to Nigeria, wafted there by Lagos-based traders and visitors keen to be rid of the religious nuisance Crowther was deemed to be.

Partly in belated response to the Wood Report, a commission sat in Bonny in August 1890, to take action. Twelve of the fifteen Africans in the Niger Mission were summarily dismissed at the commission's hearings, largely at the sole direction of its secretary, Revd F. N. Eden. It was all Crowther could do to contain himself as he witnessed his principal men being taken down over his head. For the sake of the record, he challenged the secretary of the commission to say whether he "alone is empowered to dismiss and suspend and do everything in the Mission. . . . Will you write down, say, please, Bishop Crowther expresses surprise at the statement of the Secretary that he has power as the representative of the CMS to suspend any clergyman from his duty. . . ."[28] Eden responded by reprimanding Crowther for defending the censured pastors, charging him with conduct unworthy of his sacred office. Crowther was dismissed from the commission. He died on 31 December 1891.

Reaction and Resistance

During the years of turmoil, beginning with the Commission of Inquiry set up in 1880, and continuing to 1891, Africans had watched with dismay as the CMS, pressured by the Lagos traders, allowed the props to be pulled from underneath the Niger Mission. However, the Niger Mission episode illuminates a deeper antislavery logic than being merely cannon fodder for patriotic struggle. Andrew Walls describes the historical background:

> European thought about Africa had changed . . . the Western powers were now in Africa to govern. Missionary thought about Africa had

28. Cited in Ajayi, *Christian Missions*, p. 253.

changed since the days of Henry Venn; there were plenty of keen, young Englishmen to extend the mission and order the church; a self-governing church had now seemed to matter much less. And evangelical religion had changed since Crowther's conversion; it had become more individualistic and more otherworldly. A young English missionary was distressed that the old bishop who preached so splendidly on the blood of Christ could urge on a chief the advantages of having a school and make no reference to the future life.[29]

It is the theme of Crowther as a recaptive leading the Christian movement among Africans that the Niger Mission existed to promote but in the end threatened to subvert.

When the reaction came to Crowther's demise, the Nigerian Baptists led the way. The path was cleared for them by the temporary withdrawal of Southern Baptist missionaries during the American Civil War, so that by the time the missionaries were able to resume work in the 1870s, local Baptists had assumed control of the mission. Although there was at that stage no breakaway movement among the Baptists, the stage was ready for one, lacking only a *casus belli*. That was supplied when African leaders in the Baptist church saw the provocative way in which Crowther was being brought down by white agents like Townsend, Ashcroft, Wood, Kirk, and others, with Hutchinson authorizing the attack. The local Baptists, reacting to this experience, decided in March 1888 to splinter off as the Native Baptist Church, taking with them all the great African pioneers of Baptist work in Nigeria. The Baptist secession had "ushered in a new era of Christianity among the Yoruba. A spell had been broken"[30] and the example could, therefore, spread with cumulative effect.

Within Anglicanism, the Africans' response eventually led in 1892 to the establishment of an independent Niger Delta Pastorate (NDP), staffing it themselves, and launching a major fundraising drive to underwrite it. Five of those dismissed by Eden joined it as leaders, thus keeping alive the flame Venn lit with his plan for native Christian leadership, not for rehabilitating chiefly structures.

29. Andrew F. Walls, "The Legacy of Samuel Ajayi Crowther," *International Bulletin of Missionary Research* 16, no. 1 (January 1992), pp. 19-20.

30. James Bertin Webster, *The African Churches among the Yoruba: 1888-1922* (Oxford: Clarendon Press, 1964), pp. 56, 61.

Appraisal and Conclusion

By forging a successful, pivotal alliance with antislavery, evangelical religion imbued slaves and other social victims with the powerful idea of
the nobility of human personhood.[31] Yet evangelical religion was less
successful in securing the commitment of traders, as the conflict between Lagos and Abeokuta showed. The motive spring of this evangelical idealism was described by William Wilberforce. Writing in 1797 he
expressed it forcefully thus:

> Is Christianity then reduced to a mere creed? Is its practical influence
> bounded within a few external plausibilities? Does its essence consist
> only in a few speculative opinions, and a few useless and unprofitable
> tenets? And can this be the ground of that portentous distinction,
> which is so unequivocally made by the evangelist between those who
> accept and those who reject the Gospel: He that believeth on the Son
> hath everlasting life: and he that believeth not the Son shall not see
> life; but the wrath of God abideth on him?

31. It can be argued that the critical alliance between Puritan doctrine and
the new politics of Elizabethan England has its counterpart in a corresponding alliance between evangelical doctrine and the social activism of antislavery. Accordingly, Michael Walzer's description of Puritan political radicalism echoes many of
the features of the religion of the community of ex-slaves and ex-captives in
Freetown and elsewhere. He writes: "Their 'plain speaking' and matter-of-fact
style; their insistence upon education and independent judgment; their voluntary
association outside the corporate church; their emphasis upon methodical, purpos-
ive endeavor; their narrow [emancipated] sense of order and discipline — all this
clearly suggested a life-style very different from that of a feudal lord, a Renaissance
courtier or even an Anglican archbishop. This new style was first developed and
tested on the margins and in the interstices of English society by men cut off from
the traditional world, angry and isolated clerics, anxiously seeking, a new order. It
was by no means the entirely spontaneous creation of these sturdy London merchants and country gentlemen who later became its devoted advocates; it was something they learned. . . . The automatic burgher values — sobriety, caution, thrift —
did not constitute the significant core of Puritan morality in the seventeenth century; the clerical intellectuals had added moral activism, the ascetic style, and the
quality of high-mindedness and taught these to their followers. In politics, too, the
'advanced' intellectuals, committed representatives of a Cause, developed a new
style [of organization] and taught it to those who came after." Michael Walzer, *The
Revolution of the Saints* (Cambridge, Mass.: Harvard University Press, 1965), pp.
124-25. This description has echoes in the religious and moral life of Freetown and
Abeokuta as antislavery settlements.

Wilberforce went on to assert that the "morality of the Gospel is not so slight a fabric," that Christianity's practical precepts were no less pure than its doctrines were sublime, that Christianity called for reliance on the promises of God and for vigilant, unrelenting struggle against the works of sin, and that such an activist solidarity with the downtrodden and dispossessed in the name of God was, he insisted, universal and uncompromising.[32] The practical life, committed to good news to the poor, release of the captives, and liberty for the oppressed (Luke 4:18f.), was the prerequisite of evangelical activism rather than abstract speculation about doctrine. Nor, for that matter, should evangelicals defer to establishment prerogatives to advance the cause.[33]

In spite of setback and contradiction, then, Crowther's leadership was crucial for the continuity of CMS's evangelical heritage as it was for the redefinition of the Niger Mission. A new world order came into being in Africa, not, as Lord Rosebery asserted, with military might but with belief in the power of redeemed and sanctified persons, who as slaves, captives, and other downtrodden members of society, male and female, the chiefly structures exploited and repressed, and yet whose freedom, dignity, and enterprise evangelical religion championed as its own. And so it happened that the small trickle started in 1837 by two Hausa ex-slaves, rising in Trinidad and spreading to Freetown and finally to Badagry, grew into the checkered movement that opened up Nigeria to antislavery and to the emergence of a resurgent class of recaptives. A major change thus came to transpire in Nigeria on account of it. Ajayi reflects on this deeper historical logic and argues that the importance of the recaptive emigrants in Nigerian history was out

32. William Wilberforce, *A Practical View of the Prevailing Religious System of Professed Christians in the Higher and Middle Classes in This Country Contrasted with Real Christianity* (London: SCM Press, 1958), pp. 57ff. Wilberforce wrote this work as his religious manifesto in 1797 when he was thirty-seven. The work was an instant bestseller on both sides of the Atlantic. By popular demand it was translated into German, Italian, Spanish, and Dutch.

33. The evangelical movement in England was a factor that helped liberalize religious laws, one consequence of seeking to free the church of state control. Thus in 1797 Wilberforce supported opening the militia to Catholics after an Act of 1793 limited their admission to the army to a rank below that of colonel. In 1812 and 1813 Wilberforce again supported the admission of Catholics to Parliament, a very un-Tory thing to do. However, the coming of Catholic emancipation with the Irish question complicated Wilberforce's logic of tolerance. Élie Halévy, *A History of the English People in the Nineteenth Century*, vol. 1, *England in 1815* (London: Ernest Benn; New York: Barnes & Noble, 1961), pp. 476-85.

of all proportion to their number. The missionary movement they led kept them a cohesive, self-motivated group and focused them on a few strategic centers. Had they been scattered, each left to pursue his or her own personal interest and inclination, their impact would have been diluted and their legacy weakened. As it was, traders, catechists, evangelists, and schoolmasters found themselves bound together by the same purpose and goal and united in the same enterprise. It was they who brought the cause to Nigeria, and they who remained indispensable to its future success.[34] With the encouragement and support of Britain and the CMS behind them, this recaptive achievement turned a significant corner for antislavery and antistructure in Africa.

34. Ajayi, *Christian Missions*, pp. 51-52.

8. Culture and Ecclesiology: The Church Missionary Society and New Zealand

ALLAN K. DAVIDSON

In 1992, ninety years after the Church Missionary Society withdrew from New Zealand, the Anglican Church in Aotearoa, New Zealand, and Polynesia approved a constitution to replace the one drawn up in 1857.[1] Central to the revised constitution was the tikanga structure that recognized the autonomy of three distinctive streams: Tikanga Maori — Te Pihopatanga o Aotearoa; Tikanga Pakeha — dioceses in New Zealand; Tikanga Pasefika — the diocese of Polynesia.[2] These three groupings consisted of: Maori, the indigenous people of Aotearoa; Pakeha, those of European and other descent; Polynesia, particularly people from Fiji, Tonga, and Samoa. In 1997 there were five Maori episcopal regions, seven Pakeha dioceses, and one Polynesian diocese.

The ethnic and cultural identity of the tikanga reflected their distinctive yet interweaving historical relationships. This emphasis on ethnic diversity and at the same time commitment to partnership expressed in the unity of the church of Jesus Christ as one, holy, catholic, and apostolic and acceptance of a common mission statement was a response from the church within its context. The Anglican tradition, expressed in the fundamental provisions of the constitution, appropriated by differ-

1. Aotearoa is the commonly accepted Maori name for New Zealand.
2. "Tikanga" means "stream" or "cultural way."

198

ent cultural groups and influenced by the particularities of time and place, was given new ecclesiastical expression through the 1992 constitution. In many ways this was a long-overdue response to unresolved issues that had their origin in the nineteenth century.[3] This chapter surveys those historical developments and in particular the contribution of the Church Missionary Society to the shaping of the church in New Zealand.

A Prologue — Building the Church — Rangiatea

In New Zealand there are many wooden church buildings dating from last century. When people came to erect places of worship they often used the cheapest materials closest to hand. These buildings have distinctive characteristics that clearly mark them as churches: bell towers, lancet windows, steep roofs, porches, vestries, and crosses. Some of the buildings have considerable architectural merit and are now considered treasures that need to be preserved as part of New Zealand's heritage. Although they reproduced many of the distinctive features familiar to the missionaries and settlers who came from England in the nineteenth century, there was a considerable contrast between the stone churches of "home" and the wooden churches of the new world. They represented both the continuity and discontinuity of tradition and context.

That continuity with the church building tradition of England and the discontinuity in the use of new materials and cultural adaptations was seen most clearly in some of the churches built by Maori communities. The most famous was Rangiatea, erected near the CMS station at Otaki between 1848 and 1851. Apart from the encouragement of the CMS missionaries, Octavius Hadfield and Samuel Williams, the erection of the church was undertaken by local Maori. The great Ngati Toa warrior chief, Te Rauparaha, who was never baptized, gave his "mana," or prestige, to the building of the church.

Giant totara trees were secured from the forest for the huge ridge pole, some seventy-two feet long, and three massive pillars, more than thirty-six feet tall. Soil from the island of Rai'atea, believed to be the homeland of Maori ancestors, several thousand miles away in the Pacific, was placed under the altar. The interior of the church was deco-

---

3. *Proceedings of the Special Session of General Synod (PGS)* (1990), S.12-26a; *PGS* (1992), p. 22.

rated with large panels of traditional Maori weaving or tukutuku using the purapura whetu (star-dust)' design said to have been chosen by Te Rauparaha to signify his hope that the followers of Christianity would soon be as numerous as "the stars in the heavens." The rafters were embellished with the painted design or kowhaiwhai of the "hammerhead shark pattern . . . [denoting] great power and prestige." An elaborate altar rail was carved by men from different tribes.[4] From the outside the church was quite plain, but inside, the Maori embellishments blended with the English influence to create a unique bicultural building. While it was built by Maori, "it was intended that the church should serve both" Maori and Pakeha.[5]

An illustration of Rangiatea in the *Church Missionary Intelligencer* in 1854 (see p. 202) showed a Maori congregation gathered around the pulpit listening to Hadfield preach. The artist captured the grandeur of the building with its three massive pillars and Maori painted designs and weaving.[6] The accompanying article asked the question: at what point and how should a missionary society withdraw from a country where its operation had seemingly been successful? New Zealand was seen as a success story with the rapid extension of Christianity:

> The Maori race, abandoning its ancient heathenism, has assumed a profession of Protestant Christianity. Great changes have been accomplished. National vices are repressed — in some cases extirpated. Cannibalism is extinct: the war spirit wonderfully softened down. Christian ordinances are generalized over the island. The conclusion seems evident: having fulfilled its work, the Society's Mission has terminated.[7]

Using the experience of missionaries in Hawaii, it was argued that the New Zealand Mission needed to be strengthened in two areas: the education of Maori and the development of a native pastorate.[8] The author advocated the use of the Maori language that "for another generation, will continue to be the language of the heart" and pointed out that "Maori Christianity can never become aught else than a servile, creep-

---

4. Sharon Dell, "Rangiatea," in *Historic Buildings of New Zealand: North Island,* ed. Francis Porter (Auckland: Methuen, 1983), p. 255.

5. Eric Ramsden, *Rangiatea: The Story of the Otaki Church, Its First Pastor, and Its People* (Wellington: A. H. & A. W. Reed, 1951), p. 146.

6. *CMI* (Dec. 1854), p. 267.

7. *CMI* (Dec. 1854), p. 269.

8. *CMI* (Dec. 1854), p. 279.

Figs. 20 and 21. *Above,* Interior of Maori house;
below, exterior of Maori house (no date).
Church Mission Society, London

ing plant, if prevented from developing itself in the vigorous and health-
ful action of Christian ministrations."[9] This optimistic article represented a high point in the assessment of the success of Christianity in
New Zealand. While aware of defects, the author concluded that "the

9. *CMI* (Dec. 1854), p. 282.

Fig. 22. The interior of Rangiatea church,
Otaki (engraving 1854).
Church Mission Society, London

time undoubtedly has arrived for the Church Missionary Society to prepare for its eventual removal from New Zealand."[10]

In 1854 the CMS had been active in New Zealand for forty years.
It was to be another forty-eight years before the CMS officially withdrew in 1902. While the church at Otaki, Rangiatea, symbolized the
blending of English and Maori styles of building, together with the adaptation from English materials to those available in New Zealand, the
church in New Zealand as an institution was very much an English
transplant. The failure of the CMS and the Anglican Church fully to de-

10. *CMI* (Dec. 1854), p. 283.

Fig. 23. Maori church, Turanga, New Zealand, 1851.
Church Mission Society, London

velop and encourage indigenous patterns of leadership and organization left unresolved tensions that the church in the late twentieth century was still seeking to address.

The Early Ecclesiology of the CMS

Being part of the Church of England was important to the founders of
The Society for Missions to Africa and the East. John Venn suggested in
1799 that it "ought to be founded upon the *Church principle,* not the
high-Church principle."[11] In Hennell's view, Venn meant that "The new
society was to be controlled by its own committee, not by bishops."[12]
Anglican evangelicals, as "members of the Established Church," were
committed to working within the Church of England at a time when

11. J. H. Pratt, ed., *The Thought of the Evangelical Leaders* (Edinburgh: Banner of Truth Trust, 1978), p. 97.
12. Michael Hennell, *John Venn and the Clapham Sect* (London: Lutterworth, 1958), p. 233; Stock, vol. 1, pp. 65-67.

they were considered theologically suspect. The popular title, "Church Missionary Society," used officially from 1812, distinguished the "Church" society from other Protestant missionary organizations. Anticipating the difficulty of recruiting clergy as missionaries, Venn suggested that they should send lay catechists: "If it be objected that this is contrary to the strict rules of the Establishment, I reply, that I would do a great deal to keep up the Establishment, but not sacrifice the good of souls." Catechists would "instruct the people" and "gather a Church together," and clergy would be provided later.[13]

Early CMS ecclesiology was shaped by missionary pragmatism and activism as well as establishment loyalty. Lay leadership and the society's voluntary organization reflected evangelical principles. The evangelical ecclesiology underlying this was not clearly articulated. The Evangelical Eclectic Society, for example, during its 260 meetings between 1798 and 1814, was concerned with practical issues and "not once did they discuss the nature of the church."[14]

Activism and pragmatism were clearly seen in Claudius Buchanan's promotion of the English ecclesiastical establishment and missionary cause in India. Buchanan served in India, 1797-1808, as one of the notable evangelical military chaplains. His *Memoir of the Expediency of an Ecclesiastical Establishment for British India; Both as the Means of Perpetuating the Christian Religion Among Our Own Countrymen; and as a Foundation for the Ultimate Civilization of the Natives,* published in 1805, promoted the integration of colonial and missionary episcopacy thirty-five years before this became a popular cause.[15] Buchanan was a major contributor to the evangelical and missionary lobby in the 1813 East India Company charter debate that resulted in the appointment of a bishop and three archdeacons and a clause lifting restrictions on missionary efforts in India.[16] For Buchanan the English

13. Pratt, *The Thought of the Evangelical Leaders,* p. 97.

14. Robert Glen, "Those Odious Evangelicals: The Origin and Background of the CMS Missionaries in New Zealand," in *Mission and Moko: Aspects of the Work of the Church Missionary Society in New Zealand, 1814-1882,* ed. Robert Glen (Christchurch: Latimer Fellowship, 1992), p. 23.

15. Buchanan, *Memoir* (London: Cadell & Davies, 1805), is reproduced in Allan K. Davidson, *Evangelicals & Attitudes to India, 1786-1813: Missionary Publicity and Claudius Buchanan* (Appleford: Sutton Courtenay Press, 1990). See also Claudius Buchanan, *Christian Researches in Asia . . . ,* 5th ed. (London: Cadell & Davies, 1812), pp. 270-90.

16. Davidson, *Evangelicals & Attitudes to India,* pp. 229-61. Claudius Bu-

ecclesia was to be transplanted to serve both colonial and missionary ends.

Missionary activity was largely a new thing and viewed suspiciously by most church leaders. Missionary methodology was in a pioneering phase. Given the initial difficulties in recruiting English missionaries, the first CMS missionaries were seven German Lutherans who went to West Africa. New Zealand was chosen as its second mission field due to the advocacy of Samuel Marsden, the evangelical chaplain in New South Wales.

CMS Beginnings in New Zealand, 1814-1824

Marsden judged Maori "to be a very superior people in point of mental capacity," but believed "nothing . . . can pave the way for the introduction of the gospel, but civilization." In 1807 he proposed that the CMS appoint "three mechanics," because "to preach the gospel without the aid of the Arts will never succeed amongst the heathen."[17] The first English CMS missionaries, William Hall and John King, were designated for New Zealand in 1809, and Thomas Kendall followed in 1813.

Ruatara, a Maori chief, whom Marsden befriended, provided a significant point of contact. Marsden held his first service in Ruatara's tribal area and the CMS established their base there in 1814. Marsden reported:

> I saw the English flag flying, which was a pleasing sight in New Zealand. I considered it as the signal and the dawn of civilization, liberty, and religion, in that dark and benighted land. I never viewed the British Colours with more gratification; and flattered myself they would never be removed, till the Natives of that island enjoyed all the happiness of British Subjects. . . . it being Christmas Day, I preached from the Second Chapter of St. Luke's Gospel, and tenth verse — *Behold! I bring you tidings of great joy, &c.*[18]

---

chanan, *Colonial Ecclesiastical Establishment* . . . , 2d ed. (London: Cadell & Davies, 1813).

17. Allan K. Davidson and Peter J. Lineham, *Transplanted Christianity: Documents Illustrating Aspects of New Zealand Church History,* 3d ed. (Palmerston North: History Department, Massey University, 1993), p. 27.

18. *Missionary Register* (Nov. 1816), p. 471.

Marsden brought together his Christian commitment and English identity. Gospel and culture were inextricably intertwined from the beginning of CMS involvement in New Zealand. Although Maori could not understand Marsden's sermon, Ruatara translated, indicating that "they would understand by and bye; and that he would explain my meaning as far as he could." The gospel was being shaped by two cultures, that of the preacher and the translator.[19]

Church structures were of little importance to the first missionaries. Their priorities were learning the Maori language and surviving in an alien, sometimes hostile environment. Marsden was an occasional visitor, living at Parramatta in New South Wales, some 1,250 miles away.[20] He was not a CMS missionary, but acted on behalf of the society. The missionaries faced isolation, difficulties with communication, interpersonal strife, and Maori disinterest in their message. They were largely dependent on local Maori for protection, land, food, and travel. John Butler, a deacon, the first resident clergyman, arrived as superintendent in 1819. His presence created tension, leading Kendall to go to England in 1820, without permission, where he was ordained deacon and priest. Kendall returned to New Zealand in 1821 and was dismissed by Marsden for musket trading and adultery in 1823. Butler was suspended for "improper conduct" and left in 1823 after Marsden informed him that "he could not officiate as a clergyman in these settlements under his present disgrace."[21]

Marsden supervised the mission through its difficult first ten years. Few signs of missionary success were evident, but relations were established with Maori and progress made in understanding and writing their language. Henry Williams, who had been ordained a priest in 1822 "for the cure of souls in his majesty's foreign possession," even although New Zealand was not a British territory, arrived in 1823 and took over the leadership of the mission.[22]

---

19. *Missionary Register* (Nov. 1816), p. 471.

20. Marsden made seven visits: 1814-15, 1819, 1820, 1823, 1827, 1830, 1837.

21. John Rawson Elder, *The Letters and Journals of Samuel Marsden* (Dunedin: Coulls Somerville Wilkie, 1932), pp. 412, 413.

22. Robin Fisher, "Henry Williams," in *Dictionary of New Zealand Biography*, ed. W. H. Oliver (Wellington: Allen & Unwin, 1990), vol. 1, p. 593.

Te Hahi Mihinare — The Missionary Church, 1825-40 •

Williams, a former naval officer, gave firm direction, forbidding trade and emphasizing evangelization in place of Marsden's civilizing concern. The mission worked in the 1820s amidst internecine tribal warfare exacerbated by access to muskets. Under Williams the mission became more independent of Maori patronage, with its own transport and food supplies. Isolation and distance from England gave the mission considerable practical autonomy. Between 1814 and 1840, forty men were employed, in many cases assisted by their wives and families. Only eight were ordained, pointing to the heavy reliance on lay "assistant industrial agents" or "catechists."[23] Evangelism was emphasized rather than priestly or even pastoral ministry.

The remarkable growth of the Maori church dates from the baptism of Christian Rangi in 1825. By 1842 more than three thousand Maori had been baptized in the area where the mission commenced.[24] George Clarke estimated in 1845 "that out of a total Maori population of 110,000 about 43,000 attended Anglican services regularly, 16,000 attended Methodist services, and 5,100 were associated with the Catholic mission."[25] Historians have debated the reasons for this sudden interest in Christianity.[26] Among the most significant factors were the response of Maori to literacy seen in the translation of the Prayer Book and Bible, the way in which Maori themselves became evangelists, and the expansion of the mission to new areas.

The emerging church was called Te Hahi Mihinare, the missionary church. While the prayers, hymns, sermons, and the Bible were heard in Maori, the forms were shaped by Anglican and evangelical influences. Conversion was dynamic and complex. Maori were recipients and active participants, imitating the missionaries and taking over their message. In 1833 Williams went as the first European to a village and commencing the evening service was surprised "when we heard our whole congregation join, and correctly sing with us; and in the prayers also

23. CMS, *Register of Missionaries . . . from 1804 to 1904* (London: CMS, n.d.), no. 90; Glen, ed., *Mission and Moko*, pp. 194-212.

24. Fisher, "Henry Williams," p. 593.

25. Davidson and Lineham, *Transplanted Christianity*, p. 46. For other population estimates see note 59 below.

26. For bibliographical references see Allan K. Davidson, *Christianity in Aotearoa: A History of Church and Society in New Zealand*, 2d ed. (Wellington: Education for Ministry, 1997), pp. 14-16; notes 6, 17, 21, 22, 25-27; pp. 206-7.

the responses were given by all as the voice of one man." Three Maori from Williams's station had returned home and spontaneously acted as teachers.[27] At the other end of the spectrum, Maori were reinterpreting the missionaries' message for themselves. An early example was Papahurihia's teaching in 1833. Williams responded that "The new doctrine has been brought forward by some, who after residing awhile with us and obtained a superficial knowledge, have gone forth two-fold more the child of the Devil than they were before."[28]

For Anglicans, the relationship between church and state came under increasing pressure in the late 1820s and early 1830s. The Oxford movement sharpened ecclesiological awareness and divisions and promoted debate over the nature of the church. The New Zealand missionaries, influenced by traditional Protestant anti-Catholic hostility and anxiety over developing Catholic tendencies among some Anglicans, viewed these debates with considerable foreboding.

The missionaries' ecclesiology was shaped by their Anglican evangelicalism and their desire to protect the emerging Maori church. That was complicated, and the missionary message was undermined, by growing European involvement in New Zealand by traders and whalers. Missionaries, to defend their interests, in 1831 encouraged thirteen Maori chiefs to petition the king for protection against the possibility of French annexation. Williams and Clarke witnessed the 1835 Declaration of Independence drawn up by James Busby, the British Resident, and signed by thirty-four chiefs. In 1837 the missionaries obtained more than two hundred signatures from British nationals petitioning the British Crown for "that relief which may appear most expedient to your Majesty."[29] The CMS, informed by missionary accounts, petitioned Parliament in 1838 opposing the proposed colonization of New Zealand as "a violation of the Rights and Liberties of the Natives" and as undermining the beneficial missionary efforts.[30] The CMS, given the activist evangelical involvement in politics, seen in the abolition of the slave trade, eschewed erastianism but worked closely with the Colonial Office in the 1830s to achieve their own evangelical ends.

Faced with the inevitability of colonization the missionaries

27. Davidson and Lineham, *Transplanted Christianity*, p. 45.
28. Davidson and Lineham, *Transplanted Christianity*, pp. 43-44. For bibliographical references see Davidson, *Christianity in Aotearoa*, pp. 205, 207.
29. Davidson, *Christianity in Aotearoa*, p. 21.
30. Davidson and Lineham, *Transplanted Christianity*, p. 55.

played a critical role in gaining Maori acceptance of the Treaty of Waitangi in 1840 that secured New Zealand as a British possession. Williams cooperated with William Hobson, the British Crown's representative and first governor of New Zealand, translating the treaty and the negotiations at Waitangi and with other missionaries securing the adherence of the majority of Maori chiefs who signed it. William Colenso, however, questioned whether Maori really understood what they were signing and was concerned that this might come back to haunt the missionaries.[31] Orange noted that "missionary influence was significant simply because many Maori trusted the missionaries' good intentions." Williams brought a "spiritual and temporal" interpretation to the treaty so that it could "be construed as a covenant between the Maori people and the Queen [Victoria] as the head of the English Church and state."[32]

The visit in 1839 of William Broughton, bishop of Australia, to the Bay of Islands, the center of CMS work, where he ordained Octavius Hadfield a priest, pointed to the anomalous nature of Anglican ecclesiology. Legally, as determined by his letters patent, New Zealand was outside Broughton's episcopal jurisdiction.[33] Little troubled by this, the CMS were more concerned that missionaries and native converts should "enjoy the full privileges of a Christian Church, by participating in the benefits of the exercise of the Episcopal office," including confirmation and ordination, arguing that these functions were "inherent in the Episcopal office" and independent "of the prerogatives attached to it by the law of England."[34] This coincided with Broughton's views.[35] At this point CMS and traditional High Church ecclesiology, which recognized that episcopal powers were derived from consecration rather than law, coincided.

31. William Colenso, *The Authentic and Genuine History of the Signing of the Treaty of Waitangi, New Zealand, February 5-6, 1840* (Wellington: Government Printer, 1890), p. 33.

32. Claudia Orange, *The Treaty of Waitangi* (Wellington: Port Nicholson, 1987), p. 90.

33. G. P. Shaw, *Patriarch and Patriot: William Grant Broughton, 1788-1853* (Melbourne: Melbourne University Press, 1978), pp. 97-98.

34. Stock, vol. 1, p. 412.

35. Shaw, *Patriarch and Patriot*, p. 126.

Missionary and Colonial Christianity, 1841-1857

According to Peter Nockles, "It was the old High Churchmen rather than the advanced Tractarians who espoused a pan-Anglicanism associated with the rise of colonial churches."[36] C. J. Blomfield, bishop of London, established the Colonial Bishoprics Fund in 1840 so that "every band of settlers, which goes forth from Christian England" should "take with it not only its civil rulers and functionaries, but its bishops and clergy."[37] The CMS desire to have bishops make good the deficiency of the churches emerging from their missionary activity paralleled this colonial concern.

Colonial expansion coincided with the ecclesiological divisiveness stimulated by the Oxford movement and the demands of missionary and colonial churches. Henry Venn's contribution was critical for the CMS. He became honorary clerical secretary in 1841 and during the next thirty years he articulated CMS policy. Alongside the "central aim of the *plantatio ecclesiae*," Venn can be seen pursuing a policy of accommodation to the expanding ecclesiastical framework of the Anglican communion during the period.[38] There was a provisional dimension to Venn's ecclesiology that reflected his pragmatic response to the demands placed on the society's funds by the needs of their mission fields.

The CMS adopted Venn's statement on "Ecclesiastical Relations" in 1839, claiming that its "constitution and practice . . . are in strict conformity with Ecclesiastical principles."[39] Ordained missionaries were to be licensed to the bishop who determined their sphere of labor and superintended their ecclesiastical duties.[40] The missionaries' services were to be "in strict conformity with the Ritual and Discipline of

---

36. Peter B. Nockles, *The Oxford Movement in Context: Anglican High Churchmanship, 1760-1857* (Cambridge: Cambridge University Press, 1997), p. 182.

37. *Incorporated Society for the Propagation of the Gospel in Foreign Parts: Report for the Year 1840*, p. 104.

38. Timothy E. Yates, *Venn and Victorian Bishops Abroad: The Missionary Policies of Henry Venn and Their Repercussions upon the Anglican Episcopate of the Colonial Period, 1841-1872* (Uppsala: Swedish Institute of Missionary Research, 1978), p. 17. See also Stock, vol. 1, pp. 400-426; Hans Cnattingius, *Bishops and Societies: A Study of Anglican Colonial and Missionary Expansion, 1798-1850* (London: SPCK, 1952); C. Peter Williams, *The Ideal of the Self-Governing Church: A Study of Victorian Missionary Strategy* (Leiden: E. J. Brill, 1990).

39. *Proceedings of the CMS* (1859-60), p. xv.

40. *Proceedings of the CMS* (1859-60), p. xvi.

the Church" and missionary operations were considered "temporary and preparative" and "to be gradually but eventually superseded by a different order of things."[41]

The consecration of George Augustus Selwyn as bishop of New Zealand in 1841, the first appointee of the Colonial Bishoprics Fund, brought the missionary and colonial churches together as uneasy bedfellows. The Oxford movement's ideal of the "missionary bishop" combining both missionary and colonial roles threatened CMS independence. The aspirations of the missionary and colonial churches were intrinsically incompatible, making it impossible to bring them together without sacrificing the autonomy of one to the other.[42]

The New Zealand Association, who were interested in colonization, urged the appointment of a bishop in 1837. This was taken up by the New Zealand Company and the Church Society of New Zealand, who looked to the SPG for support. Although the CMS had no say in choosing Selwyn, they had pressed the Colonial Office since 1839 to make an appointment.[43] The CMS cooperated with Selwyn, reporting in 1842 "that the full benefits of our Ecclesiastical Constitution have thus been provided for the infant Church in those Islands."[44] They agreed to pay six hundred pounds a year, half Selwyn's stipend, the remainder coming from the Colonial Office, with endowments from the SPG and SPCK. Venn was concerned about the dangers of episcopal autocracy, the need to safeguard the Protestant heritage by retaining strong links with the church in England, and maintaining the society's exclusive missionary focus.

Selwyn accepted a position as a CMS vice president in 1841. His churchmanship, however, was somewhat ambiguous. He was "influenced by the traditional High Church outlook" and while "in sympathy with some of the concerns of the Tractarians about the doctrine of the Church and episcopal authority, he never identified himself fully with the movement."[45] Selwyn was an exemplar of robust Victorian muscu-

---

41. *Proceedings of the CMS* (1859-60), p. xvii.

42. Allan K. Davidson, "The Interaction of Missionary and Colonial Christianity in Nineteenth-Century New Zealand," *Studies in World Christianity* 2, no. 2 (1996), pp. 145-66.

43. Stock, vol. 1, pp. 412-14.

44. Stock, vol. 1, p. 416.

45. Allan K. Davidson, *Selwyn's Legacy: The College of St. John the Evangelist, Te Waimate and Auckland, 1843-1992, A History* (Auckland: The College of St. John the Evangelist, 1993), p. 10.

lar Christianity. This, together with his commitment to Maori, initially won the missionaries' admiration. Although willing to work with Selwyn, the missionaries were suspicious of his Tractarian sympathies and his acceptance of "Catholic" practices like altar candles and were critical of his autocratic tendencies. In the light of this, it is ironic that John Keble, who nevertheless thought Selwyn a great bishop, should comment: "he makes me shiver now and then with his Protestantisms, crying up the Ch. Miss. Society."[46]

Writing in 1842, Selwyn reflected his strong sense of episcopal authority: "I find myself placed in a position such as was never granted to any English Bishop before, with a power to mould the institutions of the Church from the beginning according to true principles."[47] These "true principles" included freedom from state control. Selwyn believed his consecration gave him inherent episcopal powers, which were in no way compromised by the fact of his Crown appointment. His initial cooperation with the work of the CMS was seen in his choice of Waimate mission station for his first episcopal residence and collegiate enterprise and his appointments of CMS missionaries as archdeacons: William Williams in 1842 to East Cape, A. N. Brown to Tauranga in 1843, and Henry Williams in 1844 to Waimate. Selwyn quickly, however, alienated Wesleyan missionaries in New Zealand, referring to them as "schismatics" and treating their baptisms "as the act of laymen."[48] The evangelical ecumenism of an earlier generation was being replaced by denominational allegiance.[49] The comity Selwyn was willing to practice in the Pacific, he was unwilling to extend to New Zealand. This was confusing to Maori in the north where family ties crossed Anglican and Methodist boundaries.

46. J. T. Coleridge, *A Memoir of the Revd John Keble,* 2 vols. (Oxford: Parker, 1869), vol. 2, p. 408.

47. [George Augustus Selwyn], *New Zealand. Part I . . . ,* 3d ed. (London: SPG, 1847), pp. 11-12.

48. Selwyn to the Wesleyan Missionaries of the Southern District, Rotorua, 31 October 1843, quoted by John Whiteley to Wesleyan Missionary Society Secretaries, 2 December 1843, in Davidson and Lineham, *Transplanted Christianity,* p. 65. Tensions had already begun to appear between the CMS and Wesleyan missionaries over the matter of territorial boundaries.

49. Selwyn at Lambeth in 1867, following the devastation experienced by both Methodist and CMS missions among Maori, reflected a very different position. He questioned, "Am I authorized by this Conference representing the whole Church to admit that the sacraments are duly administered by ministers of the Wesleyan persuasion?" Lambeth Palace Library, MS LC 1, p. 59, Lambeth Conference Papers, Proceedings 1867, 24 September 1867.

Selwyn convened a synod with nine clergy at Waimate in September 1844. Some in England saw it as breaching royal prerogative, but for Selwyn it was intended "to frame rules for the better management of the mission and the general government of the Church."[50] There was no thought of involving lay missionaries or Maori in these discussions. The missionaries were keen to work with Selwyn when it would advance their missionary cause, such as ordaining their catechists. But Selwyn unrealistically required his priests to know Greek as well as Maori. He also wanted to disperse "his clergy" as he saw fit, even although this conflicted with his 1841 agreement with the CMS. When he demanded a pledge of obedience from his ordinands regarding their stationing, the CMS felt "bound to state with all explicitness their determination to maintain the principles of the Society inviolate" and withdrew their candidates from ordination.[51] Selwyn, as a gesture of goodwill, retracted the preordination pledge to mark the CMS jubilee in 1849.

The missionaries' independence was seriously compromised by the support Selwyn gave to Governor Grey's accusation in 1846 over their land purchases. Selwyn, supported by the CMS, demanded that the missionaries should own no more than 2,560 acres. For Henry Williams this was a matter of integrity. He had bought land, the titles for which had been investigated and approved, to provide a future for his children. The CMS dismissed Williams, Clarke, and Kemp. Selwyn had played into the hands of the governor who wanted to destroy the influence of the missionaries in the north following the outbreak of war in 1844-45. Williams was reinstated in 1854 following his brother's intervention and with the support of Grey and Selwyn — the authors of his dismissal.[52]

Selwyn proved a considerable disappointment to the CMS in advancing "native ministry." He had ambitious plans for multilevel education at St. John's College for Maori and Pakeha but in 1853 the col-

---

50. H. W. Tucker, *Memoir of the Life and Episcopate of George Augustus Selwyn*, 2 vols. (London: Gardner, 1879), vol. 1, p. 158.

51. St. John's College (SJC), Misc. Arch. 9/10, typescript copy, Henry Venn to G. A. Selwyn, 4 November 1845. See also Yates, *Venn and Victorian Bishops*, pp. 58-63.

52. E. O. Sheild, "The New Zealand Episcopate of George Augustus Selwyn (1842-1867) with Special Reference to Bishop Selwyn's Part in the Dispute with Archdeacon Henry Williams in Respect of the Latter's Land Claims" (B.D. thesis, University of Oxford, 1981); Yates, *Venn and Victorian Bishops*, pp. 63-72.

lege was closed. The missionaries had already shown their lack of confidence in Selwyn's scheme by withdrawing and then refusing to send students.[53] In 1851 Venn criticized the attempts "to train up native missionaries and pastors by an European education, and in collegiate establishments." He called for the selection "from among the native catechists those who have approved themselves faithful and established Christians, as well as 'apt to teach,' and by giving to such persons a special training in Scriptural studies, in the vernacular language."[54]

The delay in ordaining Maori has often been attributed to Selwyn's supposed demand that Maori, like his Pakeha clergy, needed a knowledge of English, Latin, and Greek, but this has been greatly exaggerated.[55] Selwyn certainly had a poor record, not ordaining his first Maori deacon, Rota Waitoa, until 1853. This delay prevented Maori from giving clerical leadership at a critical period of their history. The reasons for this delay, however, were more complex than Selwyn's critics allowed. William Williams, who ordained Waitoa as the first Maori priest in 1860, indicated in 1856 that Selwyn "does not ask for anything beyond Scriptural knowledge expressed in the New Zealand language" of the Maori candidates.[56] Georg Kissling, who was entrusted with training Maori in the 1850s, endorsed this and indicated that the failure to produce Maori ministers arose from "the lack of suitably qualified candidates and the inability of the missionaries to develop a unified system of primary and central schools and a training institution for clergy."[57]

T. S. Grace, one of the younger missionaries, reported in 1851 that "Outwardly they [Maori] have embraced the Gospel, but ere there has been time for it to become rooted and grounded in their hearts, colonization has burst upon them with all the evils which in modern times it has brought upon the different aboriginal races."[58] The growth of the

53. Davidson, *Selwyn's Legacy*, pp. 24-81.
54. Wilbert R. Shenk, *Henry Venn — Missionary Statesman* (Maryknoll, N.Y.: Orbis Books, 1983), p. 119.
55. *CMI* (Dec. 1868), pp. 353-64; (Oct. 1879), pp. 577-99.
56. Watson Rosevear, *Waiapu: The Story of a Diocese* (Hamilton: Paul's, 1960), p. 54; see also pp. 52-55.
57. Davidson, *Selwyn's Legacy*, p. 80.
58. S. J. Brittan, ed., *A Pioneer Missionary among the Maoris, 1850-1879, Being the Letters and Journals of Thomas Samuel Grace* (Palmerston North: Bennett, n.d.), pp. 17-18.

Maori church in the 1840s and 1850s coincided with the impact of Pakeha settlement. It is estimated that there were only about 2,000 Pakeha in the country in 1840 compared to some 70,000 Maori. By 1858 Maori numbers had dropped to 60,000, while by 1861 there were 99,000 Pakeha. When the Maori population reached its nadir in 1896 at 42,000, the Pakeha population was more than 700,000.[59]

Given this context, it became difficult to give institutional expression to the Maori church apart from the Pakeha church. Selwyn was increasingly preoccupied with devising a method of church government that would safeguard the church's familial link with the Church of England but maintain its autonomy in a self-governing colony. In 1847, at his second synod, he acknowledged that "The Missionary must always expect that colonization will follow in his train, that he will not be allowed to retain his own authority unimpaired, nor to draw a line around his native converts, within which no contamination shall be allowed to enter."[60]

Venn, by contrast, in his 1851 Minute declared that the "ultimate object of a mission, viewed under its ecclesiastical aspects," was "to be the settlement of a native Church, under native pastors, upon a self-supporting system" resulting in "the euthanasia of a mission."[61] The CMS were initially suspicious of Selwyn's plans and in 1851 warned their missionaries to "abstain from identifying themselves with the proposed scheme."[62] During his visit to England in 1854, Selwyn met with the CMS, reassuring them that the integrity of the Anglican Church would be maintained and indicating his desire to divide his diocese and have three missionaries appointed bishops. The CMS now agreed that they did "not wish their missionaries to be regarded as a separate body

---

59. Figures taken from: James Belich, *Making Peoples: A History of the New Zealanders from Polynesian Settlement to the End of the Nineteenth Century* (Auckland: Allen Lane, Penguin, 1996), pp. 177-78; W. H. Oliver, ed., *The Oxford History of New Zealand* (Wellington: Oxford University Press, 1981), p. 117; Ian Pool, *Te Iwi Maori: A New Zealand Population Past, Present & Projected* (Auckland: Auckland University Press, 1991), p. 76; Davidson and Lineham, *Transplanted Christianity*, p. 179.

60. George Augustus Selwyn, *A Charge Delivered to the Clergy of the Diocese of New Zealand, at the Diocesan Synod, in the Chapel of St. John's College, on Thursday, September 23, 1847* (London: Rivington, 1859), p. 17.

61. Shenk, *Henry Venn*, p. 119.

62. W. P. Morrell, "Selwyn's Relations with the Church Missionary Society," in *Bishop Selwyn in New Zealand, 1841-68*, ed. W. E. Limbrick (Palmerston North: Dunmore Press, 1983), p. 89.

in the New Zealand Church." They desired to "assist the Bishop and clergy in consolidating and establishing" the church "upon that Protestant and Evangelical basis upon which all its prosperity, under God, depends."[63]

The Pakeha Church and Maori, 1857-81

Selwyn summoned a constitutional convention in 1857 that included five missionaries. The constitution established the church on the basis of "voluntary compact" and included "fundamental provisions" that entrenched its Anglican identity. It provided for a General Synod to meet nationally and diocesan synods in which bishops, clergy, and laity would take part voting in separate houses. For its time it was a creative response to the colonial context, but it was a document shaped without any Maori involvement. While the convention was meeting, Lord Chichester, the CMS president, wrote to the Colonial Office that the society wished to withdraw from New Zealand and "leave the Native Christians under Native Pastors . . . as an organised self-supporting Native Church" and use its funds elsewhere. He was disappointed "in the amount of assistance" they had received from Selwyn in "raising up a Native Ministry, and otherwise preparing the Native population for self support."[64]

At the first General Synod in 1859, Selwyn asked what was "the best mode of drawing our Native brethren into closer bonds of Christian fellowship with ourselves?"[65] He looked forward to William Williams's consecration and his "missionary diocese of Turanga" widening "the basis of Native ordination."[66] He was convinced "that the time has come when a united action between the two branches of our Church is absolutely necessary" and that "it will be found impossible to carry on a double government for the Colonial and Missionary Church." While he described "the blending of the one into the other" as "a gradual work" that "ought to be begun immediately," he declared that "The Euthanasia of the Mission cannot be a sudden death."[67]

Williams was consecrated bishop of Waiapu in 1859. Hadfield de-

63. Stock, vol. 2, p. 89.
64. SJC, Misc. Arch. 9/4, Lord Chichester to H. Labouchere, 2 June 1857.
65. *PGS* (1859), pp. 17-18.
66. *PGS* (1859), p. 18.
67. *PGS* (1859), p. 19.

clined the offer of Wellington but was its second bishop from 1870 to 1893. Williams gave priority to developing a Maori ministry. By 1872 he had ordained ten of the first twenty-three Maori clergy.[68] He also held four synods between 1859 and 1865 in the Maori language and encouraged Maori parishes to become self-supporting. This was, however, too little, too late. The wars of the 1860s and the rapid growth of Maori religious movements contributed in 1865 to the murder of C. S. Volkner, the missionary at Opotiki, and the destruction of Williams's headquarters. Williams noted, "It is a sad conclusion, after twenty-five years of labour, to be obliged then to leave."[69] Sanderson argues that "What Williams saw as a complete about-face was for a large number of East Coast Maori simply a statement of their autonomy, both political and spiritual. It was an assertion of 'Maoriness,' not an outright rejection of Christianity."[70]

The development of ecclesiastical structures was set within the context of the contrary forces at work in New Zealand politics. The missionary voice, notably heard in the protests of Hadfield, Selwyn, and others over the illegal purchase of Maori land, could not prevent the destructive North Island wars in the 1860s. Some Maori tribes, through the King movement, partly inspired by the Bible, attempted to express their "rangatiratanga," or sovereignty, but this was rejected by the missionaries. The idea of the sovereignty of the Maori King, existing alongside that of the Queen, was anathema to most loyal Pakeha Anglicans. Many Maori, both Anglicans and former Anglicans, however, objected to praying for the Queen. The rejection of missionary Christianity and the development of Maori religious movements such as Pai Marire, Hau Hau, and Ringatu were seen by most missionaries and Pakeha as aberrations. Some missionaries, notably James Stack and T. S. Grace, had glimmers of insight, seeing them as attempts to give an indigenous voice and institutional expression to an amalgam of traditional customs and recently gained Christian insights.[71]

Selwyn's language of "blending" represented the assimilationist thinking that dominated attitudes toward Maori for the next hundred years or more. Venn's ideal about the native church becoming self-governing was submerged in the colonial context. Maori culture and lan-

68. Stock, vol. 2, p. 640.
69. *Church Missionary Record* (Sept. 1865), p. 264.
70. Kay Sanderson, "Maori Christianity on the East Coast, 1840-1870," *New Zealand Journal of History* 17, no. 2 (Oct. 1983), pp. 166-67.
71. Davidson, *Christianity in Aotearoa*, pp. 39-49.

guage retained its integrity in local settings but was excluded from synodical structures. The Waiapu diocesan headquarters, for example, were shifted to Napier in 1867 where "From being an almost purely Maori gathering, with the only Europeans the English missionaries, Synod became for the next thirty years virtually an English gathering, with the only Maoris the occasional Maori clergyman."[72]

The missionaries met without Selwyn in June 1866 to consider "whether the Society shall withdraw & leave its Mission to be completed by the Ecclesiastical authorities of New Zealand."[73] Burrows, reflecting on the war, recorded that "The painful fact that the great majority of the Natives have entirely put aside Christianity as taught them from the Scriptures and have either embraced Hauhauism or are living without any religious service whatever, was one that no member of the conference wished to discuss."[74] The exclusive Maori focus of some missionaries was compromised by their withdrawal from their mission stations and their appointment as military chaplains or as ministers to Pakeha congregations.

The missionaries asked for continued CMS support. Selwyn endorsed this, repeating that euthanasia "cannot be a sudden death. The Parent must provide for his children; assigning portions to those who are still in infancy." He suggested that CMS annual grants might be "commuted into permanent endowments" for two of the North Island bishoprics and some CMS property be held in Trust, "thus binding upon all future Bishops of the Dioceses the obligations of watching over the interests of the Native Church." The native clergy he viewed "like the children still in infancy, requiring not only maintenance but also guidance and control."[75]

Venn "became increasingly sceptical of the missionary capacity to trust the emerging church and consequently to give it real independence."[76] His minutes, adopted in 1861 and 1866, developed the idea of the self-governing, self-supporting, self-extending native church.[77] In 1866 the CMS resisted Selwyn's suggestion that it should "make over its Church property to the Synod or tie it up by partial endowments."

72. Rosevear, *Waiapu*, p. 75.
73. SJC, Misc. Arch. 9/7, CMS Secretaries to R. Burrows, 26 February 1866.
74. W. P. Morrell, *The Anglican Church in New Zealand* (Dunedin: Anglican Church of the Province of New Zealand, 1973), pp. 81-82.
75. Davidson and Lineham, *Transplanted Christianity*, p. 142.
76. Williams, *Ideal of the Self-Governing Church*, p. xiii.
77. Shenk, *Henry Venn*, pp. 118-29.

Venn viewed "with many fears . . . the amalgamation of the two races in one Synod," ruefully noting that "the great need of the Mission in the past years has been the extension of the Native pastorate. Instead of 10 native ministers there should have been & might have been 50." Given organization and support "the native church would have presented a much firmer resistance to the evils which have well nigh ruined it."[78] The New Zealand Mission had "not become nationalized."[79] The CMS secretaries rejected the idea of resigning their work to "the Church in New Zealand as at present constituted . . . for the next generation there must be a Native Church organization independent of the New Zealand Church organization. Ultimately an amalgamation may take place. But if the amalgamation is pressed too soon the Native Church will suffer."[80]

Peter Williams has concluded that Venn's "ideology had manifestly not wrestled sufficiently with the ecclesiological implications within itself." In the nineteenth century, "To have two churches in the same place, separated on the grounds of race, offended not only some obscure church tradition but also the plain understanding of the nature of the body of Christ. There were few appropriate models of 'unity in diversity.' "[81] In New Zealand, Venn's native church was sacrificed on the altar of colonial ecclesiology. Underlying this were monocultural attitudes that, as the century progressed, were reinforced by Social Darwinism and an implicit racism antagonistic toward the earlier humanitarianism of the missionary movement.[82]

At his final General Synod in 1868 Selwyn reflected on the way the missionaries "governed by the Laws of their own Society, might have been unable to unite with us in the same system of Church Government." The society had removed this difficulty by advising "its Missionaries to assist the bishop and the rest of the Clergy in organising the institutions of the infant Church in New Zealand."[83] Although the CMS wanted to defend its independence, it was already

78. SJC, Misc. Arch. 9/7, Henry Venn to R. Burrows, 26 December 1866.
79. *Church Missionary Record* (Dec. 1868), p. 406.
80. SJC, Misc. Arch. 9/7, H. Venn and C. Fenn, to R. Burrows, 1 September 1868.
81. Williams, *Ideal of the Self-Governing Church*, p. 259.
82. John Stenhouse, "The Darwinian Enlightenment and New Zealand Politics," in *Darwin's Laboratory,* ed. R. Macleod and P. F. Rehbock (Honolulu: University of Hawaii Press, 1994), pp. 395-425.
83. *PGS* (1868), p. 3.

institutionally compromised by its involvement in the church organization.

This was seen in the "Local Boards . . . in Maori Districts for the better management of Church affairs among the natives."[84] They became important meeting places for Maori clergy and laity but their powers were prescribed by diocesan synods. Grace noted in 1877 that one Maori minister refused to attend these synods saying, " 'What is the use of going there to stand like a post?' . . . Maoris have minds and tongues of their own; to have expected the Native to be present at a Synod, where only English is spoken, was an affront, and clearly this man felt it to be so."[85] Lay Maori representation at diocesan synods was approved in 1898 but legislation in 1901 and 1913 providing for direct Maori General Synod representation failed.[86]

The failure to elect a Maori bishop concerned some. Hemi Matenga noted in 1877 that there were Maori clergy, members of Parliament, and magistrates. Aware that Africans had a bishop in Samuel Crowther, he questioned, "Why is there no Maori bishop, since the Natives of these Islands have for a considerable time past embraced Christianity?" In obtaining a successor to William Williams they were looking only "in the ranks of the English clergy." A great deal of the bishop's work was "with the Maori portion of the Church. Let it not be said because a man is a Maori he is unfit to be a bishop."[87] Grace was virtually a lone Pakeha voice, declaring, "We ought to give Native Churches Native Bishops."[88]

The Auckland Maori Church Board's proposal in 1880 to appoint a coadjutor bishop for the Maori church[89] was rejected initially by the General Synod on financial grounds.[90] Assimilationist thinking was reflected in the final motion, which looked to "the oneness which exists between the English and Maori portions of the Church . . . hoping that they will be brought yet closer together in worship and Church organisation."[91] In the same year, the CMS notified their New Zealand agents

84. *PGS* (1868), p. 40.

85. Brittan, *Pioneer Missionary,* p. 287.

86. *PGS* (1898), pp. 45-46; (1892), pp. 28, 34; (1895), pp. 54-55; (1901), p. 37; (1913), p. 32.

87. Davidson and Lineham, *Transplanted Christianity,* p. 146.

88. Brittan, *Pioneer Missionary,* p. 256.

89. *Church Gazette* (Apr. 1880), p. 32; (Feb. 1880), p. 12.

90. *PGS* (1880), p. 39.

91. *PGS* (1880), p. 40.

that due to financial difficulties it was necessary to accelerate the "dimi-nution of our expenditure in New Zealand" and "leave the Mission-aries and Native X's [sc. Christians] of each diocese, under the guidance of their respective Bishops, to manage to a great extent their own af-fairs."[92]

The *Church Missionary Intelligencer* indicated in 1881 that the fundamental principle of the society was "the conversion of heathen Natives, almost to the exclusion of ministrations among Europeans." Defending the native church, the author argued that Selwyn, "under the absorbing fancy of a territorial Episcopate, strove to fuse Europeans and Natives into a common Church." The careful study of this "ought to convey . . . a never-failing lesson of the extreme impolicy of prema-ture fusion between a handful of Englishmen and masses of Natives."[93] While acknowledging the help of "territorial bishops," it declared "they have of necessity been outsiders to the Native Church." The au-thor's unqualified preference was for "tribal or linguistic bishops as su-perintendents of Native Churches."[94] This declaration, however, came too late for the Maori church.

The Withdrawal of the CMS, 1882-1902

In 1882, the CMS gave notice of its intention to withdraw, identifying New Zealand with other areas where indigenous races were becoming minorities in colonial societies. Unlike India and China they could not look forward to developing into independent native churches. "Maori Christians are already in some respects absorbed in the Colonial Church" so that the society could transfer its work as it became "more settled and pastoral . . . to the Colonial Dioceses." The CMS looked forward to leaving its "Maori children to the care of the English Bishops, with the happy consciousness that by God's good blessing its work will then be done."[95]

A New Zealand Mission Board, established in 1882, formalized as the Mission Trust Board in 1889, administered the society's diminishing grant, property, and revenue. No provision was made for Maori mem-

92. SJC, Misc. Arch. 9/2, C. Fenn to R. Burrows, 20 May 1880.
93. *CMI* (March 1881), p. 135.
94. *CMI* (March 1881), p. 136.
95. *Proceedings of the Synod of the Diocese of Waiapu* (1883), pp. 20-21.

bership. This reinforced the paternalistic control of Maori resources and contributed to making Maori financially dependent. The board gave priority to training Maori clergy by establishing Te Rau College in Gisborne in 1883. Between 1853 and the end of the century, some seventy Maori had been ordained. The ministry training reflected the needs of Maori communities to worship in their own language, although students were increasingly pushed to undertake the English examinations of the Board of Theological Studies. After 1920 Maori were integrated at St. John's College, resulting in a great decrease in cultural and linguistic emphases.[96]

Stock, reinterpreting Venn, wrote in 1899 that "In New Zealand . . . there will continue to be one Church; but there the white colonist is, and will be, dominant. The Maori section must more and more be relatively small and dependent."[97] This reinforced the 1897 Lambeth report which accepted that Maori and North American Indians were diminishing and would "be absorbed in white races." There was "no need for the separate organisation of a Maori Church."[98] Faced with the CMS withdrawal, a General Synod sessional committee in 1901 warned that "unless the Church of New Zealand is roused to a sense of the responsibility now resting upon her, and makes a vigorous effort to discharge her obligations to the Maori in our midst, the work of the Church among Christian Maories will crumble to the dust."[99] There was concern particularly about the inadequate Maori clergy stipends. An appeal and a generous donation from Samuel Williams were only short-term expedients. The General Synod's failure to provide for ongoing Maori work was symptomatic of the priority New Zealand was giving Maori in society. A New Zealand Church Mission Association, founded in 1893, devoted its energy largely to supporting missionary work overseas.

---

96. Davidson, *Selwyn's Legacy,* pp. 164, 182-85, 210-12, 229-31; J. L. P. Te Paa, "Kua Whakatungia Ano a Te Rau Kahikatea: An Historical Critical Overview of Events Which Preceded the Re-establishment of Te Rau Kahikatea, Theological College of Te Pihopatanga o Aotearoa" (Master's thesis, Auckland, 1995).

97. Stock, vol. 3, p. 558.

98. R. T. Davidson, *The Five Lambeth Conferences* (London: SPCK, 1920), p. 232.

99. W. G. Cowie, *To the Clergy and Laity of the Church of the Province of New Zealand* (New Zealand Mission Trust Board, 1901).

The Maori Church After the CMS, 1902-92

After eighty-eight years in New Zealand, the CMS terminated their connection in 1902. The next ninety years were to see various attempts to restructure Maori work. Significant aspects are highlighted here indicating the way in which the nineteenth-century ecclesiastical legacy cast a long shadow over the Maori church.

M. R. Neligan, bishop of Auckland, in 1903 suggested the appointment of a Pakeha who could speak Maori, as suffragan to the three North Island bishops to take charge of Maori work. "In all probability," he informed the archbishop of Canterbury, "25 years hence no such need will exist; for the Maori will be absorbed by the Pakeha."[100] Unaware "of any appropriate precedent," Archbishop Davidson saw great difficulty in this, suggesting that the suffragan should be attached to one bishop and receive commissions from the others.[101] Neligan accepted this as "the only feasible" option, but no action was taken.[102] Instead a Provincial Maori Mission Board was established in 1904 to supervise and finance Maori work.[103] It was ineffective, lacking diocesan support. In 1913 it was replaced by the Provincial Board for Missions that distributed diocesan-raised funds within New Zealand and overseas.[104]

After the First World War, T. W. Ratana's healing movement challenged Anglican complacency. Initially welcomed by the bishop of Waiapu, it was increasingly seen as heretical. North Island bishops issued a pastoral letter in 1925 excommunicating Anglicans who accepted Ratana's teaching.[105] By 1926 more than 18 percent of Maori, many formerly Anglican, were identified with the Ratana Church.[106] A Pakeha commission was appointed — the Maori politician and lay Anglican (Sir) Apirana Ngata was later added — to inquire into Maori

100. Lambeth Palace Library, Davidson Papers, vol. 430 ff. 205-7, M. R. Neligan to Archbishop Davidson, 20 July 1903.

101. Lambeth Palace Library, Davidson Papers, vol. 430 ff. 208-10, R. T. Davidson to Bishop of Auckland, 4 September 1903.

102. Lambeth Palace Library, Davidson Papers, vol. 430 ff. 212-13, M. R. Neligan to Archbishop Davidson, 19 Oct. 1903.

103. *PGS* (1904), pp. 77-78.

104. *PGS* (1913), pp. 19-20.

105. *PGS* (1913), pp. 164-65.

106. Davidson and Lineham, *Transplanted Christianity*, p. 172.

work, "self-expression," and "the control and government of the work of the Church amongst" Maori.[107]

After a conference that included Maori representatives, a special General Synod sought to implement the commission's recommendation that a Maori diocese be created with the bishop having diocesan status.[108] Archbishop Averill questioned whether there was any precedent for diocesan bishops divesting "themselves of any part of their jurisdiction except by consensual compact" to enable another bishop to take charge of this jurisdiction. He concluded that this "should not of itself deter us from creating a precedent if we are satisfied that such action would not conflict with Catholic order."[109] The Lambeth discussions, recognizing that differences of race and language sometimes required special provisions, were noted.[110] Averill rejected any suggestion that the diocese was being established on the basis of color. The motivating idea was "the spiritual welfare of the Maori race, so that it may be enabled to make its full contribution to the fulness of the Holy Catholic Church."[111]

Legislation established a diocese of Aotearoa but it was never given effect. The North Island bishops nominated Herbert Williams, a Pakeha, grandson of the first and son of the third bishop of Waiapu, but Maori, led by Ngata, insisted that a Maori should be appointed. Averill claimed that the nominating bishops had no objection "to a Maori because he is a Maori" but claimed "no Maori has had sufficient experience as yet to hold the position." If this was true, it was a sad indictment on the church that had been in New Zealand for 112 years. Averill noted that "Maoris desire a Maori bishop for the sake of racial dignity I think. There are Maori MPs, doctors, lawyers etc and Maori feel that they should have a Maori bishop."[112] Ngata indicated that "the constitutional position" was secondary: "It is enough that one of our people will be called to this high office and that the responsibility is at last on the race to make good. . . . They have been asking us to fash-

---

107. *PGS* (1925), pp. 28, 123-24.

108. *PGS* (1925), p. 453.

109. *PGS* (1925), p. 432.

110. Davidson, *The Five Lambeth Conferences* (1867), p. 71; (1897), pp. 203, 232; (1908), p. 377; (1920), pp. 79-90, 86.

111. *PGS* (1925), p. 438.

112. Lambeth Palace Library, Davidson Papers, vol. 430 ff. 232-34, A. W. Averill to Bishop of Edinburgh, 23 June 1926; *PGS* (1925), vol. 438 ff. 235-36, Averill to Archbishop of Canterbury, 23 June 1926.

ion things after a likeness seen through pakeha eyes. . . . They were not the things we wanted, nor were they moulded by our unfettered hands, to any design near our hearts."[113]

The 1928 General Synod reached a compromise. F. A. Bennett, a Maori, was consecrated suffragan to the bishop of Waiapu as bishop of Aotearoa.[114] Ngata wrote, "We wanted a Maori as the nucleus of a movement and of an eventual organisation that he will create gradually from below — the natural growth rooted in the Maori heart & mind & shaped to suit the characteristics of the people."[115] Ngata's desire for a Maori bishop was unassailable in principle, but the diocesan status provided under the 1925 proposal was lost. The limitations of the assistant status soon became evident. The bishop of Aotearoa could attend a General Synod only if elected as a clerical representative from his diocese. His ministry in other dioceses depended on their bishops. W. J. Simkin, bishop of Auckland, 1940-60, the diocese with the largest Maori population, would not give the bishop of Aotearoa free access to Maori. He wrote in 1946 that "The clergy of my Diocese cannot observe two loyalties and a clash between the Bishop and myself would be almost inevitable and not in the best interests of the Church."[116] While welcomed by Maori throughout the country, the bishop of Aotearoa's role was circumscribed by ecclesiastical restrictions and an underlying assimilationist mind-set.

In 1964 the bishop of Aotearoa was given a seat on the General Synod in his own right.[117] The encouragement given to nonstipendiary ministry, *minita-a-iwi,* from the 1970s, with local training, gave a great boost to Maori ministry. The General Synod in 1978 established Te Pihopatanga o Aotearoa, the Bishopric of Aotearoa, with its own council and provided for its bishop to be "licensed by the Primate to share with the Bishop of each Diocese the episcopal oversight of the Maori people." A commission was still required from each diocesan bishop.[118] Manu Bennett, third bishop of Aotearoa, noted that the new relation-

113. M. P. K. Sorrenson, ed., *Na to Hora Aroha: From Your Dear Friend. The Correspondence Between Sir Apirana Ngata and Sir Peter Buck, 1925-50* (Auckland: Auckland University Press, 1986), vol. 1, p. 88.

114. *PGS* (1928), pp. 122-24.

115. Sorrenson, *Na to Hora Aroha*, p. 87.

116. W. J. Simkin to Secretary, Diocese of Waiapu, 24 September 1946.

117. *PGS* (1964), p. 101.

118. *PGS* (1978), pp. 53-54.

ship provided "the Church with a proper Maori voice and fuller participation in its processes."[119]

Antiracist movements, initially concerned about apartheid in South Africa, began in the 1970s to examine the deep roots of racism in New Zealand. A Maori renaissance was associated with the preservation of Maori language and culture, claims for the recovery of alienated land, and greater involvement in political and economic life. Attention to New Zealand's foundation gave increasing prominence to the importance of the Treaty of Waitangi, in which the CMS missionaries played a critical role, as a founding charter for relations between Maori and Pakeha. A Bicultural Commission on the Treaty of Waitangi, set up in 1984, reported to the General Synod in 1986. The Synod adopted "the principles of partnership and bicultural development" and agreed to revise the church's constitution to express and entrench them.[120] The ministry of Te Pihopa o Aotearoa, the bishop of Aotearoa, was redefined "to provide episcopal care and oversight of Maori people throughout the Province." Episcopal commissions were no longer required, giving Te Pihopa the same status as diocesan bishops.[121]

Reshaping the Church, 1992

When the church's revised constitution was adopted in 1992, Archbishop Brian Davis introduced it as a "visionary" document providing "for the one Church of Aotearoa, New Zealand and Polynesia, to express its life and serve its common mission through three cultural partners — Maori, Pakeha and Polynesian." He acknowledged that its implementation would "demand massive canonical change and the review of almost every aspect of our common life as a church." Pointing to the ultimate goal, he emphasized: "We must keep our mission calling and objective sharply focussed before us — and we must remember that all institutional change can be justified by one criterion only — that the Church will as a consequence be more obedient to God and more faithful to Christ's mission."[122]

119. Manuhuia Bennett, "The Bishopric of Aotearoa — a Maori Dimension," in *He Toenga Whatiwhatinga: Essays Concerning the Bishopric of Aotearoa*, ed. John Paterson (Rotorua: Te Pihopatanga o Aotearoa, 1983), p. 17.
120. *PGS* (1986), p. 31.
121. *PGS* (1986), p. 116.
122. *PGS* (1986), p. 7.

Underlying the development of the Anglican Church in Aotearoa and New Zealand have been issues of culture and ecclesiology. The ecclesiology of the early missionaries was shaped by their English culture and traditions, evangelical activism, and missionary pragmatism. These gave rise to Te Hahi Mihinare, a developing missionary church, in which the language and people were Maori but the forms and content were largely English and Anglican. The colonial society brought pressure on Maori. The demands of settler ministry and ecclesiastical organization overwhelmed the emerging Maori church before its leadership could be developed and consolidated. Henry Venn's hopes for a self-governing native church were swamped by assimilationist thinking and the paternalistic dominance of the colonial church and territorial episcopate. Maori retained a voice in their local church and their own world and through their religious movements. The Anglican Maori Church survived the assimilationist period. Gradually accommodation and greater autonomy were given and claimed so it could undertake its mission. Whakahuihui Vercoe, bishop of Aotearoa, welcoming the revised constitution, declared, "We Maori are now responsible for the conduct of the Church's business in our own tradition and customs."[123]

In the late twentieth century, the church has put in place structures that recognize cultural diversity and identity but also emphasize the need for partnership. This has meant forging new ecclesiastical structures that take account of tradition and context. There are ecclesiological tensions, as old as the church itself, in allowing for ethnic diversity (Jews and Greeks, Maori and Pakeha), while holding on to unity in one Lord, faith, baptism, and ministry. Church structures are human attempts to embody the mission, which calls the people of God together and helps them undertake their commission to witness to the world. The future of the Anglican Church in Aotearoa, New Zealand, and Polynesia will be shaped by the way in which it gives ecclesiological expression to its faithfulness in holding these tensions together within the wider ecumenical spirit and mission of the gospel.

123. General Synod/Te Hinota Whanui Communications Team, *The Anglican Church in Aotearoa, New Zealand and Polynesia* (1992), p. 2.

9. India: Missionaries, Conversion, and Change

GEOFFREY A. ODDIE

A lthough the first CMS Corresponding Committee organized in India was established in Calcutta in 1807, it was not until ten years later that the first CMS missionaries arrived in the country to begin, or continue, the work of evangelization. This chapter will explore the nature and ramifications of this expanding activity with special reference to three of the most important inquiry/conversion movements associated with the CMS in the first half of the nineteenth century. The first of these was a movement that gained momentum among the peasantry in the Krishnagar district about one hundred miles north of Calcutta in the 1830s and 1840s. A few small groups of baptized and long-term inquirers were suddenly joined by hundreds of poor Hindu and Muslim families affected by floods and famine, and a "mass movement," which from the missionaries' point of view appeared initially to be full of promise, ended in stagnation, disappointment, and failure. The second movement we shall examine, which developed prior to the first, but was not totally unconnected with it, involved members of the Kartabhaja (Vaishnava) sect, a devotional cult that, attracting both Hindus and Muslims, arose in the socio-economic and political turmoil of the eighteenth century. The third movement, or rather series of movements, were those that took place primarily among the shanars (subsequently known as nadars) in the Tirunelveli district in South India.

Any discussion of the complexities involved in the development and extension of Christian faith in modern history almost invariably raises questions about the role and importance of foreign missionaries in facilitating the Christian movement. For example, Frederick Downs in his discussion of the explosive power of Christian movements in North-East India has argued that there was little relationship between the number of missionaries present and the spread of Christianity in that part of the world.[1] Furthermore, Robin Horton, the anthropologist who has written extensively on the subject of African conversion, raises similar questions when he argues that what mattered more than anything else were the preexisting worldviews together with intellectual, social, and other changes that were already taking place prior to the reception of Christianity and Islam.[2] How important then were the missionaries as a factor in the spread of Christianity in the CMS fields under consideration? What was the role of the Indians themselves? And to what extent were these developments (including the growth of Christian churches) a response to deeper social, economic, political, and other changes already taking place in early colonial society?

The Context of Early British Rule

All three movements that make up the subject of this chapter arose and developed in the context of early British rule and at a time when the introduction of colonial administration was beginning to affect village relationships and life. The East India Company, which administered British Indian possessions until 1858, was especially concerned about constructing a new environment of peace and stability in which it could pursue and extend its trade and commerce. Company officials were already in the process of negotiating land revenue settlements in Bengal and Tirunelveli (or Tinnevelly) district — a process that, if anything, tended to strengthen the power and control of the dominant classes, including the zamindars, or landlords, over the peasant population. At the same time the authorities were not unaware of the need to develop or even improve the legal system, together with courts of appeal, which could be used (so it was thought) to settle disputes and curb the excessive power of landlords and others determined to exact whatever they could from the peasant population.

1. F. S. Downs, *Christianity in North-East India* (Delhi: ISPCK, 1983).
2. R. Horton, "African Conversion," *Africa* 41, no. 2 (1971), pp. 85-108, and "On the Rationality of Conversion, Part 1," *Africa* 45, no. 3 (1975), pp. 219-35.

Associated with these developments was an increase in the number of Europeans in India and a growth in the number of Indians employed in company business or in the lower echelons of the company's administration. As a result of the changes in the company's policy facilitating the admission of Christian missionaries, European officials, merchants, and others already in India were joined by a slowly increasing number of Protestant missionaries. Although they usually observed the rules of comity (respect for each other's territory) among themselves, the same restraints did not apply to Catholics, who in their activity had always aimed at the conversion of Protestants, as well as "pagans." Hence CMS missionaries competed with Catholics in different parts of India including both the Krishnagar and Tirunelveli districts. In contrast to this, their attitude toward Anglican missionaries of the SPG in Tirunelveli (representing more of a High Church tradition than that of the CMS) was very different — the CMS coming to an agreement with their Anglican colleagues whereby the district was subdivided, three-fifths going to the CMS and two-fifths (the southeastern corner) to the SPG.[3]

Though the towns and cities were becoming more conspicuous as centers for different types of European activity, the situation was somewhat different in the countryside where the appearance of the European district officers and other "sahibs" was a less common occurrence. Planters as well as missionaries sometimes settled in the remoter parts of the country, but it was the missionaries more than other Europeans who tended to "itinerate," making contact with a broader section of the population. In some outlying districts the missionary represented the only visible sign of the European presence, a reminder of the country's recent past of European conquest, power, and control. But if, on the one hand, they symbolized a superior authority, they were also bearers of cultural difference — a difference that many Hindus (especially the higher castes) interpreted as a sure sign of the Europeans' basic inferiority. For many Brahmans, for example, this inferiority was reflected in the Europeans' tendency to eat meat, consume alcohol, and neglect the very basic rules of personal hygiene.[4] But while, through fear of pollution, many high-caste Hindus shunned the company of Eu-

3. R. Caldwell, *Lectures on the Tinnevelly Missions* (London: Bell & Daldy, 1857), pp. 15-16, 55.
4. For eighteenth-century high-caste Tamil comment on European habits and customs, see H. Grafe, "Hindu Apologetics at the Beginning of the Protestant Era," *Indian Church History Review* 6, no. 1 (June 1972), pp. 43-70.

ropeans, especially in the early nineteenth century, the lower castes and classes, such as the shanars, had no such misgivings.[5] It was therefore much easier for Europeans (free from caste prejudice) to mingle with them, enter their homes, and gain an insight into the way in which they lived.

CMS Beginnings and Early Kartabhaja Converts in Krishnagar District

In 1832 the CMS opened schools in the town of Krishnagar (the district headquarters) and in Nadia, which was on the opposite side of the Jellinghy river, an ancient center celebrated as the birthplace of Chaitanya, the leader of a Bengali devotional movement that flourished in the sixteenth century.[6] Christian scriptures were introduced and read. In 1835 William Deerr, a man fluent in Bengali and who had spent thirteen years in neighboring districts, returned from Europe. Leading a team comprising himself, a Bengali school teacher, and two Bengali catechists ("native" co-workers), he commenced preaching in the town of Krishnagar and surrounding villages. In 1835, in the course of their preaching, the two catechists, Paul and Ramathon, visited the village of Dipchandrapore about six miles west of Krishnagar. The people mostly interested in what the catechists had to say were Kartabhajas led by an educated village blacksmith called Chandy. In this case the Kartabhajas had already publicly renounced idol worship and were suffering some degree of annoyance and persecution from Hindu neighbors. The catechists presented them with a portion of Christian scripture and left. This visit was followed up by Deerr, who had further discussions with Chandy and others on several occasions.

The Christian movement among the Kartabhajas began at Dipchandrapore, or as H. C. L. Krückeberg (CMS) explained, Dipchandrapore was the "first and moving point" of conversion to Christianity in the Krishnagar district (at least among Protestants). Many of the Christian movements elsewhere in India began with local initiative, indigenous leaders seeking out the Christian missionaries. In this case,

---

5. Caldwell, *Lectures*, pp. 58-59.

6. For these and other details see the author's paper "Old Wine in New Bottles? Kartabhaja (Vaishnava) Converts to Evangelical Christianity in Bengal. 1835-1845," in *Religious Conversion Movements in South Asia: Continuities and Change*, ed. Geoffrey A. Oddie (Richmond: Curzon Press, 1997), pp. 57-77.

however, it was Bengali Christian preachers who stumbled across a village where the people were especially willing and anxious to listen, and it was Chandy, the Kartabhaja leader, who played a key role in discussion with the missionaries.

In 1836 about thirty persons, including Chandy, were baptized. This event created a great deal of interest especially among the converts' relatives. Persecution increased, but so too did interest in the Christian movement. Visitors came to the village and news spread among relatives in other villages nearby. In 1838 leading men in ten villages belonging to the Kartabhaja sect, along with their families (four to five hundred people) embraced Christianity. By this time the movement had spread extensively among Kartabhajas — at least fifty miles northeast of Dipchandrapore and in and around centers such as Solo, Joginda, and Ranaband.

The Krishnagar "Mass Movement": Opportunities, Crisis, and Disappointment

It was at this point that the whole character and tone of the movement was suddenly transformed and came to include not only Kartabhajas, but many other Hindus as well. Toward the end of 1838, as a result of unusually heavy rain, all the flats alongside the Jellinghy river were heavily flooded.[7] Everyone, Hindus, Muslims, and Christians alike, lost almost all their crops and faced starvation. Deerr and his catechists, who had limited resources, decided to do what they could to relieve "the suffering Christians" who had been without food for days. But while Deerr in his account seems to imply that the boats carrying supplies of rice distributed relief to the Christians alone, this may not have been the case, for according to a missionary colleague and after extensive inquiries, it appeared that relief was handed out not only for Christians but "especially for those who had expressed or had declared their desire to embrace Christianity."[8] Whatever the truth of this allegation and the further claim that "temporal relief" and missionary preaching went hand in hand, the message was much the same. If you are starving

7. For one of the best accounts of these events see J. Long, *Hand-book of Bengal Missions* (London: John Farquhar Shaw, 1848), pp. 183-86.

8. Long, *Hand-book*, p. 185; M. Wylie, *Bengal as a Field of Missions* (London: W. H. Dalton, 1854), p. 201.

and need food and other assistance, join the Christians. Deerr may have had the best of intentions and a deeply felt pastoral concern for his Christian flock, but his actions (including his subsequent raising of loans and distribution of seeds for Christian communities) could only have reinforced the idea among suffering and desperately poor people that Christianity would always provide material help and other types of assistance in times of need. This impression was reinforced by Daniel Wilson, bishop of Calcutta, who visited the district in October 1839 when there were already several thousand inquirers and baptized Christians. According to the bishop of Victoria, Hong Kong (one of those subsequently involved in investigations into events connected with the movement), when the bishop of Calcutta, "a lord sahib," speaking through an interpreter addressed them as "dear brethren and friends," "the poor ryots (peasants) deemed themselves henceforth secure against the oppression of zamindars and the future incursions of want — their European protectors had taken them under their tutelage and support; and as long as these impressions lasted, the native population to the number of 3,000, continued to seek and receive baptism."[9] Furthermore, if there was any notion that bishops and missionaries were somehow separate from British administration, the bishop did little to enlighten the people at Chapra when, after the death of an inquirer, he assured the Christians that "whatever the British law could do in the way of protection would be afforded them, although, from false witnesses, justice might for a time be perverted."[10]

Perhaps an inevitable consequence of a movement that, according to the CMS report of 1851-52, contained "a considerable proportion" of inquirers "actuated only by worldly desires and hopes"[11] was that when circumstances changed, and when the people's hopes and expectations were no longer met, they lost interest in Christianity. By the early 1840s the movement was losing momentum and was beginning to peter out. The floods and famine had abated and the countryside was returning to normal.

The Calcutta Corresponding Committee, increasingly aware of the risks involved in giving material assistance and of the churches being flooded with purely nominal adherents, began to tighten up the sys-

9. George Smith, "The Krishnagurh and Tinnevelly Missions," *CMI*, 1854, p. 16.

10. Daniel Wilson, ed., *Bishop Wilson's Journal Letters* (London: J. Nisbet, 1863), p. 367.

11. Quoted in Wylie, *Bengal as a Field of Missions*, p. 200.

tem of loans and other forms of assistance.[12] The missionaries themselves, who had very few trained catechists and had to establish and
organize churches from the very beginning, were becoming increasingly
disillusioned and disappointed with what they felt was a lack of genuine spiritual progress among baptized Christians. Their annual reports
to the Calcutta committee became increasingly a litany of sorrows.
Complaints that the Christians gave "more sorrow than joy," that they
mostly wanted temporal relief, that they did not care for the word of
God, that they were disappointing, "weak and unsteady" and that the
mission was faced with "the great darkness and deadness of the mass"
are words and phrases that begin to emerge in correspondence.[13] In line
with these comments were reports of CMS Christians becoming Roman
Catholics and of others returning to Islam and Hinduism. Moreover,
the Anglican hierarchy, missionaries, and lay supporters of the CMS
were also beginning publicly and openly to face the problems and disappointment. What had begun with such promise left a legacy of about
four thousand Christians, mostly nominal adherents, to be pastored
and taught the basics of evangelical Christianity. A series of visitations,
interviews, and inquiries in Krishnagar followed. These included inquiries by Archdeacon Dealtry who conducted extensive interviews with
missionaries, converts, and others, and visits and further inquiries by
Bishop Spencer of Madras and the bishop of Hong Kong. The movement was and has remained the largest movement focused on Protestant Christianity in Bengali history. Its apparent "failure," which was
referred to by Stock in his history of the CMS,[14] appears to have reinforced a long-standing conviction among Protestant missionaries of all
denominations, at least up until the 1880s, that mass movements were
fraught with danger and were likely to lead to the incorporation of adherents with what they regarded as "unworthy" motives.

Although, as a result of the movement of 1838-39, there was a
great deal of gloom and disappointment, the missionaries tended to ignore indirect results, such as the effect of Christian teaching on the people who remained or returned to Hinduism or Islam. Indeed a great

12. George Spencer (Bishop of Madras), *A Brief Account of the Church Missionary Society's Mission in the District of Krishnagur in the Diocese of Calcutta*
(London, 1846), p. 18; St. Paul's College Calcutta archives, Calcutta Correspondence, Proceedings, 1839-1842.

13. Calcutta Corresponding Committee, twenty-fifth to thirty-second annual
reports.

14. Stock, vol. 1, pp. 315-16.

deal more research is required into popular religious movements in Bengal in the nineteenth century, including their links with Christianity. Furthermore, by way of contrast with the movement of the poor, disempowered peasantry preoccupied with "temporal affairs" was the movement of Kartabhajas into the Christian fold, which, as already mentioned, *preceded* the floods and famine and which appears to have involved converts who were on a spiritual journey and trying to make sense of the changing world around them.[15]

Kartabhaja Fulfillment in the Christian Gospel

After the floods and during the period from about 1839 to 1840, a few more Kartabhajas were swept into the fold, along with the thousands of other Hindu and Muslim inquirers. Among these latter-day Kartabhaja converts were at least seven gurus who commanded the allegiance of numerous disciples scattered in villages throughout the district. However, by this time the character and earnest tone of the Kartabhaja movement appears to have been already established.

It was, as I have shown, the Kartabhajas who first responded to missionary preaching, and it was these people who persevered in spite of the suffering and persecution that occurred in the early stages of the movement. Moreover, as the missionaries most closely associated with the movement declared, it was the Kartabhajas who were the most consistent Christians, the best and steadiest, and those who gave the missionaries the greatest satisfaction. When asked to give an account of why they were involved in the new religion, it was the Kartabhajas who constantly pointed to the nature of their religious journey and the way in which Christianity seemed to satisfy long-felt religious needs and make sense in the light of their own Kartabhaja system of beliefs. Indeed, it is through the Kartabhaja movement that we can see more clearly than in many other cases of Christian conversion in India, the way in which preconversion ideas predisposed indigenous groups in favor of Christianity. In their case, it does not appear to have been a yearning for security and material comforts, but a yearning of the spirit for meaning and satisfaction that was the primary reason for their engagement with Christian teaching.

15. For this account, including references to sources, see Oddie, "Old Wine in New Bottles?"

GEOFFREY A. ODDIE

The Kartabhaja movement was from the beginning a fairly open, fluid, and eclectic movement — absorbing and reflecting a wide variety of influences as it developed in the late eighteenth and early nineteenth centuries. Its somewhat amorphous and heterogeneous character, reflected in a variety of subdivisions, was partly a consequence of the fact that the traditions which began to develop under their chief guru Dulalchand (1775-1832) were not committed to writing until the 1880s. Nevertheless, it is clear that these traditions, incorporated in what was known as the *Bhaver Gita* (not to be confused with the *Bhagavadgita*) and recounted in missionary and other sources, placed a consistent emphasis on certain central teachings. Among these was an insistence that the Kartabhaja sect was a legitimate extension of the Bengali Vaishnava movement and that its roots lay in Chaitanya's *bhakti,* or devotional movement, of the sixteenth century. Together with the Bengali Vaishnavas, the Kartabhajas affirmed at least two basic ideas that bore some similarity with Christian teaching. The first of these was belief that at some time God had come to earth in human form. According to this tradition, Vishnu or God, the creator of all things, is a beneficent deity who, whenever the world is out of joint, takes the form of a creature, usually an animal or human, to visit the world and save humankind. As the *Bhagavadgita* has Krishna (an incarnation of Vishnu) say, "in every age I come back to deliver the holy, to destroy the sin of the sinner, to establish righteousness" (chap. 4, st. 8). The second teaching propounded by Chaitanya and subsequent Kartabhaja gurus was not only the claim that they themselves were incarnations of Krishna or Vishnu and therefore God, but the simple message of *moksha,* or salvation, through devotion or love for God. Priestly rituals, learning, or logic were all unnecessary. As in evangelical Christianity the stress appears to have been on the accessibility of salvation, which is open to all irrespective of religion, social status, or background — a radical doctrine in a country where ideas of caste hierarchy were well entrenched. And as was the case in all forms of Christianity, Chaitanya and the Kartabhaja gurus appear to have adopted some form of congregational worship.

The Kartabhajas, however, appear to have developed both teachings and practice even more in line with Christianity than other Bengali Vaishnavas. Like Christians they rejected idol worship and not only questioned concepts of hierarchy in the caste system, but challenged it through intercaste forms of congregational worship. As the Baptist missionary, Joshua Marshman, pointed out, for Kartabhajas, caste was nothing, idols were nothing, and Brahmans were nothing.

236

Followers, drawn from different caste backgrounds, met perhaps weekly or once a month, but in the strictest secrecy lest they be discovered and excommunicated from Hindu or Muslim society. J. J. Weitbrecht of the CMS, who had several discussions with the leader and other members of the sect in Burdwan, wrote that:

> They meet every Thursday in certain villages, after sunset, two or three hundred together; sitting cross-legged, in a circle, on the ground. They sing hymns in praise of their Creator. Every distinction of caste ceases at these nightly meetings; the Brahmin is sitting in brotherly fellowship by the side of the Sudra or the Mahomedan. They break bread together and a cup passes round the circle, from which all are drinking.[16]

William Deerr, who had considerable knowledge of Kartabhaja ideas and practice in the Krishnagar district, explained that there, after the hymn, they "admonish each other to be virtuous, and inculcate the doctrine that God is pure, Merciful & Holy." Referring to the love feast that he argued "seems to form the principal part of their worship," he described the ignoring of caste distinctions, the atmosphere of mutual love and support, and the fact that during the feast they not only took food from each other's hands, but frequently put rice in each other's mouth — a clear violation of caste taboos.

Any refusal to perform image worship or observe the usual caste distinctions in public was extremely dangerous as it invited ostracism and persecution. In practice, therefore, most Kartabhajas lived a double life. When the meeting was over, they reverted to the practices that operated in everyday life. As Deerr pointed out, the Brahman became once more the Brahman and the Muslim resumed his life as a Muslim. Except for a few occasions when they joined in secret with other members of the sect, Kartabhajas continued to observe the rules of social behavior, rituals, and forms of worship which they had always followed prior to their involvement in the movement — the women of Hindu background, for example, continuing to play a prominent role in keeping up Hindu rituals in the home. The Protestant missionaries tended to regard this type of behavior as hypocrisy, and Kartabhaja converts who had not already been made outcasts were expected publicly and openly to renounce caste and all forms of idolatrous worship.

16. J. J. Weitbrecht, *Protestant Missions in Bengal Illustrated* (London: John F. Shaw, 1844), pp. 321-22.

In spite of disappointment that the Kartabhajas had not come further in their rejection of the caste system, many of the missionaries underlined the extent to which Kartabhaja teachings and life style were already in accordance with Protestant Christianity. As the Christian weekly newspaper, the *Friend of India,* remarked, the Kartabhajas recognized two of the main principles of true religion — "the spirituality of divine worship and the obligation to mutual good will and love." But in spite of these parallels with Christianity, there were also differences. The parallels in thought and teaching certainly facilitated understanding, but it was the perception of difference that seemed to make the transfer of faith and eventual conversion to Christianity worthwhile.

While some members of the sect were satisfied with the stage they had reached in faith and practice, others were restless and still searching for something further. Indeed the idea of openness and of seeking truth was an influential impulse among them and in the 1830s and 1840s, in a period of continued change and disruption, some of them, still trying to make sense of the world around them, became increasingly interested in what they heard of Jesus. As we have seen, like hosts of other Bengalis, they had their own gurus. But what sort of guru was Jesus? Was he like the Karta or subordinate gurus in the Kartabhaja sect, or was he different? Notwithstanding their possession of a mantra and formal allegiance to the Karta or head of the sect, some of those involved in the Kartabhaja movement had doubts about whether they really had found "the true guru," without whom no one could hope "to cross the river of life."

According to much in Kartabhaja teaching, gurus were not supposed to be caught up in worldliness or immoral behavior. The *Bhaver Gita* declares, for example, that "one must practise both modesty and poverty if one is to realise God." There can be little doubt, however, that Dulalchand, the third leader of the sect, lived in considerable luxury. Describing a visit to his residence in 1802, Joshua Marshman wrote that "Dulal's handsome and stately house, exceeding that of many Rajahs, and his garners around filled with grain, all the gifts of his deluded followers, convinced us of the profitability of his trade."[17]

Dulalchand's sons and successors (Iswarchandra and Indra Narayan) were singled out and especially condemned by Bengali writ-

---

17. Joshua Marshman's Journal, in *Periodical Accounts Relative to the B.M.S.,* vol. 11, p. 266.

ers as not living up to the highest of moral standards. And this was precisely at the time the largest number of Kartabhajas were converted to Christianity. Even if allegations of greed, corruption, and sexual immorality leveled against them were largely untrue, these allegations must have created further unease among more ordinary members of the Kartabhaja sect.

What is very clear is that some of those Kartabhajas who began to think about adopting Christianity, already had doubts about the integrity or moral standing of the Kartabhaja gurus. For them there was a contrast between what they knew of contemporary gurus and the Jesus of the Gospels. Two of these converts were Krishna Pal, the Baptist convert, and Peter Chandy, the first, best known, and most highly respected convert of the CMS Krishnagar mission. Like Pal, Chandy was convinced that the true guru would be a man of great love and humility. When in the 1830s a certain fakir proclaimed himself as the true heir of the Rajah of Burdwan and deliverer of the people, many Kartabhajas rallied in support of the rising ruler. However, after giving him his initial support, Chandy decided that the fakir could not be the expected messiah, as he was quite clearly "subject to hatred and pride."

Interest in Jesus as the true guru was not only linked with growing disappointment with Kartabhaja gurus, but was tied in with an atmosphere of messianic expectation that was widespread in Bengal in the late eighteenth and early nineteenth centuries. As I have noted, it was a period of great instability, turbulence, and change, not to mention the economic hardship and suffering among ordinary people who naturally longed for some kind of leader who would deliver them from all their trouble. Messianic ideas, including the idea that God would come again, were quite explicit in the Vaishnavite tradition. Nor were they unknown in Islam, especially in Shiah and Sufi circles, including among Sufi preachers in the Krishnagar district in the early nineteenth century. A commonly held view among Kartabhajas was that God would appear in human flesh — perhaps through some extraordinary public intervention or perhaps in a more personal way whereby the individual would "see" God through the inner eye and thereby achieve salvation.

In 1839 Deerr, when visiting the Kartabhajas at Dipchandrapore, declared that their chief principle was that "by devotion God will give them eyes, and that they will obtain a sight of Him, and through that sight salvation." Although by this the Kartabhajas apparently meant that they would see God "through the inner eye," some inquirers elsewhere, including those of Muslim origin, had somewhat different hopes and expectations anticipating God's intervention in an outward and physical form.

No matter what the questions were about God's activity, the Bengali catechists and CMS missionaries were faced with the task of convincing persistent inquirers and also critics that Christian scripture and Christianity were relevant to their situation and provided at least some answers. It certainly does not appear that either Deerr or Krückeberg (the two CMS missionaries most involved in negotiations with the Kartabhajas) believed in an imminent Second Coming or that God would act in the near future in some unusual way. But what is clear is that the missionaries and their assistants were able to point to three of the basic claims in Christian scripture in order to attempt to satisfy messianic hopes and expectation. In the Old Testament there was the prediction that God would raise up a Messiah for his people; in the New Testament there was the claim that this had come to fulfillment through the advent, life, and death of Jesus Christ and also the promise that he (the risen Christ) would come again. All of these themes were exploited in missionary preaching among the Kartabhajas. For example, when preaching to Christians and non-Christians alike at Dipchandrapore in August 1837, Krückeberg read and explained Isaiah, chapter 9, "by which they seemed to be much edified." This includes the well-known verses that describe God as being on the side of the oppressed and where the prophet predicts God's coming as the Messiah who will rule in justice for ever more. The message, one can safely assume, was that this promised Messiah had already come, that Kartabhaja longings could be satisfied through worship of him, and that his rule was (as verses 4 and 5 clearly state) associated with justice for oppressed and exploited people. In developing the Christian idea of the incarnation, Deerr honed in on the Kartabhaja quest for a sight of God by referring to the passage in St. John's Gospel, 14:9, where Jesus says, "he that hath seen me hath seen the Father." According to Deerr, Jesus was God "manifest in the flesh" and all that the Kartabhajas were seeking was in the gospel. Nor did the missionaries ignore the doctrine of the Second Coming. J. J. Weitbrecht, referring to his conversation with a Kartabhaja leader, noted that the latter "was exceedingly pleased to hear that Christ was to appear a second time, and that all true believers in him await for his advent." There is clear evidence then that missionaries made a deliberate attempt to link preexisting beliefs with the presentation of the Christian gospel.

240

Thus Kartabhaja interest in Christianity was somewhat different from that of most other groups who joined the Protestant churches in large numbers in Bengal in the first half of the nineteenth century. Unlike the mass-movement converts who joined the churches later (1839-41) after the floods and handouts, the Kartabhajas were attracted especially to the theological and other ideas associated with Christian teaching and the Christian way of life.

In common with many other oppressed and low-caste peoples, they had been uprooted and forced to move. They had been searching for a new and better place in which to live and, as was the case with many of their fellow travelers, their physical journey was not unrelated to an open-mindedness and spiritual quest. As the Christian missionaries might well have said, their search was for "a new heaven and a new earth." Among other things they were seeking "the true guru," a messiah, or a saving vision of God, a more accepting, less hierarchical fellowship, and rituals and forms of worship more expressive of their changing views of God and the world around them. Though many of them found what they wanted in the Kartabhaja religion, others were less strongly committed, and, for them, participation in the movement was only one stage in an ongoing journey. For those who found in Christianity greater religious and conceptual satisfaction, the Kartabhaja experience was, nevertheless, an important stage in their religious and conceptual journey. It was at least one of the factors that predisposed them more in favor of Christian teaching. As we have seen, Kartabhaja belief and doctrine provided striking parallels with Christian belief. And because they already shared many of the same basic assumptions, values, and beliefs, the Kartabhajas were in a better position than most of their Hindu and Muslim neighbors to be able to understand and respond to evangelical claims about God and the Christian message of salvation.

Although it is likely that belief or intellectual conviction was not the only factor in Kartabhaja conversion, there can be little doubt that pre-Christian ideas played a crucial role in the conversion process and that, when linked with Christian teaching, were a powerful incentive in encouraging Kartabhajas to accept the Christian faith. The ideas of incarnation, the search for the true guru, and longings for a messiah who would usher in an era of equality and justice were also ideas which emerged in other religious movements in India in the nineteenth century, for example, among followers of the Rajayoga sect in Andhra Pradesh, who became Christian in the 1860s and 1870s.

Tirunelveli Nadars and Conversion

The third and final movement or series of movements under consideration were mainly an outcome of nadar interest in Christianity and took place in the south. The nadars, known as shanars in the early nineteenth century, were not a sect like the Kartabhajas (united across caste lines on the basis of shared religious belief) but were a caste community that one inherited rather than joined and that possessed a traditional occupation, rules relating to marriage, commensalism, and a vague position somewhere toward the lower end of the Hindu caste hierarchy.[18] According to Robert Caldwell, who spent many years as an SPG missionary among them, they could be described as "belonging to the highest division of the lowest classes, or the lowest of the middle classes: poor, but not paupers, rude and unlettered, but by many degrees removed from the savage state."[19] Unlike the Kartabhajas and other converts in the Krishnagar district who were mainly tenants and landless laborers engaged in paddy cultivation, the nadars' principal occupation and source of income was the cultivation of the palmyra palm, which was to them what rice was in Bengal. "During the hottest part of the year, from March to September [wrote Caldwell] the principal occupation of the men is the climbing of the palmyra, a tall mast-like palm, with only a few fan shaped leaves at the top. The object of this labourious task is to obtain the juice which flows from the bruised flower stalk of the tree, and which is collected as it drops, in little pots tied to the stalk."[20] The sweet juice could be drunk, but, more often, was used for commercial purposes, being boiled down into "jaggery" (a coarse sugar) or allowed to ferment and then sold as toddy or country liquor. The leaves of the tree, as well as the wood, were also valued — these being used as writing material, for thatching houses and the making of mats, baskets, and vessels of almost every description.[21]

The nadar community itself was subdivided. The nadans, who were the most powerful group, claimed signorage or ultimate rights of control over the lands and even the dwellings of the rest of the population. In

18. For the best and most comprehensive analysis on the development of the nadar community, see Robert L. Hardgrave, *The Nadars of Tamilnad: The Political Culture of a Community in Change* (Berkeley: University of California Press, 1969).

19. R. Caldwell, *The Tinnevelly Shanars* (Madras, 1849), p. 4.

20. Caldwell, *Tinnevelly Shanars,* p. 56.

21. Caldwell, *Lectures,* pp. 31-36.

spite of this, however, most ordinary shanars (the group that showed most interest in Christianity) had acquired some land and were described by Caldwell as proprietors of a small patch of ground on which they grew the palmyra. While they climbed their own trees or were hired to climb the trees of others, there was a third group in the community who were engaged in trade, for example in selling the country liquor.

As R. E. Frykenberg's analysis has so clearly shown, when the first CMS missionaries, C. T. E. Rhenius and L. B. E. Schmid, arrived in Tirunelveli district in the early 1820s, they took over the supervision of congregations that, in spite of persecution and a decline in numbers, still retained considerable vitality.[22] They had already benefited a great deal from the assistance of experienced Indian catechists and workers from the Tanjore mission and had developed largely as self-directing autonomous communities. A new spurt of conversions and period of expansion took place from about 1825 to 1835 and again in the 1840s. In some ways these conversions, which occurred largely among the nadar community, followed patterns similar to the conversions in the Krishnagar district and in subsequent mass-movement areas. Rather than involving the individual in action independent of others, they were movements of groups and families into the Christian churches. By way of contrast with what often happened in urban areas and among higher-caste converts where individuals usually had to break with members of their own caste and family, the emphasis in these lower-caste conversions was on family and corporate action. Describing the nature of these movements among the shanars, Caldwell wrote that

> individuals and single families are rarely found to relinquish heathen-ism and join the Christian church. They wait till favourable circum-stances influence the minds of their relatives or neighbours: and then they come in as a body. In like manner, if through any cause a new learner should wish to return to heathenism, he generally waits till he can succeed in engaging on his side the sympathies of a portion of the congregation.[23]

22. Robert Eric Frykenberg, "The Impact of Conversion and Social Reform upon Society in South India during the Late Company Period: Questions Concern-ing Hindu-Christian Encounters with Special Reference to Tinnevelly," in *Indian Society and the Beginnings of Modernisation, c. 1830-1850,* ed. C. H. Philips and Mary Doreen Wainwright (London: School of Oriental and African Studies, 1976), pp. 187-243.

23. Caldwell, *Tinnevelly Shanars,* p. 69. See also Caldwell, *Lectures,* p. 46.

One of the key questions in relation to nadar conversion is why such an unusually high proportion of the community adopted the Christian faith. Though Christianity spread among some other castes higher or lower on the social scale, the number of shanars who placed themselves under Christian instruction was, by the 1850s, greater than that of all the other converts in India in connection with Protestant missions.[24] Indeed, the shanars formed the bulk of the congregations in almost every part of Tirunelveli and, in some areas, the Christian church was almost exclusively the shanar church. Explaining the peculiar accessibility of the shanars, Caldwell declared that they were "without priests; without a written religious code; without sacred traditions; without historic recollections; without aversion to Christianity as a foreign religion which other classes evince" and that the chief obstacle to their evangelization was the depth of their ignorance.[25] Apart from these considerations, a crucial factor in their conversion may well have been the village structure and the comparative ease with which they were able to respond to the Christian message. Castes such as pallars and pariahs, lower than shanars in social status, were more closely integrated within the traditional village system.[26] In many parts of Tamilnadu, for example, the pariahs were expected to beat the village drum during religious festivals and bury the dead, as well as work for their village masters as agricultural laborers. When converted to Christianity there was usually some concern that the new converts would neglect their traditional duties — a feeling reinforced by what often looked like a new spirit of independence. The shanars, however, tended to live in or near palmyra forests in comparative isolation. And while an interest in Christianity might displease and threaten some members of their own community, it did not have all of the same threatening implications for the higher-caste Hindus who had very little to do with shanars in everyday life.

In spite of the comparative ease with which shanars were able to respond to Christianity, it should not be imagined they were entirely free from problems and persecution once they decided to join the Christians. When the missionaries first arrived in some villages, they stepped into a minefield of local disputes. Some of these involved the higher

24. Caldwell, *Tinnevelly Shanars,* p. 71; *Lectures,* pp. 31, 44.
25. Caldwell, *Tinnevelly Shanars,* p. 71.
26. Caldwell, *Tinnevelly Shanars,* pp. 5, 32, 62-63.

castes and shanars long before Christianity arrived — one complaint being, for example, that the higher castes, acting as agents for shanar landholders, were gradually appropriating the land for themselves.[27] Furthermore, in some cases, Christianity was seen as a threat to the establishment nadans and other landlords feeling alarm that they were losing control over Christian tenants who seemed to be becoming increasingly assertive.[28] Those who owned the palmyra trees and employed Christians as climbers could no longer be sure they would work on Sundays.[29] In some villages, headmen feared disunity and endless quarrels while there was also anger and concern at the Christians, refusal to pay the usual taxes in support of traditional religious activities.[30] Writing in 1827 C. T. E. Rhenius and Bernard Schmid pointed out, for example, that "When the people were in Heathenism, they paid certain taxes to idol temples for the performance of idolatry, and other contributions for the maintenance of dancing girls, travelling sunnyasies, etc: now, becoming Christians, they think themselves justly freed from such contributions; but the accountant comes and asks the same from them as from the Heathen: they, of course, refuse; and instantly have to suffer for it."[31]

Thus while, at least initially, shanars were in a better position to respond to Christianity than many of the other low-caste Hindus integrated in a more tightly knit village system, many of them still had to face troubles and persecution even after they had placed themselves under Christian instruction or joined Christian congregations. In these circumstances it is not surprising that some inquirers returned to traditional religious life and practice while others, more strongly committed, persevered as catechumens or baptized Christians.

Although the conversion accounts of individual high-caste Hindus (many of them educated in mission schools) may suggest some parallels with evangelical conversion accounts, for example in Britain, the conversion experience of most mass-movement converts to Christianity in India in rural areas was probably very different. Self-conscious individualism was not a feature of shanar society and, for this reason alone, it

27. *Missionary Register* (Oct. 1826), p. 491 and (Oct. 1828), p. 521.
28. Hardgrave, *The Nadars of Tamilnad*, p. 48; George Pettitt, *The Tinnevelly Mission of the Church Missionary Society* (London: Seeley, 1851), pp. 187-92.
29. *Missionary Register* (Oct. 1826), p. 259.
30. Pettitt, *The Tinnevelly Mission*, p. 240.
31. *Missionary Register* (Oct. 1828), p. 523.

is hardly surprising that the missionary sources on the shanars are marked by a comparative dearth of references to individual conversion. This includes accounts of conversion in the sense of an individual's sudden turnaround or transformation such as the Pauline-type of experience described in A. D. Nock's book, where the convert declares that "the old was wrong and the new is right."[32] In contrast to this, the process as described in missionary records was more of a corporate process involving the slow and very gradual incorporation of new ideas, patterns of worship, and lifestyle into an ongoing village life and activity. It was not easy for converts, even if they wished, to forget all that had gone before. After his eight years of work and experience among the shanars, Caldwell wrote that

> Converts from demonolatry cannot all at once forget, though they may have abandoned, the system in which they were trained. They will necessarily bring with them into the Christian church much of their materialism, their superstitious fear, and their love of rude excitements. The mind cannot slough off its old ideas and associations in a day. . . . It is only when religion becomes a passion, or a habit, that old things pass away and all things become new. It is surely not to be supposed that of the 40,000 souls connected with the Missions in Tinnevelly all are Christians in earnest. The public has often been told that the majority, though converted from heathenism to Christianity, do not appear to have been converted from sin to God; that the faith of the majority is only an intellectual assent to half-understood truths; and that the number of persons who appear to be sincerely pious is small. It follows that in the majority, or at least in a large proportion of cases, the superstitious fear of the old demonolatry must have survived conversion to the new theology; or at least that the roots of the old system remain.[33]

Shanar beliefs and understandings of the world around do not appear to have played such a crucial role in stimulating an interest in Christianity in Tirunelveli as Kartabhaja views and traditions did in arousing an interest in Christianity in Bengal. Nevertheless, shanar tra-

---

32. A. D. Nock, *Conversion. The Old and New in Religion from Alexander the Great to Augustine of Hippo* (Oxford: Clarendon Press, 1933), p. 7. For a more recent but broadly based interpretation of the religious conversion phenomenon see Lewis R. Rambo, *Understanding Religious Conversion* (New Haven: Yale University Press, c. 1993).

33. Caldwell, *Tinnevelly Shanars*, p. 31.

ditions provided some ideas that could be used to facilitate the introduction of the Christian gospel. While, for example, the shanars did not
believe in life after death, there were "traces among them of a vague
traditionary belief in the existence of God."[34] And while their active
and everyday worship and propitiation of devils (spirits that, according
to missionary accounts, always inflicted evil and never good on human
beings) appeared to offer the missionary or evangelist little that could
be used as a foundation for Christian teaching, the idea of bloody sacrifice and of giving a life for life served as a basis for the doctrine of ever-
lasting redemption through the sacrifice of Christ. Moreover, fear of
devils (a potent and persistent feeling in the life of shanars) was also a
basis for teachings about the true nature of the Christian God. The missionaries could explain that he was, in contrast with the devils, essentially constructive, moral and good; and that he, being more powerful
even than the most powerful devils, could protect them from whatever
harm the devils might want to inflict.[35]

But aside from religious considerations, what other factors appear
to explain shanar interest in Christianity? Referring to his experience of
work among them, the CMS missionary, George Pettitt, explained that
one could "scarcely expect whole families, and perhaps villages to
abandon the religion of their youth, and of their ancestors, for one
which they would have had but few opportunities to understand —
without some impulse of a worldly kind."[36] In Caldwell's view these
considerations included:

> the expectation of receiving from the missionary of their district ad-
> vice on difficulties, sympathy in adversity, and help in sickness, and of
> being at all times friendly inquired after and kindly spoken to; the de-
> sire of being connected with a rising, united body, guided by Euro-
> pean intelligence, and governed by principles of Christian justice; the
> expectation of being protected in some measure from the oppressions
> of their wealthy neighbours; the fact that Native Christians appear af-
> ter a few years to acquire a higher standing and to enjoy more peace
> and prosperity than they had as heathens; the desire of advancement
> on the part of the lower castes, who find that they are considered by

---

34. On shanar beliefs and relationship with Christian teachings see Caldwell,
Tinnevelly Shanars, pp. 6-31; Pettitt, *The Tinnevelly Mission,* pp. 483-501; and Edward Sargent's account in *CMI* (1849), pp. 34-37, 60-62, 84-85.

35. Caldwell, *Lectures,* p. 50, and *Tinnevelly Shanars,* p. 43.

36. Pettitt, *The Tinnevelly Mission,* p. 512.

the missionaries as capable of advancement and taught to feel that they are men.[37]

One of the major differences between CMS converts in Bengal and Tirunelveli in the first half of the nineteenth century was that the latter had a better idea of what was involved in becoming Christian. In Krishnagar in the 1830s and 1840s there were fewer well-established and active Christian communities than there were in Tirunelveli which could serve as models or as pointers to what it would be like if individuals or families joined the Christian church. The CMS missionaries in Tirunelveli had the advantage of following in the footsteps of other evangelists and could always point to "healthy" preexisting congregations, whereas, in many cases, the Bengal missionaries (who were also less well resourced) had to build from scratch and did not always have the advantage of being able to point inquirers to developing or well-established local congregations.

The importance of models, or "the demonstration effect," was emphasized by Caldwell when he remarked that

> The surrounding heathen too often refuse to be made acquainted with the doctrines of Christianity; but they cannot refuse to become acquainted with the visible embodiment of those doctrines in the Christian Church. The Church's unity, her discipline, her zeal for justice and truth, her care for her poor members, her exertions in behalf of the oppressed, her unwearied instructions, her daily prayers, her solemn services, her corporate life, her progressive prosperity, her universal claims — these characteristics of the Church render her visible in Tinnevelly, even to heathen eyes.[38]

It would perhaps be surprising if the shanars were equally impressed with all of these so-called characteristics. But at least two of the considerations that appear to have weighed heavily in their minds were the capacity of missionaries and catechists to offer some kind of help and protection in adversity, and the non-Christian shanars' sense that the Christians were outstripping them in prosperity and progress.

As early as 1826, Rhenius remarked that his influence with higher officials, and the attention that grievances of the Christians subsequently received from the magistrate, "became known . . . all over this

37. Caldwell, *Lectures*, p. 77.
38. Caldwell, *Lectures*, p. 64.

part of the district; and was probably one of the causes which excited many more villages to listen to Christian Instruction and renounce Idolatry."[39] Writing some twenty years later, Pettitt stated his opinion that one of the most important temporal reasons for continuing interest in Christianity was the help and advice missionaries and catechists were able to give to Christians in times of oppression or persecution and in the settlement of local disputes. Success in these efforts, he wrote, "showed that the poor Shanar and even the Pariah could, in connection with the Mission, obtain protection and enjoy security."[40]

Also highly significant was the feeling that the Christian shanar community was making rapid progress, economically, socially, and in other ways in comparison with non-Christian members of the same caste. Contemporary observers all seem to be agreed that shanar Christians were making rapid progress intellectually, in habits of industry, materially, in improved cleanliness, dress, and quality of housing, in their tendency to move into new and rising occupations and in their upward social mobility.[41] After visiting shanar Christians in Tirunelveli in 1843, J. Tucker (CMS) wrote that, in his opinion, "the effect of Christianity on the people is visible in their more cleanly appearance — more industrious habits — and, the natural and legitimate consequence, more wealth, and more independence of character."[42] Some years later, Caldwell remarked that "in every case with which I am acquainted, villages which have held fast and valued the Christianity they received, have risen, sometimes in the first generation, always in the second, to the enjoyment of greater prosperity and comfort, and to a higher position in the social scale, than any heathen village of the same caste."[43]

By the 1840s, Christian shanars were already expanding their economic activities to include work in sugar refineries in Cuddalore or on coffee plantations in Ceylon, as a result of which they were sending money back to relatives in Tirunelveli district. Progress in education and an improving economic position, evident in these and other economic activities, were accompanied by a growing self-awareness and improvements in social status. In fact, as early as 1849,

39. *Missionary Register* (Oct. 1826).
40. Pettitt, *The Tinnevelly Mission*, pp. 513-15.
41. Pettitt, *The Tinnevelly Mission*, p. 514.
42. J. Tucker, "Report on Tinnevelly Mission" (Aug. 1843). *Pamphlets on Indian Missions*, no. 1, p. 13.
43. Caldwell, *Lectures*, p. 40.

Caldwell, in his work *The Tinnevelly Shanars,* noted that "generally
. . . conversion to Christianity is found to raise rather than lower
them in the social scale." Unlike higher-caste converts, the shanars,
who converted in groups together, did not lose status, and were not
usually ejected from the broader caste community. They therefore
continued to intermingle with non-Christian shanars, working with
them and, in many cases, acting as leaders in attempts to improve and
raise the level of the whole community.[44] Hence for shanars, conversion was not opting out of one community and joining another, but
simply joining an additional specifically Christian association. Not
only did they not lose caste, but, as Hardgrave has pointed out, having connections with the CMS or other Protestant missions provided
them with a network of opportunities in education and in other activities that had the effect of greatly improving the community's social
standing.[45]

Missionaries and Autonomy in Christian Movements: Some Conclusions

I have discussed three different types of inquiry/conversion movements
associated with the CMS in the first half of the nineteenth century. How
important were the foreign missionaries as a factor in facilitating the
spread of the Christian gospel?

Frist, my investigation is a further illustration of the idea that if
one wants to understand what was happening in the mission field then
it is important to start with the converts' world rather than with the
missionaries. Political, economic, social, religious, intellectual, and
other changes already taking place influenced the way in which people
(in this case the poorer classes of Krishnagar and Tirunelveli) heard, understood, and responded to Christian preaching. These changes, reaching into India's history, included religious developments such as the introduction of Catholic and early Protestant Christianity and the rise of
the Kartabhaja sect in the eighteenth century, economic and political
turbulence that encouraged migration and the settlement of peoples
along the banks of the Jellinghy river, and the further consolidation of
British rule in South India as well as in Bengal.

44. Caldwell, *Tinnevelly Shanars,* pp. 64-65.
45. Hardgrave, *The Nadars of Tamilnad,* pp. 90-94.

All the movements I have discussed were largely independent, spontaneous expressions of people's will and agenda — the desire for salvation from floods and famine, the long search for spiritual meaning, the desire for protection and security, a longing for recognition, the aspiration and desire for a generally better way of life, and other hopes and aspirations. Of course the missionaries were partly responsible for these movements in the sense that they or their forebears, together with Indian Christians, had been preaching far and wide. They had established schools, for example, in Krishnagar and Palamcotta; prepared and distributed pamphlets, handbills, and portions of scripture in Bengali or Tamil (for those few who could read); and made their presence felt and recognized as a possible source of help and authority in times of trouble. Furthermore, their influence and ability to attract the attention of local people was enhanced by the fact that they were white Europeans, or sahibs, and were therefore associated in the mind of the population (especially the more ignorant) with the power and possible benefits of British rule.

Whatever the reasons for the attractiveness of Christianity and whatever the motives, a crucial issue was the Indian Christian and missionary response. How these parties reacted to the phenomenon of inquirers wanting to put themselves under Christian instruction could determine the future shape and destiny of the Christian movement. What role then did the CMS missionaries play in this process of Christian instruction, baptism, and the organization and consolidation of local churches?

It was primarily the missionaries (perhaps more so in Krishnagar than Tirunelveli) who acted as a filter that determined who among the inquirers was acceptable for baptism and who was not. In other words, it was they who, to a very large extent, determined the boundaries of missionary Christianity on the basis of intellectual, moral, and possibly even cultural criteria. In both Bengal and Tirunelveli, however, they appear to have been fairly inclusive in their approach, being prepared to accept and baptize most of those who came for instruction. In Krishnagar, for example, J. J. Weitbrecht complained that the baptisms taking place in 1839 were "too hasty,"[46] while in Tirunelveli, Pettitt explained that "the great point" with the missionaries was "whether persons or parties are really willing to give up heathenism, to join the Christian body, and submit to its rules and discipline without reserve,

---

46. Wylie, *Bengal as a Field of Missions*, p. 202.

Fig. 24. Church at Suveshishapuram, Tirunelveli (engraving, no date).
Church Mission Society, London

and without any *intention* of drawing back, when, perhaps, some temporal advantage is gained."[47] This statement, however, raises the questions: What was "heathenism"? And which particular practices were acceptable and which were not? Furthermore, what were the rules of discipline and how far were these a reflection of Victorian views of what was expected of Christian behavior?

The role of the missionaries in further Christian instruction was often indirect. While in Bengal they were faced with a lack of assistants and often acted as pastors directly responsible for the new congregations, the situation was somewhat different in the south. From the commencement of CMS mission work in Tirunelveli, Rhenius depended on the aid and support of Christian workers, selected and trained in a well-organized seminary. The work of these men and women, he acknowledged, was crucial for the progress of Christianity. Nearly twenty years later, Pettitt also emphasized the importance of Indian subordinates, explaining to his readers in England that the Tirunelveli catechists were

47. Pettitt, *The Tinnevelly Mission*, pp. 517-18.

able to carry out the work of instructing their own people more effectively than foreign missionaries.[48]

While some tasks were delegated, the power exercised by missionaries in determining the character and direction of mission churches was therefore considerable in that they were the ones who generally selected, trained, and employed the Indian catechists and pastors. Furthermore, missionaries who were understanding of, and sensitive to, local languages and culture were also capable of making decisions that could facilitate an understanding of the gospel or enhance and strengthen congregational life. Deerr, Weitbrecht, and Krückeberg in Bengal were sufficiently skillful to be able to explain the relationship between Kartabhaja and Christian teachings, while in Tirunelveli, the missionaries, instead of destroying all the devil temples and the preexisting system of village panchayats (councils), kept them in place, using the temples as places of worship and the traditional village committee as a type of parish council that would make decisions about discipline and temporal issues affecting the life and welfare of members of the congregation.[49] All of these decisions appear to have greatly strengthened and consolidated the Christian movement.

However, the importance of foreign missionaries in shaping the nature and direction of Christianity in India can and has been seen in more negative terms and in ways that eventually brought some of them into conflict with Indian Christians. Like Christians in every age, the missionaries were, to a greater or lesser degree, victims of their cultural background and influenced by their sense of power and control. All the churches reflected European denominational divisions. Tirunelveli, even to this day, is dotted with parish churches which look remarkably like Anglican parish churches in Victorian England; and though more indigenous clergy were ordained in Tirunelveli district than anywhere else in the Protestant mission field, it was a very long time before Azariah, a native of Tirunelveli, was consecrated as the first Indian bishop of the Anglican Church in India. In the meantime, Tirunelveli and possibly other parts of CMS territory witnessed the rise and formation of independent and more truly nativistic expressions of the Christian gospel. But that is another complex and still unfolding story.

48. Pettitt, *The Tinnevelly Mission*, p. 506.
49. Caldwell, *Lectures*, pp. 66-70.

10. The Role of Kikuyu Christians in Developing a Self-Consciously African Anglicanism

JOHN KARANJA

Introduction

This chapter seeks to highlight the early Kikuyu Christians' contributions to the creation of a distinctively African-Anglican church in central Kenya between 1900 and 1932. It identifies two possible levels of analysis — the formal and the informal — and concludes that there was, in the appropriation of Christianity in its Anglican form, a considerable degree of continuity with Kikuyu culture, even where there was conflict. At the more conspicuous formal level, the church grew up as an organized institution with its own regulations, doctrine, liturgy, and form of ministry. From this perspective, the Kikuyu Anglican Church became a replica of its English mother church adhering to the Thirty-Nine Articles, the Book of Common Prayer, and the threefold order of ministry. This chapter is, in part, an analysis of how a mission became a church. The period of study starts with the arrival of the first Anglican missionary in 1900 and ends in 1932 with the young church having overcome its first major crisis. The question is, what sort of a church had it become?

At this second, popular, or grassroots, level, the church consisted of communities of Christians struggling to come to terms with their total environment. This struggle involved a creative response to the tensions produced by the encounter between Kikuyu culture and mission Christianity. It is argued that the Kikuyu response to, and appropriation of, Christianity derived its force and vitality from indigenous models and experiences.[1] The study focuses on three features of Kikuyu culture that shaped its response: its conflict-resolving mechanism, its pragmatic nature, and its desire to master and exercise power. I focus on central Kenya because it is inhabited by a relatively homogeneous people. The sources, oral and written, are readily obtainable.

The Setting

The Kikuyu,[2] who are the subject of this chapter, constitute a large group of Bantu-speaking people in the Central Province of Kenya. At the end of the nineteenth century, they numbered about half a million. Their ancestral land is a highland area measuring about one hundred miles north to south and fifty miles east to west. The altitude ranges from three thousand to nine thousand feet.[3] The Kikuyu hills are cut by numerous streams and rivers that have created a distinctive topography of high, narrow ridges and deep valleys. Kikuyuland enjoys fairly heavy and reliable rainfall. Mean annual rainfall ranges from forty inches in the low-lying areas to seventy inches in the higher areas. The temperatures are generally moderate, ranging from forty-five to eighty-five degrees Fahrenheit.

Kikuyu social organization was based on two fundamental principles: kinship and age grading.[4] The principle of kinship found its direct expression in the *mbari*. This was a descent group extending to several known generations, mostly named after its founder and jointly owning a piece of land. Each *mbari* selected from among its most able members a *muramati* (trustee of family land), whose primary responsibility was to control the allocation and use of the land. The *muramati* was usually the senior member of the *mbari*. All male, circumcised, and married

---

1. This interpretation is based on Richard Gray, *Black Christians and White Missionaries* (New Haven: Yale University Press, 1990), chap. 1.
2. This study covers the Kikuyu and their eastern neighbors, the Embu.
3. The main source of information on physical features and climatic conditions is *The National Atlas of Kenya*. 3d ed. (Nairobi: Government Printers, 1970).
4. What follows is only a brief summary of Kikuyu society. Several aspects will be expanded at appropriate places below.

members of the *mbari* formed a council that, under the *muramati's* leadership, regulated *mbari* affairs.[5]

Besides being the basic social and economic unit, the *mbari* was also the basic religious unit. A Kikuyu family included not only those living in the physical world, but also the dead, who were remembered by the living and whose assumed wishes were taken into account in decisions affecting the *mbari* as a whole. The family group was thus the basic link between the generations, those living in the physical world, the unborn, and those living in the spirit world. The *muramati* usually presided over family religious ceremonies. The principle of age grading cut across clan and lineage affiliations. Through circumcision, all Kikuyu were admitted to membership of an age grade at some suitable time after reaching adolescence. Membership of an age grade carried with it powerful obligations of brotherhood and sisterhood toward all other members. In this way, it unified the clan and family groups of that particular age grade throughout the whole territorial unit.

Kikuyu religious beliefs may be classified into two separate but related areas: belief in *Ngai* (the High God) and belief in ancestral spirits.[6] *Ngai* was regarded as omnipotent and omniscient. He was the creator and sustainer of all things. Kikuyu believed that the ancestors, though dead, continued to exercise their influence over the living through their *ngoma* (spirits). Kikuyu recognized three types of spirits: the spirits of the immediate forebears, the spirits of the clan, and the age-group spirits. Sacrifices were the most solemn form of worship. Their chief function was to maintain a healthy relationship between the physical and spiritual worlds.[7]

Although Kikuyuland lay close to the northern caravan route from the Indian Ocean coastal ports to the interlacustrine area of what became Uganda, it was largely untouched by Westernizing influences before 1890. This was mainly because Britain, which maintained a naval presence on the East African coast, was reluctant to become directly

---

5. Jomo Kenyatta, *Facing Mount Kenya* (London: Secker & Warburg, 1938), p. 33; J. Middleton and G. Kershaw, *The Central Tribes of the North-Eastern Bantu: The Kikuyu and Kamba of Kenya,* Ethnographic Survey of Africa, East Central Africa, Part 5 (London: International African Institute, 1965), p. 26.

6. In this section, I wish simply to distinguish between them. Details of Kikuyu beliefs and how those beliefs contrasted with Christianity will be reserved for later discussion.

7. J. S. Mbiti, *African Religions and Philosophy* (London: Heinemann, 1969), p. 59.

involved in East Africa. Kikuyu isolation from Europeans ended after the Imperial British East Africa Company (IBEAC) was granted a royal charter to operate within the region, which later came to be known as Kenya.[8] The company set up a chain of posts along the northern route to Uganda. One such post was established at Dagoretti in the Kikuyu country in 1890. The fort, which was intended to serve as a staging post for the caravans bound for Uganda, was moved farther into the Kikuyu country and named Fort Smith in 1892. The strategic location of Kikuyuland, coupled with availability of surplus food and other goods, led the company to establish formal contacts with Kikuyu. In 1895, the IBEAC handed over the administration of the country to the British Foreign Office, which set up a protectorate. Between 1895 and 1906, the protectorate government extended its authority to the whole of Kikuyu country mainly through a series of military campaigns euphemistically called "punitive expeditions." The expeditions were intended to punish dissident African groups and to elevate collaborating African leaders.[9]

Missionary Occupation of Central Kenya

The establishment of the British Protectorate and, more importantly, the building of the Uganda Railway, paved the way for extensive missionary upcountry penetration.[10] The CMS was at the forefront of this expansion. Between 1900 and 1913, the mission set up seven stations in Kikuyuland: Kabete (1900), Weithaga (1903), Kahuhia (1906), Kabare (1910), Kigari (1910), Mutira (1911), and Gathukeine (1913). Kabete was always seen as the mother church. Its close proximity to Nairobi and the Kikuyu station of the Church of Scotland Mission, together with its sponsorship by the remarkable chiefs Koinange and Njonjo, ensured that it would never be far from political controversy. Weithaga was characterized by the early vigor of its immigrant converts but was soon overtaken as an educational center by the more easily accessible Kahuhia farther down the hill. The last four stations were founded in a

8. The IBEAC was a private company chartered by the British government in 1888, partly to trade and partly to further British interests in the area.

9. R. Tignor, *The Colonial Transformation of Kenya* (Princeton: Princeton University Press, 1976), p. 15.

10. On the building of the Uganda Railway, see M. G. Mill, *The Permanent Way*, 2 vols. (Nairobi, n.d).

second wave of expansion in which to some extent the CMS found it-self overextended. In subsequent years, these younger stations were less often staffed than older ones. All these contrasts are relevant to later discussion.

Three other Protestant missions established work in the area: the Church of Scotland Mission (CSM), the Africa Inland Mission (AIM), and the Gospel Missionary Society (GMS). The CSM was the first to open a station in the Kikuyu country in 1898. The AIM, which had started work at Ukambani in 1895, set up its headquarters at Kijabe on the Southern Kikuyu Escarpment in 1901. The GMS, which was ini-tially affiliated with the AIM, established its first station in Kikuyuland in 1902.[11]

Thus by 1915, there were four Protestant missions working in central Kenya, with a total of fifteen stations. The CMS stations and those of the GMS and the AIM (with the exception of Kijabe) were "one-man" stations, three or four missionaries being the most ever resi-dent. The CSM missions operated along different lines. The aim of the CSM leaders was to found fewer but larger stations, each complete with medical facilities and with a relatively large staff of missionaries.[12] The location of four Protestant missions in close proximity to each other was bound to produce friction and cause overlapping and confu-sion. Hence in 1902, the CSM and CMS agreed to divide the Kikuyu area into two spheres, with the CMS getting the territory to the east of a line from Ngong to Mount Kenya and the CSM the area to the west. Similar arrangements were eventually worked out with the other Protestant missions operating in the area.[13] For many years, the policy of mission spheres succeeded in removing competition in evangelism among Protestant missions. However, this policy could continue to work satisfactorily, after Kikuyu began to move about and to learn other ways, if in general the same methods of work were followed by all the missions. Once Africans realized that some missions with less-

11. R. McPherson, *The Presbyterian Church in Kenya* (Nairobi: East African Publishing House, 1970), chaps. 3, 5; R. Oliver, *The Missionary Factor in East Af-rica* (London: Longman, 1952), p. 171.

12. M. G. Capon, *Towards Unity in Kenya: The Story of Co-operation be-tween Missions and Churches in Kenya, 1913-1947* (Nairobi: Christian Council of Kenya, 1962), p. 6.

13. CMSA, G3A5/1902/111. Minutes of Executive Committee, 6-7 August 1902; G3A5/1909/134, Peel to Baylis, 8 November 1909; Capon, *Towards Unity*, chaps. 2, 3.

advanced schools happened to insist on stricter standards of personal living among their adherents, they began to call for freedom of choice in religion. This chapter explores why many chose to become Anglican and how they made Anglicanism Kikuyu.

Kikuyu Cosmology and Encounter with Missionary Culture

The story of the origins of the Anglican Church in central Kenya is a story of family and clan conflicts. These conflicts had a twofold source. First, within pre-Christian Kikuyu society, there already existed differences and disagreement over certain practices and customs.[14] These disagreements were exacerbated with the coming of missionaries. Second, the missionary worldview posed additional challenges and problems to the traditional Kikuyu worldview. There were two primary expressions of this conflict: in the relationship between individuals and society, and in the sphere of personal moral growth. But it is important to understand that Kikuyu culture was dynamic and not static. The society consisted of immigrant groups who were not fully settled at the time of the British occupation. As they struggled to come to terms with their new environment, the immigrants evolved a highly utilitarian culture. The experimental and adaptive nature of that culture enabled Kikuyu to resolve some of their conflicts with mission Christianity.

All religious belief has within it a tension between absolute demands and the need to exist in this world. The missionary message had a prominent eschatological component: it emphasized radical discontinuity between the demands of this world and of the world to come. On the other hand, the Kikuyu worldview, while not totally lacking in eschatology, did not exhibit a sharp distinction between the world of human experience and the spirit world. Just as Kikuyu culture was adaptive, so too the early missionaries had to accommodate their eschatological message to the realities of Kikuyu culture if they were to succeed in their task of evangelism. The Kikuyu Anglican Church was therefore the product of a two-way exploration of the tensions between what could and could not be negotiated in belief and practice.

14. For a fictional portrayal of precolonial Kikuyu conflicts, see Ngugi wa Thiong'o, *The River Between* (London: Heinemann, 1965).

Conflict in the Area of Relationship
between Individual and Society

Like other societies, Kikuyu had laws and customs that regulated their social life and behavior and to which every member was expected to conform. Individuals who failed to observe a particular custom or law risked bringing shame, and possibly disaster, to themselves, their families, and the entire community. Tough sanctions were therefore imposed on them. The fear of such sanctions prompted some offenders to seek an alternative settlement outside Kikuyu society. For such individuals, mission stations provided welcome havens. The stories of Parmenas Githendu Mukiri[15] and Emily Mumbi[16] will serve to illustrate this point.

Githendu was born around 1900 at Chui in Murang'a district, of non-Christian parents. He belonged to Ethaga, one of the nine Kikuyu clans.[17] Custom forbade all Kikuyu from eating the meat of wild animals, except in the case of boys before circumcision and those who adopted a hunting mode of life. Among Ethaga in particular, the prohibition was extended to all members of the clan.[18] The reason for this prohibition is not clear. There is insufficient evidence to link it with totemism as some scholars have attempted to do.[19] A more plausible explanation is to be found in the Kikuyu desire to tame the soil and enjoy its fruits. Hunting was generally regarded as an occupation of poor people with little in the way of stock or property who, as soon as their economic status improved, abandoned it and took to agriculture.[20] Those who thus graduated adopted the Kikuyu taboo against eating wild animals.

Young Githendu spent his early days herding his father's flock. One day in 1914, as he and other boys were looking after cattle, he killed and ate a partridge, thus violating an eating taboo of his clan. The act, if detected, carried a double punishment: he would be beaten

15. Interview with Miriam Wanjiku Githendu, Milka Waigwe Githendu, and Grace Wanjiku Githendu, 11 June 1991.

16. Interview with Emily Mumbi Shadrack, 23 August 1989.

17. According to Kikuyu tradition, the whole tribe descended from one man, Gikuyu, and his wife Mumbi. The couple gave birth to nine daughters, who are regarded as the ancestors of the nine major Kikuyu clans.

18. Interview with Miriam Githendu, Milka Waigwe Githendu, and Grace Wanjiku Githendu, 11 June 1991; Mugo wa Gatheru, *Child of Two Worlds* (London: Routledge & Kegan Paul, 1964), p. 5.

19. See, for example, C. Cagnolo, *The Akikuyu* (Nyeri, 1933), p. 22.

20. L. S. B. Leakey, *The Southern Kikuyu before 1903,* 3 vols. (London: Academic Press, 1977), vol. 1, p. 441.

by his father for disobedience; and he and his family would be subjected to discipline by his clan. The exact form of punishment for this offense is not clear. Nevertheless, it was serious enough to precipitate the family crisis discussed below.

When the news of Githendu's misconduct reached his father that evening, the latter became furious and gave the boy a thorough beating. He also promised to carry the punishment on to the next day. In an effort to preempt a further beating, Githendu sought refuge at the CMS station at Gathukine, five miles away. This station had been founded the previous year by the CMS missionary A. E. Clarke. Fearing that members of Githendu's clan might search for him at Gathukine, Clarke transferred the boy to Nairobi, sixty miles away. There, Githendu attended the only African school in the town, which had been started in 1906 by George Burns, a CMS missionary from Australia.

Githendu's story is important in that it brings out the correlation between social conflicts and church growth. Individuals who fell out with society for failing to observe the established laws and customs occasionally sought refuge at the nearest mission station. Such people often stayed on to play an important part in the growth of the church. In the case of Githendu, he was engaged as a teacher at the CMS Kahuhia primary school between 1925 and 1936.[21] During that period, he played an important part in molding the character of the students entrusted to him.

The story of Emily Mumbi illustrates how some Kikuyu girls were first drawn to the missions. At first, Kikuyu were strongly opposed to girls attending the missions for two reasons. It conflicted with the role assigned to women by society. Although it was the men's responsibility to protect the home, women were essentially homemakers.[22] While the men were on war raids, it was the women's duty to care for the home. Mission attendance was fiercely resisted because it tended to divert women from this role. Kikuyu also feared that mission attendance would offer the girls unwarranted freedom that might express itself in their going to Nairobi to become prostitutes.[23] This would both bring shame to the girls' parents

21. Kenya National Archive (KNA): DC/FH4/6, Chiefs and Headmen Record Book, vol. 1, 1937-54.

22. W. S. Routledge, *With a Prehistoric People* (London: Edward Arnold, 1910), p. 121.

23. Interviews with G. Kaniaru and E. Mureithi, 24 August 1989; Emily Mumbi Shadrack, 23 August 1989. Kevin Ward, "The Development of Protestant Christianity in Kenya" (Ph.D. thesis, University of Cambridge, 1976), p. 117.

and upset their chances of a good brideprice.[24] Mumbi was born around 1888 at Kabete in Kiambu district. Her parents died during the great famine of 1900.[25] According to Kikuyu custom, the responsibility of providing for her passed to her paternal uncle, Chege Kanyi, a rich village headman. Mumbi found life at her paternal uncle's home hard and difficult to cope with. She felt overworked and not sufficiently rewarded for her labor. She thought that Chege's biological children did far less work than she and got better rewards for it. Mumbi attributed this supposed discrimination to the fact that Chege was not her biological father and therefore had no affection for her.

The latent conflict between Mumbi and Chege came into the open over the issue of marriage. In theory, Kikuyu did not practice forced marriages; boys and girls were left to choose their partners without undue parental pressure. In practice, however, this was not always the case. There were times when parents, in search of good connections and wealth, arranged for their daughters to marry wealthy and famous individuals without considering the girls' wishes. In a sense, such marriages were forced.[26]

In 1907, Chege made arrangements with a wealthy polygamist to marry his foster daughter. The arrangements were made behind Mumbi's back. To Chege's embarrassment, Mumbi rejected the man chosen for her. This provoked open hostility between her and her uncle since custom allowed Chege to make marriage arrangements for his foster daughter without consulting her. (Arranged marriages did take place in traditional Kikuyu society, though on a limited scale.) Mumbi was well aware of this. What she questioned were her paternal uncle's motives in arranging for her marriage. Since she had grown to mistrust Chege's attitude to her, she could not help believing this to be another instance of exploitation by an unscrupulous foster father. In refusing to marry the old man, Mumbi was rebelling against what she perceived as her uncle's perpetual exploitation. For Chege, Mumbi's behavior was an act of insubordination intended to humiliate him and to deny him a good brideprice. Their conflict was therefore inevitable.

24. St. Michael's Church Gathukeine: CMS Gathukeine Station Log Book.
25. The great famine of 1899-1900 acquired the name Ng'aragu ya Ruraya (famine of Europe) because most of the relief was understood to have come from abroad. See E. N. Wanyoike, *An African Pastor* (Nairobi: East African Publishing House, 1974), pp. 19-20.
26. Routledge, *With a Prehistoric People*, pp. 124-25; Leakey, *Southern Kikuyu*, vol. 1, p. 10; Kenyatta, *Facing Mount Kenya*, p. 165.

While living with her relatives away from Chege, Mumbi met Shadrack Njuguna, her future husband. He had been born around 1886 and was among the first Kikuyu to join the CMS Kabete mission. His entry into the mission was as fortuitous as that of Parmenas Githendu. It was the responsibility of Kikuyu boys to keep the birds away from millet fields. One day in 1901, Njuguna neglected this duty by going to watch a Kikuyu dance. During his absence, birds invaded the field and devoured the millet crop. Fearing the prospect of a severe punishment from his foster father (his biological father had also died during the great famine), he sought refuge at Fort Smith, the temporary CMS station purchased from the IBEA Company. He was welcomed so warmly that he decided to stay on.[27] Njuguna was among the first Kikuyu to be baptized in 1905. At the time he met Mumbi, he was a pupil-teacher at the CMS Kabete school.[28] Non-Christian girls wishing to marry male mission adherents were required first to enroll for baptism. In order to fulfill this requirement, Mumbi enrolled as an inquirer in 1908.[29] She was married to Njuguna in 1910, theirs being the first African Christian wedding at Kabete mission.[30] In accordance with Kikuyu custom, Njuguna paid brideprice to Chege. This served to bring reconciliation between Mumbi and her foster father.

A family conflict over marriage, coupled with desire to marry a man of her own choice, had led Mumbi to join the CMS Kabete mission. Hers was not an isolated case. The bulk of the women who joined the missions during the pioneering period were motivated by these two factors. Like Mumbi, a significant number of those women were fleeing marriages arranged by their foster parents and not their actual parents.[31] This gives substance to Mumbi's suspicion of being exploited by

27. Interview with Emily Mumbi Shadrack, 23 August 1989.

28. A pupil-teacher was a student selected and engaged by the manager of an elementary school to assist the teachers in maintaining discipline and imparting instruction. The pupil-teachers also received instruction in subjects of general education.

29. Interview with Emily Mumbi Shadrack, 23 August 1989.

30. St. Paul's Church Kabete: Diocese of Mount Kenya South, Partners in Mission Consultation Report, 1987, p. 4. The document erroneously states that their wedding took place in 1905.

31. For more cases of this nature, see my interview with Miriam Wanjiku Githendu, 11 June 1991, and Florence Nyakio Nduranu, 25 March 1991. Miriam joined the CMS Kahuhia mission to avoid a forced marriage arranged by her brother, to whom dowry had been paid by a wealthy elderly man. Florence joined Kabete mission in 1930 after discovering that her step-brother was planning to sell

Chege. Foster parents were likely to be less affectionate toward children under their care than actual parents. Among Kikuyu, foster parenthood was common due to high mortality rates resulting from famine and disease.

Conflict in the Sphere of Personal Moral Growth

Conflict between missionary and Kikuyu worldviews often manifested itself in the lives of the early mission adherents. Through contact with missionary culture, many *athomi*[32] (mission adherents) came to renounce aspects of the traditional worldview that seemed to contradict missionary teaching. For any ceremony to be valid, all family members had to be present.[33] The *athomi's* refusal to participate in many ceremonies threatened both the validity of those ceremonies and the relationship between the physical and spiritual worlds. Upsetting that relationship was considered detrimental to the community's well-being. The *athomi* behavior therefore created conflict between themselves and non-Christians.

As Kikuyu youths grew up, they were required to undergo various rites marking their movement from one stage of life to the next. Each rite had its own significance. For instance, the "second birth" marked the breaking of the special ties between a child and its mother, and circumcision marked the entry into adulthood. Some mission adherents' refusal to participate in these ceremonies set them at odds both with their immediate family members and with the entire society. This point will be illustrated by the stories of Paul Mbatia[34] and Aram Ndaari.[35]

Mbatia's case is of special significance for three reasons. First, it is a further illustration of conflicts that existed within pre-Christian Kiku-

---

her also to an old man. Both women were orphans at the time of their entry into the mission.

32. The Kikuyu word *athomi* means "readers." It is derived from the Swahili word *Kusoma*, which means "to read." The early mission adherents acquired the name *athomi* due to their literacy skills.

33. Leakey, *Southern Kikuyu*, vol. 1, pp. 1-2.

34. Interview with Ezbon Mbatia and Samuel Mbatia, 19 June 1991; KNA: Weithaga Log Book, entry for 18 March 1906; *Proceedings of the CMS*, 1906-7, pp. 72-73.

35. Interview with Aram Ndaari, 6 June 1991. The story of Ndaari's entry into the mission is widely known at Kahuhia.

yu society and that led some individuals to join the mission stations. Second, it demonstrates the existing conflict between missionary and Kikuyu worldviews and the manner in which some early *athomi* resolved it. Third, Mbatia grew to become a prominent church leader. It is therefore important to know something of his family background and early struggles.

Mbatia was born c. 1888 at Kiruri, about ten miles west of the CMS Weithaga mission. His father, Gakobo, was a *mundu mugo* (medicine man)[36] and thus belonged to the most important professional class among Kikuyu. The special status of a *mundu mugo* derived from his knowledge and skill in religious matters. That expertise was acquired after a considerable period of apprenticeship. The duties of a *mundu mugo* included divination, offering sacrifices and prayers during times of crisis, performance of cleansing ceremonies to remove ritual uncleanness, curing diseases that had failed to respond to herbal treatment, and making charms and medicines to counter misfortune. Gakobo's reputation as a *mundu mugo* incurred the hostility of the local chief, Karuri wa Gakure.[37] Karuri resented popular people because they seemed to threaten his power. He therefore employed various methods to frustrate and humiliate Gakobo, such as forcibly removing him from his birth place.[38] Mbatia entered the mission as a result of this antagonism between his father and Chief Karuri. During the pioneering period, it was common for missionaries to ask the local chiefs to assist them in recruiting school children. Some chiefs cooperated, hoping that the government would look in favor on their support of the missions. Many parents were against their sons' attendance at the mission because it conflicted with the boys' role of herding the cattle. When chiefs were asked to provide boys for instruction, some sought such boys from the homes of their enemies.[39] It was precisely for this reason that Karuri forced Gakobo, his old rival, to provide a boy for instruction.

Young Mbatia began schooling in 1903. He experienced his first serious crisis during his third year at the CMS Weithaga mission. In

---

36. For more details on medicine men, see Routledge, *With a Prehistoric People,* pp. 249-81; Leakey, *Southern Kikuyu,* vol. 3, chap. 26; S. K. Gathigira, *Miikarire ya Agikuyu* (London: Sheldon Press, 1952), chap. 10.

37. For a biography of Karuri, see Charles Mucuha, "Karuri wa Gakure." University College Nairobi, History Department: Research Project Archives (UCN/HD-RPA) B/2/2/2/1968.

38. Interview with Ezbon Mbatia and Samuel Mbatia, 19 June 1991.

39. Interview with Ezbon Mbatia and Samuel Mbatia, 19 June 1991.

March 1906, his parents called him home to fulfill an undisclosed family responsibility. When he arrived home, Mbatia discovered that his parents wanted him to undergo circumcision.[40] This important Kikuyu ceremony was performed on boys at the age of seventeen or eighteen. For Kikuyu, circumcision had a twofold significance: it marked an individual's passage from childhood to adulthood, and the beginning of the individual's participation in the affairs of the community outside the family.

The rite of circumcision consisted of three basic elements. First, there were the preliminary ceremonies that started several weeks before the actual day of circumcision. They included animal sacrifice to ensure God's protection and culminated in a great ceremonial dance held on the eve of the actual operation. Second, there was the physical operation, which involved cutting off the foreskin. Third, the operation was followed by a short period of seclusion during which the neophytes retired to temporary huts for recovery. Mbatia refused to undergo circumcision, prompting his parents to attempt suicide. Later, he promised to cooperate on condition that he would not be required to take part in sacrifices. Neither his parents nor the community at large could contemplate a circumcision ceremony without the accompanying rituals. Thus Mbatia's condition for participation was rejected. A deadlock ensued that was broken only by the intervention of a missionary named Arthur Wallace McGregor.[41] The missionary managed to persuade Mbatia's parents to postpone the ceremony and to allow their son to return to the mission.[42]

A few comments may be made on the incident. The conflict between Mbatia and his parents did not center on the surgical aspect of the custom. Both parties recognized the social significance of the operation; indeed Mbatia was circumcised in the same year at the CSM Kikuyu mission.[43] The bone of contention was the accompanying rituals. For Mbatia's parents, as indeed for all non-Christian Kikuyu, the rituals and the operation were inseparable. Mbatia's case was all the more

---

40. A large body of literature exists on Kikuyu circumcision. Among the works consulted were Gathigira, *Miikarire*, chap. 9; Leakey, *Southern Kikuyu*, vol. 2, chap. 16; Middleton and Kershaw, *The Central Tribes*, pp. 56-59.

41. Arthur Wallace McGregor was the pioneer CMS missionary in Kikuyuland who set up stations at Kabete (1900) and Weithaga (1903). He remained at Weithaga until his resignation in 1925.

42. *Proceedings of the CMS*, 1906-7, pp. 72-73.

43. Interview with Ezbon Mbatia and Samuel Mbatia.

disturbing because he was the first member of his community to refuse to cooperate in this area.

It is significant that after staying at the mission for fewer than three years, Mbatia had developed sufficient courage to take on the Kikuyu worldview by refusing to participate in circumcision with rituals. This was partly because during his short stay at Weithaga, Mbatia had come to interact with a small but influential Christian community consisting of McGregor, the resident missionary, and a few *athomi* who had joined the mission a few years before him. The previous year, two members of that community had shown their defiance of Kikuyu custom by burying a dead man and not undergoing the necessary cleansing ceremony.[44] From this community, Mbatia came to learn that Christ's death on the cross obviated all animal sacrifices.

But another factor should also be taken into account: Mbatia's character, especially his strong moral courage. Twenty years after this crisis, he was to become the first Kikuyu from Murang'a to renounce female circumcision. Not all the early *athomi* had the courage to withstand family and social pressure on matters of custom. When time came for their circumcision, many of them left the mission to undergo the rite together with their non-Christian counterparts.[45]

Aram Ndaari did not have an illustrious career like that of Mbatia. However, the story of his entry into the mission is important in that it reveals the remarkable, yet often overlooked, influence of the early *athomi* on the wider non-Christian community. Ndaari was born in 1908 near the CMS Kahuhia mission. Ndaari did not join the mission until 1919, but he maintained a close friendship with several of his contemporaries who were schooling at the mission. It was through them that he first came into contact with missionary teaching. In their conversations, the young mission adherents attacked various aspects of Kikuyu culture that they thought contradicted missionary teaching. Among such customs was the symbolic second birth. This was a mandatory childhood rite usually performed at the age of five but some-

44. CMSA, G3A5/1906/7, Annual letter from A. W. McGregor, 1905. For death and burial rites, see C. W. Hobley, *Bantu Beliefs and Magic* (London: H. F. & G. W. Witherby, 1922), pp. 97-102; Leakey, *Southern Kikuyu*, vol. 2, chap. 22.

45. See, for example, Amos Maina, "The Coming of Christianity in My Home Area," typescript deposited at St. Paul's Theological College Archives, n.d., p. 2. KNA: CMS1/639: Kabare Station Log Book, entry for 11 July 1913. It was precisely for this reason that the CMS decided to postpone male baptism until after circumcision.

times postponed to a later date depending on the father's ability to provide the necessary sacrificial goat.

For Kikuyu, the rite of second birth had a two-fold significance. First, it marked the severing of the ties that bound a child to its mother and identified the child with her. Until the ceremony had taken place, the child had no separate identity of its own. Secondly, a child who had not gone through the second birth could not assist in the disposal of his father's body after death, be initiated, or inherit property. The essential part of the rite was a reenactment of the birth: the child was placed naked between the mother's legs, and bound to her by a goat's intestine. The intestine was cut and the child imitated the cry of a newborn child. The mother's head was then shaved, the hut swept out, and a formal visit made to the fields to collect arum lily roots.[46] The young *athomi* found the rite of second birth unacceptable for two reasons. First, it involved animal sacrifice, which they believed was idolatrous. Secondly, the requirement of a child to sit naked between its mother's legs appeared to them ridiculous and embarrassing. Since Ndaari had not undergone the rite, he listened to his friends' arguments with keen interest. He found those arguments so persuasive that he decided never to participate in the ceremony.

One evening in 1919, Ndaari's father arrived home to inform his son that he would soon be undergoing the second birth. In order to avoid the ceremony, Ndaari fled to Kahuhia mission where Handley Hooper, the resident missionary, sheltered him. Fearing his father, Ndaari stayed away from his home for five years. During that period he lived at the mission, where he attended school. Ndaari's rift with his father was not healed until 1924, the year he was circumcised at the mission. Hearing the news of his son's circumcision, Ndinu began to seek reconciliation with him, as Mbatia's father had.

Although the cases discussed here are spectacular, they are by no means exhaustive. Apart from those mentioned, there were many people who joined the missions for other reasons.[47] Nevertheless, besides their sensational nature, these cases bring out the correlation between the nature of Kikuyu society and the beginning of the Anglican Church in central Kenya. Conflicts were inherent in traditional Kikuyu society;

46. Middleton and Kershaw, *The Central Tribes*, p. 56.
47. For a fuller discussion on motives for joining the missions, see J. K. Karanja, "The Growth of the African Anglican Church in Central Kenya" (Ph.D. thesis, University of Cambridge, 1993).

before the coming of missionaries, the most common way of resolving them was for one party to leave the community and settle elsewhere. The arrival of missionaries provided a new destination for those seeking an alternative settlement. Just as those who left home were reconciled with their relatives after a period of separation, so too, those who joined the mission after a family disagreement were later reconciled with other family members. For Mbatia, Githendu, and Ndaari, reconciliation with their parents came after initiation. For Mumbi, it came after her Christian husband agreed to pay brideprice to Chege. Movement, time, and fulfillment of the necessary cultural obligations helped to bring reconciliation.

The struggles of the early *athomi* laid the foundation for the Kikuyu Anglican Church. The customs they rejected, such as animal sacrifices and second birth, were rejected by the church. Those which they approved, such as male circumcision without rituals or, later in life, the payment of brideprice, were accepted. Kikuyu decisions, rather than missionary rules, seem to have given the church its particular character. If one goes back to Mbatia's case, it was due to his heroic courage that the CMS introduced a modified form of circumcision. Missionaries were following a Kikuyu lead rather than exercising their authority.

At this point it is worthwhile to reiterate my earlier remark that the Kikuyu Anglican Church was a product of a two-way exploration of the tensions between what could and what could not be negotiated in belief and practice. This tension was partly due to the differences in emphasis between mission Christianity and Kikuyu religion. The missionary message was dualistic; it emphasized radical discontinuity between the demands of this world and of the world to come. On the other hand, the Kikuyu worldview did not emphasize a sharp distinction between the physical and spiritual worlds. It was important for mission Christianity to accommodate itself to the realities of Kikuyu culture if it was to survive, let alone make an impact on society.

Realizing this difference in worldviews and its implication for evangelism, the CMS missionaries came to classify Kikuyu beliefs and practices into two broad categories. First, there were those that were incompatible with Christian principles and therefore unacceptable. They included witchcraft, sacrifices, adultery, polygamy, and sexually motivated dances. Second, there were those practices that, though undesirable, were allowed to continue because they were not explicitly prohibited by Scripture. They included circumcision, drinking alcohol, and payment of brideprice. In between the acceptable and the unacceptable customs as defined by missionaries, African Christians identified a gray area within which they exercised their discretion. It covered such practices as disposal of the dead and second birth. Although the *athomi* privately decided to renounce certain Kikuyu customs, they did so with the knowledge that their mentors expected to see change in their behavior.[48] Yet Kikuyu Christians did not always follow missionary prescriptions. This was mainly because there was a limit as to how far they could go in antagonizing their non-Christian neighbors. Against missionary wishes, they continued to pay brideprice and undergo circumcision, albeit without rituals. Missionaries, too, did not attempt to pressure their adherents to repudiate all Kikuyu customs, lest they renounce Christianity.

Thus the early *athomi* relationships with missionaries and with non-Christian society were marked by an informal debate on cultural and religious issues. It was a result of that debate that the Kikuyu Anglican Church assumed its cultural character.

The Pragmatic Nature of Kikuyu Culture

Like many African societies, Kikuyu were a dynamic and mobile people. The society consisted of immigrant groups who first settled in Murang'a in the sixteenth century and later spread northward into Nyeri and southward into Kiambu. The southward movement was still in progress at the time of the British occupation.[49] As they struggled to come to terms with their environment, the immigrants evolved a highly experimental and adaptive culture. This was reflected in their pragmatic approach to supernatural powers. At times of prolonged crises, Kikuyu individuals were willing to experiment with new rituals. The best example was the ritual exchange of identity from one guild to another within Kikuyu society in order to improve one's fortune.[50] This pragmatic nature of Kikuyu culture often served to enhance the missionary cause. Individuals who lost confidence in traditional beliefs and

48. Missionaries described this change as evidence of "new birth." See, for example, CMSA, G3A5/1907, Annual letter of A. W. McGregor, 1907; E. M. Crawford, *By the Equator's Snowy Peak* (London: CMS, 1913), p. 169.

49. For a detailed study of Kikuyu migration, see G. Muriuki, *A History of the Kikuyu* (Nairobi: Oxford University Press, 1974).

50. S. G. Kibicho, "The Continuity of the African Conception of God into and through Christianity: A Kikuyu Case-Study," in *Christianity in Independent Africa,* ed. E. Fashole-Luke et al. (London: Rex Collings, 1978), p. 386.

Fig. 25. A Kikuyu village (1950s?).
Royal Commonwealth Society Collection, University of Cambridge

practices sometimes joined the missions in search of a better alternative. A case in point is Nuhu Kanyingi,[51] who was born at Kiambuthia in Muranga'a district c. 1890. In 1918, he settled in Nyandarua, where he was employed as a forest ranger. His problems started in 1923, the year he became a *mundu mugo*. Between 1923 and 1928, his wife gave birth to several children, all of whom died soon after birth. Each time this happened, he consulted a fellow medicine man, who assured him that the tragedy would not be repeated. The fact that misfortunes continued dogging him despite the medicine men's assurances shook his confidence in the efficacy of Kikuyu religion.

One day in 1928, on his way to consult another medicine man, Kanyingi encountered a group of Christians holding an open-air meeting. He drew near to listen to them. In their message, they emphasized that faith in Christ removed all worries and cares. They singled out the fears of witchcraft, superstitions, and persistent misfortunes as some of the problems from which their audience needed deliverance. The mes-

51. Interview with Isaac Kamau and Stanley Kagiri, 22 May 1991; "A History of St. Mark's Church, Kiambuthia, 1935-90," typescript, n.d.

271

Fig. 26. Senior chief Njiri,
oldest colonial chief of the Kikuyu, 1955.
Royal Commonwealth Society Collection, University of Cambridge

sage had an immediate impact on Kanyingi. He canceled his visit to the medicine man, gave up his own practice, and joined the new faith. The following year he returned to Kiambuthia and enrolled as a baptismal candidate. He was baptized in 1936. Thus Kanyingi joined the mission as a result of disappointment with Kikuyu traditional religion and out of a desire to test the new faith. Mission Christianity passed his test: his subsequent children survived. This may have been due to improvement in medical science and/or other physical factors. However, Kanyingi was convinced that Christianity had ended his misfortunes. He remained a staunch Anglican until his death in 1983.

Fig. 27. W. H. Cantrell teaching students at the
Kahuhia Normal School (1950s?).
Royal Commonwealth Society Collection, University of Cambridge

Kanyingi's decision to abandon his profession and become a Christian might seem strange considering his special status in traditional Kikuyu society. It should be seen, however, as a good illustration of the fact that even for people who were committed to old beliefs and derived their livelihood from them, Kikuyu culture was adaptive enough to overcome their vested interests. Moreover, by virtue of his profession, the medicine man was better placed than other people to reflect deeply on supernatural power.[52]

The pragmatic nature of Kikuyu culture was not manifest only in personal crisis; it was also evident during times of social crisis. There is the famous case of Herbert Butcher,[53] the resident missionary at Mutira between 1919 and 1926. Situated at Ndia division in the TransTana

52. For a similar view, see T. Ranger and J. Weller, *Themes in the Christian History of Central Africa* (Berkeley: University of California Press, 1975), p. 11.

53. Interview with Canon Johana Njumbi, 19 April 1991; Mariko Kangi, 26 April 1991; and Gerishon Matiti, 16 May 1991.

Fig. 28. T. F. C. Bewes with Kikuyu children at the
Kahuhia [?] convention, *c.* 1952.
Royal Commonwealth Society Collection, University of Cambridge

district,[54] the Mutira station was started in 1911. Missionary work at
Mutira was greatly hindered by three factors: absence of a European
missionary for a considerable period of time, opposition from local
chiefs, and competition from medicine men. During Butcher's incum-
bency, Ndia division experienced two severe droughts — in 1921 and
1924 — that threatened human and animal life. Efforts of ritual experts
failed to bring down the rain. On both occasions, Butcher successfully
prayed for the rain, thus helping the community to avert a major crisis.
His successful prayers produced predictable results. Large numbers of
people streamed into the Mutira mission. Among them were several
prominent medicine men who gave up their practice and surrendered
their divining equipment to be burnt. Perhaps the medicine men gave

54. After independence, Ndia, Mwea, and Gichugu divisions were grouped
together to form Kirinyaga district.

up their profession and joined the mission partly in recognition of Butcher's superior power and partly out of fear that the new faith would soon make them redundant. Both considerations would emphasize the pragmatic nature of Kikuyu culture.

Desire to Master and Exercise Power

Pre-Christian Kikuyu society was marked by competition for power and wealth. In particular, large landowning *mbari* competed vigorously with each other to increase their land holdings, the number of wives they married, the children they produced, and the number of tenants they supported and hence were economically and politically allied with. With the coming of Christianity, a new form of power emerged. Missionaries introduced literacy, which greatly fascinated Kikuyu. The new skill was important because it seemed to give special power to an individual that other members of society did not possess. In fact, some Kikuyu were drawn to missions by a quest for literacy, which was widely perceived as the "white man's magic." Gideon Mugo,[55] a leading evangelist and politician from Kahuhia, joined the local CMS mission in order to learn the "miracle" of reading and writing. This happened after his younger brother, who had joined the school before him, sent him a letter from Embu. Gideon's brother, Mariko Kuhutha, had settled at the CMS Kigari mission as one of the assistants to T. W. W. Crawford,[56] the pioneer missionary there. At that time, Gideon was illiterate, so he asked Livai Gachanja, the head of the mission adherents at Kahuhia, to read the letter for him. The subject matter of the letter was only known to the two brothers and Gideon was greatly surprised to hear Livai reading it from the paper. At that moment he resolved to join the mission and learn "to talk to a paper."

In describing literacy as the white man's magic, Kikuyu were placing the new skill within the scope of their cultural experience. They believed that there was an inherent power or energy pervading the universe that could be tapped in various ways to the advantage or disadvantage of the

55. For a profile of Gideon Mugo, see "Rugano rwa Mutigaire Gideon Mugo Kagika"; typescript, n.d, privately held by this writer.

56. Dr. T. W. W. Crawford belonged to the Canadian CMS. He joined the CMS Kenya mission in 1904. He was the pioneer missionary at Kahuhia (1906-9). When he left Kahuhia in 1910 to begin a mission in Kigari, he was accompanied by five assistants among whom was Mariko Kahutha.

individual or community.[57] Literacy, though originating with the white man, was seen as a manifestation of that mystical power. Just as medicine men had to undergo a formal training before they were fully admitted into the profession, so Gideon had to go through a period of instruction in mission schools before he could secure the new power.

Later, when the church grew in numbers and respectability, it also became a new arena for the exercise of power. This was mainly the case after World War I and was due largely to two reasons. First, the boundaries that formerly insulated Kikuyu society from the wider world were weakening through increased interaction with other communities.[58] In particular, World War I took thousands of Kikuyu men beyond their local boundaries. For those young men, Kikuyu traditional religion with its emphasis on ancestral spirits (that were relevant only to their home locality) seemed incapable of explaining the wider world in which they suddenly found themselves.[59] On the other hand, Christianity, with its emphasis on the High God who directs the affairs of the whole world, seemed best able to explain the larger world. The pragmatic nature of Kikuyu culture facilitated this transition from Kikuyu religion to Christianity.

Second, the war experience, coupled with the increase in settler population after the war, heightened Kikuyu awareness of the permanence of European rule and the new social order created by that rule. Realizing that their interests could no longer be safeguarded by continued resistance to that system, they began to explore the best means of exploiting the opportunities provided by it. Western education seemed to provide the answer. Literacy resulted not only in relatively well-paid employment in government and private sectors, it also effected a new social status, both respected and feared. Since education was controlled largely by missionaries, those wishing to acquire it enrolled in mission schools. This accounts for most of the dramatic rise in mission attendance immediately after the war.

57. McPherson, *The Presbyterian Church in Kenya,* pp. 9-10.

58. This interpretation, which is based on Robin Horton's theory of African conversion, was confirmed by my informants. See R. Horton, "African Conversion," *Africa* 41, no. 2 (April 1971), pp. 85-108.

59. Evidence of the weakening hold of Kikuyu religion on society after World War I was the declining fear of ritual pollution and with it the old restraints, resulting in all manner of crime "from which the old heathen beliefs have been a remarkable safeguard" (CMSA, G3A1/1917-34, Annual letter from Handley Hooper, 1918).

This new interest in Western education manifested itself in the establishment of out-schools. Since the CMS lacked sufficient funds to buy all the land required, or to build and maintain schools over wide areas, it had to depend on the cooperation of the local people in the provision of land and construction and maintenance of buildings. By 1924, a definite pattern of establishing and running out-schools had emerged. After the local elders had agreed to start a school, a local resident provided the plot on which to build it. In most cases the land was given by a mission adherent; in other cases it was provided by a *muramati*. The plot often remained part of that family's property and could be reclaimed when needed. Building materials and labor were all donated and the erection of the building was carried out communally. Sometimes the community paid the teachers' salaries and provided them with a house. The mission was mainly responsible for training, allocation, and supervision of teachers. The raison d'être of the out-schools was promotion of evangelism. They provided basic literacy to enable the students to read Christian literature in the vernacular. During weekdays, the schools served as centers for literacy and religious instruction. On Sundays they were used as prayer houses.

Two distinct categories of out-schools emerged after World War I: those started by locally educated mission adherents and those founded by migrant workers returning mainly from Nairobi and Mombasa.[60] The former constituted the vast majority. They adhered to strict discipline, were highly dependent on missionary guidance, and were confined within the spheres agreed upon between European missionaries or enforced by government regulations. The latter, of which there were only a few before the 1930s, were less strict on matters of discipline, showed a remarkable degree of independence from missionary guidance, and upset the agreed spheres of influence. In fact, the two types of out-schools symbolize the tension in the growth of the church between missionary guidance and Kikuyu initiative.

The difference between the two categories of schools may largely be explained by the backgrounds of their founders. Locally educated mission adherents spent many years at a mission station receiving religious instruction. As a result, they developed a keen sense of church

60. Migrant laborers working in Nairobi enrolled at the CMS school popularly known as Kwabanji ("Burns' corner") after its founder. Those working in Mombasa enrolled at Buxton High School, a CMS school started in 1904 primarily to counter the spread of Islam. Besides attending literacy classes, these workers also attended baptismal classes.

discipline and great dependence on missionary guidance. On the other hand, returning migrant workers had little contact with missionaries besides a brief period of instruction for baptism. Being less instructed in matters of church discipline, they did not make abstention from alcohol or renunciation of tobacco conditions for joining their community. Moreover, exposure to impersonal urban life enabled them to work more independently than their mission-educated counterparts.

The importance of the out-schools cannot be overestimated. They were the chief means through which Christianity spread in Kikuyuland after World War I. They provided the bulk of mission adherents. In 1924 McGregor reported that the sixteen out-schools within his district "provide 75 percent of our converts."[61] The out-school system led to an increase in the number of female mission adherents. This was mainly because the schools served the needs of "women and children who cannot be reached from a distance but will respond to out-schools, which "offered great scope for African work in their immediate neighbourhood."[62] The out-schools offered great scope for African Christians to exercise church leadership without too much missionary supervision. According to Handley Hooper, "the school provides for them the first vision of a native Church and it engenders a native enthusiasm which was not possible while the control and direction of the Church was immediately in the hands of a benevolent foreigner."[63]

Conclusion

The growth of the Kikuyu Anglican Church was similar, in many ways, to that of mission-founded churches elsewhere in Africa. This was mainly because Kikuyu society shared many common features with other African communities, such as a dynamic and competitive culture and a strong desire to overcome evil. Nevertheless, in detail, the African experience of Christianity varied from place to place. This was partly because of the different institutions that African communities brought into Christianity and through which they appropriated the new faith, and partly because of their colonial experience. To illustrate this variation, I briefly compare the growth of the Kikuyu Anglican Church with

61. CMSA, Annual letter from McGregor, 1924.
62. CMSA, Annual letter from Hooper, 1919.
63. CMSA, Annual letter from Hooper, 1919.

that of the Buganda church. The latter has been chosen because John Taylor's classic study, *The Growth of the Church in Buganda*,[64] provides an excellent framework for comparison. Before turning to this comparative framework, two points of contrast between these two contexts need to be noted. First, the structures of the two societies were different and this had important implications for the spread of the gospel. To quote M. P. K. Sorrenson, the New Zealand historian: "Unlike the Ganda, the Kikuyu were an extremely segmented society, with no centralised political institutions. There was no Kikuyu Constantine — or Kabaka — to capture and thus no possibility of conversion from the top. In the Kikuyu country and elsewhere in the British East African Protectorate the missionaries had to start from the bottom."[65]

Second, although Christianity preceded colonial rule in Buganda, in Kikuyuland colonial rule preceded Christianity. This meant that in Buganda in the pioneering period, missionaries were more dependent on African rulers than in the Kikuyu country. Moreover, since Baganda chiefs were the natural leaders of their people, they commanded more respect from both society and missionaries than their Kikuyu counterparts. In fact the first Baganda deacons, who were mainly recruited from the ranks of chiefs, were treated by missionaries as colleagues and not as protégés. By contrast, the first generation of Kikuyu pastors, who rose from the ranks of catechists and teachers, remained much more subservient to their mentors.

Two aspects of Taylor's work are especially relevant to this study: his analysis of the processes of church growth and his examination of the Baganda contribution to the evangelization of neighboring areas. Regarding the processes of church growth in Buganda, Taylor identifies four consecutive components: congruence, detachment, demand, and crisis.[66] *Congruence* involved "a fitting together and contact of the new community and the new teaching with the old structure and the complex of ideas which already existed." *Detachment* meant the gradual loosening of the ties that bound people to the old ways. *Demand* meant the challenge that people felt the gospel made upon them. *Crisis* referred to the conflict of loyalties among Baganda Christians resulting

64. J. V. Taylor, *The Growth of the Church in Buganda* (London: SCM Press, 1958).

65. M. P. K. Sorrenson, *Origins of European Settlement in Kenya* (Oxford: Oxford University Press, 1968), p. 254.

66. Taylor, *Growth*, pp. 43-59; J. V. Taylor, *Processes of Growth in an African Church* (London: IMC Research Pamphlets, 1958).

from the upheavals of 1879-92. I focus on the first and the last of these components because they show clearly the difference in the development of the two churches.

Within Baganda society, there were some institutions that proved to be congruent with the structure of a mission station. On the other hand, within Kikuyu society, this congruence was less obvious. In Buganda, the mission stations resembled the Kabaka's palace and chiefs' households with their clusters of retainers and dependents. In Taylor's words, "the new thing could, apparently, be described in familiar categories and therefore, recognized and accepted. It belonged, and therefore one could belong to it."[67] By contrast, there was no Kikuyu equivalent of a mission station. Perhaps the closest parallel was a *mbari,* but the similarity between local Kikuyu organization and *mbari* did not become obvious until the church gained respectability. Moreover, while it was common practice for ambitious Baganda parents to send their sons away to be servants of chiefs or of the Kabaka, Kikuyu did not have a similar custom. Kikuyu adults did attach themselves to wealthy patrons, but they did this primarily out of poverty and misfortune rather than out of ambition. This lack of obvious congruence may initially have hindered the growth of the Kikuyu church.

The tension between individual Christian commitment and the demands of society has already been mentioned. This tension assumed different forms at different phases of church growth. During the pioneering period (1900-1914), Kikuyu society as a whole saw Christians as individually delinquent people. Thus there was no congruence between Kikuyu society and the church. Congruence came in the early 1920s with the realization that Christian literacy provided a new arena for *mbari* politics. However, while *mbari* Christians (Christians who sought to advance the interests of their *mbari* through the church) sought to make Christianity congruent with Kikuyu society, station Christians (those most dependent on missionaries) continued to emphasize incompatibility between the two. This tension continued and ensured that when crisis came, it would be very different from that experienced by the Buganda church.

Both Baganda and Kikuyu Christians experienced serious crises that called for a clear definition of their stand in relation to society. These crises, however, were far from identical because of the difference in social structures and in the societies' experience of colonial rule. The

67. Taylor, *Processes,* p. 8.

crisis of Buganda was political. It challenged all Christians to decide where their primary loyalty lay; whether with the Kabaka or with the new community, which was both political and religious. "Some adhered to the new community, endured persecution and gripped more tightly to the Church. Others flew back to the old allegiance."[68] In the end, after years of civil war in the 1890s, the Baganda found a political solution to a political problem by turning Christianity into two political religions, one "English" and the other "French."

In Kikuyuland, by contrast, indigenous rulers could not demand absolute loyalty from Christians partly because such a demand would have had no cultural justification (Kikuyu society was acephalous), but more importantly because Kikuyu chiefs operated within the restricted context of colonial rule. Therefore the crisis of the Kikuyu church regarding female circumcision was cultural and not political. It involved conflict between the need to obey the missionary ruling against female circumcision and the desire to maintain solidarity with non-Christian society by continuing with the practice.[69] Within the CMS communities, the crisis was resolved through the typically Kikuyu process of compromise and negotiation. Indeed, the circumcision crisis enabled Kikuyu Christians to distinguish between the inherent demands of the gospel and the extraneous demands of the missionaries. In this way, the crisis enabled the *athomi* to resolve the tension between individual demands of Christianity and social demands of Kikuyu culture.

Baganda Christians were more committed to the evangelization of the neighboring districts than their Kikuyu counterparts. Again this can be explained in political terms. First, precolonial Baganda society was used to extending its influence to neighboring areas through military conquests while Kikuyu society did not embark on expansionist programs. Among the Baganda, evangelization of the neighboring districts resembled the extension of the Baganda supremacy. In her book, *Black Evangelists,* Louise Pirouet observes that the places to which Baganda catechists went, with the exception of Sukumaland (in modern Tanzania), were places in which Buganda had political interests.[70] By con-

68. Taylor, *Processes,* p. 10.

69. The best work on the Kikuyu female circumcision crisis (1929-32) so far remains Jocelyn Murray, "The Female Circumcision Controversy, with Special Reference to the Church Missionary Society's Sphere of Influence" (Ph.D. thesis, UCLA, 1974).

70. M. L. Pirouet, *Black Evangelists: The Spread of Christianity in Uganda, 1891-1914* (London: Rex Collings, 1978), p. 36.

trast, Kikuyu did not attempt to extend their supremacy over their neighbors. It is true that Kikuyu individuals migrated to new areas, but the process of settlement in those areas involved negotiations with their new neighbors rather than military conquests. Nor did Kikuyu immigrants seek to impose their beliefs and values on their neighbors. Thus among Kikuyu, the concept of evangelization lacked a cultural equivalent.

The discussion has centered on differences in the growth of the Buganda and Kikuyu churches in order to bring out the distinctive features of the Kikuyu Anglican Church. It is my conviction that the uniqueness of Kikuyu Christianity was rooted in the institutions that Kikuyu brought into Christianity. Such customary institutions included the symbolic second birth, *ituika,* and circumcision. The first two customs were peculiar to Kikuyu.[71] They were both abandoned after a prolonged period of controversy among mission adherents themselves and between Christians and non-Christians. The *athomi* rejected the second birth partly because it involved animal sacrifice, which denied the efficacy of the Great Sacrifice of Christ, and partly because it was embarrassing. *Ituika* was abandoned because it was considered irrelevant to the new social order. Male circumcision continued in a modified form after missionary protest.

Thus the significance of this study lies in the light it casts on Kikuyu society's ability to negotiate and compromise over specifically Kikuyu institutions. It was this readiness to consider and renounce objectionable and irrelevant customs and to modify the adaptable ones, that gave the Kikuyu Anglican Church its distinctively indigenous character.

---

71. Before the coming of Europeans, alternate generation sets held judicial authority over the Kikuyu for thirty to forty years. The handing over of power from one generation set to another took place in a prolonged ceremony known as *ituika.* For more details, see Leakey, *Southern Kikuyu,* vol. 3, pp. 1278-84; B. Berman and J. Lonsdale, *Unhappy Valley* (London: James Currey, 1992), p. 344.

PART 3

CHANGING PERSPECTIVES
ON MISSION IN BRITAIN

11. *Mission and the Meeting of Faiths: The Theologies of Max Warren and John V. Taylor*

GRAHAM KINGS

Introduction

You'll be amused to hear that the Swedish missionary society have asked me for a paper on "Christians and Other Faiths" and as they gave me a month's notice, I have told them I can only let them have a reduced Kelham paper . . . but privately, and just between you and me, and the door of your study, I am rather thrilled that some folk on the continent are interested in my views on this subject. The origin of their curiosity is my introduction to the "Christian Presence Series" which, so it appears, are very widely read in Scandinavia.

Max Warren wrote this letter on 18 January 1969 to his daughter Pat and son-in-law Roger Hooker, CMS missionaries at Bareilly in North India. The letter is part of an extraordinary fortnightly correspondence, between 1965, when they went to India, and 1977, when Warren died.[1] When he wrote this letter, Warren was a canon at West-

---

1. I am very grateful to the late Roger Hooker, John V. Taylor, Kenneth Cragg, and Christopher Lamb for the stimulation of their discussions in preparation for this chapter. I would like to thank Roger and Pat Hooker for permission to use these letters (the originals are housed in the CMS archives). For further extracts

minster Abbey, but from 1942 to 1963 he had been general secretary of the Church Missionary Society.[2]

The quotation manifests various aspects of Warren's character and life's work. It is personal and witty: "just between you and me, and the door of your study" concerns a key theme in his thinking, "Christian Presence," and shows the sort of lecture invitations he was receiving at the time. It also demonstrates his enthusiastic delight in his wider influence: "I am rather thrilled that some folk on the continent are interested in my view on the subject."

In the same month, John V. Taylor, Warren's successor as general secretary of the CMS (1963-74), addressed the theme of "the Cross and Pakistan" in his influential monthly *CMS News-letter*. He wrote: "He did not call his disciples to brandish the cross but to carry it on their shoulders" and went on to point out the importance of "the sign of the broom," for in Pakistan the name Christian is synonymous with "sweeper."[3]

As the CMS celebrates its bicentenary thirty years after these writings, it has been fascinating to discern and trace the works and influence of Warren and Taylor on the subject of mission and the meeting of faiths. Both of them included in their thinking and writing a range of subjects that related to the mission of God. After the Second World War, Warren wrote prophetically about the rise of nationalism and the demise of colonialism, seeing key issues well before many politicians. Taylor, in the late 1960s, advocated the strategic development of small

from this correspondence see Graham Kings, "Max Warren: Candid Comments on Mission from His Personal Letters," *International Bulletin of Missionary Research* 17, no. 2 (Apr. 1993), pp. 54-58, and Graham Kings, "Immigration, Race and Grace: Max Warren's Letters to Pat and Roger Hooker, 1965-1977," in *Mission in a Pluralist World*, ed. Aasulv Lande and Werner Ustorf (Frankfurt am Main: Peter Lang, 1996), pp. 127-51.

2. As a CMS missionary in his younger days, Warren (b. 1904) had experienced only ten months working among Muslims in northern Nigeria before being invalided home with bovine TB in 1928. After convalescence and a post as youth officer for Winchester Diocese, he was appointed vicar of Holy Trinity Church, Cambridge (1936-42), before becoming general secretary of the CMS.

3. John V. Taylor (b. 1914) had two curacies in England, before serving with the CMS as warden of Bishop Tucker Theological College, Mukono, Uganda (1944-54). After a year's deputation he joined the research department of the International Missionary Council, then became Africa secretary of the CMS (1959-63) and finally general secretary (1963-74). He served as bishop of Winchester from 1975 to 1985, and continues to write, lecture, and preach in his retirement.

ecclesial groups for mission. Yet the key issue in both missiological and theological debate at the end of the twentieth century is this subject of Christianity and people of "other faiths," and both Warren and Taylor have made significant contributions to the development of an open approach that is centered on Christ.[4]

In this chapter I consider first the people who helped shape Warren and Taylor's thinking before I look at their writing and their influence on British and world Christianity at the end of the twentieth century.

Background Influences on Warren and Taylor

In his autobiography, *Crowded Canvas,* Warren described inviting a famous missionary to tea in 1927 in his student rooms at Ridley Hall, Cambridge:

> Among many memories of that happy four terms was the privilege I had of entertaining Temple Gairdner of Cairo, already a hero for me long before Constance Padwick's magnificent biography which appeared in 1929. It was as stimulating as it was humbling to have this experienced veteran of work in the Muslim world listening to my ambitions for literature work in the Western Sudan, this being my pri-

---

4. I am very wary (and weary) of using the adjectives "exclusive," "inclusive," and "pluralist" for various positions on this issue, although they have been widely used since the publication of Alan Race, *Christians and Religious Pluralism: Patterns in the Christian Theology of Religions* (London: SCM Press, 1983). Some people may, in the past, have found them useful as a grid for general "mapping" and they appear in Gavin D'Costa, *Theology and Religious Pluralism* (Oxford: Basil Blackwell, 1986), pp. 22, 52, 80. D'Costa provides the following concise summaries of these now outdated categories:

> The exclusivist paradigm has been characterized as maintaining that other religions are marked by humankind's fundamental sinfulness and are therefore erroneous, and that Christ (or Christianity) offers the only valid path to salvation. . . . The inclusivist paradigm has been characterized as one that affirms the salvific presence of God in non-Christian religions while still maintaining that Christ is the definitive and authoritative revelation of God. . . . The pluralist paradigm has been characterized as one that maintains that other religions are equally salvific paths to the one God, and Christianity's claim that it is the only path (exclusivism), or the fulfilment of other paths (inclusivism) should be rejected.

Fig. 29. Max A. C. Warren (1904-77), general secretary of the CMS, 1942-63.
Church Mission Society, London

vate dream, and kindly encouraging me to follow the dream as a not impossible one.[5]

Temple Gairdner (1873-1928), a CMS missionary in Cairo from 1899, was the author of *"Edinburgh 1910": An Account and Interpretation of the World Missionary Conference* (1910) and the pioneering *The Reproach of Islam* (1909) that he later retitled *The Rebuke of Islam* (1920). He was an important forerunner of the respectful witness to Muslims that was developed by Kenneth Cragg. When he died, his

5. Max Warren, *Crowded Canvas: Some Experiences of a Lifetime* (London: Hodder & Stoughton, 1974), p. 49. Furey, who wrote his dissertation on Warren's theology of mission, cited a letter to him from Warren in which he acknowledged Gairdner to be one of the formative influences on his thinking, "giving me a vision of just how rich and wide a true understanding of Evangelism and mission could be." Francis Eamon Furey, "The Theology of Mission in the Writings of Max Warren" (L.S.T. thesis, Louvain, 1974), p. 3.

288

Fig. 30. John V. Taylor (b. 1914), general secretary of the CMS, 1963-74, with his wife, Peggy.

Church Mission Society, London

colleague in Cairo, Yusef Effendi Tadras, commented: "Other teachers taught us how to refute Islam; he taught us how to love Muslims."[6] This was also to epitomize the approach of Warren and Taylor.

In his *CMS News-letter* for December 1973, Taylor described appreciatively the significance of Gairdner:

> Hardly has one man enriched the mission of the Church with such diversity of talents. The fastidious musician, and collector of Near Eastern airs, the writer and producer of plays, the Christian apologist versed in the thought of Islam, the Arabic scholar and author, the creator of a profoundly beautiful and vivid worship, the great inventor of games and family celebrations, the perceptive lover of books and places and peculiar people, were all equally and totally at the disposal of the Living Christ and his Gospel.

The spirit of Gairdner's approach to Christian witness in a Muslim society was crucial to Warren and Taylor's own thinking about the

6. Constance E. Padwick, *Temple Gairdner of Cairo* (London: SPCK, 1929), p. 302.

meeting of faiths. Even in the 1960s, however, it was felt to be dangerously radical and alarming as far as many in the Church of England were concerned. This is illustrated by a review in the *Church Times* of a superb collection of Muslim prayers edited by Constance Padwick, who can be identified as a second background influence.[7] Padwick (1886-1968) was one of the leading British women missionaries in the twentieth century. She made her way in the Middle East on her own, having been rejected by the CMS, but was in very close liaison with various CMS personnel and continued to be in contact with Warren in the 1950s.[8] As well as the biography of Gairdner, she also wrote the lives of Henry Martyn and Alexander Mackay.

Kenneth Cragg, himself a missionary scholar continuing the tradition of Gairdner and Padwick, wrote to Warren on 8 March 1961:

> The "Church Times" of February 25th . . . included a rather adverse review on Constance Padwick's "Muslim Devotions." It strongly disapproved the S.P.C.K. publication of a book which it described as wholly unchristian and argued that such interest in other faiths tended towards "religious indifference."[9]

Cragg enclosed a copy of the sharp letter he wrote to the *Church Times* in response to this attack, which manifested his own approach:

> It would seem that "religious indifference" lies squarely with the reviewer. When has it been a principle of apostolic Christianity to ignore whole stretches of human experience or to secure its exclusiveness by a studied repudiation of interest in everything outside its own interior confines?[10]

---

7. Constance E. Padwick, *Muslim Devotions: A Study of Prayer-manuals in Common Use* (London: SPCK, 1961; Oxford: One World, 1996).

8. Padwick wrote to Warren: "I greatly appreciate your Newsletter and always wonder how you find time for all the reading involved. I was delighted when a young American missionary pounced upon the letter saying 'We always saw that at Hartford'" (Hartford Seminary, Connecticut) Roger Hooker Archives, MACW/1/1, C. Padwick to M. A. C. Warren, 23 January 1959. See also Cragg's chapter on Padwick in Kenneth Cragg, *Troubled by Truth: Life Studies in Inter-Faith Concern* (Edinburgh: The Pentland Press, 1992).

9. Roger Hooker Archives, MACW/1/3, K. Cragg to M. A. C. Warren, 8 March 1961.

10. Roger Hooker Archives, MACW/1/2, K. Cragg to the editor of the *Church Times*, 26 February 1961.

Later in the letter he commented on the review attributing to him an advocacy of the "need to regard Muhammad as a true prophet."

> This is one of those unhappily ambiguous sentences, which might mean an acceptance of the truth of all the prophet ever said or claimed. There are numerous things, most notably the claim to the superceding of our Lord, which for the Christian are manifestly untrue. But that is not to disqualify the deep and positive content of the Qur'an in such areas as the Divine unity, the created order, the dignity of man, the enormity of idolatry and the fact of nature as a realm of Divine "signs" to be taken with reverent gratitude. Not to acknowledge these is to repudiate one's Christianity.[11]

Kenneth Cragg (b. 1913) had profound influence on Warren from the time of the publication of his book *The Call of the Minaret*.[12] Cragg was never technically a CMS missionary but was part of the tradition developed by Gairdner, and he remained in close contact with CMS leaders. T. E. Yates has commented that "copies of Warren's *News-letter* were studded with references to this book and appeals to his readers to acquire it."[13] The *News-letter* for March 1957 took it as its text and quoted freely from it:

> Part at least of the deepest significance of Dr. Cragg's book is that it prepares us for the possibility that a genuinely Christian encounter with Islam will be almost as much a discovery for the Christian as a revelation for the Muslim.[14]

---

11. Roger Hooker Archives, MACW/1/2, K. Cragg to the editor of the *Church Times*, 26 February 1961.

12. Kenneth Cragg, *The Call of the Minaret* (London: Oxford University Press, 1956; London: Collins, 1985). For an excellent exploration of Cragg's thought, see Christopher Lamb, *The Call to Retrieval: Kenneth Cragg's Christian Vocation to Islam* (London: Grey Seal, 1997).

13. Timothy Yates, *Christian Mission in the Twentieth Century* (Cambridge: Cambridge University Press, 1994), p. 141, listed the following mentions in the *News-letters* for March 1957, June 1957, October 1958, February 1959, January 1961, and March 1963. Cragg stated in his autobiography, with a twinkle in his pen, that Warren gave the book almost lyrical acceptance in a double issue of his *News-letter* "though he sobered me later by observing that 'the Irish were given to strange enthusiasm.'" Kenneth Cragg, *Faith and Life Negotiate: A Christian Story-Study* (Norwich: The Canterbury Press, 1994), p. 119.

14. Max Warren, "The Muslim, the Christian and the Christ," *CMS News-letter* 192 (March 1957), p. 1.

In the three main sections of his book, Cragg set out the contemporary political and economic environment of the Muslim peoples since 1945.[15] He then went on to play with the ambiguity of the word "call" by showing a deep understanding of what it meant to a Muslim to hear the call to prayer, and what the call of the minaret demanded for a Christian. Part of this final section was a "call to retrieval," which for Cragg involved redeeming the failures of love in the past centuries of tragic Christian encounter with Islam by witnessing to a new future of relationships possible in Christ. His concern was not to have the map more Christian, but to have Christ more widely known. Near the end of the book there was a call to patience. In commending it to his readers, Warren ended his *News-letter* with this quotation from Cragg:

> If Christ is what Christ is, He must be uttered. If Islam is what Islam is, that "must" is irresistible. Wherever there is misconception, witness must penetrate: wherever there is the obscuring of the beauty of the Cross it must be unveiled: wherever men have missed God in Christ He must be brought to them again.[16]

The fourth influence on Warren was his son-in-law, Roger Hooker, through their regular correspondence between 1965 and 1977. Hooker's ministry in North India was first as a teacher at Bareilly Theological College and then as a student of Sanskrit at the Sanskrit University, Benaras (Varanasi), which also involved deep friendships with Hindus and Muslims. This sensitive, pioneering post had been set up by John V. Taylor. Hooker later became the bishop of Birmingham's adviser for Inter-Faith Relations based in the inner-city area of Smethwick, where he died in 1999. Hooker had also been influenced by Gairdner and Cragg, as well as by Warren and Taylor.[17]

Warren bore witness to the importance of these letters in the fore-

---

15. Warren commented, in the light of the Suez crisis, "I wish that every member of the House of Commons, and some other legislatures, could read the first thirty pages." Max Warren, "The Muslim, the Christian and the Christ," *CMS News-letter* 192 (March 1957), p. 1. Contemporary political issues are deeply affected by understanding or misunderstanding of religions. Warren reached some fourteen thousand readers with his *News-letter;* see *CMS News-letter* 194 (May 1957).

16. Cragg, *The Call of the Minaret,* p. 304.

17. R. Hooker to M. A. C. Warren, 24 April 1969: "I feel that now after ten years I am fulfilling, just a little, that vision I first caught at Wycliffe from reading Temple Gairdner and *The Call of the Minaret* for the first time."

word to his final book, *I Believe in the Great Commission:* "the letters
have 'kept me in touch with the actual life and work of a foreign missionary. In particular, I have been enabled to live, if only at second
hand, in the creative experience of meeting with men of other
Faiths.' "[18] In one of the letters he commented:

> Now here is a point where in our discussions (you with me) we need
> to be clear how very great are my limitations. I know a little about Is-
> lam and Judaism and Western Agnosticism (secularism if you like). I
> know nothing about Hinduism or Buddhism. . . . [Through our corre-
> spondence] my assumptions are always being very properly chal-
> lenged by the reminder that there is another "universe of discourse"
> where they cannot be applied simpliciter.[19]

These four influences were all English. What of European, American, and non-Western missiologists? Ossi Haaramäki, who wrote a dissertation on *The Missionary Ecclesiology of Max Warren* commented:

> Though reviewing in his monthly publication of the *CMS Newsletter*
> of 1942-1963 the contemporary literature of European and American
> missiology, Warren after all seldom carried out real theological dia-
> logue with missiologists of his day (Kraemer, Freytag, Sundkler and
> Hoekendijk). He did quote them in his writings, yet this reflection
> had surprisingly little impact on his thought structure.[20]

This comment is perceptive and generally fair, though Warren's
friendship with Walter Freytag was important. Freytag was professor of
Missiology and Ecumenical Relations at Hamburg from 1953 to 1959
and they met at various ecumenical mission conferences. In an intriguing
article for Freytag's *Festschrift*,[21] after admitting that he did not know
German, Warren went on to describe four emphases of Freytag that he
had learnt from personal conversations, and his own detailed records of

18. Max Warren, *I Believe in the Great Commission* (Grand Rapids: Eerdmans, 1976). Foreword pages unnumbered.
19. M. A. C. Warren to R. Hooker, 26 October 1971.
20. Ossi Haaramäki, *The Missionary Ecclesiology of Max A. C. Warren: A
Systematic Research on the Warren Production of 1942-1963* (Helsinki: The Finnish Society for Missiology and Ecumenics, 1982), p. 159.
21. Max Warren, "The Thought and Practice of Missions: Notes on Walter
Freytag's Contribution," in *Basileia: Walter Freytag zum 60. Geburtstag*, ed. Jan
von Hermelink and Hans Jochen Margull (Stuttgart: Evang. Missionsverlag
GMBH, 1959), pp. 158-65.

Freytag's addresses at those conferences. They were the corporate nature of Christian witness and mission, eschatology, the relationship between church and mission, and the importance of missiological research. It is clear from this essay that Freytag had influenced Warren, but interestingly the subject of the meeting of faiths was not mentioned.

The most significant non-Western (or Indo-European) scholar to influence Warren was Raymond (Raimundo) Panikkar (b. 1918). Born in Barcelona, the son of a Hindu father and a Spanish Catholic mother, he was brought up in a Hindu-Catholic environment, learning the Hindu scriptures alongside the Bible. As a Catholic priest, he taught in India and the United States. His classic book, *The Unknown Christ of Hinduism*,[22] and his personal friendship helped develop Warren's thought and phraseology in the late 1960s.

Warren, and the other previously mentioned scholars, also fed into the stream of Taylor's learning (although Taylor has been more critical of Panikkar's thought). Soon after Warren had been appointed general secretary in 1942, he helped Taylor find his missionary vocation as principal of Bishop Tucker College, Mukono, Uganda. Later he was appointed as Africa secretary of the CMS.[23] Taylor was profoundly influenced by his students at Mukono and by the village people in Uganda among whom he lived while researching his book *The Growth of the Church in Buganda*.[24] This bore abundant fruit in *The Primal Vision*, which includes quotations from the works of Walter Freytag.[25]

Warren's Theology of Christian Presence and of Attention

Christian Presence Series

"Christian presence" surfaced as a theme in the Catholic worker-priest movement in France after the Second World War, where close, incarna-

---

22. Raymond Panikkar, *The Unknown Christ of Hinduism* (London: Darton, Longman & Todd, 1964), revised and enlarged as *The Unknown Christ of Hinduism: Towards an Ecumenical Christophany* (Maryknoll, N.Y.: Orbis Books, 1981).

23. See John V. Taylor, "My Pilgrimage in Mission," *International Bulletin of Missionary Research* 17 (Jan. 1993), p. 59.

24. John V. Taylor, *The Growth of the Church in Buganda: An Attempt at Understanding* (London: SCM Press, 1958).

25. John V. Taylor, *The Primal Vision: Christian Presence amid African Religion* (London: SCM Press, 1963, 1982), pp. 36, 42, 129.

tional involvement with workers alienated from the church produced a call for a radically new approach to mission in an industrialized society.[26] It also came to be important in European Protestant theology engaging with issues of a secular society following Bonhoeffer's influence. Warren, inspired by Cragg's *Call of the Minaret*, developed and edited his own series, published by SCM Press between 1959 and 1966, which focused mainly on other faiths. He invited Cragg to write the first book, *Sandals at the Mosque*.[27] Others followed on Buddhism by George Appleton, Japanese religions by Raymond Hammer, African traditional religion by John V. Taylor, Judaism by Peter Schneider, Hinduism by William Stewart, and Secularism by Martin Jarrett-Kerr.[28]

Account needs to be taken of the context in which the series was initiated (before Vatican II encouraged a new openness to other faiths) in order fully to appreciate the extraordinary openness of approach. Warren aimed to invigorate a major shift in attitude toward other faiths, but one that was still authentically biblical. Each book began with a general introduction by Warren, at the end of which was a comment on that particular volume. He outlined the new opportunities and challenges at the "end of Empire" and moved from there to the "coexistence with other religions" (a strange-sounding phrase today). His fundamental emphasis was on respect and humility:

> When we approach the man of another faith than our own it will be in a spirit of expectancy to find how God has been speaking to him and what new understandings of the grace and love of God we may ourselves discover in this encounter.
>
> Our first task in approaching another people, another culture, another religion, is to take off our shoes, for the place we are approaching is holy. Else we may find ourselves treading on men's dreams. More serious still, we may forget that God was here before our arrival. We have, then, to ask what is the authentic religious content in

---

26. Owen C. Thomas, ed., *Attitudes Towards Other Religions: Some Christian Interpretations* (London: SCM Press, 1969), p. 219.

27. Kenneth Cragg, *Sandals at the Mosque: Christian Presence amid Islam* (London: SCM Press, 1959).

28. Warren's remark cited on p. 285 makes clear that this series was well read in Scandinavia. See also Aasulv Lande, "Witness as Presence," in *Contemporary Issues in Mission,* ed. J. Andrew Kirk (Birmingham: Department of Mission, Selly Oak Colleges, 1994), pp. 67-79, and Aasulv Lande, "Contemporary Missiology in the Church of England," in *Mission in a Pluralist World*, ed. Aasulv Lande and Werner Ustorf (Frankfurt am Main: Peter Lang, 1996), pp. 25-61.

the experience of the Muslim, the Hindu, the Buddhist, or whoever he may be. We may, if we have asked humbly and respectfully, still reach the conclusion that our brothers have started from a false premise and reached a faulty conclusion. But we must not arrive at our judgement from outside their religious situation. We have to try to sit where they sit, to enter sympathetically into the pains and griefs and joys of their history and see how those pains and griefs and joys have determined the premises of their argument. We have, in a word, to be "present" with them.[29]

This became a famous quotation. Stephen Bevans, a Catholic missiologist in Chicago, cited it in his book *Models of Contextual Theology,* and continued:

These words express perhaps more clearly than any I know the central and guiding insight of the anthropological model: Human nature, and therefore human culture, is good, holy, and valuable. It is within human culture that we find God's revelation — not as a separate supracultural message, but in the very complexity of culture itself, in the warp and woof of human relationships, which are constitutive of cultural existence.[30]

The phrase "Christian presence" came to have a slightly different meaning in the student world, with greater stress on anonymity in witness and on social justice. In 1964 the World Student Christian Federation adopted the idea of "Christian presence" in a policy statement that defined the phrase as follows:

[The word "presence"] tries to describe the adventure of being there in the name of Christ, often anonymously, listening before we speak, hoping that men will recognise Jesus for what he is and stay where they are, involved in the fierce fight against all that dehumanizes.[31]

---

29. Max Warren's general introduction to the Christian Presence series in Cragg, *Sandals at the Mosque,* pp. 9-10.

30. Stephen B. Bevans, *Models of Contextual Theology* (Maryknoll, N.Y.: Orbis Books, 1992), p. 49.

31. *Student World* 58 (1965), p. 233. This was cited in *Attitudes Towards Other Religions,* p. 219. The last chapter of this book was devoted to the concept of presence in the work of Warren and Taylor and included extracts. Other chapters had extracts from the works of, amongst others, Schleiermacher, Troeltsch, Barth, Hocking, Tillich, and Küng.

Warren's own use of the phrase also developed. In the series he used the word to refer to the Christian being present; in his later thought, influenced by Panikkar, he used the word "presence" to refer to Christ's presence.[32]

Ecumenical Lectures in Israel

In 1967 Warren prepared four lectures which were read at an ecumenical conference in Israel in March. (He was unable to attend after having a heart attack.) The first two lectures concerned other religions.[33] In the first lecture, "A Christian Theology of Attitude Towards Other Religions," his biblical theology led him into various "insights" (his preferred word to the overdefined "doctrines").

He showed that the good news of the cross is part of the *whole* story of redemption: "God did not start loving the world at the Incarnation of our Lord" and more controversially "there is a deep and profound sense in which we can claim that because what happened at Calvary happened once and for all, all men have been redeemed. The difference between men is that some know it and some do not know it." He then introduced the concept of the "uncovenanted" Christ:

> Assuming the word "cosmic" to refer to the whole world, or in more modern parlance, to the whole created order, I would propose to speak of the "uncovenanted" Christ, that is the Christ who was not pre-figured in the Old Covenant with Israel, and is only hinted at in the New Covenant with the New Israel.[34]

Warren then referred to John 1:9: "The true light that enlightens every man was coming into the world."

> That enlightening, I want to suggest, is much more than the provision of conscience. It should, I believe, be understood as the activity of the

32. See Taylor's comments below on p. 311 and our consideration of the Lausanne Covenant on p. 313.

33. The other two lectures were on ecumenism. Roger Hooker, "CMS and Other Faiths — Some Lessons from Our History" (unpublished paper for CMS, 1987), included summaries and quotations from these lectures. They were circulated in facsimile type print in Israel under the title "Ecumenical Horizons: The Full Report of the Conference on Ecumenical Principles and the Christian Encounter with Other Faiths, held in Israel, 6-7 March, 1967."

34. Cited in Hooker, "CMS and Other Faiths," p. 8.

uncovenanted Christ seeking to make *de facto* that authority over all the world which is his *de iure*. . . . Dare we limit this attempt to make it *de facto* to the activities of his church? If he is thus active, then when I go to meet the man of some other religious faith, I go to meet Christ. He is already there in that other man, unrecognised no doubt, but there nonetheless.[35]

In his second Israel Lecture, "A Christian Theology of Practice in Relation to Other Religions," after stressing the importance of service, he came to the distinction between dialogue and evangelism:

In Dialogue we do not aim to evangelise. Rather we aim to establish a relationship of mutual understanding and respect on the basis of a common humanity and an equally genuine shared search for the truth. In quite other circumstances, perhaps of great personal need, we bear witness to Christ as the one who can meet the need. . . . Between such a witness and the encounter through Dialogue there is no conflict. The same person can engage in both. But he resolutely refuses any attempt to confuse them. Each has its proper place.[36]

A Theology of Attention

The particular phrase "A Theology of Attention" was used first in a lecture to the annual CMS School of Mission in January 1970, which was later published in *Face to Face: Essays on Inter-Faith Dialogue*,[37] and republished in India by the Indian SPCK together with two other essays, "Attention and the Problem of Idolatry" and "The Universal Christ and the Problem of Interpretation."[38] These three essays form a coherent presentation of Warren's thought at that time. He drew on the compelling work of a German missionary monk in India, Klaus Klostermaier,[39] and in particular his chapter "Theology at 120 Degrees Fahrenheit," to which Warren added "in the Shade."

35. Hooker, "CMS and Other Faiths," p. 9.

36. Hooker, "CMS and Other Faiths," p. 9.

37. John V. Taylor et al., *Face to Face: Essays on Inter-Faith Dialogue* (London: The Highway Press, 1971).

38. Max Warren, *Theology of Attention* (Madras: Christian Literature Society and ISPCK, 1971).

39. Klaus Klostermaier, *Hindu and Christian in Vrindaban* (London: SCM Press, 1969).

Warren answered his rhetorical question, why he had substituted the word "attention" for "dialogue," thus:

> My reason is fundamental to all that follows. The essence of true dialogue is that it is an activity of listening, mutual listening. Unless that attitude is recognised as basic there will always be the danger of dialogue becoming an argument and even degenerating into a shouting match, however discreet the shouting, neither party to the dialogue paying serious attention to what the other is saying.[40]

He developed his theme with reference to Christ:

> When you and I venture to listen to another person "in the name of Jesus Christ" there is an unseen listener present, Jesus himself. We have to listen to him listening. We have to know Jesus and be ready to learn all his meanings too. And in the context of this listening it may be that he will have something new to say, something we have never heard before. And if we listen very carefully, with concentrated attention, it is likely that we will hear him speaking through the lips of a Hindu, a Muslim, a Buddhist, a Jew, a man or woman of some tribal religion — or perhaps a Marxist or humanist. Jesus, now as always, is very full of surprises.[41]

Warren suggested that our humility should be shown in three ways: toward God, toward people of other faiths, and in our questioning. All these comments were based on years of regular reading, rereading, and notetaking during his early morning Bible studies. Primarily Warren was an historian, but the biblical theology movement flowed in his blood. He stressed that redemption must be seen in the context of creation and cited passages that have now become well known in ecological reflections (Ps. 50:10-11; Ps. 19:1) and in recent discussions concerning people of other faiths.[42]

For redemption he focused on Colossians 1:15-20 and Ephesians 1:10 and raised the issue of the Omnipresent Christ. His section on God the Sanctifier was, interestingly, weaker: it needed Taylor to develop this theme in depth.

---

40. Warren, *Theology of Attention*, p. 1.
41. Warren, *Theology of Attention*, p. 6.
42. Amos 9:7 "Did I not bring Israel from the land of Egypt, and the Philistines from Capthor and the Syrians from Kir?" and Isaiah 19:23-24 where Egypt is called "my people" and Assyria "the work of my hands."

In Warren's second way, of humility toward people of other faiths, he advanced a tentative distinction between the two Pauline phrases "Christ in you, the hope of glory" and "being in Christ." The former, he suggested, was wider and included unconscious and inarticulate experience of the "Christ-presence" while the latter concerned being consciously incorporated into Christ.[43] It seems to me that a distinction between conscious and unconscious response to Christ is valid, but not warranted by the distinction between these Pauline phrases. "Christ in you, the hope of glory" refers to the extraordinary context of the Gentiles receiving Christ.[44]

The third section raised key questions on idolatry, universalism, and the uncovenanted Christ, which were developed in later chapters of the Indian edition. First, he stressed that the Old Testament prophetic denunciations of idolatry were mainly focused "inwards," as a warning to Israel, rather than "outwards," commenting on the Gentiles' behavior. Warren developed this theme in the chapter "Attention and the Problem of Idolatry":

> The attack is made upon those who know better, *not* on those who know no other way. In defending Israel's belief about God, all idols have to be attacked, and within the historical context of the Old Testament this involved an attack upon idolaters.[45]

This emphasis is no doubt correct, though not all biblical texts support it, particularly those that indulge in heavy sarcasm.

Second, with regard to the "universalist" texts in Romans (5:18; 3:23-24; 11:32-36), Warren commented that he was not "arguing for a facile universalism," but asked: "can we seriously believe that there are

---

43. There is a fascinating marginal note in Warren's own copy of Barth's *Epistle to the Romans* (in the Henry Martyn Centre, Cambridge). He marked on the cover that he bought it in April 1953 and at the top of page 164 where Barth commented on Romans 5:9-11, Warren wrote: "Surely with Barth's contempt for all human consciousness he unwittingly prepares the way for the view that more may stand 'unconsciously' in the light of Christ, that a 'good' Muslim or Hindu may in fact be *very* near the kingdom. If this is so it is an important conclusion for our thinking about the 'other' religions. Barth cannot really have it both ways."

44. Warren's New Testament mentor, C. F. D. Moule, indicated a reservation in a footnote that Warren, with humility, included in *Face to Face* (p. 27), and Warren made a point of noting this in his own handwritten bibliography of his work on other faiths.

45. Warren, *Theology of Attention,* p. 31.

any men anywhere unaffected by this all-embracing redemption?"[46] Warren discussed this question with Hooker in his letter of 17 October 1971:

> I am always grateful for being challenged on "universalism." But with you I believe in paradox. I'm sure that two mutually inconsistent ideas may have to be held in tension in this our time of ignorance. I wholly agree that God only wants the free response of man and that must involve the possibility of a free rejection. Yet I find myself increasingly perplexed as to what to do with the multitudes in ever increasing number who are not free to reject because they know of no one to accept. Isn't this one of the vastest problems of today. . . . This, so it seems to me, gives a dimension of depth to all one's thinking about "Universalism" and the ultimate destiny of man and the meaning of anakephalaiosis. . . .[47]
>
> So you see what a long chase your paragraph on "Universalism" has taken me. Keep up this challenge — you are, as I said in my last letter, the only person with whom a regular conversation is possible.

The twin strands of judgment and the promise of "all things being summed up in Christ" (Ephesians 1:10 was a fundamental text for Warren) can, perhaps, be brought together if judgment is seen as "annihilation," banishment into nothingness.[48] This would mean that all who remain (with many, many surprises, including people of other faiths) will indeed be summed up in Christ. As a stone dropped into a pond causes ripples in all directions, so the cross of Christ, at the epicenter of history, has effects backward to the patriarchs as well as forward to us and outward to those who have not yet fully heard of Christ, but are open to God as they know him. Salvation by faith (not by religious observances), by Christ (even if unknown), and by the cross (which challenges all claims on God) seem to me to be "three themes in one" that bring the promise of God's hope.

Warren's third key question related to this discussion. It considered the prologue of John's Gospel, "the light of men" and the "uncov-

46. Warren, *Theology of Attention*, p. 21.

47. *Anakephalaiosis* is the Greek word used in Ephesians 1:10 to describe the recapitulation or summing up of all things in Christ.

48. The Doctrine Commission of the Church of England, *The Mystery of Salvation: The Story of God's Gift* (London: Church House Publishing, 1995), p. 199: "Annihilation might be a truer picture of damnation than any of the traditional pictures of the hell of eternal torment."

enanted Christ." This is developed in the chapter "The Universal Christ and the Problem of Interpretation."

Warren outlined three ways of response: argument, dialogue, and empathy. As examples of the apologetics of the first way, he found illustrations in Justin, Origen, Aquinas, and especially Henry Martyn, including the story of a Persian Muslim scholar who came to faith. As an example of dialogue he pointed to Gairdner.[49] He presented the vital importance of friendship (". . . he taught us how to love Muslims"), a favorite theme of Warren's, which surfaced again and again in his letters to Hooker:

> We shall not get very far with our meeting, with arriving at a "mutual courtesy of respect" unless we forget all about dialogue in the sheer enjoyment of making friends. Friendship without any *arrière pensée* is to be our first achievement.[50]

In this chapter Warren quoted four times from Hooker's letters to him. On 4 October 1969 Hooker wrote about a visit to a *satsang*, a weekly Hindu meeting consisting of loving devotion to Ram and Sita and expositions of the Bhagavadgita:

> Simply to proclaim the gospel to these people would simply be an exercise in insensitive futility. I think that the way must lie in "listening and asking them questions." What was thrilling was to be accepted so readily and completely into their circle.[51]

Warren also mentioned another important influence on him:

> A dear friend of mine, priest of the Roman Obedience, Fr. Raymond Panikkar, of the Hindu University of Varanasi,[52] wrote some years ago a work with the title *The Unknown Christ of Hinduism* in which he seeks to show something of the unexpectedness of the way Christ himself is to be discovered in Hindu spirituality.[53]

49. For sources for both of these, Martyn and Temple Gairdner, he shows again the influence of Constance Padwick, quoting from Constance E. Padwick, *Henry Martyn: Confessor of the Faith* (London: SCM Press, 1923), p. 270, and Padwick, *Temple Gairdner*, pp. 108, 148-49, 158-59.

50. Warren, *Theology of Attention*, p. 54.

51. Warren, *Theology of Attention*, p. 56.

52. Varanasi was also where the Hookers were based.

53. Warren, *Theology of Attention*, p. 58. Warren focused further some of his ideas from his ecumenical lectures in Israel in Max Warren, "Presence and Procla-

As an example of his third way of response, empathy, Warren quoted Klostermaier's incisive insight, "Christ does not come to India as a stranger, he comes into his own. Christ comes to India not from Europe, but directly from the Father."[54] He then gave the example of Charles de Foucauld and the Little Brothers of Jesus[55] and ended with the words of de Foucauld that focus on a theme dear to his own heart. "Being present amongst people, with a presence willed and intended as a witness of the love of Christ."[56]

The Debate with John Hick on Uniqueness

Finally, in considering Warren, I come to his debate with John Hick on the uniqueness of Christ. A working party of the British Council of Churches had asked Warren for a memorandum on this subject. It was later published in *The Modern Churchman*,[57] and his biographer, F. W. Dillistone, reckoned it to be one of the finest articles Warren ever

---

mation," a paper read by proxy at the European Consultation on Mission Studies, at Selly Oak Colleges, April 1968, unpublished in English but in German "Präsenz und Verkündigung," *Evangelische Missions Zeitscrift* 25.3 (Aug. 1968), pp. 158-71. He showed the key influence of Panikkar again in quoting him: "The Christian attitude is not ultimately one of bringing Christ *in*, but of bringing him *forth*, of discovering Christ; not in command but of service. Or, in other words, Christ died and rose again for all men — before and after him — his redemption is universal and unique." Warren, "Presence and Proclamation," p. 8, citing Panikkar, *Unknown Christ*, p. 45. Warren concluded: "Dwell on that thought of the 'present' individual unveiling the 'present Christ.' When I go to meet the man of another Faith I do not, in any sense whatever, precede Christ. He is there before me. . . . He is the Way, the Truth and the Life. There is no other way, no other truth, no other life but he." Warren, "Presence and Proclamation," p. 13.

54. Klostermaier, *Hindu and Christian in Vrindaban*, p. 112.

55. Charles de Foucauld (1858-1916) was a Catholic hermit who, during the last years of his life, lived in the Sahara, Algeria, among the Muslim Tuaregs. He won their respect, compiled their first grammar and dictionary, translated the Gospels, and transcribed proverbs and songs. Through a tragic misunderstanding, he was shot by an anti-French Tuareg in 1916. After his death, the Little Brothers followed a rule that he had composed. See R. Voillaume, *Seeds of the Desert: The Legacy of Charles de Foucauld* (London: Burns & Oates, 1955); the author was one of the Little Brothers order.

56. Cited in Voillaume, *Seeds of the Desert*, p. 120.

57. Max Warren, "The Uniqueness of Christ," *The Modern Churchman* 18 (winter 1974), pp. 55-66.

wrote.[58] Warren endeavored to show that the uniqueness of Christ consisted of the fact that Jesus' intimate relationship with his Father, and supremely the cross and resurrection, explicitly demonstrated what had been felt after, or even implicitly believed, by other faiths.

He accepted the need for a "Copernican revolution" but not such a one as expressed by Hick in *God and the Universe of Faiths*.[59] "The new centre is not a theological term — God — . . . but an historical person Jesus in whom God is to be recognised as uniquely revealed."[60] Hick wrote a short comment that was also published.[61] Warren stressed the personal nature of God and the importance of the incarnation. He was first of all an historian, and although acknowledging the need for a major rethink in theology, he argued as an historian with Hick, the philosopher of religion, who denied the coherence of holding to the uniqueness of Christ in the modern world.

At the close of the twentieth century and the beginning of the next, the real focus of debate is between those who follow the line developed by Hick and those who, like Warren and Taylor, hold to the finality, ultimacy, and distinctiveness or uniqueness of Christ.[62]

Taylor's Theology of the Go-between Spirit and the Meeting of Faiths

In a letter to Pat Hooker dated 26 April 1973, Warren gave a wonderfully witty pen portrait of John V. Taylor:

> He is head and shoulders spiritually and mentally above any of his contemporaries and is one of the few Anglicans with a capacity for

58. F. W. Dillistone, *Into All the World: A Biography of Max Warren* (London: Hodder & Stoughton, 1980), p. 202.

59. John Hick, *God and the Universe of Faiths* (London: Macmillan, 1973).

60. Warren, "Uniqueness of Christ," p. 61.

61. Warren's letter in reply, in which he used the word "distinctive" rather than "unique," may be found as Appendix II in Dillistone, *Into All the World*.

62. The so-called "pluralist" case has been set out in John Hick and Paul Knitter, eds., *The Myth of Christian Uniqueness: Toward a Pluralist Theology of Religions* (Maryknoll, N.Y.: Orbis Books, 1987); the case against this "pluralism" has been set out in Gavin D'Costa, ed., *Christian Uniqueness Reconsidered: The Myth of a Pluralistic Theology of Religions* (Maryknoll, N.Y.: Orbis Books, 1990), and, from a more conservative position, in Vinoth Ramachandra, *The Recovery of Mission Beyond the Pluralist Paradigm* (Carlisle: Paternoster Press, 1996).

seeing 6 feet in front of his nose and then a little more. What is more he doesn't possess the peculiar Anglican Ecclesiastical squint which gets virtually every important issue out of focus.

The Primal Vision

Warren invited Taylor to write in his Christian Presence series and this produced *The Primal Vision*. Earlier in the century, the missionary scholars Placide Tempels (Belgian Catholic) and Edwin Smith and Geoffrey Parrinder (both British Methodist) had pioneered studies on African religion in a sensitive way.[63] Taylor developed their work. He presented Christ as "the Coming One," elucidating the widespread African myth of the "lost presence of God," the divine withdrawal. The "Coming One" renews that presence:[64]

> The "pagan" sees the *Erchomenos,* the Coming One, standing in the midst of his own world-view and presenting to him several points of reference so relevant and yet so startlingly new as to command immediate recognition and immediate resistance.[65]

> He that should come, the Emmanuel of Africa's long dream, is, I believe, this God who has been eternally committed to, and involved in, the closed circle, even to the limit of self-extinction. His symbol is not the cross above the orb, but the cross within the circle. His is the lost Presence that the primal faith of man has always sensed. In the meeting of the Christian with the man who clings to that faith it may be that he will show himself to them both.[66]

Taylor began the book by drawing on his experience of living, during his research for *The Growth of the Church in Buganda,* in a

---

63. Placide Tempels, *La Philosophie Bantoue* (Elizabethville: Editions Lovania, 1945); Edwin W. Smith, *African Beliefs and Christian Faith* (London: United Society for Christian Literature, 1936); Edwin W. Smith, ed., *African Ideas of God* (Edinburgh: Edinburgh House Press, 1959); Geoffrey Parrinder, *West African Religion* (Oxford: Oxford University Press, 1949); Geoffrey Parrinder, *African Traditional Religion* (London: Hutchinson, 1954).

64. In a discussion between Taylor and the author in July 1997 on *The Primal Vision,* he commented, "I felt that Christ must make his own way into African religion: it is not that he is already there, nor that we bring him in, but that he needs to make his own way in."

65. Taylor, *The Primal Vision*, p. 120.

66. Taylor, *The Primal Vision*, p. 92.

thatched hut for several months close to a bush school in Uganda. After discussing whether one religion had to cede to another, he went on:

> Ruthlessness has had a long run in Africa, and so long as the mission-ary encounter is conceived of as a duologue one will have to "cede to the other." But may it not be truer to see it as a meeting of three, in which Christ has drawn together the witness who proclaims him and the other who does not know his name, so that in their slow discovery of one another each may discover more of him?[67]

Taylor went on to argue that the two key surprises that Christ brings to the African worldview are the recognition of a *direct* relationship with God and the solidarity of all humanity, the discovery of "Adam" when "the first ancestor in most African myths is, strictly speaking, the equivalent of Abraham."[68]

In *The Primal Vision*, Taylor manifested his close affinity with African spirituality, which came out of years of profound involvement and engagement with the African worldview.

The Go-between God

In chapter 9 of his classic book *The Go-between God: The Holy Spirit and Christian Mission*[69] entitled "Meeting: the Universal Spirit and the Meeting of Faiths,"[70] Taylor set out his underlying conviction:

> We are citizens of a forgiven universe. Being-in-Christ is a more primary and essential condition of a man's existence than is his ignorance of Christ. It follows that any and every movement of his mind and spirit which can be called an act of faith is truly faith in Christ, even though Christ is still the unknown magnetic pole which draws him. Evangelism, therefore is, inviting a man to become what he is, helping him to accept the fact that he is *already* accepted in the beloved.[71]

67. Taylor, *The Primal Vision*, pp. 34-35.
68. Taylor, *The Primal Vision*, p. 122.
69. John V. Taylor, *The Go-between God: The Holy Spirit and Christian Mission* (London: SCM Press, 1972).
70. A portion of it first appeared in Taylor et al., *Face to Face* and many of the ideas were developed originally in his *CMS News-letter*.
71. Taylor, *The Go-between God*, p. 180.

Then he developed a careful, fascinating definition of religion. He criticized a static view of religion as "primarily a body of propositions and regulations, standing over against people who either believe or do not believe" and then continued:

> But I believe it is truer to think of a religion as a people's tradition of response to the reality the Holy Spirit has set before their eyes. I am deliberately not saying that any religion is the truth which the Spirit disclosed, nor even that it contains that truth. All we can say without presumption is that this is how men have responded and taught others to respond to what the Spirit made them aware of.[72]

For Taylor, therefore, religion was "a tradition of response." When he turned to dialogue he mentioned two particular truths he had learned from his own experience in dealing with disagreements: "Firstly, I would say, pay attention to the real conviction that underlies the precise point at which disagreement appears and then try to turn mere confrontation of opposites into a real and possible choice."[73] After mentioning the differences between the response of Jesus and Muhammad to violence, he continued:

> The gulf between is seen, as it were, in cross section. Both I and the Muslim may go forward either on the one side or the other. I said "cross section"; for it is nothing less than the cross which is now demanding our decision. Once more we see the evangelism of the Holy Spirit consists in creating occasions for choice.[74]

He described the second truth, "I must be patient enough to listen and learn until I begin to see his world through his eyes," before discussing what is beginning to happen within the very life of these other faiths themselves, "a fervent, a subtle change, brought about by the influence of Jesus Christ upon them, far beyond any conscious impact that Christians are making."[75]

The Go-between God was written during the early period of the influence of the charismatic movement in Britain and had a sympathetic chapter on world Pentecostalism; yet in his treatment of other faiths,

72. Taylor, *The Go-between God,* p. 182.
73. Taylor, *The Go-between God,* p. 187.
74. Taylor, *The Go-between God,* p. 188.
75. Taylor, *The Go-between God,* pp. 189, 194.

Taylor sensitively challenged some of the attitudes that have been characteristic of that movement.

Lambeth Inter-faith Lecture

Finally I come to Taylor's Lambeth Lecture: this was the first Lambeth Inter-faith Lecture and was delivered on 2 November 1977.[76] He began with the fundamental insight that "respecting an opinion that conflicts with one's own without itching to bring about a premature and naive accomodation" is what is entailed in "loving one's enemies."[77] He went on to make several carefully crafted points, which built on and developed the discussion in the Go-between God. He described how "past isolation has bred ignorance and suspicion," defined religion again as a "tradition of response by ordinary people" (pointing out that this response included disobedience as well as obedience), outlined "the open, inclusive view in Christian theology" (quoting biblical passages, among others, cited in Warren's Theology of Attention), and insisted on the Christian claim for "an absolute centrality for Jesus Christ" including the conviction, based on the biblical phrase "before the foundation of the world," that this is a "pre-forgiven universe": "In other words, wherever we see people enjoying a living relationship with God and experiencing his grace we are seeing the fruits of Calvary though this may neither be acknowledged nor known."[78]

The next section was headed with a phrase that became widely known, "Every religion has its jealousies." He meant "those points in every religion concerning which the believers are inwardly compelled to claim a universal significance and finality."[79]

> One of the most significant things we have in common on which to
> build our mutual understanding is the experience of having a convic-

76. John V. Taylor, "The Theological Basis of Interfaith Dialogue," International Review of Mission 68 (Dec. 1979), pp. 373-84; also published in J. Hick and B. Hebblethwaite, eds., Christianity and Other Religions (London: Collins, 1980), pp. 212-33.

77. Taylor, "The Theological Basis of Interfaith Dialogue," International Review of Mission, p. 373.

78. Taylor, "The Theological Basis of Interfaith Dialogue," International Review of Mission, p. 379.

79. Taylor, "The Theological Basis of Interfaith Dialogue," International Review of Mission, p. 380.

tion that by definition precludes the other person's belief, and being unable to accommodate it with integrity. . . . So I would plead with those who want to make all intractable convictions relative and level them down for the sake of a quick reconciliation: Leave us at least with our capacity for categorical assertion, for that is what we have in common.[80]

The lecture, given in the wake of the "Myth of God Incarnate" debate,[81] continued with "some experiences that have to be absolute and universalized," focused on the incarnation, and finished with a plea to "expose our experience to one another's questionings" and a summary of "things we have in common." Twenty years later, in reflecting on these issues in a letter, Taylor commented:

The historic Christ, the Logos fully revealed, comes as a story that must be told and an image reflected in other human lives — but he does not come as a stranger. He has been there all along, but his footprints were not on the most frequented paths and he is recognized as a face seen in half-forgotten dreams like that of the Suffering Messiah foreshadowed in the Old Testament but neglected in the on-going tradition of Judaism. He comes to his own in the other faiths in another way also, in that he, the Logos incarnate once for all in Jesus of Nazareth, matches the need and fulfils the promise of each traditional world-view as though he had emerged from within it with no less relevance than he did within Judaism. We who stand outside the other traditions may only guess how this may be.[82]

It can be seen that Taylor's thought on other faiths was more developed than Warren's and that his tone was different, in that he considered the theological structure of religion itself and sought to work out a theology of religions.

---

80. Taylor, "The Theological Basis of Interfaith Dialogue," *International Review of Mission*, p. 381.

81. This debate had been launched with the publication of John Hick, ed., *The Myth of God Incarnate* (London: SCM Press, 1977). The book criticized traditional belief in Christ's divinity from philosophical, New Testament, and patristic perspectives. Maurice Wiles, one of the contributors, later gave a critique of Taylor's concept of "jealousies" in this lecture, in Maurice Wiles, *Christian Theology and Inter-Religious Dialogue* (Philadelphia: Trinity Press International, 1992), pp. 31-35.

82. Taylor's letter to the author, 27 July 1997, cited with permission, and thanks.

Conclusions: Warren and Taylor's Influence in World Christianity in the Later Part of the Twentieth Century

In concluding, some similarities and contrasts between Warren and Taylor will be suggested, before considering their influences on British and world Christianity.

Similarities and Contrasts

Warren and Taylor shared much in common, including their education at Cambridge,[83] their great gift for friendship across cultures and for keeping in touch with friends, their early prophetic insights that became accepted orthodoxies, their insistence on the context of politics, their invigorating encouragement of younger missionaries and scholars,[84] their stress on the "personal" as a priority in all mission, and their courteous, respectful, patient attitude to people of other faiths that could be summed up as "implicit universalism focused on Christ."[85] Both rejoiced in the adjective "evangelical," but refused to hyphenate it when pressed by conservatives for further definition.[86] It is interesting to note that both of them had more firsthand African than Asian experience, which is unusual for those who write on other faiths, and both also had to return to Britain from Africa before they had hoped to do so.

The general contrasts between the two are also significant. Warren's formative subject discipline was history, and Taylor's was English and then theology. Warren had ten months in Nigeria as a missionary overseas, and Taylor had ten years in Uganda plus other periods of research. Warren had little appreciation for the arts and wrote only in prose, whereas Taylor has great insights into music and art, writes po-

83. They were also both appointed honorary fellows of their Cambridge colleges: Warren of Jesus College and Taylor of Trinity College.

84. In his memory, Max Warren Fellowships were set up by CMS to fund the "immersion" of young scholars in the cultures of other faiths.

85. This phrase tries to describe their desire to combine the openness of seeing God at work in people of other faiths, with a belief that ultimately God will indeed be the savior of *all* people, through his son Jesus Christ, who was, and is, fully divine as well as fully human.

86. Tim Yates, "Evangelicalism without Hyphens: Max Warren, the Tradition and Theology of Mission," *Anvil* 2 (July 1988), pp. 231-45.

etry and even his prose is poetic. Warren focused on Christ; Taylor developed a distinctive theology of the Holy Spirit. Warren was outgoing in personality but essentially a layman in a clerical collar, preferring to work on the creative margins of church structures as a "backroom boy" and refusing to become a bishop. Taylor, by contrast, is rather shy in nature, but eventually became bishop of Winchester and influenced the Church of England from the center as chairman of the Doctrine Commission.

What of Taylor's views on the contrasts between them? In discussing the difference between Warren's early use of the term "Christian presence" and its later missiological use by others, and also Warren's phrase "the uncovenanted Christ," Taylor has commented:

> The difference lay between what I expressed in that book [*The Primal Vision*] and the meaning which other people gave to the phrase "Christian Presence," a meaning that Max seemed to endorse in some of his *later* writing. . . . What I meant, and mean, by the term is Christians being present in a profound sense to adherents of other faiths or ideologies, and I believe that is what Max had in mind when he launched the series of books. But it fairly quickly became a shorthand for the concept of a non-historical, "cosmic" Christ being inherently present within the beliefs and traditions of all religions, a concept towards which Max seemed to be veering when in 1967 . . . he proposed for his Israel lectures the strange term, "the uncovenanted Christ."

Taylor later continued:

> To call the timeless Logos "Christ" is to fasten upon him, as we should, the historical identity which he took upon himself in his incarnation. His universality was not diminished by that identification; rather was his eternal likeness revealed in sharper focus. If, therefore, our use of such terms as cosmic, unknown or uncovenanted Christ serve to bring the image into softer focus and make it more conveniently undefined I am doubtful of their value. And yet I wholly endorse Klostermaier[87] and have done ever since I introduced his manuscript to the SCM Press.[88]

---

87. Klostermaier, *Hindu and Christian in Vrindaban*.
88. Taylor's letter to the author, 27 July 1997.

Christianity in Britain

Several missiologists in Britain have been influenced by both Warren and Taylor in their writings on this subject — for example, Kenneth Cracknell, who served with the Methodist Missionary Society in Nigeria before working for the British Council of Churches. Included among those who have served overseas with the CMS are Roger Hooker, Christopher Lamb, Philip Lewis, Andrew Wingate, and Colin Chapman. To varying degrees and in different directions, these may see themselves developing the Warren/Taylor tradition in ecumenical contexts.[89] The Church of England's Doctrine Commission's book, *The Mystery of Salvation,* specifically mentioned this tradition in its chapter on other faiths, which was drafted by Wingate, who was a consultant.[90] As noted above, Taylor, while bishop of Winchester, became the chairman of the Church of England Doctrine Commission.[91] Other bishops who have written on other faiths and have served with the CMS include David Brown, David Young, Simon Barrington-Ward, and Michael Nazir-Ali.[92]

89. See the bibliography for a selection of their works. Roger Hooker has been mentioned above (note 33); Christopher Lamb served in Pakistan and became officer for Other Faiths in the Council of Churches for Britain and Ireland and in the Church of England; Philip Lewis also served in Pakistan and was appointed adviser to the bishop of Bradford on Inter-Faith Issues; Colin Chapman served in Egypt and Lebanon, later became director of Faith to Faith, an (evangelical) Christian consultancy service for interfaith concerns, and represents an articulate conservative position of many CMS members; Andrew Wingate served in India and later as principal of the United College of the Ascension, the joint USPG and Methodist training college in Selly Oak.

90. Doctrine Commission, *Mystery of Salvation,* pp. 157ff.

91. Also on that commission was John Bowker, then Fellow of Trinity College, Cambridge, and prolific writer on other faiths including the new *Oxford Dictionary of Religions* (Oxford: Oxford University Press, 1997). He was greatly influenced by Warren, who had nearly succeeded in encouraging him to serve in Nigeria with CMS.

92. David Brown served in the Sudan and became bishop of Guildford; David Young served in Sri Lanka and became bishop of Ripon; Simon Barrington-Ward served in Nigeria and was Taylor's successor as general secretary (1975-85) and later bishop of Coventry; Michael Nazir-Ali, previously bishop of Raiwind in Pakistan, became general secretary of CMS (1989-94) and then bishop of Rochester.

World Christianity

What then of responses to their writings and their influence on others in world Christianity in the later part of the twentieth century? The fact that three dissertations, in the universities of Pretoria, Louvain, and Helsinki, have been written on Warren's missiology shows a widespread interest in his work. These were by Meiring, an Afrikaans-speaking Dutch Reformed missiologist; Furey, an Irish Catholic missionary; and Haaramäki, a Finnish Lutheran pastor. Haaramäki's work has been published.[93] In considering the wider stream of influence, the international evangelical movement and Roman Catholic missiology will be examined, before considering a personal letter from an ecumenical Indian theologian and the writings of a leading Presbyterian theologian from Ghana.

The Lausanne Covenant of 1974 has acted as a significant confessional statement for international evangelicalism and represents a conservative position concerning attitudes toward people of other faiths. However, paragraph 4, titled "The Nature of Evangelism," did have an echo of Warren's terms:

> Our Christian presence in the world is indispensible to evangelism, and so is that kind of dialogue whose purpose is to listen sensitively in order to understand. But evangelism itself is the proclamation of the historical, biblical Christ as Saviour and Lord, with a view to persuading people to come to him personally, and so be reconciled to God.[94]

The shape and wording of the covenant were greatly influenced by its architect, John Stott, who chaired the drafting committee. In his book *Christian Mission in the Modern World*,[95] based on addresses at

---

93. Pieter G. J. Meiring, "Max Warren as Sendingwetenskaplike" (D.D. diss., Pretoria, 1968); Francis Eamon Furey, "The Theology of Mission in the Writings of Max Warren" (L.S.T. thesis, Louvain, 1974); Ossi Haaramäki, *The Missionary Ecclesiology of Max A. C. Warren: A Systematic Research on the Warren Production of 1942-1963* (Helsinki: The Finnish Society for Missiology and Ecumenics, 1982). The Afrikaans and Finnish dissertations have short concluding summaries in English.

94. John Stott, ed., *Making Christ Known: Historic Mission Documents from the Lausanne Movement, 1974-1989* (Grand Rapids: Eerdmans, 1996), p. 20.

95. John Stott, *Christian Mission in the Modern World* (Downers Grove: IVP, 1975).

the Lausanne Congress and the Chevasse Lectures at Oxford, Stott showed how the above wording specifically responded to Warren's thought (and perhaps also to the development of the concept of presence noted above by the World Student Christian Federation):

> The notion of the "Christian Presence"[96] has not always commended itself because its advocates have sometimes spoken of a "silent presence" or an "authentic silence." No doubt there are occasions when it is more Christian to be silent than to speak. Yet Christian presence in the world is intended by God to lead to Christian proclamation to the world.[97]

In his chapter on dialogue, Stott showed Warren's influence also on paragraph 3 of the Covenant: "Dialogue, however, to quote Canon Max Warren 'is in its very essence an attempt at mutual "listening," listening in order to understand. Understanding is its reward.' " It is this point which was picked up in the Lausanne Covenant.[98]

The majority of Western and non-Western Protestant mission personnel in the world today are evangelicals, with conservative attitudes to other faiths. Most have probably not heard of either Warren or Taylor, whose works are now little quoted in their literature, partly because not much of Warren and Taylor's writing was published in the United States and also because of the generational gap. Since South Korea is providing a growing proportion of mission personnel, perhaps more of Warren and Taylor's work should be translated into Korean?

Paul F. Knitter, a Roman Catholic professor of theology at Xavier University, Cincinnati, represents a radical theology of religions. In his

---

96. Later, in a chapter on dialogue, Stott mentioned the series. He mentioned Cragg with approval, noting that his dialogical approach seemed to have been "the main inspiration of the series of 'Christian Presence' books that Canon Max Warren has edited." *Christian Mission*, p. 76.

97. Stott, *Christian Mission*, p. 55.

98. Stott, *Christian Mission*, p. 73. The quotation of Warren was from his paper "Presence and Proclamation." Stott went on to cite the two references to dialogue in the Covenant: "On the one hand it says firmly that we 'reject as derogatory to Christ and the gospel every kind of syncretism and dialogue which implies that Christ speaks equally through all religions and ideologies' (para. 3). But on the other it says with equal firmness that 'that kind of dialogue whose purpose is to listen sensitively in order to understand' is actually 'indispensable to evangelism' (para. 4)." Stott, *Christian Mission*, p. 73.

fair-minded and comprehensive survey *No Other Name?*,[99] he outlined four models of Christian attitudes toward the world religions: "Conservative Evangelical (one true religion)," "Mainline Protestant (salvation only in Christ)," "Catholic (many ways, one norm)," and "Theocentric (many ways to the center)." It is interesting to note that, as a Catholic, Knitter treated Warren, Cragg, and Taylor as a group and included them under the Catholic model, in the section "A Mainline Christian Model." This positioning is both ironic (in that they come from the evangelical Anglican tradition), but also perceptive in that they would not fit particularly easily into the mainline Protestant model (where Knitter placed Lesslie Newbigin and Stephen Neill). Knitter, who had studied under Karl Rahner (a key influence at Vatican II), commented:

> Typical of the Anglican tradition, these theologians speak with admirable respect for the spiritual values of other religions. They advocate a method of dialogue called "Christian presence"; it requires a long, respectful listening before trying to converse with members of other faiths.
>
> When these theologians take up that conversation, however, they restate much of Rahner's theory of anonymous Christianity.[100] Warren speaks of "the unknown Christ" who saves even when "unrecognized as the Savior."[101]

Knitter's linking of their thought with Rahner's is significant. They all represented different aspects of similarly open positions, but were part of independent streams of investigation that came to converging conclusions, using different language. In a letter to Hooker, dated 7

99. Paul F. Knitter, *No Other Name? A Critical Survey of Christian Attitudes Toward the World Religions* (Maryknoll, N.Y.: Orbis Books, 1985).

100. For a lucid, nuanced elucidation of Rahner's (often misunderstood) concept of "anonymous Christianity," see Knitter, *No Other Name?*, pp. 128-30: "In showing that other believers can be called 'Christians without a name,' Rahner tries to break through Christian exclusivism. . . . It states not only that there is saving grace within other religions but also that this grace is Christ's. . . . Especially in his earlier writings, Rahner clearly sets a time limit for the validity of religions. Once a religion really confronts the gospel — once the gospel is translated into the new culture and embodied in community — then that religion loses its validity. It must make way for him who is greater." For Rahner's own foundational treatment of the subject, see Karl Rahner, "Christianity and the Non-Christian Religions," in *Theological Investigations*, vol. 5 (London: Darton, Longman & Todd, 1966), pp. 115-34.

101. Knitter, *No Other Name?*, p. 135.

March 1969, Warren mentioned that he had just completed reading Rahner's three-volume *Mission and Grace:*[102]

> This is coming to be very much the new R. C. approach to the other religions. I am hoping, some of these days, to do a study of contemporary Roman Catholic "Missionary" writing. In some ways it has gone an astonishingly long way. I'm not sure that it is not going to be the real break-through out of the bondage of much Roman legalistic thinking.

I turn now to a criticism of the Christian Presence series from an Indian scholar, writing in the year that Warren died. On 4 July 1977, Stanley Samartha, then director of the WCC unit "Dialogue with People of Living Faiths and Ideologies," replied to a letter of Warren's and commented:

> I know that 15 years ago you asked Stewart[103] to write a volume on Hinduism in the Christian Presence series. My immediate reaction then — as it is now — was why ask a British missionary to write such a book rather than an Indian Christian theologian? I have great respect for Bill Stewart who was my predecessor as Principal of Serampore College. But my point is that while missionaries from other countries have a contribution to make it is more important now for people to struggle with these questions from within their own cultural situation. The intellectual decolonisation of our minds seems to be a much slower process than the geographical retreat of colonialism.[104]

The point was well made. The 1970s introduced a new context in theological writing, and writers "from within their own cultural situation" did indeed produce such works, including Samartha himself and his successor, Wesley Ariarajah, both of the Church of South India.[105]

---

102. Karl Rahner, *Mission and Grace,* 3 vols. (London: Sheed & Ward, 1964).

103. William S. Stewart, a Church of Scotland missionary, was principal of Serampore College, India, from 1959 to 1967.

104. Roger Hooker Archives, MACW/1/4, S. Samartha to M. A. C. Warren, 4 July 1977.

105. Stanley Samartha, *One Christ — Many Religions: Towards a Revised Christology* (Maryknoll, N.Y.: Orbis Books, 1991); S. Wesley Ariarajah, *Hindus and Christians: A Century of Protestant Ecumenical Thought* (Grand Rapids: Eerdmans, 1991). For an excellent critique of the radical theologies of Samartha, Pieris, and Panikkar, see Ramachandra, *The Recovery of Mission.*

Current writing on other faiths from Asia refers little to the works of Warren and Taylor, both of whom, as noted above, had focused more on Africa.

African theologians have regularly returned to Taylor's *Primal Vision* as an early example of a white man's sensitive appreciation of African traditional religions. Kwame Bediako (director of the Akrofi-Kristaller Memorial Centre, Akropong, Ghana), in an exciting book on African theology, commented in a discussion concerning ancestors:

> Conceivably it could happen, as John V. Taylor wrote nearly thirty years ago, with great insight and deep African sympathy, that: "when the gaze of the living and the dead is focused on Christ Himself, they have less compulsive need of one another." However, Taylor felt able also to add: "But need is not the only basis of fellowship; and Christ as the second Adam enhances rather than diminishes the intercourse of the whole community from which he can never be separated."[106]

Bediako himself built on the concept of presence and described Christ, present in Africa, calling in missionaries from outside:

> In missiological terms, this is another way of saying that the cross-cultural transmission did not *bring* Christ into the local African situation. If that were to be the case, then, in African terms, Christ would be a disposable divinity, actually able to be taken, carried and brought . . . and presumably also, disposed of if not needed. The deeper insight is, however, that Christ, already present in the situation, called in His messengers so that by proclamation and incarnation, He might be made manifest.[107]

This chapter has considered the contributions of Warren and Taylor to the subject of mission and the meeting of faiths, with discussions of earlier influences on them and of later responses to them, in the setting of world Christianity. It has been argued that, although their particular writings are not widely known to the majority of mission partners at the end of the twentieth century, their key ideas of "presence" and "attention," of "awareness" and "jealousies" have entered the stream of thinking of various theologians, missiologists, and statements from different traditions.

106. Kwame Bediako, *Christianity in Africa: The Renewal of a Non-Western Religion* (Maryknoll, N.Y.: Orbis Books, 1995), p. 228.
107. Bediako, *Christianity in Africa*, p. 226.

The writer of the epic *The Lord of the Rings*, J. R. R. Tolkien, commented on his earlier book, *The Hobbit*, "One writes such a story out of the leaf-mould of the mind."[108] Perhaps the ideas of Warren and Taylor have bedded down in the fertilizing leaf-mould of past missiological thinking and are silently enriching new and growing plants?

---

108. Cited in Humphrey Carpenter, *J. R. R. Tolkien: A Biography* (London: George Allen & Unwin, 1977), p. 178.

12. CMS and Mission in Britain: The Evolution of a Policy

JOHN CLARK

The Church Missionary Society had been formed for missionary work "in Africa and the East." It was only in 1973, nearly two hundred years after the creation of the society, that it was resolved to bring missionaries *to* Britain. This was at the first meeting of the society's newly created General Council.[1] Although a background paper for that meeting stated that the change was made "not as a sharp change of tack, but as a logical consequence in today's world of its 175 years of commitment to world mission," the decision was, in fact, a major development in the policy of the society.[2] Within the next twenty years the CMS was to develop, alongside its long-standing work of sending missionaries overseas, a number of programs that involved either taking people to Britain or sending them overseas to gain experience that would subsequently help them in work within Britain. The CMS Annual Report for 1997 could speak of "new partners in Britain from Uganda, Pakistan, Sierra Leone and North India, with one more promised from the Philippines."[3] The contrast to 1897, with its focus on its "foreign mission work," when CMS had more than 480 clergy and lay-

---

1. Resolution 6, CMS General Council Minutes 1973, p. 6.
2. CMS Standing Committee *Report for 1973* to April 1974 General Council, p. 1.
3. Church Mission Society, *Report and Accounts*, 31 January 1998, p. 5.

men and more than 530 married and single women missionaries on its 483 mission stations, was dramatic.[4]

The contribution of the churches formed in the traditional mission fields of British Anglican missionary societies to the life and mission of the Anglican churches within the United Kingdom has yet to be systematically investigated and assessed.[5] This is partly because until recently the main focus of the societies' work has been overseas and such contribution as they may have made to the mission of the church in Britain has been an incidental by-product of another purpose. By contrast the overseas work and policies of the societies have been the subject of many studies, as have their support and training structures in this country.

This chapter makes a preliminary contribution to that investigation, first by suggesting some areas of church life that might be investigated and second by identifying, in some detail, the factors that led to the development by the CMS of a policy for mission in Britain. It sets this in the wider context of changes in the Anglican communion. It also looks at the early ways in which the policy was implemented and some of its consequences for the CMS in the 1980s.

The Contribution of Returned Missionaries to Church Life in Britain

In addition to the crucial importance of deputations by staff and missionaries on leave, a great industry of missionary magazines, books, pictures, and later slides was developed in the nineteenth century to keep supporters in touch with the work overseas.[6] Notice boards in parish churches list the missionaries sent out from or supported by the congregation through the decades, often describing them as "our own missionaries."[7] The missionary societies formed one of the major chan-

4. *Church of England Yearbook,* 1898.

5. The impact of the churches of the Continent and North America on the life of the British churches is increasingly recognized.

6. For nineteenth-century examples see, for example, Stock, vol. 3, pp. 54-72. For the early twentieth century see Hewitt, vol. 2, pp. 445-54. For post–Second World War plans, see the important *Invitation to Adventure: Some Outlines for a Post-War Plan on Behalf of CMS and Its Work* (London: CMS, 1946).

7. The missionary board of a major CMS-supporting church like St. Michael's Church, Blackheath Park, south-east London, is not untypical. Its first vicar

nels by which information about other cultures and other faiths was introduced to people in Britain. The networks of CMS associations, often transcending parish boundaries and denominations, and the activities undertaken to raise funds were a significant way in which ordinary Christians could become involved in the life of the church and a major aspect of the great expansion of voluntary activity undertaken by the Victorians. This network of support was one of the consequences of the interest in "foreign missions" and although it may have not been so intended, it provided a way for tens of thousands to participate actively in the life of the Anglican churches in Britain. Recent regional studies of churches have emphasized the importance of these home support networks both in parish life and ecumenically across denominations.[8]

The engagement with missions overseas also introduced many for the first time to people of other cultures. From the earliest days, the CMS took people from overseas to Britain. These were often the sons (for almost invariably they were male) of local leaders, taken for education with the intention that they should return to lead churches in their own societies. There were also visitors like Bishop Samuel Crowther, one of the only two black African bishops of the nineteenth century. Their successors in the late nineteenth and twentieth centuries were the bursars who went to study in Britain then return to leadership positions in their own churches and communities. But the intention has always been that they should give information about the work overseas as well as being a sign of the success of the missions themselves.

There were other ways in which the missionaries and the nascent church overseas had an impact on the church in Britain. Of great importance was the publicity and campaigning about situations of serious concern such as the early campaign for the abolition of slavery, followed by Thomas Fowell Buxton's parliamentary inquiries into the treatment of indigenous peoples. Subsequently the CMS continued to raise concerns about situations in New Zealand, South Africa, and In-

---

(from 1829-78), Joseph Fenn, was a CMS missionary in India and strongly supported the society in Blackheath. Of the fifty-seven missionaries named as being connected with the parish between 1829 and 1982, forty-six served with CMS or CEZMS.

8. See, for example, the references to missionary societies and their influence in Jeffrey Cox, *The English Churches in Secular Society: Lambeth 1870-1930.* (New York: Oxford University Press, 1982), and Mark Smith, *Religion in Industrial Society: Oldham and Saddleworth, 1740-1865* (Oxford: Clarendon Press, 1994).

dia. In this century, from time to time both the CMS and the SPG (later USPG) have had occasion to campaign on issues such as racism, colonial policy in Kenya during the Mau Mau period, apartheid in South Africa, UK immigration policy, the Brandt report on economic disparities between North and South, and, most recently, international debt and the Jubilee 2000 campaign.

Second there was the impact on the evolution of the Church of England in its official response to situations that arose through the church's missionary and colonial expansion overseas. The first Lambeth Conference was called partly as a result of pressures from the Anglican Church in Canada and within the leadership of the Church of England for some international forum at which pressing issues within the colonial church and emerging Anglican communion could be addressed.[9] The influence of the Episcopal Church in the United States has been particularly significant. It provided the model, for example, for the rediscovery, within the colonial Church of England, of the synod as a body in which a bishop could take counsel with clergy and lay representatives. This was pioneered, in the mid nineteenth century, in New Zealand by Bishop Selwyn and then by Bishop Gray in Capetown. The concept of a "missionary bishop" came into the life of the Church of England through the influence of American Episcopal Church practice on Bishop Samuel Wilberforce.[10] The first such English bishop was Charles Mackenzie, consecrated by Bishop Gray in 1861 for work in Central Africa for which UMCA provided support. It was the Episcopal Church that provided the terms of the 1887 Chicago/Lambeth Quadrilateral as the basis for approaching unity talks with other churches. In the twentieth century, issues of women's ordination and unity have been pressed on British Anglican churches by experiences in churches of the communion — Macao in 1944 and South India in 1948.[11]

A third aspect of the impact of the overseas churches on British religious and national life has been the experience of those who served as missionaries overseas. They brought back with them both the reality of

9. For the role of the SPG in the origins of the Lambeth Conference, see H. G. G. Herklots, *The Church of England and the American Episcopal Church* (London: Mowbray, 1966), pp. 154-77.

10. Gavin White, "The Idea of the Missionary Bishop in Mid-Nineteenth Century Anglicanism" (M.S.T. thesis, General Theological Seminary, New York, 1968).

11. W. L. Sachs, *The Transformation of Anglicanism* (Cambridge: Cambridge University Press, 1993), pp. 299-302.

their experience and, at their best, used it in their ministry within the church at parish level, but also in raising concerns with government.[12] Recent studies have stressed that the experience of mission overseas during the Victorian and Edwardian period had profound implications for the development of religion in Britain, in particular in the revision of traditional theology and in attitudes to people of other faiths.[13] Experience overseas has been particularly significant in the development of the role of women in the life of the church. Overseas women missionaries often were able to undertake tasks that were not possible in Britain and on their return they often were given roles in speaking that were in practice denied to residents.[14]

A fourth contribution has been in the realm of liturgy. In this century the publication of the eucharist of the Church of South India (CSI) in 1952 has been described as "an immensely significant influence in the development of alternative patterns of liturgy."[15] It provided a new model for liturgical development combining a careful blend of elements from existing traditions and awareness of the tradition of the primitive church, with a recognition of the needs of the local community. Its production led to the 1958 Lambeth Conference encouraging a process of liturgical revision in the provinces and a virtual endorsement of the structure of the CSI liturgy. Leslie Brown was a CMS missionary in India, where he chaired the CSI's liturgical committee. He went on to become bishop of Uganda in 1953 and was in-

12. The CMS estimates that more than seven thousand missionaries have served with the society, the majority of whom have returned to live in England. For a comparatively recent investigation of the impact of missionaries stimulated by CMS see two publications by Richard and Helen Exley, *In Search of the Missionary* (London: Highway Press, 1970) and *The Missionary Myth: An Agnostic View of Contemporary Missionaries* (London: Lutterworth, 1973).

13. See, for example, John Wolffe, ed., *Religion in Victorian Britain,* vol. 5, *Culture and Empire* (Manchester/New York: Manchester University Press, 1997); and Kenneth Cracknell, *Justice, Courtesy and Love — Theologians and Missionaries Encountering World Religions, 1846-1914* (London: Epworth Press, 1995).

14. See, for example, Jeffrey Cox, "The Missionary Movement," in *Nineteenth-Century English Religious Traditions,* ed. D. G. Paz (Westport, Conn.: Greenwood Press, 1995), p. 209; J. Cox, "Independent English Women in Delhi and Lahore, 1860-1947," in *Religion and Irreligion in Victorian Society,* ed. R. W. Davis and R. J. Helmstadter (London: Routledge, 1992), pp. 166-84; Brian Heeney, *The Women's Movement in the Church of England, 1850-1930* (Oxford: Clarendon Press, 1988).

15. W. M. Jacob, *The Making of the Anglican Church Worldwide* (London: SPCK, 1997), p. 281.

volved in the liturgical section of the 1958 Lambeth Conference and in the production of *Eucharist for Africa,* based on the CSI model. The CSI influence on the Church of England's Alternative Service Book is very evident, but the CSI service also gave added momentum to a process of developing more contextual liturgies throughout the communion.[16]

The preceding paragraphs suggest some of the areas that could be further investigated to assess the contribution of overseas missionary connections to the witness of the church in Britain. A more detailed study of the factors that led the CMS to take a clear policy decision to engage in mission in Britain provides a specific case study of the society making a major policy change and to this I now turn.

The Aftermath of World War Two

The dramatic transformation in the global situation in which British missionary societies operated since the Second World War has been well summarized by Brian Stanley:

> The thirty years . . . between 1962 and 1992 witnessed a fundamental transformation in the global context within which Christian mission was conducted . . . [previously] it had been possible to conceive of the missionary enterprise as an essentially one way flow of personnel, funds and ideas from a broadly Christian Western world to a broadly non-Christian, non-Western world. Both the theology and the practice of the Christian attempt to bridge this gulf between two worlds were ultimately fashioned by Westerners (although indigenous Christians had always done most of the spade work of evangelism in the mission fields). In Protestant circles the contours of thinking about mission were set by the boards of the historic denominational missionary societies, which found their collective voice in the International Missionary Council. All this missionary activity took place within a political context in which the supremacy of the European or

16. For Leslie Brown's role at and after the 1958 Lambeth Conference, see Colin Buchanan, ed., *Modern Anglican Liturgies, 1958-1968* (London: Oxford University Press, 1968), pp. 19-26; and on the "Liturgy for Africa," Colin Buchanan, ed., *Modern Anglican Liturgies,* pp. 48-56. In *One Word, Three Worlds* (London: Rex Collings, 1981), pp. 75-79, Leslie Brown outlines the principles behind the CSI Communion.

North American — exercised either through formal colonial rule or through the more subtle mechanisms of cultural hegemony — was only rarely challenged and never wholly overturned.[17]

During the years of rapid decolonization in the late 1950s and early 1960s, the World Council of Churches and its departments provided platforms in which the voices of leaders of the new and growing churches of the Third World could be expressed. Their desire to be independent of their Western founders and their challenge to them to attend to the situation in their own countries were clear. At New Delhi in 1961 the International Missionary Council was integrated into what became the Commission of World Mission and Evangelism (CWME) of the WCC, further contributing to the shift in the balance of power away from the historic Western churches and their societies. In 1963 the Mexico meeting of the CWME called for "Mission on Six Continents," stressing the oneness of the Christian mission everywhere. At the WCC Assembly in Uppsala in 1968 radical challenges were made to traditional understandings of mission as evangelism and conversion, while the 1973 Commission on World Mission and Evangelism in Bangkok declared that the missionary era had ended and the era of mission (of Christian responsibility to the world) had begun. Meanwhile the self-confidence of churches in Britain seemed to be sapped by the theological questioning, the radicalism of social change, the severe decline in church attendance, and the reduction in income caused by the inflation of the 1970s.

The period after the Second World War also saw dramatic change for the Church of England's missionary societies. Much was a result of the growth in the number of independent provinces[18] in the Anglican communion and the dismantling of the British Empire. The spirit of national autonomy transformed the relationships between Britain and the newly independent nations of the evolving Commonwealth. During the Second World War, Max Warren had foreseen two major trends, and he

17. Brian Stanley, *The History of the Baptist Missionary Society, 1792-1992* (Edinburgh: T. & T. Clark, 1992), p. 502.

18. A "province" in Anglican terminology refers to a collection of autonomous dioceses united under a presiding bishop or an archbishop, and with full authority. It is often coterminous with the boundaries of a state, to form the Anglican Church presence in there. But, rather confusingly, the term "province" is also used of a subdivision within that national church unit — thus the Church of England has two provinces, York and Canterbury.

gave time to preparing the CMS to face them. First, he said, the growth of nationalism and the rise of independent nations would require the CMS to divest itself of its property and mission stations overseas and hand them over to newly independent Anglican churches. Second, the growth of state concern for the welfare of its citizens would lead to many of the medical and educational tasks undertaken by missionaries being taken over by governments. The period was characterized for the CMS by the need to adjust to the growth of newly independent Anglican churches and discover the implications for the society. One of these was the gradual realization of the need for the society to engage as a matter of policy in mission in the British Isles. Two broad streams contributed to the emergence of the society's policy for mission in Britain. One was the changing face and structure of the Anglican communion producing the programs "Mutual Responsibility and Interdependence" and then "Partners in Mission." The other was the growth of black and Asian communities in Britain.

The Development of Partnership

The 1950s and 1960s saw a rapid growth in independent provinces of the communion often in advance of state independence.[19] Archbishop Fisher showed great interest in this development and often sought the advice of the missionary society general secretaries, Max Warren in particular.[20] But the growth of provinces and the rapid expansion of churches within them raised questions of how a communion of independent churches and provinces could be held together and provide mutual care, support, and missionary involvement. Since 1867 the decennial Lambeth Conference had provided an occasion for deliberation and consultation among bishops, the sole communion-wide forum for handling such major issues. In 1948 the conference set up an Advisory

19. P. A. Welsby, *A History of the Church of England, 1945-1980* (Oxford: Oxford University Press, 1984), p. 91.

20. Edward Carpenter in his life of Fisher points to the wise advice of the "knowledgeable" Warren in matters of the Anglican Church in East and West Africa, the Middle East, and China: *Archbishop Fisher: His Life and Times* (Norwich: Canterbury Press, 1991); see index references under Warren. Max Warren in his autobiography *Crowded Canvas* (London: Hodder & Stoughton, 1974), p. 169, pays tribute to Fisher's "farsighted" role in "hastening the creation of new Ecclesiastical Provinces."

Council on Missionary Strategy,[21] established a central college for the Anglican communion at St. Augustine's Canterbury, welcomed the idea of an Anglican Congress (held first in 1954), and created an Anglican Cycle of Prayer. In 1958 the conference recommended the establishment of an Anglican Consultative Council (ACC) to continue the work of the conference between sessions. Although it was not formally set up until after the 1968 conference, a significant step was taken in the appointment of Bishop Stephen Bayne of Olympia, Washington, as the first full-time executive officer of the Anglican communion.

For more than two years, Bishop Bayne traveled widely round the communion carrying out a survey of the needs, resources, opportunities, and problems of the burgeoning churches. He reported on the huge disparity in financial resources, the needs for clergy training, and the need to help the newly formed provinces gain the capability to work as provinces.[22] His report formed the basis for the only major meeting of the Advisory Committee on Missionary Strategy at Huron in 1963, preceding the Second Anglican Congress in Toronto, Canada.[23] Out of these meetings came the call to *Mutual Responsibility and Interdependence* (MRI), "the aim of which was to mobilize the resources of the Anglican Communion in such a way that help could be given where and when it was most needed."[24] It called for a comprehensive review of needs and resources throughout the communion and for each church to give increased support in finance and manpower. A special call was issued to raise 5 million pounds above regular budgets to fund special developments, particularly in theological education.[25]

Within the Church of England, the MRI call was taken on enthusi-

21. It was never provided with a staff or budget and so met only around the time of Lambeth Conferences. Its only major meeting was before the 1963 Anglican Toronto Congress, when it produced the highly influential draft statement on *Mutual Responsibility and Interdependence*.

22. See Bishop Bayne's annual reports in Stephen F. Bayne, *An Anglican Turning Point* (Austin, Tex.: Church Historical Society, 1964), pp. 25-97.

23. Both Max Warren, then ending his period as CMS general secretary, and his successor designate (then) Canon John V. Taylor were consultants at these meetings. Warren provided the first keynote address at the congress.

24. Welsby, *Church of England,* p. 183.

25. Stephen F. Bayne's (ed.) *Mutual Responsibility and Interdependence in the Body of Christ* (London: SPCK, 1963) contains the basic text and background documents. Barry Till explained the background, underlying principles, and implications for the Church of England in *Change and Exchange: Mutual Responsibility and the Church of England* (London: Church Information Office, 1964).

astically. A Lent study program, *No Small Change,* was initiated by the missionary societies as a major attempt to "make mission central to the life of the Church of England. It reached an unusually large number of parish study groups, and was a real attempt to communicate to both lay people and clergy that mission must be central in the life of the Church, and not just something done 'over there.' "[26]

The provinces of the communion made their needs known through "Directories" in the hope that other churches would help finance them. The northern churches had difficulty identifying their own mission needs and responded with financial gifts to the needs expressed by the poorer churches.[27] The concept of mutual support and interdependence tended thus to be reduced to a focus on financial needs rather than on exchange of less tangible aspects of faith, life, and spirituality. The economic inequality between churches, part of the wider economic imbalance in the world, has been a constant problem in relations between churches. It has reinforced the image of financially wealthier churches as "givers" and the poorer as "receivers." Nevertheless the MRI call was of major practical significance in the life of the communion. It carried the reality of the worldwide communion to a wider audience than traditional missionary society supporters and widened the base of interest. MRI gave added impetus to the idea of direct companionship links between dioceses and provinces, a pattern that has subsequently become an established feature of communion life alongside the mission boards and societies.[28]

In February 1962 the CMS had launched its "Overseas Link Scheme" intended to connect parishes to the church in a specific province through the CMS missionary. This was a development of the previous "our own missionary" support scheme. It was hoped to provide a greater focus on the wider church. It was an evolution of support and

---

26. J. Murray, *Proclaim the Good News* (London: Hodder & Stoughton, 1985), p. 262. The CMS and the SPG also combined to publish a series of essays in support of MRI — see John Wilkinson, ed., *Mutual Responsibility: Questions and Answers* (London: SPCK, 1964).

27. "Although it wasn't intended to, MRI perpetuated the old idea of some Churches as givers and others as receivers, and so it often led just to a kind of 'shopping list' of requests and projects." CMS General Council, 23-25 April 1976, item 6, paper on "Partners in Mission: Some Questions Answered."

28. Companion links between dioceses of different provinces of the communion had been originated by Bishop David B. Reed in ECUSA in the late 1950s as a means of making the Anglican communion more relevant to people in the pews. Personal conversation.

interest in the missionary and the mission. Inevitably there was still a focus on the missionary since missionaries wrote the letters and received news from parishes and there was little consultation with church leadership overseas or continued discussion with them about the scheme.[29] Nevertheless it was a significant part of a process of widening interest in the newly emergent Anglican communion. With the launch of MRI the scheme was seen as an important way of emphasizing interdependence at the grass roots.

Tackling the problems of MRI, however, led to the Partners-in-Mission process, one of the early initiatives of the Anglican Consultative Council, established by the 1968 Lambeth Conference. The ACC comprised episcopal, clergy, and lay representatives of the different provinces and was originally intended to take over the role of the Lambeth Conference as a forum in which the issues facing the communion could be addressed on a regular basis. Following a review of MRI at its first meeting, the ACC launched Partners in Mission at its second meeting in Dublin in July 1973.[30] The proposals were intended to

> replace former attitudes either of independence or dependence by a common attitude of interdependence. . . . Each church should work towards financial independence in its own structures, but at the same time should be interdependent in the sharing of its spiritual and material resources in the fulfilment of God's mission.

The fundamental principles of Partners in Mission were that the church participates in the mission of God to the world. That mission is one throughout the world and is shared by the worldwide Christian community. The church in each place is primarily responsible for mission in that place, but the task is one, and since each church has gifts to offer and needs to be met, the local church needs the support, encouragement, and challenge of the wider church.[31] The practical expression of these principles was a series of consultations organized by churches and provinces to which representatives of other churches were invited to assist them in determining their priorities and to act as channels of

---

29. The whole of the February 1962 issue of *Outlook* was devoted to the new scheme.

30. The meeting took place three months after the CMS General Council resolution on mission in Britain.

31. *Partners in Mission,* Report of the Second Anglican Consultative Council Meeting, 17-27 July, Dublin 1973 (London: SPCK, 1973), pp. 55-59.

sharing between churches. Over the following twenty years these were to be highly influential in challenging the institutional structures and agencies of churches like the Church of England.[32]

The Contribution of African and Asian Communities in Britain

If the changes in the Anglican communion provided the broad context for changes in the CMS understanding of its calling in Britain, the second and more immediate factor was the immigration of black, Asian, and East African Asian people in the postwar decades. They came often at the direct invitation of British industries and government or, as in the case of the Ugandan Asians, as refugees. They were prepared neither for the hostility and racism they encountered nor the rejection that many experienced from many white British church members.[33]

The specific involvement of the CMS with immigrants had expressed itself from 1947 onward in assisting overseas students, initially through its Overseas Visitors' Department and then through the Church of England Overseas Commendation Centre, which the CMS helped to service. But CMS involvement was to broaden following interracial tensions and Enoch Powell's speech of April 1968 on the dangers of immigration. In response to growing concern from members about "what they could do at a local level to further racial harmony," a

32. The progress of the Partners in Mission process can be surveyed in the reports of the triennial meetings of the Anglican Consultative Council (ACC) — *The Time Is Now*, ACC-1, Limuru 1971; *Partners in Mission*, ACC-2, Dublin 1973; ACC-3, Trinidad 1976; ACC-4, Ontario, Canada, 1979; ACC-5, Newcastle, England; *Bonds of Affection*, ACC-6, Badagry, Nigeria, 1984; *Many Gifts, One Spirit*, ACC-7, Singapore 1987; *Mission in a Broken World*, ACC-8, Cardiff, Wales, 1990; *A Transforming Vision*, ACC-9, Cape Town, South Africa, 1992; all published in London by the ACC. By 1992 the consultation process had come largely to an end. More detailed comments are included in *Giving Mission Its Proper Place, Report of the Mission Issues and Strategy Advisory Group I (MISAG I)* (London: ACC, 1984); *Towards Dynamic Mission: Renewing the Church for Mission — Report of the Mission Issues and Strategy Advisory Group II (MISAG II)* (London: ACC, 1992); *Progress in Partnership, Report of the 1986 Mission Agencies Conference in Brisbane, Australia* (London: ACC, 1987).

33. J. Wilkinson, *Church in Black and White* (Edinburgh: St. Andrew Press, 1993), provides an historical overview of the encounter between black and white Christians in Britain. Kenneth Leech, *Struggle in Babylon* (London: Sheldon Press, 1988), outlines the history of black communities in Britain's cities.

survey of "race relations in Britain with special reference to the response of the Churches and of the CMS" was commissioned. The report *Act Now* surveyed the work of secular and church organizations and identified two broad areas for CMS involvement — the deployment of missionaries (either returned from overseas or specially selected) and the education of members. Such race relations work would be a natural extension of the society's work with overseas students. It could "mean not only working with immigrants, but also striving to help in the socially deprived areas of our large cities . . . and involve the Society with others in radical thought and action [over] some of the pressing urban and industrial problems in Britain today."[34] It was widely discussed throughout the society and the decision taken to appoint a Community Relations secretary responsible for mounting an educational program and advising members and returning missionaries about opportunities for service in community relations work.[35]

As part of the educational emphasis, articles on community relations had already begun to appear in *Outlook,* the CMS magazine, often provoking strong reactions.[36] But the major development was the appointment of Bernard Nicholls, a long-term senior staff member of the society, as Community Relations secretary in March 1971. In an early report he commented that one of the sadder aspects of his work was the

> acute contrast between missionary interest in affluent parishes focused on somewhere several thousand miles away, and the apparent indifference to the missionary situation only a few miles away. Such circumstances make a mockery of slogans like "Mission is One" and "Mission in All Six Continents." They also betoken adherence to a geographical emphasis in mission, which was never wholly valid, and in today's world is not only absurd, but also seriously neglectful of important missionary challenges.[37]

Much of his later work was to be spent in working with suburban parishes, which contained many CMS members, about issues of race

---

34. Rachel Hooper, *Act Now* (London: CMS, 1970), pp. 1, 60-68.
35. *Yes* (the CMS Members' Bulletin), no. 68, October 1970, p. 15.
36. "Foreigners in the Midst," *Outlook,* January 1969, p. 4; "Immigrants in Our Midst," *Outlook,* February 1969, p. 5; "Behind the Headlines about Race Relations in England," *Outlook,* July 1969, pp. 5-8.
37. *Yes* (CMS Members' Bulletin), no. 72, January 1972, p. 22.

and relations with people of other faiths.[38] Bernard Nicholls was to prove influential in both Anglican and ecumenical circles, serving on a number of committees and working parties of the British Council of Churches including those that discussed the use of church buildings by people of other faiths. His experience of the World of Islam Festival in 1976 led to the production by CMS of *The Way of Islam*, a filmstrip intended to help CMS members and the wider church understand and appreciate Muslims and Islam, as an essential foundation for appropriate witness. On his retirement in 1980, the CMS decided not to appoint a successor but rather to give his salary for five years as a contribution to the appointment of a field officer in the General Synod's Board for Social Responsibility. This was seen to be a means to focus the issues of race within a more central, national structure within the Church of England. Along with contributions from the USPG and other missionary societies, the CMS thus made a major contribution to the initiation of the church's Committee for Black Anglican Concerns (CBAC).[39]

In hindsight perhaps the most significant contribution to the church in Britain from overseas this century will be seen to have been that of black and Asian Christians. Some have found a home in the historic churches but the majority have felt the need to form their own denominations and fellowships, many of which are Pentecostal. Their influence in music, in vibrancy of faith, and in raising issues of practical justice and racism has posed profound questions to white British Christians.[40]

Mission Partners to Britain

The concern for community relations was growing at the same time as the CMS was preparing for its Nottingham 1970 conference — a major gathering attended by over 450 participants including most diocesan bishops, to look for "new signposts into the 70s for CMS."[41] One of

38. See, for example, his pamphlet *Letter to Mary* (London: CMS, 1979).

39. Since 1997, the committee has been known as the Committee for Minority Ethnic Anglican Concerns (CMEAC) encompassing the concerns of black, Asian, and other ethnic minority communities within the Church of England.

40. For an extended discussion see Wilkinson, *Church in Black and White*.

41. The CMS has revised and restated its goals at the end of each of the last four decades of the twentieth century. The Nottingham Congress set the agenda for the 1970s. The theme of interchange was publicized through the *Aiming to Share*

the subthemes of the conference report was a call for the CMS to support because of the changing world situation, "as full missionaries of the Society people to work in areas in the UK with an immigrant population" and also to use returned missionaries, new recruits, and people from the countries concerned. The report spoke of the need "to further the receiving of missionaries" and of a welcome for increased resources for "local experiments in evangelization, to help with the interchange of people, resources and ideas and the creation of an international missionary task force." It noted that the "Society's involvement in the well-being of people from overseas in this country is important and should be extended."[42]

After the Nottingham Congress, the CMS reformed its structures, setting up a General Council to represent the society's membership and establish broad policy.[43] When the first General Council met in April 1973, it had before it thirteen resolutions brought by different society committees. Four related to the overseas churches' connections with Britain and to mission in Britain. A small but not insignificant resolution noted the society's responsibility to "enter into new patterns of relationship with overseas Churches" and "to listen to what others were saying." It instructed that "not fewer than four Christians from Africa and Asia" should be invited to council meetings.[44] A motion on deputation asked, among other things, that attention be given to "enlisting the participation of overseas Churches in presenting the case for the support of the Church overseas."[45] A third resolution called for short training courses for society members to "help them to be more effective in evangelism."[46] Fourth, the council resolved that the CMS "give greater attention to the phrase 'mission in six continents' and, recognizing the urgent need for evangelism in this country, make provision for and in-

---

filmstrip for the 1980s. The paper *Towards a Global Policy for Mission* (1991) set new priorities for the 1990s. With the approach of the bicentenary, CMS engaged in a process of seeking vision for the next century.

42. *Yes* (CMS Members' Bulletin), no. 68, October 1970, pp. 4-6, 8.

43. Following a review of the CMS committee structure, the CMS General Council was set up in 1972 as a central representative committee of the society to lay down broad lines of policy. Initially, it held two meetings a year, one residential and one day meeting, but reduced to one residential meeting in 1977.

44. Resolution 2, General Council Minutes 1973, p. 4. The original proposal was for ten but was reduced because of the demands on overseas Christian leaders and of cost.

45. Resolution 3(c), General Council Minutes 1973, p. 4.

46. Resolution 5, General Council Minutes 1973, p. 5.

vite African and Asian missionaries to share in our mission in the UK."
The debate on the motion stressed the importance of getting the vision
of "mission on six continents" to the grass roots of the church particularly through the contribution of visiting overseas Christians.[47] The
council was also aware that a visit by three Ugandan evangelists led by
Bishop Festo Kivengere was in preparation, a visit that was to prove
highly influential for the society.

These decisions highlighted a number of issues that were to be important for the future. First, the presence and contribution of Christians
from other churches was to become an essential element at major CMS
gatherings and committees. It emphasized the importance of face-to-
face contact, allowing the direct voice of representatives of other
churches to be heard. Christians from overseas began to be appointed
to the society's staff. In 1973, for example, a Pakistani priest, Mano
Rumalshah, was appointed as a senior area secretary.[48] Second, the
stress on the mission of members in evangelism was to lead to the appointment of a Members' Training secretary with the specific task of assisting members to engage in mission and evangelism where they were
set, if possible, drawing on the experience of overseas churches. The
emphasis on enabling members to be "missionary" in Britain and not
merely supporters of overseas work, was a constant theme of the next
two decades. Third, over the next twenty years, it became more usual
for Christians visiting Britain for study or other purposes to speak at
CMS and parish meetings and services, giving information about their
church's life and often bringing pointed challenges to mission in this
country. Finally, the resolution on inviting Asian and African missionaries to Britain was to reemerge in the second General Council resolution about mission in Britain taken in 1982, after nine years of experiment and experience.

During the remainder of the 1970s, the CMS was occupied with a
number of issues that both diverted attention from mission in Britain and
also prepared the way for a more consolidated thrust in the 1980s. The
period revealed some of the tensions in the addition of an emphasis on
mission in Britain to the traditional pattern of overseas missionary sup-

47. Resolution 6, General Council Minutes 1973, p. 7. The resolution came
from the CMS Liverpool Diocese Members Group.
48. He was assistant CMS home secretary for the province of York and CMS
area secretary for the dioceses of Ripon and York, 1973-78. In 1989, he became
dean of Peshawar Cathedral, Pakistan, as a missionary with USPG; in 1994, bishop
of Peshawar; and in September 1998, general secretary of USPG.

port. The middle 1970s were years of high inflation that had a severe impact on costs and income in Britain. The resulting concern was reflected in General Council debates in 1975 calling for maintenance of "the new impetus towards world-wide inter-change in mission through recruiting . . . bursaries and inter-Church visits" and for substantial increase in income.[49] In addition to cutting costs in Britain the main factor that saved CMS from serious financial problems was the rapid decrease in the numbers of missionaries serving overseas. Annual reports to the General Council listed the numbers of inquiries, firm applications, and numbers accepted. The sending of missionaries was described as "central to the being of the Society" and commensurate efforts were made to recruit.[50] A recruiting task force was established to encourage vocations. The society's magazine, *Yes,* regularly featured some of the 150 vacant posts. But numbers coming forward were insufficient to replace those retiring, perhaps reflecting the steep decline in Church of England attendance during this decade. This recruitment thrust continued into the mid-1980s.[51]

A major new emphasis on what came to be termed "interchange" was brought by John Taylor's successor as general secretary of the society, Simon Barrington-Ward.[52] At his first General Council he spoke of how

> the idea of giving and receiving, of exchange, of interchange had become for him [a] dominant theme . . . of people entering into one another's worlds . . . a network of glowing fire, of grace, of shared joy and pain. . . . CMS was emerging as an informal personal movement of giving and receiving. . . . The new impetus that was coming through this theme of interchange called for a right balance between emphasizing our continuing role as a "sending" agency and the new possibilities of enabling people to make a contribution here.[53]

This theme of a personal interchange of gifts and experiences was to dominate Barrington-Ward's time as general secretary. It was expressed almost poetically in a number of his CMS Newsletters.[54] It

49. General Council Minutes, 18-20 April 1975, pp. 4-7.
50. Simon Barrington-Ward in General Council Minutes.
51. A major new recruitment drive began in 1998 when the number of CMS missionaries serving overseas and in Britain was less than 180.
52. CMS general secretary, 1975-85.
53. General Council meeting, 18-20 April 1975, minutes, p. 16.
54. A selection of the newsletters is published in Simon Barrington-Ward, *Love Will Out: A Theology of Mission for Today's World: CMS Newsletters, 1975-1985* (Basingstoke: Marshall Pickering, 1988).

provided the context for the statement of aims that the society formulated in 1980 and portrayed in the widely used educational filmstrip
Aiming to Share. In some ways it was a fresh expression of the trinitarian theology found in Max Warren's writings, notably his 1955
book *Partnership,* and in John Taylor's writings on the Holy Spirit,
The Go-between God, and maintained the strong CMS emphasis on
the significance of the personal and "people in relation."[55] The concept, however, was expressed practically by setting up an Interchange
Fund "to bring notable Christians from one country to another to
share their insights into the Gospel with those in another."[56] The visits were mainly but not solely to Britain.[57] The pattern of Christians
visiting Britain to share their experiences was not new. There had
been many visits in the 1960s. Seme Solomona, a youth worker from
Southern Sudan, later to become bishop of Yei, visited Britain in
1973. He had met the CMS Africa secretary, Jesse Hillman, who visited Sudan following the Addis Ababa peace agreement. Hillman recalls meeting "a group of Sudanese Christians under trees outside
Juba and being told of the 'great things God had been doing.' Seme
asked if he could come to Britain to share his experiences and made a
great impact on those who met him."[58]

What made the Interchange program distinctive was the development of such visits into a regular program "promoting visits from one
country to another by Christians who can make a specific contribution
to the life of another Church" rather than merely raising interest and
support.[59] It had small beginnings. In 1975 there was one visitor to
Britain. In 1976 the budget was raised fourfold as the number of visits
increased. But interchange was not limited to these visits. The 1976
Standing Committee Report described existing CMS activities as aspects of interchange, for example, interchange in multifaith communities, particularly through the secretary for Community Relations, interchange from Britain through widening the age range for volunteer

55. M. A. C. Warren, *Partnership* (London: SCM Press, 1955); J. V. Taylor,
The Go-between God (London: SCM Press, 1972).

56. April 1981 General Council Paper, item 6, "Mission in Britain: Information Paper," p. 2.

57. In 1977, for example, a Nigerian priest went to train clergy in the Sudan.
His report is in *Yes,* April 1979, p. 15.

58. Personal letter.

59. Statement about the Interchange Fund in Worship Booklet at CMS General Council, 23-25 April 1976.

service and through a number of visits by senior staff, interchange through bursars and from overseas to Britain.

These early examples highlight two aspects of what was to characterize the Interchange program. First there was a concern to share with Christians at parish level what God was doing in the experience of Christians overseas in order to provide a challenge and encouragement for mission in Britain and to do so face to face. Second, there was the personal impact of meeting Christians from other cultures. For many British CMS members this was the first time they had welcomed overseas Christians into their homes and parish churches and experienced the natural way so many were able to speak about God and their faith and to pray spontaneously. The CMS was not alone in providing such opportunities, but the distinction of the Interchange program was that overseas Christians had come to give; they were not in this country as students or bursars.

Partners in Mission (PIM) also had its effect on the CMS at this time. The 1973 General Council had endorsed in principle the processes commended by the ACC at Dublin to deepen the concepts of mutual responsibility and interdependence.[60] A number of the CMS secretaries represented not only the society, but the whole Church of England in the early consultations. It had been agreed among the missionary societies that one representative should go on behalf of all. In 1976 the theme, Partners in Mission, formed a major General Council discussion item in which members wrestled with the issue of how to make the concept understandable at parish level and how the Church of England as a whole could learn from other churches and hold its own consultation.[61]

The PIM process raised a serious question for the Church of England in that its newly re-formed representative, deliberative, and legislative structure of the General Synod (formed in 1970) was detached from those sections of the church that provided the practical connections with the Anglican communion overseas. Partners in Mission

> prompted developments to improve the relationship between . . . the General Synod and the various independent missionary societies. . . . Furthermore, the new understanding of mission had led to the conviction that those involved in "home" mission and those concerned with

---

60. Resolution 73.15, General Council Minutes, 13 October 1973, pp. 5-7.
61. General Council Minutes, 23-25 April 1976, pp. 4-7.

"overseas" mission must be brought together since both were integral to the one task of "world mission."[62]

Better coordination was needed among the societies and the wider Church of England represented through the Synod, enabling overseas churches to have one channel through which they could relate to the Church of England as a whole. The solution was a coordinating body, Partnership for World Mission, bringing together representatives of the General Synod and initially of eight of the recognized voluntary societies.[63]

Mission Interchange

The debate about the role of the CMS in Britain was reopened at the end of the decade following "requests for help from CMS members working in four large English cities," including an open letter from John Holden, formerly a missionary in Uganda, and then vicar of Saints Peter and Paul, Aston, Birmingham, one of the largest English urban priority parishes.[64] A discussion document prepared for the 1981 General Council outlined the current CMS involvement, including support for former missionaries working in Britain, the Interchange Fund, the work of the Members' Training and Young Adult secretaries, community relations work, the BCMS/CMS Other Faiths Theological Project, a variety of grants, and the work of the members of the field staff.[65] It stated that the distinctive contribution that CMS would seek to make would be based on the "*principle* of Interchange — namely the gaining of Christian insights through crossing cultural barriers" — operating through various forms of partnership, of which one suggestion was international interchange teams.[66] It identified possible areas of work, such as "high unemployment, high coloured *[sic]* immigration, high

62. Welsby, *Church of England*, p. 275.

63. *Partnership for World Mission*, Report of the Working Party on Relations between the Church of England, the General Synod, and the Missionary Societies (London: Board for Mission and Unity, 1977). Later the number of member societies was extended to ten and in 1992 to eleven.

64. *Yes*, July 1981, p. 8.

65. "Mission in Britain: Discussion Paper," CMS General Council, 23-26 April 1981. It was prepared by a working group set up by the CMS Standing Committee. The paper makes no mention of the 1973 council resolution.

66. "Mission in Britain: Discussion Paper," p. 3.

population density and de-population," recognizing that "most informal discussion of CMS involvement in Britain in the constituency over the last eight or 10 years has concentrated on the needs of the urban, multi-racial scene."[67] It also urged caution, for "CMS is not a large Society and any further involvement in Britain could not be on a large scale."[68] The CMS would not rival the Church Army, the Church Pastoral Aid Society, or the Society of St. Francis.

The document did recognize the divisions within the membership. Some members were deeply concerned that the society be involved in mission in Britain, convinced that

> geographical demarcation lines are an absurdity in an internationalised world. If the Church Army — founded for mission in Britain — can work abroad because the need exists, CMS founded for Africa and the East — can work in Britain if Church leaders ask it to do so. Ultimately, they feel, mission is indivisible. Other members feel equally strongly that a Society "founded for Africa and the East" would be exceeding its brief and confusing its objectives if it were to regard Britain as part of the "mission field" in which God has called us to serve.[69]

Similarly divergent views "on this controversial issue" were expressed in the April 1981 General Council debate. There was concern "lest people be deflected from mission overseas" and involvement should remain at the current level of the Interchange program. Others took the view that "mission overseas and mission in Britain should be mutually reinforcing, not in opposition" and that the society should respond to the strong call that a number of young Christians were feeling toward inner-city work. It was pointed out that "a small number of BCMS missionaries had returned to work in the UK . . . paid by local churches, but located and in some instances housed, by BCMS."[70] The CMS was not the first in the field. Those in favor believed that the CMS should build on its world connections. The decision taken was to consult the members and make a decision in 1982.[71]

67. "Mission in Britain: Discussion Paper," pp. 3-4.

68. "Mission in Britain: Discussion Paper," p. 3.

69. "Mission in Britain: Discussion Paper," p. 5.

70. The Bible Churchmen's Missionary Society (BCMS) changed its name to Crosslinks in the early 1990s.

71. General Council Minutes, 23-26 April 1981, pp. 8-10. See appendix pp. 1-3 for reports of subgroup discussions. *Yes,* July 1981, pp. 8-10, gives the public account of the council.

Response to the consultation process was high. It revealed that approximately 72 percent of the CMS associations either supported a further extension of the commitment of the CMS to mission in Britain or had no view, whereas 28 percent felt that the present commitment was sufficient. Sixty-one percent said they would be prepared to raise additional funds. The paper concluded that "there is strong, though not overwhelming, support for the Society to continue to be involved in mission in Britain in ways appropriate to its primary calling and to its stated aims."[72]

In April 1982 the CMS General Council took its second formal decision to engage in mission in Britain.[73] In the debate, Simon Barrington-Ward spoke of the challenge churches overseas were increasingly making to CMS about "what it was doing in its own country; some of them felt that the West was possibly the area in greatest need of mission today." The CMS would not decrease its primary calling to mission overseas, nor divert resources from overseas commitments. Indeed overseas work would be strengthened and "in the context of interchange, there would be mutual enrichment." CMS work would be small-scale and in the nature of pump-priming.[74] It was also pointed out that "in various ways CMS had been involved in mission in Britain throughout its history . . . now [there was proposed] a more deliberate commitment of people and funds, though even this had been foreshadowed by what had been done in the last decade."[75]

The final resolution was passed overwhelmingly. Based on the conviction that "God is calling the Society to a partnership with Christians across the world and that within this partnership it does have a missionary responsibility with the Church in Britain," it welcomed "the creative efforts the Society has already made in mission in Britain" and then resolved that "the Standing Committee shall instruct the Secretaries, to set up, where they consider it appropriate . . . fresh initiatives in mission in Britain."[76] The debate over the two years had reflected the tensions within the society. The concern lest the society lose its distinct and historic identity as an "overseas" missionary society to become one involved in "home" missions was contrasted with the challenge from overseas

72. General Council, 15-18 April 1982, paper 5, pp. 1-2.
73. The first was that of 1973.
74. General Council Minutes, 15-18 April 1982, pp. 1-2.
75. General Council Minutes, 15-18 April 1982, p. 2.
76. General Council Minutes, 15-18 April 1982, pp. 2, 5. Note the first two paragraphs were passed nem con, the last with four votes against.

churches about mission in Britain and the growing recognition of the reality and implications of mission on six continents. There was also the experience of the previous eight years and the recognition that many of the issues faced by the society's missionaries and partner churches overseas were now realities in Britain to which overseas Christians could bring experience and faith. The concept of interchange provided an undergirding theology. The need, however, to hold the membership together is reflected in the length of the consultation process, the assurances given that the CMS would not decrease its overseas commitments, and in the small-scale nature of its involvement in Britain. The CMS was dealing with the inheritance of more than 180 years during which a major focus had been on the missionary task overseas. Now the society was cautiously moving to give a greater emphasis to the missionary task irrespective of where that missionary task lay. The seeds were being sown for the change in name from Church Missionary Society to Church Mission Society that was to take place in 1995. The change was based on the principle that the society was now seeking to assist the wider church in its mission rather than to regard itself primarily as an organization whose object was to send missionaries somewhere.

Conclusion

This chapter has focused on two issues: suggestions about how the contribution of mission overseas to the life of the church in this country might be explored; and more specifically on the factors contributing to the formal decision of the CMS to engage in mission in Britain. Based as it was on the concept of interchange, that decision has had implications for all aspects of the society's life. The CMS began to see itself less as an exporter of missionaries and more as a broker enabling the exchange of the commodities of people, finance, and ideas across the world. This led to a radical restructuring of the British organization of the society in 1981. Within its publications and educational policy, the society built on previous experience to employ prayers, art, and worship material from other parts of the world to challenge and stimulate its supporters. From an early date there has been a deliberate attempt in the society's magazine, *Yes,* to ensure that the pictures chosen reflect the church around the world.[77] In *Morning, Noon and Night,* John Carden,

77. *Yes* magazine was first published in its present form in 1973 bringing to-

a missionary in Pakistan and then Asia secretary, brought a selection of prayers and meditations from around the world to a wide readership and pioneered publications from a number of sources in the 1980s.[78] Educational resources were produced with the purpose of challenging users about their own commitment to mission in Britain by connecting them to experience in other parts of the world. Area secretaries took on the task of assisting people in mission in Britain rather than just imparting information about the CMS. The concept took time to be worked through different aspects of the society's life.

Slowly a number of longer-term appointments were made. They were first known as "long-term interchange visitors," then "joint appointments" (reflecting their shared funding from CMS and local church sources), and only in 1988, "mission partners in Britain." Ken Okeke from Nigeria was the first. His task, initially for five years, was to encourage British Christians to relate to Nigerian Christians in their congregations. Soon, returned missionaries such as Roger Hooker, who, with his wife Pat, had served in India, were appointed to engage with people of other faiths. Others were appointed to assist outreach in inner-city parishes, including Aston. The priority emphases on relations with people of other faiths, urban priority areas, mission alongside the poor, and support for the witness of black and Asian Christians, drawing from the traditional areas of CMS involvement found in the CMS debates of the early 1970s, reappeared, coupled with a continued program of shorter-term visitors. Between 1980 and 1998, fifty people were appointed to serve as long-term mission partners in Britain, sixteen during the 1980s, and thirty-four in the period 1990-98, thus illustrating the gradual buildup of the program for mission partners in Britain from small beginnings.[79] Although there has been evaluation of the contribution of individuals, systematic assessment of the almost twenty years experience has yet to be undertaken. In 1988, programs were ini-

gether news for members (previously contained in a quarterly bulletin called *Yes*) and the publication *Outlook*, originally intended for a wider readership. Despite various redesigns it has retained its title to the present day (1998).

78. J. Carden, *Morning, Noon and Night* (London: CMS, 1976). Carden went on to publish *Another Day — Prayers of the Human Family* (London: SPCK, 1989) and to edit *With All God's People — An Ecumenical Cycle of Prayer* (Geneva: WCC, 1989). His latest collection is *A Procession of Prayers* (London: Cassell, 1997).

79. Seventeen were of British origin, sixteen of African, and seventeen of Asian origin. (I am grateful to Mark Oxbrow of CMS for this analysis.)

tiated to give British people experience of the life and witness of the church overseas through short-term placements and group visits, with the intention of better equipping them for witness in this country. These developments were paralleled in other Anglican societies and ecumenically in other denominations.

The period during which the CMS formally decided in principle to engage in mission in Britain and then began to work out the practical implications, has proved a watershed in the life of the society. Factors contributing to the decision included wrestling with the changed relations necessitated by the coming to birth of so many churches within the Anglican communion and more particularly the arrival of immigrant communities in Britain. The concept of interchange, of the society being an agent for the exchange of gifts of Christians across the communion, provided an overarching concept and theology for a new role for the CMS, which evolved from its traditional activities. But change took time. The end could not be seen from the beginning and in this experience, as in so many aspects of its history, the story for the CMS has been one of an organism both responding to changes in its context and developing its self-understanding in the process.

Afterword:
The CMS and the Separation of
Anglicanism from "Englishness"

BRIAN STANLEY

Bishop Bengt Sundkler began his history of the road to church union in South India with the following statement:

> The day when a church becomes a sending church, a missionary church, is among the most fateful in its history. When it moves across the seas to be transplanted in other soil, it does of necessity change, either by conscious and willing adaptation or else through its very resistance to change. The factors of growth and change are set out in sharper relief by the situation in a mission field than by the situation within the older churches of Europe and America. Transplantation means mutation.[1]

The preceding chapters of this volume have provided ample confirmation of the truth of Sundkler's dictum. When the Church Missionary Society was founded in 1799, there was little distinction between the Church of England and the Anglican Church. Since the early eighteenth century there had been a small (Protestant) Episcopal Church in Scotland, made up of those unable to accept the Presbyterian establishment, and in 1789 an Episcopal Church autonomous of the Church of

---

1. Bengt Sundkler, *Church of South India: The Movement Towards Union, 1900-1947*, rev. ed. (London: Lutterworth, 1965), p. 11.

England had been formally constituted in the newly independent United States. For obvious political and cultural reasons, however, neither of these nonestablished Episcopal churches adopted the national label "Anglican."[2] The Church of Ireland shared with the Church of England the privilege of establishment but was clearly identified as the church of the English ascendancy and thus had the allegiance of only a small minority of the Irish people. In Wales, the established church had originally been more successful in penetrating the native Welsh population, but by the end of the eighteenth century its influence was weakening in the face of resurgent Nonconformity and national sentiment.[3] There were Anglican communities in Canada and the West Indies, but they were composed almost entirely of British settlers and were constitutionally part of the Church of England. There was in 1799 but one colonial bishopric in Nova Scotia (established in 1787); elsewhere the diaspora of adherents of the Church of England remained subject to the ecclesiastical jurisdiction of the bishop of London. The term "Anglicanism" had not yet been coined in the English language, though the concept of the *Ecclesia Anglicana* was familiar enough, and the label "Anglican" was beginning to be applied to the members of that church. When the term "Anglicanism" first came into currency, in the course of the Catholic revival during the 1830s, it tended to mean not the entire religious tradition associated with the Church of England, but rather one particular (High Church) strand within it, with which the CMS had little instinctive sympathy.[4] Thirty years later, in CMS circles at least,

2. For a useful recent survey, see W. M. Jacob, *The Making of the Anglican Church Worldwide* (London: SPCK, 1997), chaps. 2-3.

3. Jacob, *The Making*, pp. 22-24, 34.

4. One of the earliest uses of the term "Anglicanism" in English was by J. H. Newman in his *Lectures on the Prophetical Office of the Church* (London: Rivington, 1837), pp. 21-22. Newman admitted that "what is called Anglicanism," namely "the religion of Andrews, Laud, Hammond, Butler, and Wilson," remained to be tried to establish whether it had any permanent identity or was "a mere modification either of Romanism or of popular Protestantism." See Peter B. Nockles, *The Oxford Movement in Context: Anglican High Churchmanship, 1760-1857* (Cambridge: Cambridge University Press, 1997), p. 40; and J. Robert Wright, "Anglicanism, *Ecclesia Anglicana*, and Anglican: An Essay on Terminology," in *The Study of Anglicanism*, ed. S. W. Sykes and John Booty (London: SPCK, 1988), p. 424. Sykes has suggested that the term may have originated as an English adaptation of the French "Gallicanism"; see S. W. Sykes, "The Genius of Anglicanism," in *The English Religious Tradition and the Genius of Anglicanism*, ed. Geoffrey Rowell (Wantage: IKON, 1992), p. 235.

Anglicanism appears to have meant little more than Englishness — part of the baggage of the missionary inheritance that the new churches of the mission field ought to jettison as quickly as possible. Only gradually, in the remainder of the nineteenth century and into the twentieth, did the term acquire anything like its modern meaning.

In 1799, to be a member of the Anglican Church was thus to affirm one's identity by birth and baptism with the established religion of the English nation and its historic relationship to the English state. Two hundred years later, Englishness and Anglicanism are no longer identical or even contiguous. The juxtaposition at the 1998 Lambeth Conference of predominantly black or brown faces with episcopal purple revealed with photographic clarity that the Church of England now constitutes only a small, and in various crucial respects unrepresentative, minority of the worldwide Anglican communion. Nevertheless, a critical observer might remark that the globalization of forms of ecclesiastical dress and polity that are rooted so firmly in the particularities of European history witnesses to the enduring cultural hegemony of the West, and especially of British imperialism, since Anglican ecclesiastical geography still corresponds quite closely to the boundaries of the former British Empire. The process charted triumphantly in Bishop Alfred Barry's 1894-95 Hulsean Lectures on *The Ecclesiastical Expansion of England in the Growth of the Anglican Communion* has, it might be claimed, continued apace in the century that followed, and with still greater rapidity and comprehensiveness.[5] Such a verdict would not be wholly foolish. Several of the authors of this volume have noted the extent to which the public face of Anglicanism in the non-Western world apparently mirrored that of the mother church in England. Allan Davidson's chapter has told the story of how the Maori church had to unshackle its own cultural identity from a missionary inheritance that for a long period made no distinction between Englishness and Anglicanism; the first church buildings erected in New Zealand reproduced the bell towers, lancet windows, and porches of the missionaries' homeland, though with some modifications consequent upon the substitution of wood for stone.[6] Similarly, in the South Indian Christian heartland of Tirunelveli, comments Geoffrey Oddie, the landscape is still "dotted with parish churches which look remarkably like Anglican parish churches in Victorian England."[7]

5. Alfred Barry, *The Ecclesiastical Expansion of England in the Growth of the Anglican Communion* (London: Macmillan, 1895); see above, p. 28.

6. See above, p. 199.

At the level of regulations, doctrine, liturgy, and form of ministry, according to John Karanja, the Kikuyu Anglican Church "became a replica of its English mother church adhering to the Thirty-Nine Articles, the Book of Common Prayer, and the threefold order of ministry."[8] How much notice, therefore, had missionaries actually taken of the stern warnings uttered repeatedly at the Liverpool Missionary Conference in 1860, and again by the *Church Missionary Intelligencer* in 1869, against producing native churches that were "nothing else than fac-similes of the mother church, and therefore disqualified from taking up a national position and exercising a national influence"?[9]

No single or simple answer can be given to that question. One factor may have been the changing pattern of CMS recruitment over the course of the nineteenth century. Paul Jenkins has reminded us in chapter 2 that in the first four decades of the society's history a very significant proportion of CMS missionaries were neither English nor Anglican. German Lutherans had to cross a frontier of national and ecclesiastical culture simply in order to serve in the society, and the case of C. T. E. Rhenius in South India indicates that their endorsement of specifically English cultural and ecclesiastical values on the mission field was neither instinctive nor uncritical. Similarly, as Kenneth Cragg points out, the Swiss Lutheran, Samuel Gobat, originally had no intention as the second Anglo-Prussian bishop of Jerusalem of creating a Palestinian Anglican church, but rather hoped, no doubt naively, to revive the ancient eastern churches to evangelical zeal.[10] By the 1860s, however, the link between Basel and London had weakened, and the national complexion of the CMS missionary force was more monochrome. Yet there were CMS missionaries forty years later, at a time when it is often assumed that Henry Venn's commitment to planting genuinely indigenous churches had been forgotten, who remained quite categorical in their insistence that imparting English cultural values was no part of their commission: "We don't want to Anglicise the Persian women, do we?" asked Winifred Westlake in 1903,[11] and the form of the question presupposes that it was still mission orthodoxy to distinguish Christianization, and now perhaps also "Anglicanization," sharply from Anglicization. How far Westlake's

7. See above, p. 253.
8. See above, p. 254.
9. See above, pp. 148, 169.
10. See above, pp. 126-27.
11. See above, p. 118.

understanding of what constituted Anglicization in the Iranian context would correspond to our own understanding remains, of course, a separate question. It is easier to find ringing missionary endorsements of the theory of inculturation from this period than to find striking examples of the theory being put into practice. But, whatever the truth about both missionary intentions and practice, the fact remains that Anglicanism in the non-Western world began through the initiatives of its new adherents to develop a face that was not simply a dark-skinned replica of its English parent.

Even the examples just cited of an apparent replication of the Church of England in non-Western contexts turn out on closer inspection to reveal a more ambiguous picture. The great Maori church at Rangiatea described by Allan Davidson in chapter 8 may have exhibited superficial conformity to English architectural patterns on the outside, but its interior displayed features that were indubitably Maori in character.[12] The numerous church buildings of Tirunelveli remarked on in chapter 9 may have been facsimiles of English models, but the shanar Christians who filled them were certainly not. The process of conversion among the shanars was substantially autonomous of missionary control and diverged too sharply from the spiritual pathway familiar to English evangelicals for that to be the case. As with the other case studies of Indian conversion presented by Geoffrey Oddie, the shanar movement to Christianity was a "largely independent, spontaneous expression of people's will and agenda."[13] Similarly, the Kikuyu Anglican Church portrayed by John Karanja, for all of its external conformity to English precedent, "derived its force and vitality from indigenous models and experiences."[14] What ultimately counted, argues Karanja, were less the rules imposed by the missionaries than the decisions made by the early *athomi* — the "readers" whose reading of where the cultural boundaries should lie between mission Christianity and Kikuyu religion proved remarkably prescriptive for the distinctive shape of Kikuyu Anglicanism.[15]

What such examples suggest is that a distinction needs to be drawn between the impact of the missionary movement as a whole on the non-Western world — which can scarcely be underestimated — and

12. See above, pp. 199-201.
13. See above, pp. 250-51.
14. See above, p. 255.
15. See above, pp. 269, 281-82.

the ability of Western missionaries to impose their particular vision on the churches they helped plant — which was often quite limited. Lamin Sanneh's analysis in chapter 7 of the Niger mission focused on the far-reaching and partly unintended implications in West Africa of the decision of the CMS to concentrate on the evangelization and consequent mobilization for evangelism of ex-slaves and ex-captives. In the person of a figure such as Samuel Crowther, who on first sight appears to be the quintessential "black European" of the Victorian missionary movement,[16] the society released what Sanneh terms the forces of "anti-structure" — an uncompromising moral imperative, rooted in his opposition to slavery, which could be as subversive of African patterns of hierarchy and oppression as of European ones. Nevertheless, Crowther's commitment to the use of Yoruba and other West African vernaculars in liturgy and his openness to indigenous cultural forms supplied the resources for later generations of Nigerian Christians to develop an African Christology.[17]

The stories told in this volume abound in ironies and ambiguities. Henry Venn, who never left the shores of Europe, is rightly depicted by Kevin Ward and Peter Williams as the chief nineteenth-century opponent of the strengthening forces of Anglicization. Yet Venn also stood in the tradition of the English Reformation, with a natural inclination to look to a measure of control by a Protestant state as the guarantee of spiritual freedom. Hence he initially resisted the arguments of such as Samuel Wilberforce for the creation of missionary bishops unfettered by the ties of establishment, supposing that constitutional control by the British Crown was necessary to prevent English bishops and clergy dominating the life of the younger churches overseas. During the 1860s, however, the case of the Ningpo bishopric reveals that Venn had come to believe that, in certain contexts at least, a missionary bishop free of state control would be less injurious to the freedom of the indigenous church than a colonial bishop.[18] Equal ironies surround the figures of Bishop Alfred Tucker of Uganda and Eugene Stock. It would be easy to dismiss Tucker as the archimperialist who gloried in the role the CMS played in the Brit-

16. See Andrew F. Walls, "Black Europeans — White Africans: Some Missionary Motives in West Africa," in *The Missionary Movement in Christian History* (Edinburgh: T. & T. Clark, 1996), pp. 102-10.

17. See above, pp. 184-87.

18. See above, pp. 26-27, 160, 168-69; C. Peter Williams, *The Ideal of the Self-Governing Church: A Study in Victorian Missionary Strategy* (Leiden: Brill, 1990), pp. 41-48.

ish annexation of Uganda in the 1890s.[19] Yet he deserves a more considered judgment (and incidentally a fuller place in this volume than he receives): Tucker was also an impassioned advocate of racial equality who fought hard, though without total success, to persuade CMS Uganda missionaries that their proper role was to serve within the structures of the Ugandan church and hence, at least in principle, under the authority of its emerging African leadership.[20] Eugene Stock, who took equal pride with Tucker in the British annexation of Uganda, and whose perspective is properly labeled by Kevin Ward as "metropolitan" and "institutionally-oriented,"[21] must take at least some of the credit for the bold step taken by the CMS in 1885-87 to reverse its previous policy and encourage the recruitment of single women on an equivalent basis to male candidates. By 1899, within fifteen years of this change, as Jocelyn Murray indicates in chapter 3, married and single women together accounted for 53 percent of the total missionary force. It was not that the CMS was ahead of its time in its attitudes to the participation of women in church government: women remained excluded from voting membership of the CMS General Committee until 1917, just as, in the Church of England as a whole, they were debarred from membership of Parochial Church Councils until 1914 and of higher representative councils until 1919.[22] Equally they were long excluded from decision-making processes on the mission field. Yet, as Murray observes, it was in an Asian diocese that owes its origins to the CMS that the first ordination of a woman to the Anglican priesthood took place in 1944.[23] Moreover, Guli Francis-Dehqani's analysis of the Persia mission in chapter 4 shows that it was not simply that female CMS personnel were often in the majority, but that they also may have had greater opportunities than men for the cultivation of individual friendships with indigenous people. In Iran such friendships with individual Muslim women began to break down the generalized stereotypes of Islam and foster the listening and learning relationships that were the necessary precondition for fruitful evangelism.

19. See above, p. 28.

20. Williams, *The Ideal of the Self-Governing Church*, pp. 243-57.

21. See above, pp. 19, 28.

22. See above, pp. 89-90. The Lower House of the Convocation of Canterbury in 1898 excluded women from membership of the new Parochial Church Councils. See Brian Heeney, "The Beginnings of Church Feminism: Women and the Councils of the Church of England, 1897-1919." *Journal of Ecclesiastical History* 33, no. 1 (Jan. 1982), pp. 89-109.

23. See above, pp. 87-88.

Francis-Dehqani's discussion of the Iran mission in terms of the contrast discernible between the vocabulary of missionary approaches to Islam in general and the reality of missionary relationships to particular Muslims may help readers less accustomed to theological discourse to form connections between the primarily historical and more theologically focused chapters of this volume. Bishop Kenneth Cragg's chapter has reflected with elegance and profundity on the nature of Christian mission as a process in which, at its best, the agents of mission are themselves discipled — instructed, challenged, and humbled — in the very act of seeking to make disciples. Those who have served in the Muslim world have found that experience of being discipled to be particularly searching. On a similar theme, Graham Kings in chapter 11 has explored the "theology of attention" expounded in his mature years by Max Warren, a theology that emphasized the necessary interconnectedness of listening and speaking in the course of Christian witness to those of other faiths. Kings also draws attention to the observation of John V. Taylor, Warren's successor as CMS general secretary, that mission encounters should be viewed from a theological perspective as a meeting, not of two, but of three parties, in which both the transmitter and the recipient of the Christian message are discipled by the presence of Christ.[24] John Clark's chapter applies the theme of "being discipled" through participation in the world mission of the church to the CMS itself and the Church of England as a whole. The growth in the 1950s and 1960s of independent provinces of the Anglican communion fostered the development of the concept of global partnership between autonomous churches in Christian mission. The influx of Caribbean, Asian, and East African people to Britain reinforced the learning process, calling sharply into question the conventional categories of domestic Christendom and overseas mission field with which the CMS, like other missionary societies, had operated since its foundation.

Most CMS missionaries (now termed "mission partners") went overseas expecting, as evangelical Christians do, to make individual disciples of Christ. Disciples of Christ were indeed forthcoming, though in varying numbers at different periods and in different locations. Those who chose to follow the Christian way, however, did so not, as the crasser versions of postcolonial orthodoxy would have it, because of the weight of British missionary numbers or influence — for such numbers and influence were generally limited — but as a result of what

24. See above, p. 306.

Geoffrey Oddie has termed "a yearning of the spirit for meaning and satisfaction."[25] Decisions to become Christian or not were most frequently taken not by individuals acting in isolation but by larger human social units. One of the most significant developments in the later thought of Henry Venn, as outlined by Peter Williams in chapter 6, was his growing conviction that the goal of the Great Commission given by Christ to the church was not simply the conversion of individuals but the discipling of the nations. Venn's hope that the missionary enterprise would lead to the multiplication of "national churches" might be interpreted as evidence of the constriction of his horizons by his membership of a national established church in England. But in application Venn's conviction was radical to the point of being subversive. It implied that each national church must be left free to determine its discipline and liturgy according to "the national taste." Williams shows how in the pages of the *Church Missionary Intelligencer* in Venn's last years the message was expounded that, rather than converts being Anglicized, Christianity must be "naturalized" in the soil in which it had been planted. "If we would propagate Christianity amongst the natives, we must be prepared to let them have it without its Anglicanism, which, however valuable for us, is unsuitable for them."[26] It is clear from the context of that article in 1869 that by Anglicanism was meant not a particular theological understanding of the Christian tradition, but a quality of inherited Englishness that the maturing younger churches needed rapidly to outgrow.[27] Nevertheless, here was a commitment to a degree of fluidity of identity within the emerging Anglican family whose implications few at the time fully grasped. One hundred and thirty years later, we are better placed to judge just how far the baggage of Englishness has in fact been jettisoned, leaving in place that pluriform and paradoxical entity of a multinational Anglicanism whose essence Anglicans themselves, let alone this non-Anglican author, still struggle to define.

25. See above, p. 235.
26. See above, pp. 167-68.
27. *CMI*, 1869, pp. 97-106; see Williams, *The Ideal of the Self-Governing Church*, p. 47. However, within twenty years the first edition of the *Oxford English Dictionary* was defining "Anglicanism" in absolute theological terms as "adherence to the doctrine and discipline of the reformed Church of England (and other churches in communion therewith), as the genuine representative of the Catholic Church"; James A. H. Murray, ed., *A New English Dictionary on Historical Principles* (Oxford: Clarendon Press, 1888), vol. 1, p. 327.

Bibliography of Printed Sources

Ajayi, J. F. A. *Christian Missions in Nigeria, 1841-1891: The Making of a New Elite*. London: Longman, 1965.

Ajayi, J. F. A. "Samuel Johnson and Yoruba Historiography." In *The Recovery of the West African Past: African Pastors and African History in the Nineteenth Century — C. C. Reindorf and Samuel Johnson,* edited by P. Jenkins. Basel: Baseler Afrika Bibliographien, 1998.

Annan, N. G. "The Intellectual Aristocracy." In *Studies in Social History: A Tribute to G. M. Trevelyan,* edited by J. H. Plumb. London: Longmans, Green & Co., 1955.

Ariarajah, S. Wesley. *Hindus and Christians: A Century of Protestant Ecumenical Thought*. Grand Rapids: Eerdmans, 1991.

Ashwell, A. R., and R. G. Wilberforce. *Life of the Right Reverend Samuel Wilberforce, DD: Lord Bishop of Oxford and Afterwards of Winchester*. 3 vols. London: John Murray, 1880-82.

Ayandele, E. A. *The Missionary Impact on Modern Nigeria, 1842-1914: A Political and Social Analysis*. London: Longman, 1966.

Barlow, Margaret. *The Life of William Hagger Barlow*. London: George Allen & Sons, 1910.

Barrington-Ward, Simon. *Love Will Out: A Theology of Mission for Today's World: CMS Newsletters, 1975-85*. Basingstoke, Hants: Marshall Pickering, 1988.

Barry, Alfred. *The Ecclesiastical Expansion of England in the Growth of the Anglican Communion*. London: Macmillan, 1895.

Bayne, Stephen F., ed. *Mutual Responsibility and Interdependence in the Body of Christ*. London: SPCK, 1963.

Bayne, Stephen F. *An Anglican Turning Point*. Austin, Tex.: Church Historical Society, 1964.

Bearth, Thomas. "J. G. Christaller: A Holistic View of Language and Culture and C. C. Reindorf's History." In *The Recovery of the West African Past: African Pastors and African History in the Nineteenth Century — C. C. Reindorf and Samuel Johnson,* edited by P. Jenkins. Basel: Baseler Afrika Bibliographien, 1998.

Bebbington, D. W. *Evangelicalism in Modern Britain.* London: Unwin Hyman, 1989.

Bediako, Kwame. *Christianity in Africa: The Renewal of a Non-Western Religion.* Maryknoll, N.Y.: Orbis Books; Edinburgh: Edinburgh University Press, 1995.

Belich, James. *Making Peoples: A History of the New Zealanders from Polynesian Settlement to the End of the Nineteenth Century.* Auckland: Allen Lane, Penguin, 1996.

Bennett, Manuhuia. "The Bishopric of Aotearoa — A Maori Dimension." In *He Toenga Whatiwhatinga: Essays Concerning the Bishopric of Aotearoa,* edited by J. Paterson. Rotorua: Te Pihopatanga o Aotearoa, 1983.

Berman, B., and J. Lonsdale. *Unhappy Valley.* London: James Currey, 1992.

Bevans, Stephen B. *Models of Contextual Theology.* Maryknoll, N.Y.: Orbis Books, 1992.

Beyerhaus, Peter, and Henry Lefever. *The Responsible Church and the Foreign Mission.* London: World Dominion Press, 1964.

Bickers, R., and R. Seton, eds. *Missionary Encounters: Sources and Issues.* London: Curzon Press, 1996.

Bishop, Eric. *Jesus of Palestine: The Local Background to the Gospel Documents.* London: Lutterworth, 1955.

Bishop, Eric. *Apostles of Palestine: The Local Background to the New Testament Church.* London: Lutterworth, 1958.

Bishop, Eric. *Prophets of Palestine: The Local Background to the Preparation of the Way.* London: Lutterworth, 1962.

Bliss, Kathleen. *The Service and Status of Women in the Churches.* London: SCM Press, 1952.

Bonhoeffer, Dietrich. *Letters and Papers from Prison.* Enlarged ed. London: SCM Press, 1971.

Bowie, Fiona, Deborah Kirkwood, and Shirley Ardener, eds. *Women and Missions: Past and Present. Anthropological and Historical Perspectives.* Providence/Oxford: Berg Publishers, 1993.

Bready, J. Wesley. *This Freedom — Whence?* New York: American Tract Society, 1942.

Brecht, Martin. "The Relationship between Established Protestant Church and Free Church: Hermann Gundert and Britain." In *Protestant Evangelicalism: Britain, Ireland, Germany, and America c. 1750–c. 1950 — Essays in Honour of W. R. Ward,* edited by K. Robbins. Studies in Church History, Subsidia 7. Oxford: Blackwell, 1990.

Brittan, S. J., ed. *A Pioneer Missionary among the Maoris, 1850-1879, Being the Letters and Journals of Thomas Samuel Grace.* Palmerston North: Bennett, n.d.

Brown, David. *All Their Splendour: World Faiths: A Way to Community.* London: Collins Fount Paperbacks, 1982.

Brown, Leslie. *One Word, Three Worlds.* London: Rex Collings, 1981.

Buchanan, Colin, ed. *Modern Anglican Liturgies, 1958-1968.* London: Oxford University Press, 1968.

Burton, Richard. *Wanderings in West Africa from Liverpool to Fernando Po.* 2 vols. London: Tinsley Bros., 1863. Reprint, New York: Dover Publications, 1991.

Byrne, Lavinia. *The Hidden Journey.* London: SPCK, 1993.

Cagnolo, C. *The Akikuyu.* Nyeri, 1933.

Cairns, H. A. C. *Prelude to Imperialism: British Reactions to Central African Society, 1840-1890.* London: Routledge, Kegan & Paul, 1965.

Caldwell, R. *Lectures on the Tinnevelly Missions.* London: Bell & Daldy, 1857.

Campbell, R. "A Pilgrimage to My Motherland: An Account of a Journey among the Egbas and Yorubas of Central Africa: 1859-60." In *Search for a Place: Black Separatism and Africa, 1860,* edited by M. R. Delany and R. Campbell. Ann Arbor: The University of Michigan Press, 1969.

Capon, M. G. *Towards Unity in Kenya: The Story of Co-operation between Missions and Churches in Kenya, 1913-1947.* Nairobi: Christian Council of Kenya, 1962.

Carden, John. *Morning, Noon and Night.* London: CMS, 1976.

Carden, John. *Another Day — Prayers of the Human Family.* London: SPCK, 1989.

Carden, John, ed. *With All God's People — An Ecumenical Cycle of Prayer.* Geneva: WCC, 1989.

Carden, John. *A Procession of Prayers.* London: Cassell, 1997.

Carey, George. "Journeying Together." Lambeth Palace, 1996.

Carpenter, Edward. *Archbishop Fisher: His Life and Times.* Norwich: Canterbury Press, 1991.

Carpenter, Humphrey. *J. R. R. Tolkien: A Biography.* London: George Allen & Unwin, 1977.

Chadwick, Owen. *The Victorian Church.* 2 vols. London: Adam & Charles Black, 1966, 1970.

Chapman, Colin. *Cross and Crescent: Responding to the Challenge of Islam.* Leicester: IVP, 1995.

Cnattingius, Hans. *Bishops and Societies: A Study of Anglican Colonial and Missionary Expansion, 1798-1850.* London: SPCK, 1952.

Colenso, William. *The Authentic and Genuine History of the Signing of the Treaty of Waitangi, New Zealand, February 5-6, 1840.* Wellington: Government Printer, 1890.

Coleridge, J. T. *A Memoir of the Revd John Keble.* 2 vols. Oxford: Parker, 1869.

Comaroff, Jean and John. *Of Revelation and Revolution.* Vol. 1, *Christianity, Colonialism, and Consciousness in South Africa.* Chicago: University of Chicago Press, 1991.

Comaroff, Jean and John. *Of Revelation and Revolution.* Vol. 2, *The Dialectics of Modernity on a South African Frontier.* Chicago: University of Chicago Press, 1997.

Conference on Missions Held in 1860 at Liverpool. London: James Nisbet, 1860.

Coquery-Vidrovitch, Catherine. *African Women: A Modern History.* London: Westview, 1997.

Cowie, W. G. *To the Clergy and Laity of the Church of the Province of New Zealand.* New Zealand Mission Trust Board, 1901.

Cox, Jeffrey. *The English Churches in Secular Society: Lambeth 1870-1930.* New York and Oxford: Oxford University Press, 1982.

Cox, Jeffrey. "Independent English Women in Delhi and Lahore, 1860-1947." In *Religion and Irreligion in Victorian Society: Essays in Honour of R. K. Webb,* edited by R. W. Davis and R. J. Helmstadter. London: Routledge, 1992.

Cox, Jeffrey. "The Missionary Movement." In *Nineteenth-Century English Religious Traditions,* edited by D. G. Paz. Westport, Conn.: Greenwood Press, 1995.

Cracknell, Kenneth. *Towards a New Relationship: Christians and People of Other Faith.* London: Epworth Press, 1986.

Cracknell, Kenneth. *Justice, Courtesy and Love: Theologians and Missionaries Encountering World Religions, 1846-1914.* London: Epworth Press, 1995.

Cragg, Kenneth. *The Call of the Minaret.* London and New York: Oxford University Press, 1956; London: Collins, 1985.

Cragg, Kenneth. *Sandals at the Mosque: Christian Presence amid Islam.* London: SCM Press, 1959.

Cragg, Kenneth. *Troubled by Truth: Life Studies in Inter-Faith Concern.* Edinburgh: Pentland Press, 1992.

Cragg, Kenneth. *Faith and Life Negotiate: A Christian Story-Study.* Norwich: Canterbury Press, 1994.

Crawford, E. M. *By the Equator's Snowy Peak.* London: CMS, 1913.

Cust, R. N. *Essay on the Prevailing Methods of the Evangelization of the Non-Christian World.* London: Luzac & Co, 1894.

Daneshvar, Simin. *Persian Requiem.* Translated by Roxane Zand. New York: George Braziller, 1992.

Davidson, Allan K. *Evangelicals & Attitudes to India, 1786-1813: Missionary Publicity and Claudius Buchanan.* Appleford: Sutton Courtenay Press, 1990.

Davidson, Allan K. *Selwyn's Legacy: The College of St. John the Evangelist, Te Waimate and Auckland, 1843-1992, A History.* Auckland: The College of St. John the Evangelist, 1993.

Davidson, Allan K. "The Interaction of Missionary and Colonial Christianity in Nineteenth-Century New Zealand." *Studies in World Christianity* 2, no. 2 (1996): 145-66.

Davidson, Allan K. *Christianity in Aotearoa: A History of Church and Society in New Zealand.* 2d ed. Wellington: Education for Ministry, 1997.

Davidson, Allan K., and Peter J. Lineham. *Transplanted Christianity: Documents Illustrating Aspects of New Zealand Church History.* 3d ed. Palmerston North: History Department, Massey University, 1993.

Davidson, R. T. *The Five Lambeth Conferences.* London: SPCK, 1920.

D'Costa, Gavin. *Theology and Religious Pluralism.* Oxford: Basil Blackwell, 1986.

D'Costa, Gavin, ed. *Christian Uniqueness Reconsidered: The Myth of a Pluralistic Theology of Religions.* Maryknoll, N.Y.: Orbis Books; London: SCM Press, 1990.

Dehqani-Tafti, Hassan. *Design of My World.* London: Lutterworth Press, 1959.

Dehqani-Tafti, Hassan. *Masih va Masihiyyat Nazd-e Iraniyan. II: Dar She'r-e Farsi, Douran-e Sabk-e Kohan (Klasik)* (Christ and Christianity Amongst the Iranians. Vol 2, In the Classical Period of Persian Poetry). London: Sohrab Books, 1993.

Dell, Sharon. "Rangiatea." In *Historic Buildings of New Zealand: North Island,* edited by F. Porter. Auckland: Methuen, 1983.

Dike, Kenneth. *The Origins of the Niger Mission: 1841-1891.* Paper read at the Centenary of the Niger Mission at Christ Church, Onitsha, 13 November 1957. Ibadan: Ibadan University Press for the CMS Niger Mission, 1962.

Dillistone, F. W. *Into All the World: A Biography of Max Warren.* London: Hodder & Stoughton, 1980.

Dillistone, F. W. "The Legacy of Max Warren." In *Mission Legacies: Biographical Studies of Leaders of the Modern Missionary Movement,* edited by G. H. Anderson and R. T. Coote. Maryknoll, N.Y.: Orbis Books, 1994.

Doctrine Commission of the Church of England. *The Mystery of Salvation: the Story of God's Gift.* London: Church House Publishing, 1995.

Douglas, Ann. *The Feminization of American Culture.* New York: Alfred A. Knopf, 1977.

Downs, F. S. *Christianity in North-East India.* Delhi: ISPCK, 1983.

Duffy, Eamon. "The Society of Promoting Christian Knowledge and Europe: The Background to the Founding of the Christentumsgesellschaft," *Pietismus und Neuzeit* 7 (1981): 28-42.

Elder, John Rawson. *The Letters and Journals of Samuel Marsden.* Dunedin: Coulls Somerville Wilkie, 1932.

Exley, Richard, and Helen Exley. *In Search of the Missionary.* London: Highway Press, 1970.

Exley, Richard, and Helen Exley. *The Missionary Myth: An Agnostic View of Contemporary Missionaries.* London: Lutterworth, 1973.

Farmaian, Sattareh Farman. *Daughter of Persia: A Woman's Journey from Her Father's Harem Through the Islamic Revolution.* London: Bantam Press, 1992.

Farrukh, Omar. *Al Tabshir wa-l-Isti'mar* [Eng. trans. Evangelism and Imperialism in Arab Lands]. Beirut, n.d.

Fisher, Robin. "Henry Williams." In *Dictionary of New Zealand Biography,* edited by W. H. Oliver. Wellington: Allen & Unwin, 1990.

Fitzgerald, Rosemary. "A 'Peculiar and Exceptional Measure': The Call for Women Medical Missionaries for India in the Late Nineteenth Century." In *Missionary Encounters: Sources and Issues,* edited by R. Bickers and R. Seton. Richmond: Curzon Press, 1996.

Francis-Dehqani, Guli. "Religious Feminism in an Age of Empire: CMS Women Missionaries in Iran, 1869-1934." Ph.D. thesis, University of Bristol, 1999.

Francis-Dehqani, Guli. "British Schools in Iran." In *Encyclopaedia Iranica.* Forthcoming.

Frykenberg, R. E. "The Impact of Conversion and Social Reform upon Society in South India during the Late Company Period: Questions concerning Hindu-Christian Encounters with Special Reference to Tinnevelly." In *Indian Society and the Beginnings of Modernisation, c. 1830-1850,* edited by C. H. Philips and M. D. Wainwright. London: School of Oriental and African Studies, 1976.

Furey, Francis Eamon. "The Theology of Mission in the Writings of Max Warren." L.S.T. thesis, University of Louvain, 1974.

Gairdner, W. H. T. *Edinburgh 1910: An Account and Interpretation of the World Missionary Conference.* Edinburgh and London: Oliphant, Anderson & Ferrier, 1910.

Gairdner, W. H. T. *The Reproach of Islam.* London: CMS, 1911.

Gairdner, W. H. T. *The Rebuke of Islam.* London: United Council for Missionary Education, 1920.

Gatheru, Mugo wa. *Child of Two Worlds.* London: Routledge & Kegan Paul, 1964.

Gathigira, S. K. *Miikarire ya Agikuyu.* London: Sheldon Press, 1952.

Gibb, H. A. R. *Whither Islam?* London: Victor Gollancz, 1932.

Gibbs, M. E. *The Anglican Church in India, 1600-1970.* Delhi: ISPCK, 1972.

Glen, Robert. "Those Odious Evangelicals: The Origin and Background of the CMS Missionaries in New Zealand." In *Mission and Moko: Aspects of the Work of the Church Missionary Society in New Zealand, 1814-1882,* edited by R. Glen. Christchurch: Latimer Fellowship, 1992.

Gobat, Samuel. *Samuel Gobat, Bishop of Jerusalem: His Life and Work.* London: James Nisbet, 1884.

Gollock, Georgina. *Eugene Stock: A Biographical Study, 1836 to 1928.* London: CMS, 1929.

Grafe, H. "Hindu Apologetics at the Beginning of the Protestant Era." *Indian Church History Review* 6, no. 1 (1972): 43-70.

Graul, Karl. *Die Stellung der evangelisch-lutherischen Mission in Leipzig zur Ostindischen Katenfrage.* Leipzig, 1861.

Gray, G. F. S. *Anglicans in China: A History of the Zhonghua Shenggong Hui.* The Episcopal China Mission History Project, 1996.

Gray, Richard. *Black Christians and White Missionaries.* New Haven: Yale University Press, 1990.

Gundert, Hermann. *Hermann Moegling.* Kottayam: DC Books, 1997.

Gundert, Hermann. *Hermann Gundert: Quellen zu seinem Leben und Werk,* edited by Albrecht Frenz. Ulm: Süddeutsche Verlagsgesellschaft, 1991.

Haaramäki, Ossi. *The Missionary Ecclesiology of Max A. C. Warren: A Systematic Research on the Warren Production of 1942-1963.* Helsinki: The Finnish Society for Missiology and Ecumenics, 1982.

Haas, Waltraud. *Erlitten und Erstritten, der Befreiungsweg von Frauen in der Basler Mission, 1816-1960.* Basel: Basileia, 1994.

Hadziantonian, G. A. *Protestant Patriarch.* London: Lucan, 1961.

Haggis, Jane. "Professional Ladies and Working Wives: Female Missionaries in the London Missionary Society and Its South Travancore District, South India in the Nineteenth Century." Ph.D. thesis, University of Manchester, 1991.

Halévy, Élie. *A History of the English People in the Nineteenth Century.* Vol. 1, *England in 1815.* London: Ernest Benn; New York: Barnes & Noble, 1961.

Hardgrave, Robert L. *The Nadars of Tamilnad: The Political Culture of a Community in Change.* Berkeley and Los Angeles: University of California Press, 1969.

Hastings, Adrian. "Were Women a Special Case?" In *Women and Missions: Past and Present. Anthropological and Historical Perspectives,* edited by Fiona Bowie et al. Providence/Oxford: Berg Publishers, 1993.

Heeney, Brian. "The Beginnings of Church Feminism: Women and the Councils of the Church of England, 1897-1919." *Journal of Ecclesiastical History* 33, no. 1 (1982): 89-109.

Heeney, Brian. *The Women's Movement in the Church of England 1850-1930*. Oxford: Clarendon Press, 1988.

Hennell, Michael. *John Venn and the Clapham Sect*. London: Lutterworth, 1958.

Herklots, H. G. G. *The Church of England and the American Episcopal Church*. London: Mowbray, 1966.

Hewitt, Gordon. *The Problems of Success: A History of the Church Missionary Society, 1910-1942*. 2 vols. London: SCM Press, 1971, 1977.

Hick, John. *God and the Universe of Faiths*. London: Macmillan, 1973.

Hick, John, ed. *The Myth of God Incarnate*. London: SCM Press, 1977.

Hick, John, and Paul F. Knitter, eds. *The Myth of Christian Uniqueness: Toward a Pluralist Theology of Religions*. Maryknoll, N.Y.: Orbis Books; London: SCM Press, 1987.

Hiebert, Frances. "Beyond a Post-Modern Critique of Modern Missions: The Nineteenth Century Revisited." *Missiology* 25, no. 3 (1997): 259-77.

Hobley, C. W. *Bantu Beliefs and Magic*. London: H. F. & G. Witherby, 1922.

Hodgins, Jack. *Sister Island: A History of the Church Missionary Society in Ireland, 1814-1994*. Dunmurry: Transmission Publication, 1994.

Hooker, Roger. *Uncharted Journey*. London, Madras: CMS, Christian Literature Society, 1973.

Hooker, Roger. *Journey into Varanasi*. London: CMS, 1978.

Hooker, Roger. *Voices of Varanasi*. London: CMS, 1979.

Hooker, Roger. "CMS and Other Faiths — Some Lessons from Our History." Unpublished paper for CMS, 1987.

Hooker, Roger. *Themes in Hinduism and Christianity: A Comparative Study*. Frankfurt am Main: Peter Lang, 1989.

Hooker, Roger H. *The Quest of Ajneya: A Christian Theological Appraisal of the Search for Meaning in His Three Hindi Novels*. Delhi: Motilal Banarsidass, forthcoming.

Hooker, Roger, and Christopher Lamb. *Love the Stranger: Christian Ministry in Multi-Faith Areas*. London: SPCK, 1986.

Hooper, Rachel. *Act Now*. London: CMS, 1970.

Hoppe, Kirk. "Whose Life Is It, Anyway? Issues of Representation in Life Narrative Texts of African Women." *International Journal of African Historical Studies* 26, no. 3 (1993): 623-36.

Horton, Robin. "African Conversion." *Africa* 41, no. 2 (1971): 85-108.

Horton, Robin. "On the Rationality of Conversion, Part 1." *Africa* 45, no. 3 (1975): 219-35.

Husein, Taha. *The Future of Culture in Egypt*. 1938. New ed. Washington: American Council of Learned Societies, 1956.

Invitation to Adventure: Some Outlines for a Post-War Plan on Behalf of CMS and Its Work. London: CMS, 1946.

Isherwood, John. "An Analysis of the Role of Single Women in the Work of the

Church Missionary Society, 1804-1904, in West Africa, India and China." M.A. thesis, University of Manchester, 1979.

Jackson, Eleanor. *"A True Mother in Israel": The Role of the Christian Mother as Evangelist in Nineteenth-Century India.* NAMP Position Paper 30. Cambridge: University of Cambridge, North Atlantic Missiology Project, 1997.

Jacob, W. M. *The Making of the Anglican Church Worldwide.* London: SPCK, 1997.

Jay, Elisabeth. *Faith and Doubt in Victorian Britain.* Basingstoke: Macmillan, 1986.

Jones, Adam. "Reindorf the Historian." In *The Recovery of the West African Past: African Pastors and African History in the Nineteenth Century — C. C. Reindorf and Samuel Johnson,* edited by P. Jenkins. Basel: Baseler Afrika Bibliographien, 1998.

Jongeneel, Jan. "European-Continental Perceptions and Critiques of British and American Protestant Missions." Paper read at North Atlantic Missiology Project Symposium, at Boston University, 1998.

Karanja, J. K. "The Growth of the African Anglican Church in Central Kenya." Ph.D. thesis, University of Cambridge, 1993.

Kenyatta, Jomo. *Facing Mount Kenya.* London: Secker & Warburg, 1938.

Kibicho, S. G. "The Continuity of the African Conception of God into and through Christianity: A Kikuyu Case-Study." In *Christianity in Independent Africa,* edited by E. Fashole-Luke et al. London: Rex Collings, 1978.

Kings, Graham. "Facing Mount Kenya: Reflections on African Traditional Religion and the Bible." *Anvil* 4, no. 2 (1987): 127-43.

Kings, Graham. "Max Warren: Candid Comments on Mission from His Personal Letters." *International Bulletin of Missionary Research* 17, no. 2 (1993): 54-58.

Kings, Graham. "Immigration, Race and Grace: Max Warren's Letters to Pat and Roger Hooker, 1965-1977." In *Mission in a Pluralist World,* edited by A. Lande and W. Ustorf. Frankfurt am Main: Peter Lang, 1996.

Kirkwood, Deborah. "Protestant Missionary Women: Wives and Spinsters." In *Women and Missions: Past and Present: Anthropological and Historical Perspectives,* edited by Fiona Bowie et al. Oxford: Berg Publishers, 1993.

Klostermaier, Klaus. *Hindu and Christian in Vrindaban.* London: SCM Press, 1969.

Knaplund, Paul. "Sir James Stephen: The Friend of the Negroes." *Journal of Negro History* 35 (1950): 368-407.

Knight, William, ed. *The Missionary Secretariat of Henry Venn.* London: Longmans, Green & Co., 1880.

Knight, William. *Memoir of Henry Venn, BD.* London: Seeley, Jackson, & Halliday, 1882.

Knitter, Paul F. *No Other Name? A Critical Survey of Christian Attitudes To-*

ward the World Religions. Maryknoll, N.Y.: Orbis Books; London: SCM Press, 1985.

Koelle, S. W. *African Native Literature, or Proverbs, Tales, Fables and Historical Fragments in the Kanuri or Bornu Language.* London: CMS, 1854.

Kord, Gohar. *An Iranian Odyssey.* London: Serpent's Tail, 1991.

Lamb, Christopher. *Belief in a Mixed Society.* Tring, Herts: Lion Publishing, 1985.

Lamb, Christopher. *The Call to Retrieval: Kenneth Cragg's Christian Vocation to Islam.* London: Grey Seal, 1997.

Lande, Aasulv. "Witness as Presence." In *Contemporary Issues in Mission,* edited by J. A. Kirk. Birmingham: Department of Mission, Selly Oak Colleges, 1994.

Lande, Aasulv. "Contemporary Missiology in the Church of England." In *Mission in a Pluralist World,* edited by A. Lande and W. Ustorf. Frankfurt am Main: Peter Lang, 1996.

Lande, Aasulv, and Werner Ustorf, eds. *Mission in a Pluralist World.* Studies in the Intercultural History of Christianity, vol. 97. Frankfurt am Main: Peter Lang, 1996.

Leakey, L. S. B. *The Southern Kikuyu before 1903.* 3 vols. London: Academic Press, 1977.

Leech, Kenneth. *Struggle in Babylon.* London: Sheldon Press, 1988.

Lewis, Philip. *Islamic Britain: Religion, Politics and Identity among British Muslims: Bradford in the 1990s.* London: I. B. Tauris Publishers, 1994.

Long, J. *Hand-book of Bengal Missions.* London: John Farquhar Shaw, 1848.

Lovett, Richard. *The History of the London Missionary Society.* 2 vols. London: Henry Frowde, 1899.

Martyn, Henry. *Journals and Letters of Henry Martyn.* 2 vols. London: Seeley & Burnside, 1837.

Mbiti, J. S. *African Religions and Philosophy.* London: Heinemann, 1969.

McGrath, Alister. "The Importance of Traditions for Modern Evangelicalism." In *Doing Theology for the People of God: Studies in Honour of J. I. Packer,* edited by D. Lewis and A. McGrath. Downers Grove, Ill.: InterVarsity Press, 1996.

McLaughlin, Eleanor. "The Christian Past: Does It Hold a Future for Women?" In *Womanspirit Rising: A Feminist Reader in Religion,* edited by C. P. Christ and J. Plaskow. San Francisco: Harper & Row, 1992.

McPherson, R. *The Presbyterian Church in Kenya.* Nairobi: East African Publishing House, 1970.

Meiring, Pieter G. J. "Max Warren as Sendingwetenskaplike." D.D. dissertation, University of Pretoria, 1968.

Middleton, John, and Greet Kershaw. *The Central Tribes of the North-Eastern Bantu: The Kikuyu and Kamba of Kenya.* Ethnographic Survey of Africa.

East Central Africa, Part 5. London: International African Institute, 1965.

Mill, M. G. *The Permanent Way.* 2 vols. Nairobi, n.d.

Miller, Jon. *The Social Control of Religious Zeal: A Study of Institutional Contradictions.* New Brunswick, N.J.: Rutgers University Press, 1994.

Mission History from the Woman's Point of View. Basel: Basel Mission, 1989.

Monroe, Elizabeth. *Britain's Moment in the Middle East.* London: Chatto & Windus, 1963.

Moorhouse, Geoffrey. *The Missionaries.* London: Eyre Methuen, 1973.

Morrell, W. P. *The Anglican Church in New Zealand.* Dunedin: Anglican Church of the Province of New Zealand, 1973.

Morrell, W. P. "Selwyn's Relations with the Church Missionary Society." In *Bishop Selwyn in New Zealand, 1841-68,* edited by W. E. Limbrick. Palmerston North: Dunmore Press, 1983.

Morrison, S. E. *The Way of Partnership.* London: Highway Press, 1936.

Morrison, S. E. *Mid-East Survey.* London: SCM Press, 1954.

Muriuki, G. *A History of the Kikuyu.* Nairobi: Oxford University Press, 1974.

Murray, Jocelyn. "The Female Circumcision Controversy, with Special Reference to the Church Missionary Society's Sphere of Influence." Ph.D. thesis, University of California Los Angeles, 1974.

Murray, Jocelyn. *Proclaim the Good News: A Short History of the Church Missionary Society.* London: Hodder & Stoughton, 1985.

Murray, Jocelyn. "Maria Newell." In *Biographical Dictionary of Christian Missions,* edited by G. H. Anderson. New York: Macmillan, 1998.

Nazir-Ali, Michael. *Islam: A Christian Perspective.* Exeter: Paternoster Press, 1983.

Nazir-Ali, Michael. *From Everywhere to Everywhere: A World View of Christian Mission.* London: Collins, 1991.

Nazir-Ali, Michael. *Frontiers in Muslim-Christian Encounter.* Oxford: Regnum Books, 1991.

Nazir-Ali, Michael. *Mission and Dialogue: Proclaiming the Gospel Afresh in Every Age.* London: SPCK, 1995.

Neill, Stephen. *A History of Christian Missions.* London: Hodder & Stoughton, 1964.

Newman, J. H. *Lectures on the Prophetical Office of the Church.* London: Rivington, 1837.

Nichols, Bernard. *Letters to Mary.* London: CMS, 1979.

Nock, A. D. *Conversion. The Old and New in Religion from Alexander the Great to Augustine of Hippo.* Oxford: Clarendon Press, 1933.

Nockles, Peter B. *The Oxford Movement in Context: Anglican High Churchmanship 1760-1857.* Cambridge: Cambridge University Press, 1997.

Oddie, Geoffrey A. "Old Wine in New Bottles? Kartabhaja (Vaishnava) Converts to Evangelical Christianity in Bengal, 1835-1845." In *Religious Conversion Movements in South Asia: Continuities and Change,* edited by G. A. Oddie. Richmond: Curzon Press, 1997.

Oduyoye, Modupe. "The Planting of Christianity in Yorubaland: 1842-1888." In *Christianity in West Africa: The Nigerian Story,* edited by O. Kalu. Ibadan: Daystar Press, 1978.

Oliver, R. *The Missionary Factor in East Africa.* London: Longman, 1952.

Oliver, W. H., ed. *The Oxford History of New Zealand.* Wellington: Oxford University Press, 1981.

Orange, Claudia. *The Treaty of Waitangi.* Wellington: Port Nicholson, 1987.

Padwick, Constance. *Temple Gairdner of Cairo.* London: SPCK, 1929.

Padwick, Constance. *Muslim Devotions.* London: SPCK, 1961; Oxford: One World, 1996.

Padwick, Constance E. *Henry Martyn: Confessor of the Faith.* London: SCM Press, 1923.

Page, Jesse. *Samuel Crowther: The Slave Boy Who Became Bishop of the Niger.* New York: Fleming H. Revell Co., 1889.

Panikkar, Raymond. *The Unknown Christ of Hinduism.* 1964. Revised and enlarged ed. with the added subtitle *Towards an Ecumenical Christophany,* Maryknoll, N.Y.: Orbis Books, 1981.

Parrinder, Geoffrey. *West African Religion.* Oxford: Oxford University Press, 1949.

Parrinder, Geoffrey. *African Traditional Religion.* London: Hutchinson, 1954.

Peel, J. D. Y. "Problems and Opportunities in an Anthropologist's Use of a Missionary Archive." In *Missionary Encounters: Sources and Issues,* edited by R. A. Bickers and R. Seton. London: Curzon Press, 1996.

Peel, J. D. Y. "Two Pastors and Their Histories: Samuel Johnson and C. C. Reindorf." In *The Recovery of the West African Past: African Pastors and African History in the Nineteenth Century — C. C. Reindorf and Samuel Johnson,* edited by P. Jenkins. Basel: Baseler Afrika Bibliographien, 1998.

Pettitt, George. *The Tinnevelly Mission of the Church Missionary Society.* London: Seeley, 1851.

Pirouet, M. Louise. *Black Evangelists: The Spread of Christianity in Uganda, 1891-1914.* London: Rex Collings, 1978.

Pirouet, M. Louise. "Women Missionaries in Uganda, 1894-1904." In *Missionary Ideologies in the Imperialist Era: 1880-1920,* edited by T. Christensen and W. R. Hutchinson. Århus, Denmark: Aros, 1982.

Pirouet, M. Louise. "Refugees and Worldwide Anglicanism." In *Anglicanism: A Global Communion,* edited by A. Wingate et al. London: Mowbray, 1998.

Pool, Ian. *Te Iwi Maori: A New Zealand Population Past, Present & Projected.* Auckland: Auckland University Press, 1991.

Powell, Avril A. *Muslims and Missionaries in Pre-Mutiny India*. London: Curzon Press, 1993.

Pratt, J. H., ed. *The Thought of the Evangelical Leaders*. Edinburgh: Banner of Truth Trust, 1978.

Prochaska, F. K. *Women and Philanthropy in Nineteenth-Century England*. Oxford: Clarendon Press, 1980.

Race, Alan. *Christians and Religious Pluralism: Patterns in the Christian Theology of Religions*. London: SCM Press, 1983.

Rahner, Karl. *Mission and Grace*. 3 vols. London: Sheed & Ward, 1964.

Rahner, Karl. "Christianity and the Non-Christian Religions." In *Theological Investigations*. London: Darton, Longman & Todd, 1966.

Ramachandra, Vinoth. *The Recovery of Mission Beyond the Pluralist Paradigm*. Carlisle: Paternoster Press; and Grand Rapids: Eerdmans, 1996.

Rambo, Lewish R. *Understanding Religious Conversion*. New Haven: Yale University Press, c. 1993.

Ramsden, Eric. *Rangiatea: The Story of the Otaki Church, Its First Pastor and Its People*. Wellington: A. H. & A. W. Reed, 1951.

Ranger, T., and J. Weller. *Themes in the Christian History of Central Africa*. Berkeley: University of California Press, 1975.

Rennie, Ian Scott. "Evangelicalism and English Public Life, 1823-1850." Ph.D. thesis, University of Toronto, 1962.

Ridgeway, Joseph. "The Memorandum of the Church Missionary Society on the Extension of the Episcopate." *Church Missionary Intelligencer* (1858): 158-67, 169-77.

Robert, Dana L. *American Women in Mission: A Social History of Their Thought and Practice*. Macon, Ga.: Mercer University Press, 1996.

Rodinson, Maxime. *Europe and the Mystique of Islam*. Seattle & London: University of Washington Press, 1987.

Rosevear, Watson. *Waiapu: The Story of a Diocese*. Hamilton: Paul's, 1960.

Routledge, W. S. *With a Prehistoric People*. London: Edward Arnold, 1910.

Sachs, W. L. *The Transformation of Anglicanism*. Cambridge: Cambridge University Press, 1993.

Said, Edward. *Orientalism: Western Conceptions of the Orient*. London: Penguin, 1995.

Samartha, Stanley. *One Christ — Many Religions: Towards a Revised Christology*. Maryknoll, N.Y.: Orbis Books, 1991.

Sanderson, Kay. "Maori Christianity on the East Coast, 1840-1870." *New Zealand Journal of History* 17, no. 2 (1983): 166-84.

Sanneh, Lamin. *Translating the Message: The Missionary Impact on Culture*. Maryknoll, N.Y.: Orbis Books, 1989.

Sanneh, Lamin. *Encountering the West: Christianity and the Global Cultural Process: The African Dimension*. London: Marshall Pickering, 1993.

Sanneh, Lamin. *The American Factor in West African Christianity: 1776-1892:*

A Study in Antislavery and Antistructure. Cambridge, Mass.: Harvard University Press, forthcoming.

Sargison, Patricia. "Elizabeth Colenso (1821-1904)." In *The Book of New Zealand Women*, edited by C. Macdonald. Wellington: Bridget Williams Books, 1991.

Schlatter, Wilhelm. *Geschichte der Basler Mission, 1815-1915*. 3 vols. Basel: Basel Mission, 1916.

Schön, James Frederick, and Samuel Crowther. *Journals*. 2d ed. London: Frank Cass, 1970.

Selwyn, George Augustus. *A Charge Delivered to the Clergy of the Diocese of New Zealand, at the Diocesan Synod, in the Chapel of St. John's College, on Thursday, September 23, 1847*. London: Rivington, 1859.

Seton, Rosemary. "'Open Doors for Female Labourers': Women Candidates of the London Missionary Society, 1875-1914." In *Missionary Encounters: Sources and Issues*, edited by R. Bickers and R. Seton. Richmond: Curzon Press, 1996.

Shafii, Rouhi. *Scent of Saffron: Three Generations of an Iranian Family*. London: Scarlet Press, 1997.

Shaw, G. P. *Patriarch and Patriot: William Grant Broughton, 1788-1853*. Melbourne: Melbourne University Press, 1978.

Sheild, E. O. "The New Zealand Episcopate of George Augustus Selwyn (1842-1867) with Special Reference to Bishop Selwyn's Part in the Dispute with Archdeacon Henry Williams in Respect of the Latter's Land Claims." B.D. thesis, University of Oxford, 1981.

Shenk, Wilbert R. "Henry Venn as Missionary Theorist and Administrator." Ph.D. thesis, University of Aberdeen, 1978.

Shenk, Wilbert R. *Henry Venn — Missionary Statesman*. Maryknoll, N.Y.: Orbis Books, 1983.

Siddiqui, Ataullah. *Christian-Muslim Dialogue in the Twentieth Century*. Leicester and London: Macmillan, 1997.

Simpson, Thomas. "Rev. Philip O'Flaherty of Ballaghadallagh, Co. Mayo and of Uganda." *The Bulletin of the Presbyterian Historical Society of Ireland* 11 (November 1981): 3-16.

Smith, Edwin W. *African Beliefs and Christian Faith*. London: United Society for Christian Literature, 1936.

Smith, Edwin W., ed. *African Ideas of God*. Edinburgh: Edinburgh House Press, 1959.

Smith, Mark. *Religion in Industrial Society: Oldham and Saddleworth, 1740-1865*. Oxford: Clarendon Press, 1994.

Sorrenson, M. P. K. *Origins of European Settlement in Kenya*. Oxford: Oxford University Press, 1968.

Sorrenson, M. P. K., ed. *Na to Hora Aroha: From Your Dear Friend. The Cor-*

respondence Between Sir Apirana Ngata and Sir Peter Buck, 1925-50. Auckland: Auckland University Press, 1986.

Spencer, George. *A Brief Account of the Church Missionary Society's Mission in the District of Krishnagur in the Diocese of Calcutta.* London: 1846.

Staehelin, Ernst. *Die Christentumsgesellschaft in der Zeit der Aufklärung und der beginnenden Erweckung.* Basel: Friedrich Reinhardt Verlag, 1970.

Staehelin, Ernst. *Die Christentumsgesellschaft in der Zeit von der Erweckung bis zur Gegenwart.* Basel: Friedrich Reinhardt Verlag, 1974.

Stamoolis, James J. *Eastern Orthodox Mission Theology Today.* Maryknoll, N.Y.: Orbis Books, 1986.

Stanley, Brian. *The History of the Baptist Missionary Society, 1792-1992.* Edinburgh: T. & T. Clark, 1992.

Stanley, Brian. "Some Problems in Writing a Missionary Society History Today: The Example of the Baptist Missionary Society." In *Missionary Encounters: Sources and Issues,* edited by R. A. Bickers and R. Seton. London: Curzon Press, 1996.

Steinmetz, Susanne. *Deutsche Gemeinden in Großbritannien und Irland: Geschichte und Archivbestände.* 1988.

Steinmetz, Susanne. *Deutsche Evangelisch-Lutherische St.-Marienkirche London, 1694-1994/St. Mary's German Lutheran Church in London.* London: St. Mary's German Lutheran Church, 1994.

Stenhouse, John. "The Darwinian Enlightenment and New Zealand Politics." In *Darwin's Laboratory,* edited by R. Macleod and P. F. Rehbock. Honolulu: University of Hawaii Press, 1994.

Stewart, William S. *India's Religious Frontier: Christian Presence amid Modern Hinduism.* London: SCM Press, 1964.

Stock, Eugene. *The History of the Church Missionary Society: Its Environment, Its Men and Its Work.* 4 vols. London: CMS, 1899, 1916.

Stock, Eugene. *The Centenary Volume of the Church Missionary Society for Africa and the East.* London: CMS, 1902.

Stott, John R. W. *Christian Mission in the Modern World.* Downers Grove: IVP, 1975.

Stott, John R. W., ed. *Making Christ Known: Historic Mission Documents from the Lausanne Movement 1974-1989.* Grand Rapids: Eerdmans; Carlisle: Paternoster Press, 1996.

Stuart, Emmeline. "The Social Conditions of Women in Muslim Lands." *Church Missionary Review* (August 1909).

Sundkler, Bengt. *Church of South India: The Movement Towards Union, 1900-1947.* Revised ed. London: Lutterworth, 1965.

Sykes, Stephen W. "The Genius of Anglicanism." In *The English Religious Tradition and the Genius of Anglicanism,* edited by G. Rowell. Wantage: IKON, 1992.

Taylor, John V. *The Growth of the Church in Buganda: An Attempt at Understanding.* London: SCM Press, 1958.

Taylor, John V. *Processes of Growth in an African Church.* London: SCM Press, 1958.

Taylor, John V. *The Primal Vision: Christian Presence amid African Religion.* London: SCM Press, 1963.

Taylor, John V. *The Go-between God.* London: SCM Press, 1972.

Taylor, John V. "The Theological Basis of Interfaith Dialogue," *International Review of Mission* 68 (December 1979): 373-84; also in *Christianity and Other Religions,* edited by J. Hick and B. Hebblethwaite, pp. 212-33. London: Collins, 1980.

Taylor, John V. *A Christmas Sequence and Other Poems.* Oxford: The Amate Press, 1989.

Taylor, John V. "My Pilgrimage in Mission." *International Bulletin of Missionary Research* 17 (January 1993): 59-61.

Taylor, John V. *The Uncancelled Mandate: Four Bible Studies on Christian Mission for the Approaching Millennium.* London: Church House Publishing, 1998.

Taylor, John V., Max Warren, David Brown, David Young, and Paul Oestreicher. *Face to Face: Essays on Inter-Faith Dialogue.* London: Highway Press, 1971.

Tempels, Placide. *La Philosophie Bantoue.* Elizabethville: Editions Lovania; Paris: Présence Africaine, 3d ed. 1949.

Thiong'o, Ngugi wa. *The River Between.* London: Heinemann, 1965.

Thomas, Owen C., ed. *Attitudes Towards Other Religions: Some Christian Interpretations.* Edited by M. E. Marty. Forum Books. London: SCM Press, 1969.

Tibawi, A. L. *British Interests in the Middle East, 1800-1901: A Study of Religious and Educational Enterprise.* Oxford: Oxford University Press, 1961.

Tignor, R. *The Colonial Transformation of Kenya.* Princeton: Princeton University Press, 1976.

Till, Barry. *Change and Exchange: Mutual Responsibility and the Church of England.* London: Church Information Office, 1964.

Tucker, Alfred. *Eighteen Years in Uganda & East Africa.* 1911. New ed. Westport, Conn.: Negro Universities Press, 1970.

Tucker, H. W. *Memoir of the Life and Episcopate of George Augustus Selwyn.* 2 vols. London: Gardner, 1879.

Ustorf, Werner. *Mission to Mission? — Rethinking the Agenda.* Selly Oak Colleges Occasional Paper, no. 9. Birmingham, 1991.

Venn, Henry. *The Missionary Life and Labours of Francis Xavier.* London: Longman, Green & Co., 1862.

Venn, Henry. *Retrospect and Prospect of the Operations of the Church Missionary Society.* 2d ed. London: CMS, 1865.

Venn, Henry. "The Negro Bishop." *Christian Observer* 69, no. 381 (1869): 641-50.

Venn, Henry. "On Nationality." In *The Missionary Secretariat of Henry Venn,* edited by W. Knight. London: Longmans, Green, and Co., 1880.

Voillaume, R. *Seeds of the Desert: The Legacy of Charles de Foucauld.* London: Burns & Oates, 1955.

Waldburger, Andreas. *Missionare und Moslems, die Basler Mission in Persien, 1833-1837.* Basel: Basileia-Verlag, 1984.

Walls, Andrew F. "The Legacy of Samuel Ajayi Crowther." *International Bulletin of Missionary Research* 16, no. 1 (1992): 15-21.

Walls, Andrew F. "Black Europeans — White Africans: Some Missionary Motives in West Africa." In A. F. Walls, *The Missionary Movement in Christian History.* Edinburgh: T. & T. Clark, 1996.

Walls, Andrew F. "Structural Problems in Mission Studies." In A. F. Walls, *The Missionary Movement in Christian History: Studies in the Transmission of Faith.* Maryknoll, N.Y.: Orbis Books; Edinburgh: T. & T. Clark, 1996.

Walzer, Michael. *The Revolution of the Saints.* Cambridge, Mass.: Harvard University Press, 1965.

Wanyoike, E. N. *An African Pastor.* Nairobi: East African Publishing House, 1974.

Ward, Kevin. *Called to Serve: A History of Bishop Tucker Theological College.* Kampala, 1989.

Ward, Kevin. "Obedient Rebels." *Journal of Religion in Africa* 19, no. 3 (1989): 194-227.

Ward, Kevin. "The Church of Uganda and the Exile of Kabaka Muteesa II, 1953-55." *Journal of Religion in Africa* 28, no. 4 (1998): 411-49.

Ward, W. R. *The Protestant Evangelical Awakening.* Cambridge: Cambridge University Press, 1992.

Ward, W. R. "Missions in Their Global Context in the Eighteenth Century." In *A Global Faith: Essays on Evangelicalism and Globalization,* edited by M. Hutchinson and O. Kalu. New South Wales: The Centre for the Study of Australian Christianity, Macquarie University, 1998.

Warren, Max. *Caesar, the Beloved Enemy.* London: Highway Press, 1955.

Warren, Max. *Partnership.* London: SCM Press, 1955.

Warren, Max. "The Muslim, the Christian and the Christ." *CMS News-letter* 192 (March 1957).

Warren, Max. "The Thought and Practice of Missions." In *Basileia: Walter Freytag zum 60. Geburtstag,* edited by Jan von Hermelink and Jans Jochen Margull. Stuttgart: Evang. Missionsverlag GMBH, 1959.

Warren, Max. *The Missionary Movement from Britain in Modern History.* London: SCM Press, 1965.

Warren, Max. *Social History and Christian Mission.* London: SCM Press, 1967.

Warren, Max. "Presence and Proclamation." Unpublished paper read at European Consultation on Mission Studies, Selly Oak Colleges, Birmingham. Published in German as "Präsenz und Verkündigung," *Evangelische Missions Zeitschrift* (August 1968): 158-71.

Warren, Max. *To Apply the Gospel: Selections from the Writings of Henry Venn.* Grand Rapids: Eerdmans, 1971.

Warren, Max. *Theology of Attention.* Madras: Christian Literature Society, ISPCK, 1971.

Warren, Max. *Crowded Canvas: Some Experiences of a Lifetime.* London: Hodder & Stoughton, 1974.

Warren, Max. "The Uniqueness of Christ." *The Modern Churchman* 18 (winter 1974): 55-66.

Warren, Max. *I Believe in the Great Commission.* Grand Rapids: Eerdmans; London: Hodder & Stoughton, 1976.

Wartburg, Beat von. *Basel 1798 — vive la République Helvetique.* Exhibition catalogue. Basel: Museum der Kulturen, 1998.

Wartenberg-Potter, Barbara von. "Women." In *Dictionary of Mission,* edited by Karl Muller, Theo Sundermeier, Stephen B. Bevans, Richard H. Bliese. Maryknoll, N.Y.: Maryknoll Publications, 1997.

Waterfield, Robin. *Christians in Persia.* London: George Allen & Unwin, 1973.

Webb, Allan Becher. *Sisterhood Life and Woman's Work in the Mission-Field of the Church.* London: Skeffington & Son, 1883.

Webster, James Bertin. *The African Churches among the Yoruba: 1888-1922.* Oxford: Clarendon Press, 1964.

Weitbrecht, H. "The Training of Women Missionaries." *Church Missionary Review* 44 (May 1913): 298-302.

Weitbrecht, J. J. *Protestant Missions in Bengal Illustrated.* London: John F. Shaw, 1844.

Welsby, P. A. *A History of the Church of England, 1945-1980.* Oxford: Oxford University Press, 1984.

Wheeler, Andrew, and William Anderson, eds. *Gateway to the Heart of Africa: Missionary Pioneers in Sudan.* Faith in Sudan, edited by A. Wheeler and W. Anderson. Nairobi: Paulines Press, 1997.

Wheeler, Andrew, and William Anderson, eds. *In Our Own Languages: The Story of Bible Translation in Sudan.* Faith in Sudan, edited by A. Wheeler and W. Anderson. Nairobi: Paulines Press, 1997.

Wheeler, Andrew, and William Anderson, eds. *Land of Promise: Church Growth in a Sudan at War.* Faith in Sudan, edited by A. Wheeler and W. Anderson. Nairobi: Paulines Press, 1997.

Wheeler, Andrew, and William Anderson, eds. *Seeking an Open Society: Inter-*

faith Relations and Dialogue in Sudan Today. Faith in Sudan, edited by A. Wheeler and W. Anderson. Nairobi: Paulines Press, 1997.

Wheeler, Andrew, and William Anderson, eds. *Struggling to be Heard: Christian Presence in Sudanese Politics 1956-96.* Edited by A. Wheeler and W. Anderson, Faith in Sudan. Nairobi: Paulines Press, 1997.

White, Gavin. "The Idea of the Missionary Bishop in Mid-Nineteenth Century Anglicanism." M.S.T. thesis, General Theological Seminary, New York, 1968.

Wilberforce, William. *A Practical View of the Prevailing Religious System of Professed Christians in the Higher and Middle Classes in This Country Contrasted with Real Christianity.* 1797. New ed., London: SCM Press, 1958.

Wiles, Maurice. *Christian Theology and Inter-Religious Dialogue.* Philadelphia: Trinity Press International; London: SCM Press, 1992.

Wilkinson, John, ed. *Mutual Responsibility: Questions and Answers.* London: SPCK, 1964.

Wilkinson, J. *Church in Black and White.* Edinburgh: St Andrew Press, 1993.

Williams, Peter. " 'Too Peculiarly Anglican': The Role of the Established Church in Ireland as a Negative Model in the Development of the Church Missionary Society, 1856-1872." In *Studies in Church History.* Vol. 25, *The Churches, Ireland and the Irish,* edited by W. J. Sheils and D. Wood. Oxford: Blackwell, 1989.

Williams, Peter. *The Ideal of the Self-Governing Church: A Study in Victorian Missionary Strategy.* Leiden: E. J. Brill, 1990.

Williams, Peter. " 'The Missing Link': The Recruitment of Women Missionaries in Some English Evangelical Missionary Societies in the Nineteenth Century." In *Women and Missions: Past and Present. Anthropological and Historical Perspectives,* edited by F. Bowie et al. Providence/Oxford: Berg Publishers, 1993.

Wilson, Daniel, ed. *Bishop Wilson's Journal Letters.* London: J. Nisbet, 1863.

Wingate, Andrew. *Encounter in the Spirit: Muslim-Christian Dialogue in Birmingham.* Geneva: WCC, 1988.

Wingate, Andrew. *The Church and Conversion: A Study of Recent Conversions to and from Christianity in the Tamil Area of South India.* Delhi: ISPCK, 1997.

Witschi, Hermann. *Geschichte der Basler Mission, 1920-1940.* Basel: Basileia, 1970.

Witts, Diana. "The Future of the Mission Agency." In *Anglicanism: A Global Communion,* edited by A. Wingate et al. London: Mowbray, 1998.

Wolffe, John, ed. *Religion in Victorian Britain.* Volume 5, *Culture and Empire.* Manchester and New York: Manchester University Press, 1997.

Women Carry More Than Half the Burden. Basel: Basel Mission, 1996.

Wright, J. Robert. "Anglicanism, Ecclesia Anglicana, and Anglican: an essay on terminology." In *The Study of Anglicanism,* edited by S. W. Sykes and J. Booty. London: SPCK, 1988.

Wylie, M. *Bengal as a Field of Missions.* London: W. H. Dalton, 1854.

Yates, Timothy E. *Venn and Victorian Bishops Abroad: The Missionary Policies of Henry Venn and Their Repercussions upon the Anglican Episcopate of the Colonial Period, 1841-1872.* Uppsala: Swedish Institute of Missionary Research; London: SPCK, 1978.

Yates, Timothy E. "Evangelicalism without Hyphens: Max Warren, the Tradition and Theology of Mission." *Anvil* 2, no. 3 (1988): 231-45.

Yates, Timothy E. "Newsletter Theology: CMS Newsletters since Max Warren, 1963-1985." *International Bulletin of Missionary Research* 12 (1988): 11-15.

Yates, Timothy E. *Christian Mission in the Twentieth Century.* Cambridge: Cambridge University Press, 1994.

Young, David. *The Open Dialogue: Buddhist and Christian.* London: The Highway Press, 1971.

Index